SQL
Database
Programming

Fifth Edition

Chris Fehily

Questing Vole Press

SQL Database Programming (Fifth Edition)
by Chris Fehily

Editor: Kevin Debenjak
Proofreader: Diane Yee
Compositor: Hiromi Yamada
Cover: Questing Vole Press

Contents

Introduction

SQL (pronounced *es-kyoo-el*) is the standard programming language for creating, updating, and retrieving information that's stored in databases. With SQL, you can turn your ordinary questions ("Where do our customers live?") into statements that your database system can understand (`SELECT DISTINCT city, state FROM customers;`). You might already know how to extract this type of information by using a graphical query or reporting tool, but perhaps you've noticed that this tool becomes limiting or cumbersome as your questions grow in complexity—that's where SQL comes in.

You also can use SQL to add, change, and delete data and database objects. All modern relational database management systems (DBMSs) support SQL, although support varies by product (more about that later in this introduction).

About SQL

SQL is:

- A programming language

- Easy to learn

- Declarative

- Interactive or embedded

- Standardized

- Used to change data and database objects

- Not an acronym

A programming language. SQL is a formal language in which you write programs to create, modify, and query databases. Your database system executes your SQL program, performs the tasks you've specified, and then displays the results (or an error message). Programming languages differ from natural (spoken) languages in that programming languages are designed for a specific purpose, have a small vocabulary, and are inflexible and unambiguous. So if you don't get the results you expect, then it's because your program contains an error—or bug—and not because the computer misinterpreted your instructions. (Debugging one's programs is a cardinal programming task.)

SQL, like any formal language, is defined by rules of **syntax**, which determine the words and symbols you can use and how they can be combined, and **semantics**, which determine the actual meaning of a syntactically correct statement. Note that you can write a legal SQL statement that expresses the wrong meaning (good syntax, bad semantics). Chapter 3 introduces SQL syntax and semantics.

Database vs. DBMS

A database is not the same as the database software that you're running; it's incorrect to say, "Oracle is a database." Database software is called a **database management system (DBMS)**. A **database**, which is just one component of a DBMS, is the data itself—that is, it's a container (one or more files) that stores structured information. Besides controlling the organization, integrity, and retrieval of data in databases, DBMSs handle tasks such as physical storage, security, backup, replication, and error recovery.

DBMS also is abbreviated **RDBMS**, in which the *R* stands for *relational*. An RDBMS organizes data according to the relational model (see Chapter 2) rather than, say, a hierarchical or network model. This book covers only relational systems, so the initial *R* is implied in *DBMS*.

```
Sub GetAuthorNames()
  Dim db As Database
  Dim rs As Recordset
  Dim i As Integer
  Dim au_names() As String
  Set db = CurrentDb()
  Set rs = db.OpenRecordset("authors")
  rs.MoveLast
  ReDim au_names(rs.RecordCount - 1, 1)
  With rs
    .MoveFirst
    i = 0
    Do Until .EOF
      au_names(i, 0) = ![au_fname]
      au_names(i, 1) = ![au_lname]
      i = i + 1
      .MoveNext
    Loop
  End With
  rs.Close
  db.Close
End Sub
```

Listing i.1 This Microsoft Access Visual Basic routine extracts the first and last names from a database table containing author information and places the results in an array.

```
SELECT au_fname, au_lname
  FROM authors;
```

Listing i.2 This single SQL statement performs the same query as the Visual Basic routine in Listing i.1. Access's internal optimizer determines the best way to extract the data.

Easy to learn. Easy compared with other programming languages, that is. If you've never written a program before, then you'll find the transition from natural to formal language to be frustrating. Still, SQL's statements read like sentences to make things easy on humans. A novice programmer probably would understand the SQL statement SELECT au_fname, au_lname FROM authors ORDER BY au_lname; to mean "List the authors' first and last names, sorted by last name," whereas the same person would find the equivalent C or Perl program impenetrable.

Declarative. If you've never programmed, then you can skip this point without loss of continuity. If you've programmed in a language such as C or Javascript, then you've used a **procedural language**, in which you specify the explicit steps to follow to produce a result. SQL is a **declarative language**, in which you describe *what* you want and not *how* to do it; your database system's optimizer will determine the "how." As such, standard SQL lacks traditional control-flow constructs such as if-then-else, while, for, and goto statements.

To demonstrate this difference, I've written programs that perform an equivalent task in Microsoft Access Visual Basic (VB, a procedural language) and SQL. Listing i.1 shows a VB program that extracts author names from a table that contains author information. You needn't understand the entire program, but note that it uses a Do Until loop to define explicitly how to extract data. Listing i.2 shows how to do the same task with a single SQL statement (as opposed to about 20 lines of VB code). With SQL, you specify only what needs to be accomplished; the DBMS determines and performs internally the actual step-by-step operations needed to get the result.

Moreover, Listing i.2 is a trivial SQL query. After you add common operations such as sorts, filters, and joins, you might need more than 100 lines of procedural code to accomplish what a single SQL SELECT statement can do.

Interactive or embedded. In interactive SQL, you issue SQL commands directly to your DBMS, which displays the results as soon as they're produced. DBMS servers come with both graphical and command-line tools that accept typed SQL statements or text files that contain SQL programs (scripts).

If you're developing database applications, then you can "embed" SQL statements in programs written in a **host language**, which commonly is a general-purpose language (C++, Java, or COBOL, for example) or a scripting language (Python, R, or PHP). A PHP script can use an SQL statement to query a MySQL database, for example; MySQL will pass the query result back to a PHP variable for further analysis or webpage display. Drawing from the preceding examples, I've embedded an SQL statement in an Access Visual Basic program in Listing i.3.

This book covers interactive SQL. In general, any SQL statement that can be used interactively also can be used in a host language, although perhaps with slight syntactic differences, depending on your DBMS, host language, and operating environment.

Standardized. SQL isn't "owned" by any particular firm. It's an open standard defined by an international standards working group, under the joint leadership of the International Organization for Standardization (ISO) and the International Engineering Consortium (IEC). The American National Standards Institute (ANSI) participates in the working groups and has ratified the standard (Figure i.1). The terms *ISO SQL*, *ANSI SQL*, and *standard SQL* are synonymous. For more information, see "SQL Standards and Conformance" on page 53.

All DBMS vendors add proprietary features to standard SQL to enhance the language. These extensions usually are additional commands, keywords, functions, operators, data types, and control-flow constructs such as if-then, while, and goto statements. Microsoft, Oracle, and IBM have added so many features to standard SQL that the resulting languages—Transact-SQL, PL/SQL, and SQL PL, respectively—are actually separate languages in their own right, rather than mere supersets of standard SQL. One vendor's extensions generally are incompatible with other vendors' products. I don't

```
Sub GetAuthorNames2()
  Dim db As Database
  Dim rs As Recordset
  Set db = CurrentDb()
  Set rs = db.OpenRecordset("SELECT au_fname,
      au_lname FROM authors;")
  '  --Do something with rs here.
  rs.Close
  db.Close
End Sub
```

Listing i.3 Here, Visual Basic serves as the host language for embedded SQL.

INTERNATIONAL STANDARD

ISO/IEC 9075-1

Fifth edition
2016-12-15

Information technology — Database languages — SQL —

Part 1:
Framework (SQL/Framework)

Technologies de l'information — Langages de base de données — SQL —

Partie 1: Charpente (SQL/Charpente)

Figure i.1 This is the cover of ISO/IEC 9075 (Part 1), which defines the SQL language officially. You can buy it in electronic format at *ansi.org* or *iso.org* if you like. Its intended audience is not SQL programmers, however, but people who design DBMS systems, compilers, and optimizers.

cover proprietary SQL extensions, but I do point out when a vendor's SQL dialect doesn't comply with the standard SQL examples in this book; see "Using SQL with a Specific DBMS" on page xiii.

Used to change data and database objects. SQL statements are divided into three categories:

- **Data manipulation language (DML)** statements retrieve, reckon, insert, edit, and delete data stored in a database. Chapters 4 through 10 cover the DML statements SELECT, INSERT, UPDATE, and DELETE. Chapter 14 covers START (or BEGIN), COMMIT, and ROLLBACK.

- **Data definition language (DDL)** statements create, modify, and destroy database objects such as tables, indexes, and views. Chapters 11 through 13 cover the DDL statements CREATE, ALTER, and DROP.

- **Data control language (DCL)** statements authorize certain users to view, change, or delete data and database objects. The GRANT statement assigns privileges to users and roles (a **role** is a named set of privileges). The REVOKE statement removes privileges. GRANT and REVOKE aren't covered in this book because they're the responsibility of database administrators. All the DBMSs (except Microsoft Access) covered in this book support GRANT and REVOKE, with variations on the SQL standard.

Not an acronym. It's a common misconception that SQL stands for *structured query language*; it stands for S–Q–L and nothing else. Why? Because ISO says so. The official name is Database Language SQL (refer to Figure i.1). Furthermore, referring to it as a structured query language is a disservice to new SQL programmers. It amuses insiders to point out that "structured query language" is the worst possible description because SQL:

- Isn't structured (because it can't be broken down into blocks or procedures)

- Isn't for only queries (because it has more than just the SELECT statement)

- Isn't a language (because it's not Turing-complete, a central concept in the theory of computation)

About This Book

Chapters 1 through 3 contain expository material about DBMSs, the relational model, and SQL syntax. Later chapters all use a learn-by-example approach to teach you how to use the SQL programming language to maintain and query database information.

You don't need prior programming experience but you must be familiar with your operating system's filesystem (the hierarchy of folders and files) and know how to issue commands at a command prompt or shell.

This book isn't an exhaustive guide to SQL; I've limited its scope to the most-used statements and functions (itself a vast topic). For information about other SQL statements, refer to your DBMS's documentation.

Typographic Conventions

I use the following typographic conventions:

Bold type introduces new terms.

Italic type represents replaceable variables in regular text.

Monospace type denotes SQL code and syntax in listings and in regular text. It also shows command-prompt text.

Bold monospace type highlights SQL code fragments and results that are explained in the accompanying text.

Italic monospace type denotes a variable in SQL code that you must replace with a value. You'd replace *column* with the name of an actual column, for example.

Syntax Conventions

SQL is a free-form language without restrictions on line breaks or the number of words per line, so I use a consistent style in SQL syntax diagrams and code listings to make the code easy to read and maintain:

- Each SQL statement begins on a new line.

- The indentation level is two spaces.

- Each clause of a statement begins on a new, indented line:

  ```
  SELECT au_fname, au_lname
    FROM authors
    ORDER BY au_lname;
  ```

- SQL is case insensitive, meaning that *myname*, *MyName*, and *MYNAME* are considered to be identical identifiers. I use UPPERCASE for SQL keywords such as SELECT, NULL, and CHARACTER (see "SQL Syntax" on page 50), and lowercase or lower_case for user-defined values, such as table, column, and alias names.

  (User-defined identifiers are case sensitive when quoted and in a few other situations for some DBMSs, so it's safest to respect identifier case in SQL programs.)

- All quote marks in SQL code are straight quotes (such as ' and "), not curly, or smart, quotes (such as ' and "). Curly quotes prevent code from working.

- Table i.1 shows special symbols used in syntax diagrams.

Table i.1 Syntax Symbols

Characters	Description
|	The vertical-bar or pipe symbol separates alternative items. You can choose exactly one of the given items. (Don't type the vertical bar.) A|B|C is read "A or B or C". Don't confuse the pipe symbol with the double-pipe symbol, ||, which is SQL's string-concatenation operator.
[ ]	Brackets enclose one or more optional items. (Don't type the brackets.) [A|B|C] means "type A or B or C or type nothing". [D] means "type D or type nothing".
{ }	Braces enclose one or more required items. (Don't type the braces.) {A|B|C} means "type A or B or C".
. . .	Ellipses mean that the preceding item(s) can be repeated any number of times.

Using SQL with a Specific DBMS

DBMS The DBMS icon flags a vendor-specific departure from the SQL standard. If you see this icon, then it means that a particular vendor's SQL dialect doesn't comply with the standard, and you must modify the listed SQL program to run on your DBMS. For example, the standard SQL operator that joins (concatenates) two strings is || (a double pipe), but Microsoft products use + (a plus sign) and MySQL uses the CONCAT() function instead, so you'll need to change all occurrences of a || b in the example SQL listing to a + b (if you're using Microsoft Access or Microsoft SQL Server) or to CONCAT(a, b) (if you're using MySQL). In most cases, the SQL examples will work as is or with minor syntactic changes. Occasionally, SQL code won't work at all because the DBMS doesn't support a particular feature.

This book covers the following DBMSs (see Chapter 1 for details):

- Microsoft Access

- Microsoft SQL Server

- Oracle Database

- IBM Db2 Database

- MySQL

- PostgreSQL

If you're using a different DBMS (such as SAP, Teradata, MariaDB, FileMaker, or SAS SQL), and one of the SQL examples doesn't work, then read the documentation to see how your DBMS's SQL implementation departs from the SQL standard.

Tip: To compare general and technical information for a number of DBMSs, read the Wikipedia article "Comparison of relational database management systems" at *wikipedia.org/wiki/ Comparison_of_relational_database_management_systems.*

What You'll Need

To replicate this book's examples on your own computer, you'll need:

- A text editor
- The sample database
- A database management system

A text editor. Typing short or ad-hoc interactive SQL statements at a prompt is convenient, but you'll want to store nontrivial SQL programs in text files. A **text editor** is a program that you use to open, create, and edit **text files**, which contain only printable letters, numbers, and symbols—no fonts, formatting, invisible codes, colors, graphics, or any of the clutter usually associated with a word processor. Every operating system includes a free text editor. Windows has Notepad, Unix and Linux have vi and emacs, and macOS has TextEdit, for example. By convention, SQL files have the filename extension .sql, but you can use .txt (or any extension) if you prefer. For programming, professional editors such as Sublime Text (*sublimetext.com*) and Vim (*vim.org*) are superior to the basic editors that come with Windows and macOS.

The sample database. The examples in this book use the same database, described in "The Sample Database" on page 39. To build the sample database, follow the instructions in "Creating the Sample Database" on page 45. If you're working with a production-server DBMS, then you might need permission from your database administrator to run SQL programs that create, update, and delete data and database objects.

A database management system. How do you get SQL? You don't—you get a DBMS that understands SQL and feed it an SQL program. The DBMS runs your program and displays the results, as described in the next chapter.

Server vs. Desktop DBMSs

A **server** DBMS acts as the server part of a client/server network; it stores databases and responds to SQL requests made by many clients. A **client** is an application or computer that sends an SQL request to a server and accepts the server's response. The server does the actual work of executing the SQL against a database; the client merely accepts the answer. If your network uses a client/server architecture, then the client is the computer on your desk, and the server is a powerful, specialized machine in another room, building, or country. Standard database access protocols and interfaces such as ODBC, JDBC, and ADO.NET define how client/server requests and responses are transmitted.

A **desktop** DBMS is a stand-alone program that can store a database and do all the SQL processing itself or behave as a client of a server. A desktop DBMS can't accept requests from other clients (that is, it can't act like a server).

Servers include Microsoft SQL Server, Oracle Database, IBM Db2 Database, MySQL, and PostgreSQL. Desktop systems include Microsoft Access and FileMaker. By convention, I use the terms *client* and *server* to refer to client and server software itself or to the machine on which the software runs, unless the distinction is important.

Running SQL Programs

You need a database management system to run SQL programs. You can have your own private copy of a DBMS running on your personal (local) computer, or you can use a shared DBMS over a network. In the latter case, you use your personal computer to connect to a DBMS server running on another machine. The computer where the DBMS is running is called a **host**.

Older DBMSs and Backward Compatibility of SQL

At this writing, the current ("stable") releases of the DBMSs covered in this book are Microsoft Access 2019, Microsoft SQL Server 2019, Oracle Database 19c, IBM Db2 Database 12, MySQL 8, and PostgreSQL 12. New releases bring new features and fixes, but also bring loss of familiarity, workflow disruptions, new bugs, dropped features, incompatibilities, installation nightmares, endless testing, revised license agreements, new prices, and a chance of data loss. Given these risks and headaches, most DBMS users, from individuals to large organizations, typically are very slow to upgrade their DBMS.

This book favors SQL code that's backward compatible, meaning it runs on older ("legacy") systems. Each new release of a DBMS brings additions (whether standard or nonstandard) to its implementation of SQL. Given a choice, opt for tried-and-true legacy SQL code, which runs on legacy and current systems. For basic SQL (SELECT, JOIN, INSERT, CREATE, and so on), the DBMS's optimizer runs legacy code at the same speed and efficiency as new-style code, so there's no disadvantage in using legacy SQL code in most cases.

DBMSs and SQL Tools

This chapter describes how to run SQL programs on these DBMSs:

- Microsoft Access
- Microsoft SQL Server
- Oracle Database
- IBM Db2 Database
- MySQL
- PostgreSQL

Microsoft Access's graphical interface lets you run only one SQL statement at a time. The other systems, all DBMS servers, let you run SQL programs in interactive mode or script mode. In **interactive mode**, you type individual SQL statements at a command prompt and view the results of each statement separately, so input and output are interleaved. In **script mode** (also called **batch mode**), you save your entire SQL program in a text file (called a **script** or a **batch file**), and a command-line tool takes the file, executes the program, and returns the results without your intervention. I use the sample database and the SQL program shown in Listing 1.1 in all the examples in the rest of this chapter. The examples give the minimal syntax of command-line tools; the complete syntax is given in the DBMS documentation.

```
SELECT au_fname, au_lname
  FROM authors
  ORDER BY au_lname;
```

Listing 1.1 This file, named listing0101.sql, contains a simple SQL SELECT statement, which is used to query the sample database in subsequent DBMS examples.

The Command Line

Most database professionals prefer to submit commands and SQL scripts through a DBMS's command-line environment rather than mousing around the menus and windows of a graphical front-end. (Database administrators don't add 1000 users by pointing and clicking.) If you're new to DBMSs, then you might find the command line to be cryptic and intimidating, but experience will show you its power, simplicity, and speed. Graphical tools do have a few advantages, though:

- Full clipboard support for cut, copy, and paste

- Boundless horizontal and vertical scrolling

- Column widths that you can change by dragging with the mouse

- Better history of the commands and results

You can find free full-featured SQL shells that work across DBMSs by searching the web for *sql front end* or *sql client*. Unix lovers stuck with Windows can use Windows Subsystem for Linux (*docs.microsoft.com/windows/wsl*). Windows PowerShell (*microsoft.com/powershell*) also provides advanced scripting.

Paths

A **path** (or **pathname**) specifies the unique location of a directory (folder) or file in a filesystem hierarchy. An **absolute path** specifies a location completely, starting at the topmost node of the directory tree, called the **root**. A **relative path** specifies a location relative to the current (or working) directory. In Windows, an absolute path starts with a backslash (\) or with a drive letter followed by a colon and a backslash (C:\, for example). In Unix or macOS Terminal, an absolute path starts with a slash (/).

C:\Program Files\Microsoft SQL Server (Windows) and */usr/local/bin/mysql* (Unix) are absolute paths, for example. *scripts\listing0101. sql* (Windows) and *doc/readme.txt* (Unix) are relative paths. Absolute paths for files and folders on a network also can begin with a double backslash and server name (*servername*, for example). If a path contains spaces, then surround the entire path with double quotes. When you specify the name of an SQL file in script mode, you can include an absolute or relative path.

To run a command-line tool from an arbitrary directory, your **PATH environment variable** must include the directory that actually contains the tool. This environment variable lists the directories (folders) that the OS searches for programs. For some DBMSs, the installer handles the PATH details; for others, you must add the tool's directory to PATH yourself.

To view the contents of the PATH variable, type `path` (Windows) or `echo $PATH` (Unix or macOS Terminal) at a command prompt. To change the PATH, add the absolute path of the directory in which the tool resides to the PATH environment variable. Search Help for *environment variable* (Windows), or modify the path command in your login initialization file, usually named .bash_login, .bashrc, .cshrc, .login, .profile, or .shrc (Unix or macOS).

Microsoft Access

Microsoft Access is a personal and commercial desktop DBMS that supports small and medium-size databases. Learn about Access at *products. office.com/access* and download a free trial copy. To determine which version of Access you're using, choose File tab > Account > About Access.

In Access, you must turn on ANSI-92 SQL syntax to run many of the examples in this book.

To turn on ANSI-92 SQL syntax for a Microsoft Access database:

1. In Microsoft Access, open the database.

2. Choose File tab > Options > Object Designers (in the left pane).

3. Below SQL Server Compatible Syntax (ANSI 92), select "This database" (Figure 1.1).

4. Click OK.

   Access closes, compacts, and then reopens the database before the new setting takes effect. You might see a few warnings, depending on your security settings.

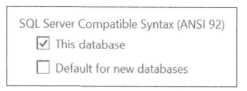

Figure 1.1 Select this checkbox to turn on ANSI-92 SQL syntax mode for the open database.

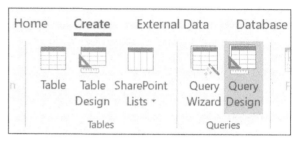

Figure 1.2 Query Design lets you skip the wizards.

Figure 1.3 You don't need to add tables graphically because the SQL statement specifies the tables.

ANSI-89 vs. ANSI-92 SQL

Be careful switching between ANSI-89 and ANSI-92 SQL syntax modes in Microsoft Access. The modes aren't compatible, so you should pick a mode when you create a database and never change it. The range of data types, reserved words, and wildcard characters differs by mode, so SQL statements created in one mode might not work in the other. The older ANSI-89 standard is limited compared with ANSI-92, so you should choose ANSI-92 syntax for new databases. For more information, see "SQL Standards and Conformance" on page 53.

DBMS | If you're using **Microsoft Access** as a front-end to query a **Microsoft SQL Server** database, then you must use ANSI-92 syntax, available in Access 2000 or later.

Figure 1.4 SQL View hides the graphical query grid and instead shows a text editor where you can type or paste an SQL statement.

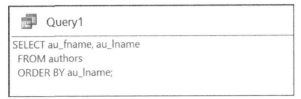

Figure 1.5 Enter an SQL statement...

Figure 1.6 ...and run it.

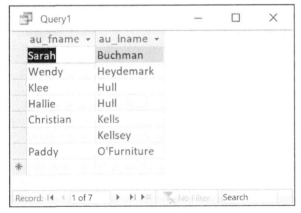

Figure 1.7 Microsoft Access displays the result of a SELECT statement.

If you're a casual Access user, then you've probably used the query design grid to create a query. When you create a query in Design View, Access builds the equivalent SQL statement behind the scenes for you. You can view, edit, and run the SQL statement in SQL View.

You can run only a single SQL statement through an Access Query object. To run multiple statements, use multiple Query objects or a host language such as Visual Basic or C#.

To run an SQL statement in Microsoft Access:

1. In Microsoft Access, open a database.

2. Choose Create tab > Queries group > Query Design (Figure 1.2).

3. Without adding tables or queries, click Close in the Show Table dialog box (Figure 1.3).

4. To run the SQL statement, choose Design tab > Results group > SQL View (Figure 1.4).

5. Type or paste an SQL statement (Figure 1.5).

6. Choose Design tab > Results group > Run (Figure 1.6).

   Access displays the result of a SELECT statement (Figure 1.7) but blocks or executes other types of SQL statements, with or without warning messages, depending on your settings.

Tip: To display a list of existing queries, press F11 to show Navigation pane (on the left), click the menu at the top of the pane, choose Object Type, click the menu again, and then choose Queries. (The Navigation pane replaced the Database window of early Access versions.)

Microsoft SQL Server

Microsoft SQL Server is a commercial DBMS that supports very large databases and numbers of transactions. It runs on Microsoft Windows and Linux operating systems and is complex enough to require a full-time database administrator (DBA) to run and maintain it.

Learn about SQL Server products at *microsoft.com/sql* and download a free trial copy of SQL Server or a (permanently) free copy of SQL Server Express. SQL Server Express is a free, limited version of SQL Server. To run SQL programs in SQL Server or SQL Server Express, you can use the SQL Server Management Studio graphical tool or the **sqlcmd** command-line tool.

To determine which version of Microsoft SQL Server you're using, run the SQL Server command-line command

```
sqlcmd -S server\instance_name -E
  -Q "SELECT @@VERSION;"
```

server\instance_name is the named instance of SQL Server to which to connect. Alternatively, run the query

```
SELECT SERVERPROPERTY('ProductVersion');
```

or

```
SELECT @@VERSION;
```

Tip: You can use the SET ANSI_DEFAULTS ON option to make SQL Server conform to standard SQL more closely.

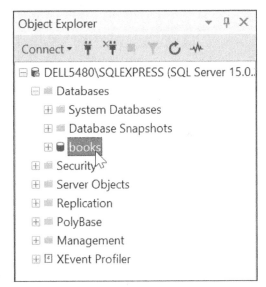

Figure 1.8 SQL Server Management Studio uses the selected database to resolve references in your SQL statements.

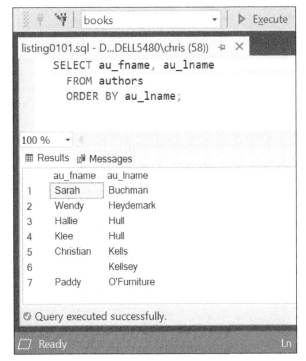

Figure 1.9 The result of a SELECT statement in SQL Server Management Studio.

To use SQL Server Management Studio:

1. On the Windows desktop, choose Start > Microsoft SQL Server Tools > Microsoft SQL Server Management Studio.

2. In the Connect to Server dialog box, select the server and authentication mode, and then click Connect.

3. In Object Explorer (the left pane), expand the Databases folder of the server that you're using, and then select a database (Figure 1.8).

   If Object Explorer isn't visible, then choose View > Object Explorer (or press F8).

4. To run SQL interactively, click New Query (on the toolbar) or right-click the database (in Object Explorer) and choose New Query in the context menu. Type or paste an SQL statement in the empty tab that appears in the right pane.

   or

   To run an SQL script, choose File > Open > File (or press Ctrl+O), navigate to and select the script file, and then click Open. The file's contents appear in a new tab in the right pane.

5. Click Execute (on the toolbar) or choose Query > Execute (or press F5).

   SQL Server displays the results in the bottom pane (Figure 1.9).

To use the sqlcmd command-line tool interactively:

1. At an administrator command prompt, type:

    sqlcmd -S *server\instance_name* -d *dbname*

    server\instance_name is the named instance of SQL Server to which to connect, and *dbname* is the name of the database to use

2. Type an SQL statement. The statement can span multiple lines. Terminate it with a semicolon (;) and then press Enter.

3. Type go and then press Enter to display the result (Figure 1.10).

To use the sqlcmd command-line tool in script mode:

1. At an administrator command prompt, type:

    sqlcmd -S *server\instance_name* -d *dbname*
     -i *sql_script*

    server\instance_name is the named instance of SQL Server to which to connect, and *dbname* is the name of the database to use. *sql_script* is a text file containing SQL statement(s) and can include an absolute or relative path.

2. Press Enter to display the results (Figure 1.11).

To exit the sqlcmd command-line tool:

*   Type exit or quit and then press Enter.

To show sqlcmd command-line options:

*   At a command prompt, type sqlcmd -? and then press Enter.

    sqlcmd tries to use a trusted connection by default. If instead you have to specify a user name and password, then add the option -U *login_id*. *login_id* is your user name. sqlcmd will prompt you for your password.

    If SQL Server is running on a remote network computer, then the sqlcmd option -S *server\ instance_name* is required to specify the SQL Server instance to connect to. Ask your database administrator for the connection parameters. The -S option also works for local connections, when SQL Server is running on your own personal computer rather than on a server elsewhere.

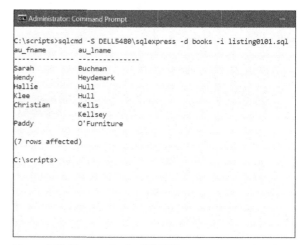

Figure 1.10 The result of a SELECT statement in sqlcmd interactive mode.

Figure 1.11 The result of a SELECT statement in sqlcmd script mode.

Tip: To open an administrator command prompt in Microsoft Windows, tap the Windows Logo Key (or click Start), type **command**, right-click "Command Prompt" in the results list, and then choose "Run as administrator" in the context menu.

```
ca. Administrator: Command Prompt - sqlplus  system@books

C:\scripts>sqlplus system@books

SQL*Plus: Release 18.0.0.0.0 - Production on Fri Jan 31 13:02
Version 18.4.0.0.0

Copyright (c) 1982, 2018, Oracle.  All rights reserved.

Enter password:
Last Successful login time: Thu Jan 30 2020 20:27:42 -08:00

Connected to:
Oracle Database 18c Express Edition Release 18.0.0.0.0 - Prod
Version 18.4.0.0.0

SQL> SELECT au_fname, au_lname
  2    FROM authors
  3    ORDER BY au_lname;

AU_FNAME         AU_LNAME
---------------  ---------------
Sarah            Buchman
Wendy            Heydemark
Hallie           Hull
Klee             Hull
Christian        Kells
                 Kellsey
Paddy            O'Furniture

7 rows selected.

SQL>
```

Figure 1.12 The result of a SELECT statement in sqlplus interactive mode.

Oracle Database

Oracle Database is a commercial DBMS that supports very large databases and numbers of transactions. It runs on many operating systems and hardware platforms and is complex enough to require a full-time database administrator (DBA) to run and maintain it.

Learn about Oracle products at *oracle.com* and download Oracle Express Edition (XE)—a free, limited version of Oracle Database. Documentation is at *docs.oracle.com*.

To determine which version of Oracle you're using, run the query

```
SELECT banner FROM v$version;
```

The Oracle version also is displayed in the initial "Connected to" message that appears when you log on to SQL*Plus.

To run SQL programs, use the **sqlplus** command-line tool.

To use the sqlplus command-line tool interactively:

1. At an administrator command prompt, type:

    ```
    sqlplus user/password@dbname
    ```

    user is your Oracle user name, *password* is your password, and *dbname* is the name of the database to connect to. For security, you can omit the password and instead type:

    ```
    sqlplus user@dbname
    ```

    sqlplus will prompt you for your password.

2. Type an SQL statement. The statement can span multiple lines. Terminate it with a semicolon (;) and then press Enter to display the result (Figure 1.12).

To use the sqlplus command-line tool in script mode:

1. At an administrator command prompt, type:

   sqlplus *user*/*password*@*dbname* @*sql_script*

   user is your Oracle user name, *password* is your password, *dbname* is the name of the database to connect to, and *sql_script* is a text file containing SQL statement(s) and can include an absolute or relative path. For security, you can omit the password, and instead type:

   sqlplus *user*@*dbname* @*sql_script*

   sqlplus will prompt you for your password

2. Press Enter to display the results (Figure 1.13).

To exit the sqlplus command-line tool:

- Type exit or quit and then press Enter.

To show sqlplus command-line options:

- At a command prompt, type sqlplus -H and then press Enter.

  This command displays pages that speed by. To view one page at a time, type

  sqlplus -H | more

  and then press Enter. Tap the spacebar to advance pages (Figure 1.14).

If you're running Oracle locally, then you can use the user name system and the password that you specified when you created the database:

sqlplus system@*dbname*

If you're connecting to a remote Oracle database, then ask your database administrator for the connection parameters.

An alternative way to start sqlplus in Windows is to choose Start > Oracle > SQL Plus.

Tip: To open an administrator command prompt in Microsoft Windows, tap the Windows Logo Key (or click Start), type **command**, right-click "Command Prompt" in the results list, and then choose "Run as administrator" in the context menu.

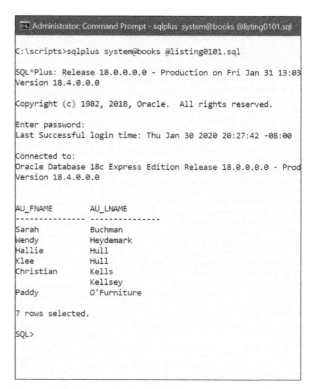

Figure 1.13 The result of a SELECT statement in sqlplus script mode.

Figure 1.14 The sqlplus help screen.

IBM Db2 Database

IBM Db2 Database is a commercial DBMS that supports very large databases and numbers of transactions. It runs on many operating systems and hardware platforms and is complex enough to require a full-time database administrator (DBA) to run and maintain it.

Learn about Db2 products at *ibm.com/db2* and download a free trial copy of Db2 or a (permanently) free copy of IBM Db2 Community Edition.

To determine which version of Db2 you're using, run the Db2 command-line command

```
db2level
```

or run the query

```
SELECT service_level
  FROM SYSIBMADM.ENV_INST_INFO;
```

To run SQL programs, use the IBM Data Studio graphical tool or the **db2** command-line processor (CLP).

To use Data Studio:

1. Open Data Studio.

   This procedure varies by platform. In Microsoft Windows, for example, choose Start > IBM Data Studio > Data Studio Client.

2. On the Administration Explorer tab (on the left), expand the All Databases folder of the object tree until you find your instance of Db2, and then select a database (below the Db2 instance).

   If the desired database doesn't appear, then right-click the All Databases folder, choose "New Connection to a Database" in the context menu, and then connect to the target database.

3. To run SQL interactively, click New SQL Script on the Administration Explorer toolbar. On the Script tab that opens, type or paste an SQL statement in the box.

   or

   To run an SQL script, choose File > Open File, navigate to and select the script file, and then click Open. On the File tab that opens, click No Connection (if it appears) to connect to the target database.

4. Choose Script > Run SQL or click ▶.

   Data Studio displays the results in the SQL Results tab (at the bottom). Click the Result tab to see the query results or click the Status tab to see query-processing information.

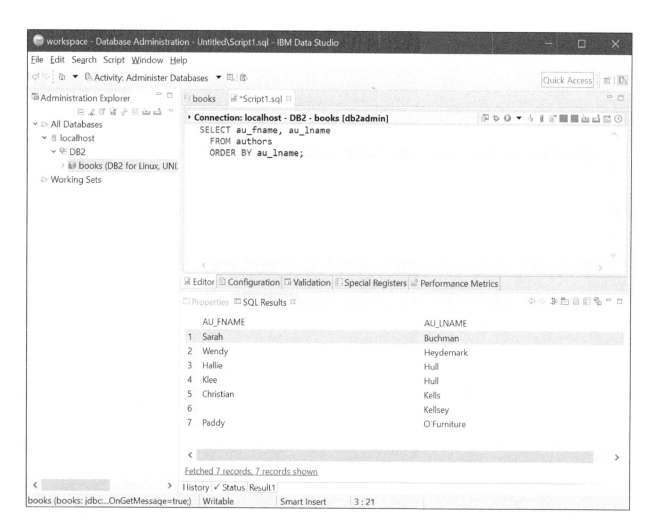

For technical reasons involving parent and child processes, (only) Microsoft Windows users must start the db2 command-line processor with a special preliminary step.

To start the db2 command-line processor in Windows:

- At an administrator command prompt, type db2cmd and then press Enter. Alternatively, choose Start > IBM DB2 DB2COPY1 (default) > Db2 Command Line Processor.

  A new DB2 CLP command-prompt window appears.

  You must use the Db2 CLP window for all db2 commands (described next). If you try to run db2 at a normal Windows command prompt, then Db2 responds with the error "Command line environment not initialized."

  If you launch a new Db2 CLP window via the db2cmd command, then you can close the original command-prompt window.

  In the Db2 CLP window, change (cd) your working directory if necessary before you run db2 commands.

To use the db2 command-line processor interactively:

1. At a command prompt, type:

   db2 -t

   and then press Enter. The -t option tells db2 that a semicolon (;) terminates statements.

   The db2 => prompt appears.

2. At the db2 prompt, type:

   connect to *dbname*;

   and then press Enter. *dbname* is the name of the database to use.

3. Type an SQL statement. The statement can span multiple lines. Terminate it with a semicolon (;) and then press Enter to display the result (Figure 1.15).

   Alternatively, you can avoid the db2 => prompt by typing commands and SQL statements right on the command line. For example:

db2 connect to books

db2 SELECT * FROM authors

If you omit the -t option, as here, then don't terminate commands and SQL statements with a semicolon.

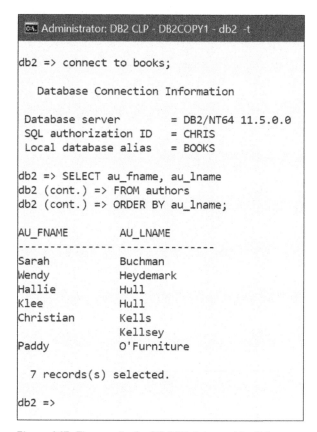

```
Administrator: DB2 CLP - DB2COPY1 - db2 -t

db2 => connect to books;

   Database Connection Information

 Database server        = DB2/NT64 11.5.0.0
 SQL authorization ID   = CHRIS
 Local database alias   = BOOKS

db2 => SELECT au_fname, au_lname
db2 (cont.) => FROM authors
db2 (cont.) => ORDER BY au_lname;

AU_FNAME          AU_LNAME
---------------   ---------------
Sarah             Buchman
Wendy             Heydemark
Hallie            Hull
Klee              Hull
Christian         Kells
                  Kellsey
Paddy             O'Furniture

  7 records(s) selected.

db2 =>
```

Figure 1.15 The result of a SELECT statement in db2 interactive mode.

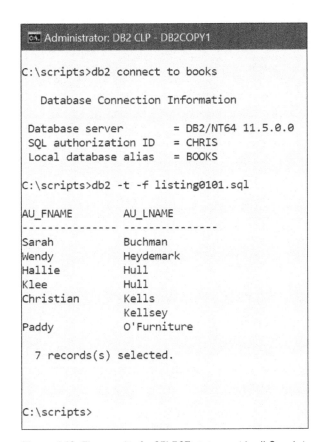

```
Administrator: DB2 CLP - DB2COPY1

C:\scripts>db2 connect to books

    Database Connection Information

 Database server        = DB2/NT64 11.5.0.0
 SQL authorization ID   = CHRIS
 Local database alias   = BOOKS

C:\scripts>db2 -t -f listing0101.sql

AU_FNAME            AU_LNAME
---------------     ---------------
Sarah               Buchman
Wendy               Heydemark
Hallie              Hull
Klee                Hull
Christian           Kells
                    Kellsey
Paddy               O'Furniture

  7 records(s) selected.


C:\scripts>
```

Figure 1.16 The result of a SELECT statement in db2 script mode.

```
Administrator: Command Prompt

c:\scripts>db2 ?  | more
db2 [option ...] [db2-command | sql-statement |
   [? [phrase | message | sqlstate | class-code]]]
option: -a, -c, -d, -e{c|s}, -finfile, -i, -lhistfile, -o, -m, -n,
        -p, -q, -rreport, -s, -t, -tdj, -v, -w, -x, -zoutputfile.
db2-command:
  ACTIVATE DATABASE      GET CONTACTS           REFRESH LDAP
  ADD CONTACT            GET/UPDATE DB CFG      REGISTER LDAP
  ADD CONTACTGROUP       GET/UPDATE DBM CFG     REGISTER XMLSCHEMA
  ADD DBPARTITIONNUM     GET DBM MONITOR SWITCHES REGISTER XSROBJECT
  ADD XMLSCHEMA          GET DESCRIPTION FOR HEALTH REORG INDEXES/TABLE
  ARCHIVE LOG            GET NOTIFICATION LIST  REORGCHK
  ATTACH                 GET HEALTH SNAPSHOT    RESET ADMIN CFG
  AUTOCONFIGURE          GET INSTANCE           RESET ALERT CFG
  BACKUP DATABASE        GET MONITOR SWITCHES   RESET DB CFG
  BIND                   GET RECOMMENDATIONS    RESET DBM CFG
  CATALOG APPC NODE      GET ROUTINE            RESET MONITOR
  CATALOG APPN NODE      GET SNAPSHOT           RESTART DATABASE
  CATALOG DATABASE       HELP                   RESTORE DATABASE
  CATALOG DCS DATABASE   HISTORY                REWIND TAPE
  CATALOG LDAP DATABASE  IMPORT                 ROLLFORWARD DATABASE
  CATALOG LDAP NODE      INITIALIZE TAPE        RUNCMD
  CATALOG LOCAL NODE     INSPECT                RUNSTATS
  CATALOG NPIPE NODE     LIST ACTIVE DATABASES  SET CLIENT
  LIST COMMAND OPTIONS   LIST APPLICATIONS      SET RUNTIME DEGREE
  CATALOG ODBC DATA SOURCE LIST DATABASE DIRECTORY SET TABLESPACE CONTAINERS
  CATALOG TCPIP NODE     LIST DB PARTITION GROUPS SET TAPE POSITION
  CHANGE DATABASE COMMENT LIST DBPARTITIONNUMS  SET UTIL_IMPACT_PRIORITY
  CHANGE ISOLATION LEVEL LIST DCS APPLICATIONS  SET WRITE
  COMPLETE XMLSCHEMA     LIST DCS DIRECTORY     START DATABASE MANAGER
-- More  --
```

Figure 1.17 The db2 help screen.

To use the db2 command-line processor in script mode:

1. At a command prompt, type:

   db2 connect to *dbname*

   dbname is the name of the database to use.

2. At a command prompt, type:

   db2 -t -f *sql_script*

   sql_script is a text file containing SQL statement(s) and can include an absolute or relative path. The -t option tells db2 that a semicolon (;) terminates statements. Add the -v option if you want to echo the contents of *sql_script* in the output.

3. Press Enter to display the results (Figure 1.16).

Tip: An alternative script tool is db2batch.

To exit the db2 command-line tool:

- At the db2 prompt, type quit; and then press Enter. (Omit the semicolon if you didn't use the -t option when you started db2.)

To show db2 command-line options:

- At a command prompt, type db2 ? and then press Enter.

  This command displays pages that speed by. To view one page at a time, type

  db2 ? | more

  and then press Enter. Tap the spacebar to advance pages (Figure 1.17).

  To get help while you're at a db2 => prompt, type ?; and then press Enter. (Omit the semicolon if you didn't use the -t option when you started db2.)

MySQL

MySQL (pronounced *my-es-kyoo-el*) is an open-source DBMS that supports large databases and numbers of transactions. MySQL is known for its speed and ease of use. It's free for personal use and runs on many operating systems and hardware platforms. You can download it at *mysql.com*.

To determine which version of MySQL you're using, run the MySQL command-line command

```
mysql -V
```

or run the query

```
SELECT VERSION();
```

To run SQL programs, use the **mysql** command-line tool.

To use the mysql command-line tool interactively:

1. At an administrator command prompt, type:

   ```
   mysql -h host -u user -p dbname
   ```

   host is the host name, *user* is your MySQL user name, and *dbname* is the name of the database to use. MySQL will prompt you for your password (for a passwordless user, either omit the -p option or press Enter at the password prompt).

2. Type an SQL statement. The statement can span multiple lines. Terminate it with a semicolon (;) and then press Enter to display the result (Figure 1.18).

Figure 1.18 The result of a SELECT statement in mysql interactive mode.

Figure 1.19 The result of a SELECT statement in mysql script mode.

Figure 1.20 The mysql help screen.

To use the mysql command-line tool in script mode:

1. At an administrator command prompt, type:

   ```
   mysql -h host -u user -p -t
       dbname < sql_script
   ```

   host is the host name, *user* is your MySQL user name, and *dbname* is the name of the database to use. MySQL will prompt you for your password (for a passwordless user, either omit the -p option or press Enter at the password prompt). The -t option formats the results as a table; omit this option if you want tab-delimited output. The redirection operator < reads from the file *sql_script*, which is a text file containing SQL statement(s) and can include an absolute or relative path.

2. Press Enter to display the results (Figure 1.19).

To exit the mysql command-line tool:

- Type quit or \q and then press Enter.

To show mysql command-line options:

- At a command prompt, type mysql -? and then press Enter.

  This command displays pages that speed by. To view one page at a time, type

  ```
  mysql -? | more
  ```

  and then press Enter. Tap the spacebar to advance pages (Figure 1.20).

  If MySQL is running on a remote network computer, then ask your database administrator for the connection parameters. If you're running MySQL locally (that is, on your own computer), then set *host* to localhost, set *user* to root, and use the password that you assigned to root when you set up or installed MySQL.

Tip: To open an administrator command prompt in Microsoft Windows, tap the Windows Logo Key (or click Start), type **command**, right-click "Command Prompt" in the results list, and then choose "Run as administrator" in the context menu.

PostgreSQL

PostgreSQL (pronounced *post-gres-kyoo-el*) is an open-source DBMS that supports large databases and numbers of transactions. PostgreSQL is known for its rich feature set and its high conformance with standard SQL. It's free and runs on many operating systems and hardware platforms. You can download it at *postgresql.org*.

To determine which version of PostgreSQL you're using, run the PostgreSQL command-line command

```
psql -V
```

or run the query

```
SELECT VERSION();
```

To run SQL programs, use the **psql** command-line tool.

To use the psql command-line tool interactively:

1. At an administrator command prompt, type:

    ```
    psql -h host -U user -W dbname
    ```

    host is the host name, *user* is your PostgreSQL user name, and *dbname* is the name of the database to use. PostgreSQL will prompt you for your password (for a passwordless user, either omit the -W option or press Enter at the password prompt).

2. Type an SQL statement. The statement can span multiple lines. Terminate it with a semicolon (;) and then press Enter to display the result (Figure 1.21).

Figure 1.21 The result of a SELECT statement in psql interactive mode.

Figure 1.22 The result of a SELECT statement in psql script mode.

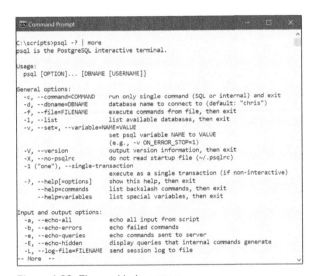

Figure 1.23 The psql help screen.

Tip: To open an administrator command prompt in Microsoft Windows, tap the Windows Logo Key (or click Start), type **command**, right-click "Command Prompt" in the results list, and then choose "Run as administrator" in the context menu.

To use the psql command-line tool in script mode:

1. At an administrator command prompt, type:

   ```
   psql -h host -U user -W
     -f sql_script dbname
   ```

   host is the host name, *user* is your PostgreSQL user name, and *dbname* is the name of the database to use. PostgreSQL will prompt you for your password (for a passwordless user, either omit the -W option or press Enter at the password prompt). The -f option specifies the name of the SQL file *sql_script*, which is a text file containing SQL statement(s) and can include an absolute or relative path.

2. Press Enter to display the results (Figure 1.22).

To exit the psql command-line tool:

• Type \q and then press Enter.

To show psql command-line options:

• At a command prompt, type psql -? and then press Enter.

   This command displays pages that speed by. To view one page at a time, type

   ```
   psql -? | more
   ```

   and then press Enter. Tap the spacebar to advance pages (Figure 1.23).

   If PostgreSQL is running on a remote network computer, then ask your database administrator for the connection parameters. If you're running PostgreSQL locally (that is, on your own computer), then set *host* to localhost, set *user* to postgres, and use the password that you assigned to postgres when you set up or installed PostgreSQL.

   You can set the environment variables PGHOST, PGDATABASE, and PGUSER to specify the default host, database, and user names used to connect to the database. See "Environment Variables" in the PostgreSQL documentation. As an alternative to the command prompt, you can use the pgAdmin graphical tool. If the PostgreSQL installer didn't install pgAdmin automatically, then you can download it for free at *pgadmin.org*.

```
au_lname       au_id au_fname
------------   ----- -------------
Hull           A04   Klee
Buchman        A01   Sarah
Hull           A03   Hallie
Heydemark      A02   Wendy
```

Figure 2.5 Rows and columns are said to be **unordered**, meaning that their order in a table is irrelevant for informational purposes. Interchanging columns or rows does not change the meaning of the table; this table conveys the same information as the table in Figure 2.4.

Columns

Columns in a given table have these characteristics:

- Each column represents a specific attribute (or property) of the table's entity type. In a table *employees*, a column named *hire_date* might show when an employee was hired, for example.

- Each column has a domain that restricts the set of values allowed in that column. A **domain** is a set of constraints that includes restrictions on a value's data type, length, format, range, uniqueness, specific values, and nullability (whether the value can be null or not). You can't insert the string value 'john' into the column *hire_date*, for example, if *hire_date* requires a valid date value. Furthermore, you can't insert just any date if *hire_date*'s range is further constrained to fall between the date that the company started and today's date. You can define a domain by using data types (Chapter 3) and constraints (Chapter 11).

- Entries in columns are single-valued (atomic); see "Normalization" on page 33.

- The order of columns (left to right) is unimportant (Figure 2.5).

- Each column has a name that identifies it uniquely within a table. (You can reuse the same column name in other tables.)

Rows

Rows in a given table have these characteristics:

- Each row describes a fact about an **entity**, which is a unique instance of an entity type—a particular student or appointment, for example.

- Each row contains a value or null for each of the table's columns.

- The order of rows (top to bottom) is unimportant (refer to Figure 2.5).

- No two rows in a table can be identical.

- Each row in a table is identified uniquely by its primary key; see "Primary Keys" on page 26.

Tips for Tables, Columns, and Rows

- Use the SELECT statement to retrieve columns and rows; see Chapters 4 through 9. Use IN-SERT, UPDATE, and DELETE to add, edit, and delete rows; see Chapter 10. Use CREATE TABLE, ALTER TABLE, and DROP TABLE to add, edit, and delete tables and columns; see Chapter 11.

- Tables have the attractive property of **closure**, which ensures that any operation performed on a table yields another table (Figure 2.6).

- A DBMS uses two types of tables: user tables and system tables. **User tables** store user-defined data. **System tables** contain **metadata**—data about the database—such as structural information, physical details, performance statistics, and security settings. System tables collectively are called the **system catalog**; the DBMS creates and manages these tables silently and continually. This scheme conforms with the relational model's rule that *all* data be stored in tables (Figure 2.7).

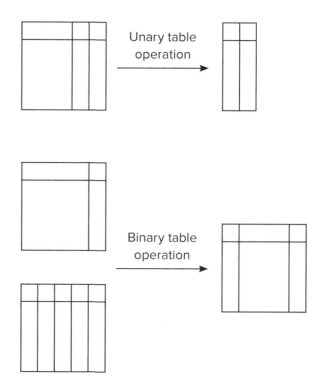

Figure 2.6 Closure guarantees that you'll get another table as a result no matter how you split or merge tables. This property lets you chain any number of table operations or nest them to any depth. **Unary** (or **monadic**) **table operations** operate on one table to produce a result table. **Binary** (or **dyadic**) **table operations** operate on two tables to produce a result table.

Name	Owner	System Object
sysdac_history_internal	dbo	True
sysdac_instances_internal	dbo	True
sysdbmaintplan_databases	dbo	True
sysdbmaintplan_history	dbo	True
sysdbmaintplan_jobs	dbo	True
sysdbmaintplans	dbo	True
sysdownloadlist	dbo	True
sysjobactivity	dbo	True
sysjobhistory	dbo	True
sysjobs	dbo	True
sysjobschedules	dbo	True
sysjobservers	dbo	True
sysjobsteps	dbo	True
sysjobstepslogs	dbo	True
sysmail_account	dbo	True
sysmail_attachments	dbo	True
sysmail_attachments_transfer	dbo	True
sysmail_configuration	dbo	True
sysmail_log	dbo	True
sysmail_mailitems	dbo	True
sysmail_principalprofile	dbo	True

Figure 2.7 DBMSs store system information in special tables called system tables. Here are some of the system tables that Microsoft SQL Server creates and maintains. You access system tables in the same way that you access user-defined tables, but don't alter them unless you know what you're doing.

Table 2.2 Object References

Platform	Address
Standard SQL	catalog.schema.object
Access	database.object
SQL Server	server.database.owner.object
Oracle	schema.object
Db2	schema.object
MySQL	database.object
PostgreSQL	database.schema.object

- In practice, the number of rows in a table changes frequently, but the number of columns changes rarely. Database complexity makes adding or dropping columns difficult; column changes can affect keys, referential integrity, privileges, and so on. Inserting or deleting rows doesn't affect these things.

- Database designers divide values into columns based on the users' needs. Telephone numbers, for example, might reside in the single column *tel_no* or be split into the columns *country_code*, *area_code*, *prefix*, and *line_number*, depending on what users want to query, analyze, and report.

- The resemblance of spreadsheets to tables is superficial. Unlike a spreadsheet, a table doesn't depend on row and column order, doesn't perform calculations, doesn't allow free-form data entry, strictly checks each value's validity, and is related easily to other tables.

- The SQL standard defines a hierarchy of relational-database structures. A **catalog** contains one or more **schemas** (sets of objects and data owned by a given user). A schema contains one or more **objects**, such as base tables, views, functions, and procedures.

- DBMS   DBMSs sometimes use other terms for the same concepts. An **instance** (analogous to a catalog) contains one or more databases. A **database** contains one or more schemas. A **schema** contains tables, views, privileges, stored procedures, and so on. To refer to an object unambiguously, each item at each level in the hierarchy needs a unique name (identifier). Table 2.2 shows how to address objects. See also "Identifiers" on page 54.

Primary Keys

Every value in a database must be accessible. Values are stored at row–column intersections in tables, so a value's location must refer to a specific table, column, and row. You can identify a table or column by its unique name. Rows are unnamed, however, and need a different identification mechanism called a primary key. A **primary key** is:

- *Required*. Every table has exactly one primary key. Remember that the relational model sees a table as an unordered set of rows. Because there's no concept of a "next" or "previous" row, you can't identify rows by position; without a primary key, some data would be inaccessible.

- *Unique*. Because a primary key identifies a single row in a table, no two rows in a table can have the same primary-key value.

- *Simple or composite*. A primary key has one or more columns in a table; a one-column key is called a **simple key**, and a multiple-column key is called a **composite key**.

- *Not null*. A primary-key value can't be empty. For composite keys, no column's value can be empty; see "Nulls" on page 72.

- *Stable*. Once created, a primary-key value seldom if ever changes. If an entity is deleted, then its primary-key value isn't reused for a new entity.

- *Minimal*. A primary key includes only the column(s) necessary for uniqueness.

Learning Database Design

To learn how to design production databases, read an academic text for a grounding in relational algebra, entity–relationship (E–R) modeling, Codd's relational model, system architecture, nulls, integrity, and other crucial concepts. I like Chris Date's *An Introduction to Database Systems*, but alternatives abound—a cheaper (and chattier) option is Date's *Database in Depth*. A modern introduction to set theory and logic is *Applied Mathematics for Database Professionals* by Lex de Haan and Toon Koppelaars. Classical introductions include Robert Stoll's *Set Theory and Logic* and the gentler *Logic* by Wilfrid Hodges. You also can search the web for articles by E. F. Codd, Chris Date, Fabian Pascal, and Hugh Darwen. All this material might seem like overkill, but you'll be surprised at how complex a database becomes after adding a few tables, constraints, triggers, and stored procedures. As in all fields, a practical grasp of theory lets you *predict* results and avoid trial-and-error fixes when things go wrong.

Avoid mass-market junk like *Database Design for Dummies/Mere Mortals*. If you rely on their guidance, then you will create databases where you get answers that you know are wrong, can't retrieve the information that you want, enter the same data over and over, or type in values only to have them go "missing." Such books gloss over (or omit) first principles in favor of administrivia like choosing identifier names and interviewing subject-matter experts.

A database designer designates each table's primary key. This process is crucial because the consequence of a poor key choice is the inability to add data (rows) to a table. I'll review the essentials here, but read a database-design book if you want to learn more about this topic.

Suppose that you need to choose a primary key for the table in Figure 2.8. The columns *au_fname* and *au_lname* separately won't work because each one violates the uniqueness requirement. Combining *au_fname* and *au_lname* into a composite key won't work because two authors might share a name. Names generally make poor keys because they're unstable (people divorce, companies merge, spellings change). The correct choice is *au_id*, which I created to identify authors uniquely. Database designers create unique identifiers when natural or obvious ones (such as names) won't work. After a primary key is defined, your DBMS will enforce the integrity of table data. You can't insert the following row because the *au_id* value A02 already exists in the table:

```
A02    Christian    Kells
```

Nor can you insert this row because *au_id* can't be null:

```
NULL    Christian    Kells
```

This row is legal:

```
A05    Christian    Kells
```

Tips for Primary Keys

- See also "Specifying a Primary Key with PRIMARY KEY" on page 336.

- In practice, the primary key often is placed in a table's initial (leftmost) column(s). When a column name contains *id*, *key*, *code*, or *num*, it's a clue that the column might be a primary key or part of one (or a foreign key, described in the next section).

- Database designers often forgo common unique identifiers such as Social Security numbers for U.S. citizens. Instead, they use artificial keys that encode internal information that is meaningful inside the database users' organization. An employee ID, for example, might embed the year that the person was hired. Other reasons, such as privacy and security concerns, also spur the use of artificial keys.

- Database designers might have a choice of several unique **candidate keys** in a table, one of which is designated the primary key. After designation, the remaining candidate keys become **alternate keys**. Candidate keys often have non-nullable, unique constraints; see "Forcing Unique Values with UNIQUE" on page 345.

- You *could* use *au_id* and, say, *au_lname* as a composite key, but that combination violates the minimality criterion. For an example of a composite primary key, see the table *title_authors* in "The Sample Database" on page 39.

- DBMSs provide data types and attributes that provide unique identification values automatically for each row (such as an integer that auto-increments when a new row is inserted). See "Unique Identifiers" on page 70.

```
au_id au_fname      au_lname
----- ------------- -------------
A01   Sarah         Buchman
A02   Wendy         Heydemark
A03   Hallie        Hull
A04   Klee          Hull
```

Figure 2.8 The column *au_id* is the primary key in this table.

Foreign Keys

Information about different entities is stored in different tables, so you need a way to navigate between tables. The relational model provides a mechanism called a **foreign key** to associate tables. A foreign key has these characteristics:

- It's a column (or group of columns) in a table whose values relate to, or reference, values in some other table.

- It ensures that rows in one table have corresponding rows in another table.

- The table that contains the foreign key is the **referencing** or **child** table. The other table is the **referenced** or **parent** table.

- A foreign key establishes a direct relationship to the parent table's primary key (or any candidate key), so foreign-key values are restricted to existing parent-key values. This constraint is called **referential integrity**. A particular row in a table *appointments* must have an associated row in a table *patients*, for example, or there would be appointments for patients who don't exist or can't be identified. An **orphan row** is a row in a child table for which no associated parent-table row exists. In a properly designed database, you can't insert new orphan rows or make orphans out of existing child-table rows by deleting associated rows in the parent table.

- The values in the foreign key have the same domain as the parent key. Recall from "Tables, Columns, and Rows" on page 22 that a domain defines the set of valid values for a column.

- Unlike primary-key values, foreign-key values can be null (empty); see "Tips for Foreign Keys" on page 29.

- A foreign key can have a different column name than its parent key.

- Foreign-key values generally aren't unique in their own table.

- The first point above is simplified: a foreign key can actually reference the primary key of its *own* table (rather than only some other table). A table *employees* with the primary key *emp_id* can have a foreign key *boss_id*, for example, that references the column *emp_id*. This type of table is called **self-referencing**.

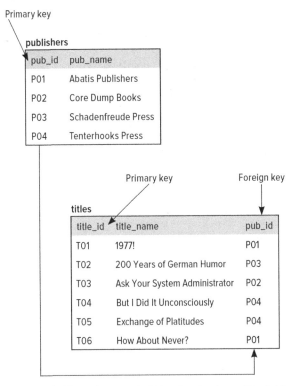

Figure 2.9 shows a primary- and foreign-key relationship between two tables.

After a foreign key is defined, your DBMS will enforce referential integrity. You can't insert the following row into the child table *titles* because the *pub_id* value P05 doesn't exist in the parent table *publishers*:

```
T07    I Blame My Mother         P05
```

You can insert this row only if the foreign key accepts nulls:

```
T07    I Blame My Mother         NULL
```

This row is legal:

```
T07    I Blame My Mother         P03
```

Tips for Foreign Keys

- See also "Specifying a Foreign Key with FOREIGN KEY" on page 339.

- SQL lets you specify the referential-integrity action that the DBMS takes when you attempt to update or delete a parent-table key value to which foreign-key values point; see "Tips for FOREIGN KEY" on page 343.

- Allowing nulls in a foreign-key column complicates enforcement of referential integrity. In practice, nulls in a foreign key often remain null temporarily, pending a real-life decision or discovery; see "Nulls" on page 72.

Figure 2.9 The column *pub_id* is a foreign key of the table *titles* that references the column *pub_id* of *publishers*.

Relationships

A **relationship** is an association established between common columns in two tables. A relationship can be:

- One-to-one
- One-to-many
- Many-to-many

One-to-One

In a **one-to-one relationship**, each row in table A can have *at most one* matching row in the table B, and each row in table B can have *at most one* matching row in table A. Even though it's practicable to store all the information from both tables in only one table, one-to-one relationships often are used to segregate confidential information for privacy and security reasons, to speed queries by splitting single monolithic tables, and to avoid inserting nulls into tables (see "Nulls" on page 72).

A one-to-one relationship is established when the primary key of one table also is a foreign key referencing the primary key of another table (Figure 2.10 and Figure 2.11).

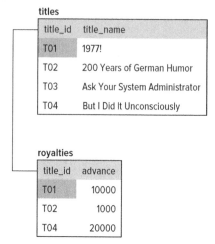

Figure 2.10 A one-to-one relationship. Each row in *titles* can have at most one matching row in *royalties*, and each row in *royalties* can have at most one matching row in *titles*. Here, the primary key of *royalties* also is a foreign key referencing the primary key of *titles*.

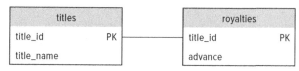

Figure 2.11 This diagram shows an alternative way to depict the one-to-one relationship in Figure 2.10. The connecting line indicates associated columns. The PK symbol indicates a primary key.

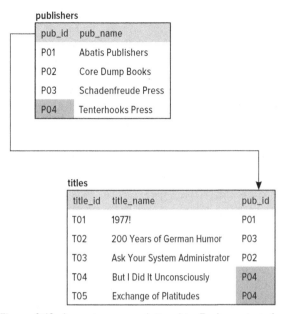

One-to-Many

In a **one-to-many relationship**, each row in table A can have *many* (zero or more) matching rows in table B, but each row in table B has *only one* matching row in table A. A publisher can publish many books, but each book is published by only one publisher, for example.

One-to-many relationships are established when the primary key of the "one" table appears as a foreign key in the "many" table (Figure 2.12 and Figure 2.13).

Figure 2.12 A one-to-many relationship. Each row in *publishers* can have many matching rows in *titles*, and each row in *titles* has only one matching row in *publishers*. Here, the primary key of *publishers* (the "one" table) appears as a foreign key in *titles* (the "many" table).

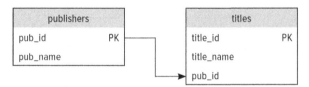

Figure 2.13 This diagram shows an alternative way to depict the one-to-many relationship in Figure 2.12. The connecting line's unadorned end indicates the "one" table, and the arrow indicates the "many" table. The PK symbol indicates a primary key.

Many-to-Many

In a **many-to-many relationship**, each row in table A can have *many* (zero or more) matching rows in table B, and each row in table B can have *many* matching rows in table A. Each author can write many books, and each book can have many authors, for example.

A many-to-many relationships is established only by creating a third table called a **junction table**, whose composite primary key is a combination of both tables' primary keys; each column in the composite key separately is a foreign key. This technique always produces a unique value for each row in the junction table and splits the many-to-many relationship into two separate one-to-many relationships (Figure 2.14 and Figure 2.15).

Tips for Relationships

- Joins (for performing operations on multiple tables) are covered in Chapter 7.

- You *can* establish a many-to-many relationship without creating a third table if you add repeating groups to the tables, but that method violates first normal form; see "Normalization" on page 33.

- A one-to-many relationship also is called a **parent–child** or **master–detail** relationship.

- A junction table also is called an **associating**, **linking**, **pivot**, **connection**, or **intersection** table.

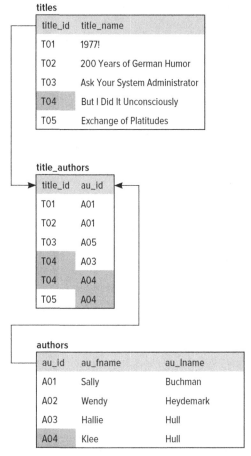

Figure 2.14 A many-to-many relationship. The junction table *title_authors* splits the many-to-many relationship between *titles* and *authors* into two one-to-many relationships. Each row in *titles* can have many matching rows in *title_authors*, as can each row in *authors*. Here, *title_id* in *title_authors* is a foreign key that references the primary key of *titles*, and *au_id* in *title_authors* is a foreign key that references the primary key of *authors*.

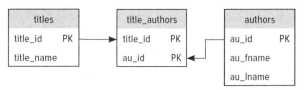

Figure 2.15 This diagram shows an alternative way to depict the many-to-many relationship in Figure 2.14. The PK symbol indicates a primary key.

Normalization

It's possible to consolidate all information about books (or any entity type) into a single monolithic table, but that table would be loaded with duplicate data; each title (row) would contain redundant author, publisher, and royalty details. Redundancy is the enemy of database users and administrators: it causes databases to grow wildly large, it slows queries, and it's a maintenance and reporting nightmare. (When someone moves, you want to change his address in one place, not thousands of places.)

Redundancies lead to a variety of **update anomalies**—that is, difficulties with operations that insert, update, and delete rows. **Normalization** is the process—a series of steps—of modifying tables to reduce redundancy and inconsistency. After each step, the database is in a particular **normal form**. The relational model defines three normal forms, named after famous ordinal numbers:

- First normal form (1NF)

- Second normal form (2NF)

- Third normal form (3NF)

Each normal form is stronger than its predecessors; a database in 3NF also is in 2NF and 1NF. Higher normalization levels tend to increase the number of tables relative to lower levels. **Lossless decomposition** ensures that table splitting doesn't cause information loss, and **dependency-preserving decomposition** ensures that relationships aren't lost. The matching primary- and foreign-key columns that appear when tables are split are not considered to be redundant data.

Normalization is not systematic; it's an iterative process that involves repeated table splitting and rejoining and refining until the database designer is (temporarily) happy with the result.

First Normal Form

A table in **first normal form**:

- Has columns that contain only atomic values

  and

- Has no repeating groups

An **atomic** value, also called a **scalar** value, is a single value that can't be subdivided (Figure 2.16). A **repeating group** is a set of two or more logically related columns (Figure 2.17). To fix these problems, store the data in two related tables (Figure 2.18).

Atomicity

Atomic values are *perceived* to be indivisible from the point of view of database users. A date, a telephone number, and a character string, for example, aren't actually intrinsically indivisible because you can decompose the date into a year, month, and day; the telephone number into a country code, area code, prefix, and line number; and the string into its individual characters. What's important as far as you're concerned is that the DBMS provide operators and functions that let you extract and manipulate the components of "atomic" values if necessary, such as a substring() function to extract a telephone number's area code or a year() function to extract a date's year.

title_id	title_name	authors
T01	1977!	A01
T04	But I Did It Unconsciously	**A03, A04**
T11	Perhaps It's a Glandular Problem	**A03, A04, A06**

Figure 2.16 In first normal form, each table's row–column intersection must contain a single value that can't be subdivided meaningfully. The column *authors* in this table lists multiple authors and so violates 1NF.

title_id	title_name	author1	author2	author3
T01	1977!	A01		
T04	But I Did It Unconsciously	**A03**	**A04**	
T11	Perhaps It's a Glandular Problem	**A03**	**A04**	**A06**

Figure 2.17 Redistributing the column authors into a repeating group also violates 1NF. Don't represent multiple instances of an entity as multiple columns.

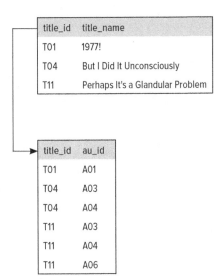

title_id	title_name
T01	1977!
T04	But I Did It Unconsciously
T11	Perhaps It's a Glandular Problem

title_id	au_id
T01	A01
T04	A03
T04	A04
T11	A03
T11	A04
T11	A06

Figure 2.18 The correct design solution is to move the author information to a new child table that contains one row for each author of a title. The primary key in the parent table is *title_id*, and the composite key in the child table is *title_id* and *au_id*.

A database that violates 1NF causes problems:

- Multiple values in a row–column intersection mean that the combination of table name, column name, and key value is insufficient to address every value in the database.

- It's difficult to retrieve, insert, update, or delete a single value (among many) because you must rely on the order of the values.

- Queries are complex and slow.

- The problems that further normalization solves become unsolvable.

Second Normal Form

A table in **second normal form**:

- Is in first normal form

  and

- Has no partial functional dependencies

A table contains a **partial functional dependency** if *some* (but not all) of a composite key's values determine a nonkey column's value. A 2NF table is **fully functionally dependent**, meaning that a nonkey column's value might need to be updated if *any* column values in the composite key change.

The composite key in the table in Figure 2.19 is *title_id* and *au_id*. The nonkey columns are *au_order* (the order in which authors are listed on the cover of a book with multiple authors) and *au_phone* (the author's telephone number).

For each nonkey column, ask, "Can I determine a nonkey column value if I know only part of the primary-key value?" A *no* answer means the nonkey column is fully functionally dependent (good); a *yes* answer means that it's partially functionally dependent (bad).

For the column *au_order*, the questions are:

- Can I determine *au_order* if I know only *title_id*? No, because there might be more than one author for the same title.

- Can I determine *au_order* if I know only *au_id*? No, because I need to know the particular title too.

Good—*au_order* is fully functionally dependent and can remain in the table. This dependency is denoted by

$$\{title\_id, au\_id\} \rightarrow \{au\_order\}$$

and is read "*title_id* and *au_id* determine *au_order*" or "*au_order* depends on *title_id* and *au_id*." The **determinant** is the expression to the left of the arrow.

For the column *au_phone*, the questions are:

- Can I determine *au_phone* if I know only *title_id*? No, because there might be more than one author for the same title.

- Can I determine *au_phone* if I know only *au_id*? Yes! The author's telephone number doesn't depend on the title.

Bad—*au_phone* is partially functionally dependent and must be moved elsewhere (probably to an *authors* or *telephone_numbers* table) to satisfy 2NF rules.

Figure 2.19 *au_phone* depends on *au_id* but not *title_id*, so this table contains a partial functional dependency and isn't in 2NF. The PK symbol indicates a primary key.

Third Normal Form

A table in **third normal form**:

- Is in second normal form

  and

- Has no transitive dependencies

A table contains a **transitive dependency** if a nonkey column's value determines another nonkey column's value. In 3NF tables, nonkey columns are mutually independent and dependent on only primary-key column(s). 3NF is the next logical step after 2NF.

The primary key in the table in Figure 2.20 is *title_id*. The nonkey columns are *price* (the book's price), *pub_city* (the city where the book is published), and *pub_id* (the book's publisher).

For each nonkey column, ask, "Can I determine a nonkey column value if I know any other nonkey column value?" A *no* answer means that the column is not transitively dependent (good); a *yes* answer means that the column whose value you can determine is transitively dependent on the other column (bad).

For the column price, the questions are:

- Can I determine *pub_id* if I know price? No.

- Can I determine *pub_city* if I know price? No.

For the column *pub_city*, the questions are:

- Can I determine *price* if I know *pub_city*? No.

- Can I determine *pub_id* if I know *pub_city*? No, because a city might have many publishers.

For the column *pub_id*, the questions are:

- Can I determine price if I know *pub_id*? No.

- Can I determine *pub_city* if I know *pub_id*? Yes! The city where the book is published depends on the publisher.

Bad—*pub_city* is transitively dependent on *pub_id* and must be moved elsewhere (probably to a *publishers* table) to satisfy 3NF rules.

As you can see, it's not enough to ask, "Can I determine A if I know B?" to discover a transitive dependency; you also must ask, "Can I determine B if I know A?"

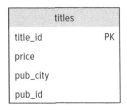

Figure 2.20 *pub_city* depends on *pub_id*, so this table contains a transitive dependency and isn't in 3NF. The PK symbol indicates a primary key.

Other Normal Forms

Higher levels of normalization exist, but the relational model doesn't require (or even mention) them. They're useful in some cases to avoid redundancy. Briefly, they are:

- **Boyce-Codd normal form** is a more rigorous version of 3NF. BCNF deals with tables that have multiple candidate keys, composite candidate keys, or candidate keys that overlap. A table is in BCNF if every determinant is a candidate key. (A determinant column is one on which some of the columns are fully functionally dependent.)

- A table in **fourth normal form** is in BCNF and has no **multivalued dependencies** (MVDs). An MVD occurs when in a table containing at least three columns, one column has multiple rows whose values match a value of a single row of one of the other columns.

  Suppose that employees can be assigned to multiple projects and each employee can have multiple skills. If you stuff all this information into a single table, then you must use all three attributes as the key because nothing less can identify a row uniquely. The relationship between *emp_id* and *proj_id* is an MVD because for each pair of *emp_id–skill_id* values in the table, only *emp_id* (independent of *skill_id*) determines the associated set of *proj_id* values. The relationship between *emp_id* and *skill_id* also is an MVD because the set of skill values for an *emp_id–proj_id* pair always depends on only *emp_id*. To transform a table with MVDs to 4NF, move each MVD pair to a new table.

- A table in **fifth normal form** is in 4NF and has no **join dependencies**, which are generalizations of MVDs. The aim of 5NF is to have tables that can't be decomposed further into any number of smaller tables. The redundancies and anomalies that 5NF cures are rare and unintuitive. In real databases, you'll see 1NF, 2NF, 3NF, and occasionally 4NF. 4NF and even 3NF tables almost always are 5NF too.

Denormalization

The increased number of tables that normalization generates might sway you to **denormalize** your database to speed queries (because having fewer tables reduces computationally expensive joins and storage throughput). This common technique trades off data integrity for performance and presents a few other problems. A denormalized database:

- Usually is harder to understand than a normalized one

- Usually makes retrievals faster but updates slower

- Increases the risk of inserting inconsistent data

- Might improve the performance of some database applications but hurt that of others (because users' table-access patterns change over time)

The need for denormalization isn't a weakness in the relational model but reveals a flawed implementation of the model in DBMSs. A common use for denormalized tables is as permanent logs of data copied from other tables. The logged rows are redundant, but because they're only INSERTed (never UPDATEd), they serve as an audit trail immune to future changes in the source tables.

The Sample Database

Pick up an SQL or database-design book, and probably you'll find a students/courses/teachers, customers/orders/products, or authors/books/publishers database. In a bow to convention, most of the SQL examples in this book use an authors/books/publishers sample database named *books*. Here are some things that you should know about *books*:

- Recall from "Tables, Columns, and Rows" on page 22 that a database appears to the user as a collection of tables (and nothing but tables). *books* contains five main tables that contain information about authors, titles they've published, their publishers, and their royalties. Figure 2.21 depicts the tables and relationships in *books* by using the graphical conventions introduced earlier in this chapter.

- *books* also contains a few additional tables that are used in specific examples. These tables are described later in the text when they're relevant.

- The SQL statements in Chapter 10 and later modify data in *books* (rather than just retrieve data). Unless otherwise noted, each new section in a chapter starts with a pristine copy of *books*. In other words, assume that database changes made in one section don't carry over to the next section.

- Some of the concepts mentioned in this section, such as data types and nulls, are covered in Chapter 3.

- *books* is a teaching tool; its structure and size don't approach the complexity of real production databases.

- To create the sample database on your own DBMS, see "Creating the Sample Database" on page 45.

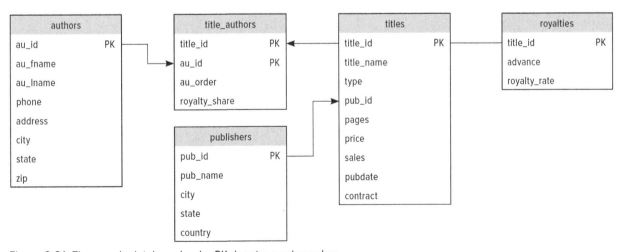

Figure 2.21 The sample database *books*. PK denotes a primary key.

The Table *authors*

The table *authors* describes the books' authors. Each author has a unique identifier (*au_id*) that's the primary key. Table 2.3 shows the structure of the table *authors*, and Figure 2.22 shows its contents.

Table 2.3 Table Structure of *authors*

Column Name	Description	Data Type	Nulls?	Keys
au_id	Unique author identifier	CHAR(3)		PK
au_fname	Author first name	VARCHAR(15)		
au_lname	Author last name	VARCHAR(15)		
phone	Author telephone number	VARCHAR(12)	Yes	
address	Author address	VARCHAR(20)	Yes	
city	Author city	VARCHAR(15)	Yes	
state	Author state	CHAR(2)	Yes	
zip	Author zip (postal) code	CHAR(5)	Yes	

```
au_id au_fname  au_lname    phone        address               city            state zip
----- --------- ----------- ------------ --------------------- --------------- ----- -----
A01   Sarah     Buchman     718-496-7223 75 West 205 St        Bronx           NY    10468
A02   Wendy     Heydemark   303-986-7020 2922 Baseline Rd      Boulder         CO    80303
A03   Hallie    Hull        415-549-4278 3800 Waldo Ave, #14F  San Francisco   CA    94123
A04   Klee      Hull        415-549-4278 3800 Waldo Ave, #14F  San Francisco   CA    94123
A05   Christian Kells       212-771-4680 114 Horatio St        New York        NY    10014
A06             Kellsey     650-836-7128 390 Serra Mall        Palo Alto       CA    94305
A07   Paddy     O'Furniture 941-925-0752 1442 Main St          Sarasota        FL    34236
```

Figure 2.22 The contents of the table *authors*.

The Table *publishers*

The table *publishers* describes the books' publishers. Each publisher has a unique identifier (*pub_id*) that's the primary key. Table 2.4 shows the structure of the table *publishers*, and Figure 2.23 shows its contents.

Table 2.4 Table Structure of *publishers*

Column Name	Description	Data Type	Nulls?	Keys
pub_id	Unique publisher identifier	CHAR(3)		PK
pub_name	Publisher name	VARCHAR(20)		
city	Publisher city	VARCHAR(15)		
state	Publisher state/province/region	CHAR(2)	Yes	
country	Publisher country	VARCHAR(15)		

```
pub_id pub_name             city          state country
------ -------------------- ------------- ----- -------
P01    Abatis Publishers    New York      NY    USA
P02    Core Dump Books      San Francisco CA    USA
P03    Schadenfreude Press  Hamburg       NULL  Germany
P04    Tenterhooks Press    Berkeley      CA    USA
```

Figure 2.23 The contents of the table *publishers*.

The Table *titles*

The table *titles* describes the books. Each book has a unique identifier (*title_id*) that's the primary key. *titles* contains a foreign key, *pub_id*, that references the table *publishers* to indicate a book's publisher. Table 2.5 shows the structure of the table *titles*, and Figure 2.24 shows its contents.

Table 2.5 Table Structure of *titles*

Column Name	Description	Data Type	Nulls?	Keys
title_id	Unique title identifier	CHAR(3)		PK
title_name	Book title	VARCHAR(40)		
type	Subject of the book	VARCHAR(10)	Yes	
pub_id	Publisher identifier	CHAR(3)		FK publishers(pub_id)
pages	Page count	INTEGER	Yes	
price	Cover price	DECIMAL(5,2)	Yes	
sales	Lifetime number of copies sold	INTEGER	Yes	
pubdate	Date of publication	DATE	Yes	
contract	Nonzero if author(s) signed contract	SMALLINT		

```
title_id title_name                             type         pub_id pages price sales    pubdate     contract
-------- -------------------------------------- ---------- ------ ----- ----- ------- ---------- --------
T01      1977!                                  history    P01      107 21.99     566 2000-08-01        1
T02      200 Years of German Humor              history    P03       14 19.95    9566 1998-04-01        1
T03      Ask Your System Administrator          computer   P02     1226 39.95   25667 2000-09-01        1
T04      But I Did It Unconsciously             psychology P04      510 12.99   13001 1999-05-31        1
T05      Exchange of Platitudes                 psychology P04      201  6.95  201440 2001-01-01        1
T06      How About Never?                       biography  P01      473 19.95   11320 2000-07-31        1
T07      I Blame My Mother                      biography  P03      333 23.95 1500200 1999-10-01        1
T08      Just Wait Until After School           children   P04       86 10.00    4095 2001-06-01        1
T09      Kiss My Boo-Boo                        children   P04       22 13.95    5000 2002-05-31        1
T10      Not Without My Faberge Egg             biography  P01     NULL  NULL    NULL       NULL        0
T11      Perhaps It's a Glandular Problem       psychology P04      826  7.99   94123 2000-11-30        1
T12      Spontaneous, Not Annoying              biography  P01      507 12.99  100001 2000-08-31        1
T13      What Are The Civilian Applications?    history    P03      802 29.99   10467 1999-05-31        1
```

Figure 2.24 The contents of the table *titles*.

The Table *title_authors*

Authors and books have a many-to-many relationship because an author can write multiple books and a book can have multiple authors. *title_authors* is the junction table that associates the tables *authors* and *titles*; see "Relationships" on page 30. *title_id* and *au_id* together form a composite primary key, and each column separately is a foreign key that references *titles* and *authors*, respectively. The nonkey columns indicate the order of the author's name on the book's cover (always 1 for a book with a sole author) and the fraction of total royalties that each author receives (always 1.0 for a book with a sole author). Table 2.6 shows the structure of the table *title_authors*, and Figure 2.25 shows its contents.

Table 2.6 Table Structure of *title_authors*

Column Name	Description	Data Type	Nulls?	Keys
title_id	Title identifier	CHAR(3)		PK, FK titles(title_id)
au_id	Author identifier	CHAR(3)		PK, FK authors(au_id)
au_order	Author name order on book cover	SMALLINT		
royalty_share	Author fractional royalty share	DECIMAL(5,2)		

```
title_id au_id au_order royalty_share
-------- ----- -------- -------------
T01      A01         1           1.00
T02      A01         1           1.00
T03      A05         1           1.00
T04      A03         1           0.60
T04      A04         2           0.40
T05      A04         1           1.00
T06      A02         1           1.00
T07      A02         1           0.50
T07      A04         2           0.50
T08      A06         1           1.00
T09      A06         1           1.00
T10      A02         1           1.00
T11      A03         2           0.30
T11      A04         3           0.30
T11      A06         1           0.40
T12      A02         1           1.00
T13      A01         1           1.00
```

Figure 2.25 The contents of the table *title_authors*.

The Table *royalties*

The table *royalties* specifies the royalty rate paid to *all* the authors (not each author) of each book, including the total up-front advance against royalties paid to all authors (again, not each author) of a book. The *royalties* primary key is *title_id*. The table *royalties* has a one-to-one relationship with *titles*, so the *royalties* primary key also is a foreign key that references the *titles* primary key. Table 2.7 shows the structure of the table *royalties*, and Figure 2.26 shows its contents.

Table 2.7 Table Structure of *royalties*

Column Name	Description	Data Type	Nulls?	Keys
title_id	Unique title identifier	CHAR(3)		PK, FK titles(title_id)
advance	Up-front payment to author(s)	DECIMAL(9,2)	Yes	
royalty_rate	Fraction of revenue paid author(s)	DECIMAL(5,2)	Yes	

```
title_id advance      royalty_rate
-------- -----------  ------------
T01         10000.00        0.05
T02          1000.00        0.06
T03         15000.00        0.07
T04         20000.00        0.08
T05        100000.00        0.09
T06         20000.00        0.08
T07       1000000.00        0.11
T08             0.00        0.04
T09             0.00        0.05
T10             NULL        NULL
T11        100000.00        0.07
T12         50000.00        0.09
T13         20000.00        0.06
```

Figure 2.26 The contents of the table *royalties*.

Creating the Sample Database

To create (or re-create) the database *books* on your own DBMS, visit *questingvolepress.com*, click the Download link for this book, and then follow the onscreen instructions. Creating *books* is a two-step process:

1. Use your DBMS's built-in tools to create a new, blank database named *books*.

2. Run an SQL script that creates tables within *books* and populates them with data.

   Listing 2.1 shows a standard (ISO/ANSI) SQL script that creates the sample-database tables and inserts rows into them.

Listing 2.1 This standard SQL script, books_standard.sql, creates the tables in the sample database *books* and populates them with data. The file that you download at the companion website includes versions of this script changed to run on specific DBMSs.

```
DROP TABLE authors;
CREATE TABLE authors
  (
  au_id     CHAR(3)     NOT NULL,
  au_fname  VARCHAR(15) NOT NULL,
  au_lname  VARCHAR(15) NOT NULL,
  phone     VARCHAR(12)        ,
  address   VARCHAR(20)        ,
  city      VARCHAR(15)        ,
  state     CHAR(2)            ,
  zip       CHAR(5)            ,
  CONSTRAINT pk_authors
    PRIMARY KEY (au_id)
  );
INSERT INTO authors VALUES
  ('A01','Sarah','Buchman','718-496-7223','75 West 205 St','Bronx','NY','10468');
INSERT INTO authors VALUES
  ('A02','Wendy','Heydemark','303-986-7020','2922 Baseline Rd','Boulder','CO','80303');
INSERT INTO authors VALUES
  ('A03','Hallie','Hull','415-549-4278','3800 Waldo Ave, #14F','San Francisco','CA','94123');
INSERT INTO authors VALUES
  ('A04','Klee','Hull','415-549-4278','3800 Waldo Ave, #14F','San Francisco','CA','94123');
INSERT INTO authors VALUES
  ('A05','Christian','Kells','212-771-4680','114 Horatio St','New York','NY','10014');
INSERT INTO authors VALUES
  ('A06','','Kellsey','650-836-7128','390 Serra Mall','Palo Alto','CA','94305');
INSERT INTO authors VALUES
  ('A07','Paddy','O''Furniture','941-925-0752','1442 Main St','Sarasota','FL','34236');
```

```
DROP TABLE publishers;
CREATE TABLE publishers
  (
  pub_id   CHAR(3)     NOT NULL,
  pub_name VARCHAR(20) NOT NULL,
  city     VARCHAR(15) NOT NULL,
  state    CHAR(2)            ,
  country  VARCHAR(15) NOT NULL,
  CONSTRAINT pk_publishers
    PRIMARY KEY (pub_id)
  );
INSERT INTO publishers VALUES('P01','Abatis Publishers','New York','NY','USA');
INSERT INTO publishers VALUES('P02','Core Dump Books','San Francisco','CA','USA');
INSERT INTO publishers VALUES('P03','Schadenfreude Press','Hamburg',NULL,'Germany');
INSERT INTO publishers VALUES('P04','Tenterhooks Press','Berkeley','CA','USA');

DROP TABLE titles;
CREATE TABLE titles
  (
  title_id   CHAR(3)      NOT NULL,
  title_name VARCHAR(40)  NOT NULL,
  type       VARCHAR(10)         ,
  pub_id     CHAR(3)      NOT NULL,
  pages      INTEGER             ,
  price      DECIMAL(5,2)        ,
  sales      INTEGER             ,
  pubdate    DATE                ,
  contract   SMALLINT     NOT NULL,
  CONSTRAINT pk_titles
    PRIMARY KEY (title_id)
  );
INSERT INTO titles VALUES
  ('T01','1977!','history','P01',107,21.99,566,DATE '2000-08-01',1);
INSERT INTO titles VALUES
  ('T02','200 Years of German Humor','history','P03',14,19.95,9566,DATE '1998-04-01',1);
INSERT INTO titles VALUES
  ('T03','Ask Your System Administrator','computer','P02',1226,39.95,25667,DATE '2000-09-01',1);
INSERT INTO titles VALUES
  ('T04','But I Did It Unconsciously','psychology','P04',510,12.99,13001,DATE '1999-05-31',1);
INSERT INTO titles VALUES
  ('T05','Exchange of Platitudes','psychology','P04',201,6.95,201440,DATE '2001-01-01',1);
INSERT INTO titles VALUES
  ('T06','How About Never?','biography','P01',473,19.95,11320,DATE '2000-07-31',1);
INSERT INTO titles VALUES
  ('T07','I Blame My Mother','biography','P03',333,23.95,1500200,DATE '1999-10-01',1);
INSERT INTO titles VALUES
  ('T08','Just Wait Until After School','children','P04',86,10.00,4095,DATE '2001-06-01',1);
INSERT INTO titles VALUES
  ('T09','Kiss My Boo-Boo','children','P04',22,13.95,5000,DATE '2002-05-31',1);
```

```
INSERT INTO titles VALUES
  ('T10','Not Without My Faberge Egg','biography','P01',NULL,NULL,NULL,NULL,0);
INSERT INTO titles VALUES
  ('T11','Perhaps It''s a Glandular Problem','psychology','P04',826,7.99,94123,DATE '2000-11-30',1);
INSERT INTO titles VALUES
  ('T12','Spontaneous, Not Annoying','biography','P01',507,12.99,100001,DATE '2000-08-31',1);
INSERT INTO titles VALUES
  ('T13','What Are The Civilian Applications?','history','P03',802,29.99,10467,DATE '1999-05-31',1);


DROP TABLE title_authors;
CREATE TABLE title_authors
  (
  title_id      CHAR(3)      NOT NULL,
  au_id         CHAR(3)      NOT NULL,
  au_order      SMALLINT     NOT NULL,
  royalty_share DECIMAL(5,2) NOT NULL,
  CONSTRAINT pk_title_authors
    PRIMARY KEY (title_id, au_id)
  );
INSERT INTO title_authors VALUES('T01','A01',1,1.0);
INSERT INTO title_authors VALUES('T02','A01',1,1.0);
INSERT INTO title_authors VALUES('T03','A05',1,1.0);
INSERT INTO title_authors VALUES('T04','A03',1,0.6);
INSERT INTO title_authors VALUES('T04','A04',2,0.4);
INSERT INTO title_authors VALUES('T05','A04',1,1.0);
INSERT INTO title_authors VALUES('T06','A02',1,1.0);
INSERT INTO title_authors VALUES('T07','A02',1,0.5);
INSERT INTO title_authors VALUES('T07','A04',2,0.5);
INSERT INTO title_authors VALUES('T08','A06',1,1.0);
INSERT INTO title_authors VALUES('T09','A06',1,1.0);
INSERT INTO title_authors VALUES('T10','A02',1,1.0);
INSERT INTO title_authors VALUES('T11','A03',2,0.3);
INSERT INTO title_authors VALUES('T11','A04',3,0.3);
INSERT INTO title_authors VALUES('T11','A06',1,0.4);
INSERT INTO title_authors VALUES('T12','A02',1,1.0);
INSERT INTO title_authors VALUES('T13','A01',1,1.0);
```

```
DROP TABLE royalties;
CREATE TABLE royalties
  (
  title_id      CHAR(3)      NOT NULL,
  advance       DECIMAL(9,2)       ,
  royalty_rate DECIMAL(5,2)       ,
  CONSTRAINT pk_royalties
    PRIMARY KEY (title_id)
  );
INSERT INTO royalties VALUES('T01',10000,0.05);
INSERT INTO royalties VALUES('T02',1000,0.06);
INSERT INTO royalties VALUES('T03',15000,0.07);
INSERT INTO royalties VALUES('T04',20000,0.08);
INSERT INTO royalties VALUES('T05',100000,0.09);
INSERT INTO royalties VALUES('T06',20000,0.08);
INSERT INTO royalties VALUES('T07',1000000,0.11);
INSERT INTO royalties VALUES('T08',0,0.04);
INSERT INTO royalties VALUES('T09',0,0.05);
INSERT INTO royalties VALUES('T10',NULL,NULL);
INSERT INTO royalties VALUES('T11',100000,0.07);
INSERT INTO royalties VALUES('T12',50000,0.09);
INSERT INTO royalties VALUES('T13',20000,0.06);
```

CHAPTER 3

SQL Basics

SQL is *based* on the relational model but doesn't implement it faithfully. One departure from the model is that in SQL, primary keys are optional rather than mandatory. Consequently, tables without keys will accept duplicate rows, rendering some data inaccessible. A complete review of the many disparities is beyond the scope of this book (see "Learning Database Design" on page 26). The upshot of these discrepancies is that DBMS users, and not the DBMS itself, are responsible for enforcing a relational structure. Another result is that the *Model* and *SQL* terms in Table 2.1 on page 22 aren't interchangeable.

With that warning, it's time to learn SQL. An SQL program is a sequence of SQL statements executed in order. To write a program, you must know the rules that govern SQL syntax. This chapter explains how to write valid SQL statements and also covers data types and nulls.

SQL Syntax

Figure 3.1 shows the syntax of an example SQL statement (don't worry about the actual meaning, or semantics, of the statement).

1. **Comment**. A **comment** is optional text that explains your program. Comments usually describe what a program does and how, or why code was changed. Comments are for humans—the DBMS ignores them. A comment is introduced by two consecutive hyphens and continues until the end of the line.

2. **SQL statement**. An SQL statement is a valid combination of tokens introduced by a keyword. **Tokens** are the basic indivisible particles of the SQL language; they can't be reduced grammatically. Tokens include keywords, identifiers, operators, literals (constants), and punctuation symbols.

3. **Clauses**. An SQL statement has one or more clauses. In general, a **clause** is a fragment of an SQL statement that's introduced by a keyword, is required or optional, and must be given in a particular order. SELECT, FROM, WHERE, and ORDER BY introduce the four clauses in this example.

4. **Keywords**. A **keyword** is a word that SQL reserves because it has special meaning in the language. Using a keyword outside its specific context (as an identifier, for example) causes an error. DBMSs use a mix of standard and nonstandard keywords; search your DBMS documentation for *keywords* or *reserved words*. The keywords in this example are SELECT, FROM, WHERE, ORDER, and BY.

5. **Identifiers**. **Identifiers** are words that you (or the database designer) use to name database objects such as tables, columns, aliases, indexes, and views. The identifiers in this example are *au_fname*, *au_lname*, *authors*, and *state*. For more information, see "Identifiers" on page 54.

6. **Terminating semicolon**. An SQL statement ends with a semicolon.

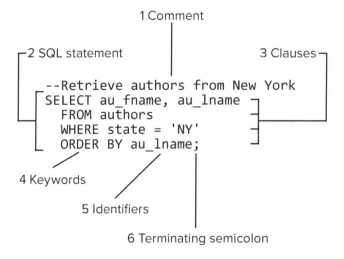

Figure 3.1 An SQL statement, with a comment.

```
select au_fname
    ,         AU_LNAME
              FROM
 authors WhErE     state
= 'NY' order
            bY
AU_lnamE
     ;
```

Figure 3.2 There aren't many rules about how to format an SQL statement. This statement is equivalent to the one in Figure 3.1.

SQL is a free-form language whose statements can:

- Be in uppercase or lowercase (SELECT, select, and sElEcT are considered to be identical keywords, for example)

- Continue on the next line as long as you don't split words, tokens, or quoted strings in two

- Be on the same line as other statements

- Start in any column

Despite this flexibility, you should adopt a consistent style (Figure 3.2). I use uppercase keywords and lowercase identifiers and indent each clause on its own line; see "About This Book" on page xii for my typographic and syntax conventions.

Common Errors

Some common SQL programming errors are:

- Omitting the terminating semicolon

- Misspelling a keyword or identifier

- Mismatched or unmatched parentheses or quotes

- Listing clauses out of order

- Not surrounding a string or datetime literal with single quotes

- Surrounding a numeric literal or the keyword NULL with quotes

- Mismatching a table and column (typing SELECT royalty_share FROM authors instead of SELECT royalty_share FROM title_authors, for example)

These errors usually are easy to catch and correct, even if your DBMS returns an obscure or unhelpful error message. Remember that the real error actually can occur well before the statement the DBMS flags as an error. For example, if you run

```
CREATE TABLE misspelled_name
```

then your DBMS will straightaway create a table with the bad name. Your error won't show up until later, when you try to reference the table with, say,

```
SELECT * FROM correct_name
```

Tip: A common way to test and fix (debug) SQL programs is to use comments to temporarily stop SQL code from being executed. If you're working on a long SQL statement and want to test only part of it, then you can **comment out** some of the code so that the DBMS sees it as comments and ignores it.

Tips for SQL Syntax

- The introductory keyword of an SQL statement is called a **verb** because it indicates an action to perform.

- Distinguish between a SELECT *statement*, which is the entire statement from SELECT to semicolon, and a SELECT *clause*, which is the part of the SELECT statement that lists the output columns.

- Some DBMSs support bracketed comments, which start with /*, continue over one or more lines, and end with */. You can nest a bracketed comment within another.

- An **expression** is any legal combination of symbols that evaluates to a single data value. You can combine mathematical or logical operators, identifiers, literals, functions, column names, aliases, and so on. Table 3.1 lists some common expressions and examples. These expressions are covered in more detail later.

Table 3.1 Types of Expressions

Type	Example
Case	CASE WHEN n <> 0 THEN x/n ELSE 0 END
Cast	CAST(pubdate AS CHARACTER)
Datetime value	start_time + '01:30'
Interval value	INTERVAL '7' DAY * 2
Numeric value	(sales*price)/12
String value	'Dear '||au_fname||','

SQL Standards and Conformance

The ISO SQL technical committee has been revising the offical SQL standard every few years since 1986. Each revision:

- Introduces new elements to the language

- Clarifies or updates the elements of earlier standards

- Drops existing elements because new elements have superseded them or they never caught on among DBMS vendors or SQL programmers

The standard is enormous—thousands of pages of dense specifications—and no vendor conforms (or ever will conform) to the entire thing. Instead, vendors try to conform to a subset of the standard called **Core SQL**. This **level of conformance** is the minimal category that vendors have to achieve to claim that they conform to standard SQL. The SQL-92 revision introduced levels of conformance, and later standards have them too, so when you read a DBMS's conformance statement, note which SQL standard it's referring to and which level. In fact, SQL-92 often is thought of as *the* standard because it defined many of the most vital and unchanging parts of the language. Except where noted, the SQL elements in this book are part of SQL-92 as well as later standards. The lowest level of SQL-92 conformance is called **Entry** (not Core).

Your programs should follow the SQL standard as closely as possible. Ideally, you should be able to write portable SQL programs without even knowing which DBMS you're programming for. Unfortunately, the SQL committee is not made up of language theorists and relational-model purists but is top-heavy with commercial DBMS vendors, all jockeying and maneuvering. The result is that each DBMS vendor devotes resources to approach minimal Entry or Core SQL conformance requirements and then scampers off to add nonstandard features that differentiate their products in the marketplace—meaning that your SQL programs won't be portable. These vendor-specific lock-ins often force you to modify or rewrite SQL programs to run on different DBMSs.

DBMS | Of the DBMSs covered in this book, **PostgreSQL** is the "purest" with respect to the SQL standard. Your DBMS might offer settings that make it better conform to the SQL standard. **MySQL** has ANSI mode, for example, and **Microsoft SQL Server** has SET ANSI_DEFAULTS ON.

Tip: For information about using SQL across different versions of the same DBMS, see "Older DBMSs and Backward Compatibility of SQL" on page 1.

Identifiers

An **identifier** is a name that lets you refer to an object unambiguously within the hierarchy of database objects (whether a schema, database, column, key, index, view, constraint, or anything created with a CREATE statement). An identifier must be unique within its **scope**, which defines where and when it can be referenced. In general:

- Database names must be unique on a specified instance of a database server.

- Table and view names must be unique within a given database (or schema).

- Column, key, index, and constraint names must be unique within a given table or view.

These rules let you duplicate names for objects whose scopes don't overlap. You can give the same name to columns in different tables, for example, or to tables in different databases.

Tip: For information about addressing database objects, see Table 2.2 on page 25.

DBMS scopes vary in the extent to which
`DBMS` they require identifier names to be unique.
Microsoft SQL Server requires an index name to be unique for only its table, for example, whereas **Oracle** and **Db2** require an index name to be unique throughout the database. Search your DBMS documentation for *identifiers* or *names*.

Standard SQL has the following **identifier rules** for names:

- Can be up to 128 characters long

- Must begin with a letter

- Can contain letters, digits, and underscores (_)

- Can't contain spaces or special characters (such as #, $, &, %, or punctuation)

- Can't be reserved keywords (except for quoted identifiers)

Standard SQL distinguishes between reserved and non-reserved keywords. You can't use **reserved keywords** as identifiers because they have special meaning in SQL. You can't name a table "select" or a column "sum", for example. **Non-reserved keywords** have a special meaning in only some contexts and can be used as identifiers in other contexts. Most non-reserved keywords actually are the names of built-in tables and functions, so it's safest never to use them as identifiers either.

You can use a **quoted identifier**, also called a **delimited identifier**, to break some of SQL's identifier rules. A quoted identifier is a name surrounded by double quotes. The name can contain spaces and special characters, is case sensitive, and can be a reserved keyword. Quoted identifiers can annoy other programmers and cause problems with third-party and even a vendor's own tools, so using them usually is a bad idea.

Here's some more advice for choosing identifier names:

- Stick to the standard rules even if your DBMS has less restrictive ones (**Oracle** names can contain # and $ symbols, for example).

- In some cases, your DBMS will be more restrictive than the standard (**MySQL** identifiers can be up to only 64 characters long, for example).

- Use lowercase letters.

- *names_with_underscores* are easier to read than *nameswithoutthem*.

- Use consistent names and abbreviations throughout the database—pick either *emp* or *employee* and stick with it.

Although you can't use (unquoted) reserved words as identifiers, you *can* embed them in identifiers. *group* and *max* are illegal identifiers, for example, but *groups* and *max_price* are valid. If you're worried that your identifier might be a reserved word in some other SQL dialect, then just add an underscore to the end of the name (*element_*, for example); no reserved keyword ends with an underscore.

DBMS You can surround **Microsoft SQL Server** quoted identifiers with double quotes or brackets ([]); brackets are preferred. In **Db2**, you can use reserved words as identifiers (but doing so isn't a good idea because your program won't be portable). **MySQL** ANSI_QUOTES mode allows double-quoted identifiers. DBMSs have their own nonstandard keywords; search your DBMS documentation for *keywords* or *reserved words*.

In **MySQL**, the case sensitivity of the underlying operating system determines the case sensitivity of database and table names.

The SQL standard directs DBMSs to convert identifier names to uppercase internally. So in the guts of your SQL compiler, the unquoted identifier *myname* is equivalent to the quoted identifier *"MYNAME"* (not *"myname"*). **PostgreSQL** doesn't conform to the standard and converts to *lowercase*. To write portable programs, always quote a particular name or never quote it (don't mix them). DBMSs aren't consistent when it comes to case sensitivity, so the best practice is always to respect case for user-defined identifiers.

Data Types

Recall from "Tables, Columns, and Rows" on page 22 that a domain is the set of valid values allowed in a column. To define a domain, you use a column's data type (and constraints, described in Chapter 11). A **data type**, or **column type**, has these characteristics:

- Each column in a table has a single data type.

- A data type falls into one of categories listed in Table 3.2 (each covered in the following sections).

- The data type determines a column's allowable values and the operations it supports. An integer data type, for example, can represent any whole number between certain DBMS-defined limits and supports the usual arithmetic operations: addition, subtraction, multiplication, and division (among others). But an integer can't represent a nonnumeric value such as 'john' and doesn't support character operations such as capitalization and concatenation.

- The data type affects the column's sort order. The integers 1, 2, and 10 are sorted numerically, yielding 1, 2, 10. The character strings '1', '2', and '10' are sorted lexicographically, yielding '1', '10', '2'. **Lexicographical ordering** sorts strings by examining the values of their characters individually. Here, '10' comes before '2' because '1' (the first character of '10') is less than '2' lexicographically. For information about sorting, see "Sorting Rows with ORDER BY" on page 83.

- Some data types, such as binary objects, can't be indexed (see Chapter 12).

- You store **literal values** (constants) in character, numeric, boolean, datetime, and interval columns. Table 3.3 shows some examples; the following sections have more examples. Be sure not to confuse the string literal *'2009'* with the numeric literal *2009*. The SQL standard defines a literal as any constant that isn't null.

Table 3.2 Categories of Data Types

Category	Stores These Data
Character string	Strings of characters
Binary large object	Binary data
Exact numeric	Integers and decimal numbers
Approximate numeric	Floating-point numbers
Boolean	Truth values: true, false, or unknown
Datetime	Date and time values
Interval	Date and time intervals

Tips for Data Types

- Use the statements CREATE TABLE and ALTER TABLE to define and change a column's data type; see Chapter 11.

- Database designers choose data types carefully. The consequences of a poor data-type choice include the inability to insert values into a column and data loss if the existing data type must be changed.

- The SQL:2003 standard dropped SQL-92's bit-string data types (BIT and BIT VARYING) in favor of binary large objects. Bit strings held smaller binary-data items than BLOBs do.

- DBMS The SQL standard leaves many data-type implementation details up to the DBMS vendor. Consequently, SQL data types don't map directly to specific DBMS data types, even if the data types have identical names. You'll find equivalent or similar DBMS data types in the tips of each of the following data-type sections. Some DBMS data types have synonyms that match the SQL standard's data-type names.

Table 3.3 Examples of Literals

Literal	Examples
Character string	'42', 'ennui', 'don''t', N'Jack'
Numeric	42, 12.34, 2., .001, -123, +6.33333, 2.5E2, 5E-3
Boolean	TRUE, FALSE, UNKNOWN
Datetime	DATE '2005-06-22', TIME '09:45:00', TIMESTAMP '2006-10-19 10:23:54'
Interval	INTERVAL '15-3' YEAR TO MONTH, INTERVAL '22:06:5.5' HOUR TO SECOND

Character String Types

Use character string data types to represent text. A **character string**, or simply **string**, has these characteristics:

- It's an ordered sequence of zero or more characters.
- Its length can be fixed or varying.
- It's case sensitive ('A' comes before 'a' when sorted).
- In SQL statements, a string is surrounded by single quotes.
- It's one of the types listed in Table 3.4.

Table 3.4 Character String Types

Type	Description
CHARACTER	Represents a fixed number of characters. A string stored in a column defined as CHARACTER(*length*) can have up to *length* characters, where *length* is an integer greater than or equal to 1; the maximum *length* depends on the DBMS. When you store a string with fewer than *length* characters in a CHARACTER(*length*) column, the DBMS pads the end of the string with spaces to create a string that has exactly *length* characters. A CHARACTER(6) string 'Jack' is stored as 'Jack ', for example. CHARACTER and CHAR are synonyms.
CHARACTER VARYING	Represents a variable number of characters. A string stored in a column defined as CHARACTER VARYING(*length*) can have up to *length* characters, where *length* is an integer greater than or equal to 1; the maximum *length* depends on the DBMS. Unlike CHARACTER, when you store a string with fewer than *length* characters in a CHARACTER VARYING(*length*) column, the DBMS stores the string as is and doesn't pad it with spaces. A CHARACTER VARYING(6) string 'Jack' is stored as 'Jack', for example. CHARACTER VARYING, CHAR VARYING, and VARCHAR are synonyms.
NATIONAL CHARACTER	This data type is the same as CHARACTER except that it holds standardized multibyte characters or Unicode characters. In SQL statements, NATIONAL CHARACTER strings are written like CHARACTER strings but have an N in front of the first quote: N'ßæþ', for example. NATIONAL CHARACTER, NATIONAL CHAR, and NCHAR are synonyms.
NATIONAL CHARACTER VARYING	This data type is the same as CHARACTER VARYING except that it holds standardized multibyte characters or Unicode characters (see NATIONAL CHARACTER). NATIONAL CHARACTER VARYING, NATIONAL CHAR VARYING, and NCHAR VARYING are synonyms.
CLOB	The character large object (CLOB) type is intended for use in library databases that hold vast amounts of text. A single CLOB value might hold an entire webpage, book, or genetic sequence, for example. CLOBs can't be used as keys or in indexes and support fewer functions and operations than do CHAR and VARCHAR. In host languages, CLOBs are referenced with a unique locator (pointer) value, avoiding the overhead of transferring entire CLOBs across a client–server network. CLOB and CHARACTER LARGE OBJECT are synonyms.
NCLOB	The national character large object (NCLOB) type is the same as CLOB except that it holds standardized multibyte characters or Unicode characters (see NATIONAL CHARACTER). NCLOB, NCHAR LARGE OBJECT, and NATIONAL CHARACTER LARGE OBJECT are synonyms.

Table 3.5 DBMS Character String Types

DBMS	Types
Access	short text, long text (in older versions: text, memo)
SQL Server	char, varchar, nchar, nvarchar
Oracle	char, varchar2, clob, nchar, nvarchar2, nclob
Db2	char, varchar, clob, nchar, nvarchar, nclob, graphic, vargraphic, dbclob
MySQL	char, varchar, nchar, nvarchar, tinytext, text, mediumtext, longtext
PostgreSQL	char, varchar, text

Unicode

Computers store characters (letters, digits, punctuation, control characters, and other symbols) internally by assigning them unique numeric values. An **encoding** determines the mapping of characters to numeric values; different languages and computer operating systems use many different native encodings. Standard U.S.-English strings use **ASCII** encoding, which assigns values to 128 (2^7) different characters—not much, and not even enough to hold all the Latin characters used in modern European languages, much less all the Chinese ideographs.

Unicode is a single character set that represents the characters of almost all the world's written languages. Unicode can encode up to about 4.3 billion (2^{32}) characters (using UTF-32 encoding). The Unicode Consortium develops and maintains the Unicode standard. The actual Unicode mappings are available in the latest online or printed edition of *The Unicode Standard*, available at *unicode.org*.

Tips for Character Strings

- Two consecutive single quotes represent one single-quote character in a string. Type 'don''t' to represent *don't*, for example. A double-quote character (") is a separate character and doesn't need this special treatment.

- The length of a string is an integer between 0 and *length*, inclusive. A string with no characters—'' (two single quotes with no intervening space)—is called an **empty string** or a **zero-length string**. An empty string is considered to be a VARCHAR of length zero.

- DBMSs often can sort and manipulate fixed-length strings faster than variable-length ones.

- Keep character columns as short as possible rather than giving them "room to grow" in the future. Shorter columns sort and group faster than longer ones.

- The SQL:1999 standard introduced CLOB and NCLOB to the SQL language (but most DBMSs already had similar data types by then).

- DBMS Table 3.5 lists character-string and similar types for the DBMSs. See the DBMS documentation for size limits and usage restrictions.

  Oracle treats empty strings as nulls; see "Nulls" on page 72.

  In **MySQL** ANSI_QUOTES mode, string literals can be quoted only with single quotes; a string quoted with double quotes is interpreted as an identifier.

Binary Large Object Type

Use the **binary large object** (**BLOB**) data type to store binary data. A BLOB has these characteristics:

- The type name is BLOB or BINARY LARGE OBJECT.

- Unlike a CLOB, which stores a long character string, a BLOB stores a long sequence of bytes. The two data types are incompatible.

- BLOBs are used mainly to store large amounts of multimedia data (graphics, photos, audio, or video, for example), scientific data (medical images or climate maps), or technical data (engineering drawings).

- BLOBs can't be used as keys or in indexes and support far fewer functions and operations than do other types. BLOBs can be compared for only equality (=) or inequality (<>) because it makes no sense for a BLOB to be "less than" another BLOB. BLOBs can't be used with DISTINCT, in GROUP BY or ORDER BY clauses, or in column functions.

- In host languages, BLOBs are referenced with a unique **locator** (pointer) value, avoiding the overhead of transferring entire BLOBs across a client/server network.

Tips for Binary Large Objects

- DBMSs don't attempt to interpret BLOBs; their meaning is up to the application.

- A binary string literal is given in **hexadecimal**, or **hex** (base 16), format. The hexadecimal system uses the digits 0 through 9 and the letters *A* through *F* (uppercase or lowercase). One hex character is equivalent to 4 bits. In SQL statements, hex strings have an X in front of the first quote, with no intervening space. The hex string X'4B' corresponds to the bits 01001011 or the **bit string** B'01001011', for example.

Table 3.6   DBMS BLOB Types

DBMS	Types
Access	ole object, attachment
SQL Server	binary, varbinary
Oracle	raw, long raw, blob, bfile
Db2	binary, varbinary, blob
MySQL	binary, varbinary, tinyblob, blob, mediumblob, longblob
PostgreSQL	bytea

- The SQL:1999 standard introduced BLOB to the SQL language (but most DBMSs already had similar data types by then).

- DBMS Table 3.6 lists BLOB and similar types for the DBMSs. See the DBMS documentation for size limits and usage restrictions.

Exact Numeric Types

Use exact numeric data types to represent exact numerical values. An **exact numerical value** has these characteristics:

- It can be a negative, zero, or positive number.

- It's an integer or a decimal number. An **integer** is a whole number expressed without a decimal point: −42, 0, 62262. A **decimal number** has digits to the right of the decimal point: −22.06, 0.0, 0.0003, 12.34.

- It has a fixed precision and scale. The **precision** is the number of significant digits used to express the number; it's the total number of digits both to the right and to the left of the decimal point. The **scale** is the number of digits to the right of the decimal point. Obviously, the scale can't exceed the precision. To represent a whole number, set the scale equal to zero. See "Tips for Exact Numeric Types" for some examples.

- It's one of the types listed in Table 3.7.

Table 3.7 Exact Numeric Types

Type	Description
NUMERIC	Represents a decimal number, stored in a column defined as NUMERIC(*precision* [,*scale*]). *precision* is greater than or equal to 1; the maximum *precision* depends on the DBMS. *scale* is a value from 0 to *precision*. If *scale* is omitted, then it defaults to zero (which makes the number effectively an INTEGER).
DECIMAL	This data type is similar to NUMERIC, and some DBMSs define them equivalently. The difference is that the DBMS can choose a *precision* greater than that specified by DECIMAL(*precision* [,*scale*]), so *precision* specifies the minimum precision, not an exact precision as in NUMERIC. DECIMAL and DEC are synonyms.
INTEGER	Represents an integer. The minimum and maximum values that can be stored in an INTEGER column depend on the DBMS. INTEGER takes no arguments. INTEGER and INT are synonyms.
SMALLINT	This data type is the same as INTEGER except that it might hold a smaller range of values, depending on the DBMS. SMALLINT takes no arguments.
BIGINT	This data type is the same as INTEGER except that it might hold a larger range of values, depending on the DBMS. BIGINT takes no arguments.

Tips for Exact Numeric Types

- Table 3.8 shows how the number 123.89 is stored for different precision and scale values.

- Don't enclose a numeric literal in quotes.

- Store numbers as strings if the numbers are not involved in arithmetic calculations. Store telephone numbers, credit-card numbers, postal codes, and U.S. Social Security numbers as strings, for example. This technique can save space and prevent data loss: if you store the postal code '02116' as a number instead of as a string, then you'll lose the leading zero.

- Calculations involving only integers are much faster than those involving decimal and floating-point numbers.

- DBMS Table 3.9 lists exact-numeric and similar types for the DBMSs. See the DBMS documentation for size limits and usage restrictions. Some DBMSs accept type names that they don't implement, converting them to suitable, supported types; **Oracle** converts INT to NUMBER(32), for example.

DBMSs usually implement SMALLINT as 16-bit values (−32,768 through 32,767), INTEGER as 32-bit values (−2,147,483,648 through 2,147,483,647), and BIGINT as 64-bit values (quintillions). The SQL:2003 standard introduced BIGINT to the SQL language (but most DBMSs already had a similar data type by then).

Table 3.8 Precision and Scale Examples for 123.89

Specified As	Stored As
NUMERIC(5)	124
NUMERIC(5,0)	124
NUMERIC(5,1)	123.9
NUMERIC(5,2)	123.89
NUMERIC(4,0)	124
NUMERIC(4,1)	123.9
NUMERIC(4,2)	Exceeds precision
NUMERIC(2,0)	Exceeds precision

Table 3.9 DBMS Exact Numeric Types

DBMS	Types
Access	byte, decimal, integer, long integer
SQL Server	tinyint, smallint, int, bigint, bit, numeric, decimal, smallmoney, money
Oracle	number
Db2	smallint, integer, bigint, decimal, numeric
MySQL	tinyint, smallint, mediumint, int, bigint, decimal, numeric
PostgreSQL	smallint, integer, bigint, decimal, numeric

Approximate Numeric Types

Use approximate numeric data types to represent approximate numerical values. An **approximate numerical value** has these characteristics:

- It can be a negative, zero, or positive number.

- It's considered to be an approximation of a floating-point (real) number.

- It typically is used to represent the very small or very large quantities common in technical, scientific, statistical, and financial calculations.

- It's expressed in scientific notation. A number in **scientific notation** is written as a decimal number multiplied by an (integer) power of 10. An uppercase E is the exponentiation symbol: $2.5E2 = 2.5 \times 10^2 = 250$, for example. The **mantissa** is the portion that expresses the significant digits (2.5 here), and the **exponent** is the power of 10 (2 here). The mantissa and exponent each can have a sign: $-2.5E{-}2 = -2.5 \times 10^{-2} = -0.025$.

- It has a fixed precision but no explicit scale. (The sign and magnitude of the exponent determine the scale intrinsically.) The precision is the number of (binary) bits used to store the mantissa. To convert from binary to decimal precision, multiply the precision by 0.30103. To convert from decimal to binary precision, multiply the decimal precision by 3.32193. For example, 24 bits yields 7 digits of precision, and 53 bits yields 15 digits of precision.

- It's one of the types listed in Table 3.10.

Table 3.10 Approximate Numeric Types

Type	Description
FLOAT	Represents a floating-point number, stored in a column defined as FLOAT(*precision*). *precision* is greater than or equal to 1 and expressed as the number of bits (not the number of digits); the maximum *precision* depends on the DBMS.
REAL	This data type is the same as FLOAT except that the DBMS defines the precision. REAL numbers usually are called single-precision numbers. REAL takes no arguments.
DOUBLE PRECISION	This data type is the same as FLOAT except that the DBMS defines the precision, which must be greater than that of REAL. DOUBLE PRECISION takes no arguments.

Tips for Approximate Numeric Types

- Don't enclose a numeric literal in quotes.

- **DBMS** Table 3.11 lists approximate numeric and similar types for the DBMSs. See the DBMS documentation for size limits and usage restrictions. Some DBMSs accept type names that they don't implement, converting them to suitable, supported types; **PostgreSQL** converts float to double precision, for example.

Table 3.11 DBMS Approximate Numeric Types

DBMS	Types
Access	single, double
SQL Server	float, real
Oracle	float, binary_float, binary_double
Db2	real, double, float, decfloat
MySQL	float, double
PostgreSQL	real, double precision

Boolean Type

Use the boolean data type to store truth values. A **boolean value** has these characteristics:

- The type name is BOOLEAN.

- The truth values are True, False, and Unknown, represented by the boolean literals TRUE, FALSE, and UNKNOWN. Truth values are described in "Combining and Negating Conditions with AND, OR, and NOT" on page 93.

- A null is equivalent to the Unknown truth value and, in practice, usually is used instead of Unknown (most DBMS boolean types don't accept the literal UNKNOWN). See "Nulls" on page 72.

Tips for Boolean Values

- Don't enclose a boolean literal in quotes.

- The SQL:1999 standard introduced BOOLEAN to the SQL language.

- DBMS Table 3.12 lists boolean and similar types for the DBMSs. See the DBMS documentation for size limits and usage restrictions. Where no boolean type is available, use the data type for storing single bits or small integers. SQL programmers often use these numeric values to represent truth values, where zero means false, 1 (or any nonzero number) means true, and null means unknown.

Table 3.12 DBMS Boolean Types

DBMS	Types
Access	yes/no
SQL Server	bit
Oracle	number(1)
Db2	decimal(1)
MySQL	boolean, bit, tinyint(1)
PostgreSQL	boolean

Datetime Types

Use datetime data types to represent the date and time of day. A **datetime value** has these characteristics:

- It's specified with respect to UTC, or Universal Coordinated Time (formerly called Greenwich Mean Time or GMT). The SQL standard requires that every SQL session have a default offset from UTC that is used for the duration of the session; –8 hours is the time-zone offset of San Francisco, California, for example.

- The rules of the Gregorian calendar determine how date values are formed. DBMSs reject values that they can't recognize as dates.

- Time values are based on a 24-hour clock, also called military time (use 13:00, not 1:00 p.m.).

- Hyphens (-) separate the parts of a date, and colons (:) separate the parts of a time. A space separates a date and time when both are combined.

- It's one of the types listed in Table 3.13.

Table 3.13 Datetime Types

Type	Description
DATE	Represents a date. A date stored in a column defined as DATE has three integer fields—YEAR, MONTH, and DAY—and is formatted *yyyy-mm-dd* (length 10) (2006-03-17, for example). Table 3.14 lists the valid values for the fields. DATE takes no arguments.
TIME	Represents a time of day. A time stored in a column defined as TIME has three fields—HOUR, MINUTE, and SECOND—and is formatted *hh:mm:ss* (length 8) (22:06:57, for example). You can specify fractional seconds with TIME(*precision*). *precision* is the number of fractional digits and is greater than or equal to zero. The maximum *precision*, which is at least 6, depends on the DBMS. HOUR and MINUTE are integers, and SECOND is a decimal number. The format is *hh:mm:ss.ssss...* (length 9 plus the number fractional digits) (22:06:57.1333, for example). Table 3.14 lists the valid values for the fields.
TIMESTAMP	Represents a combination of DATE and TIME values separated by a space. The TIMESTAMP format is *yyyy-mm-dd hh:mm:ss* (length 19) (2006-03-17 22:06:57, for example). You can specify fractional seconds with TIMESTAMP(*precision*). The format is *yyyy-mm-dd hh:mm:ss.ssss...* (length 20 plus the number fractional digits).
TIME WITH TIMEZONE	This data type is the same as TIME except that it adds a field, TIME_ZONE_OFFSET, to indicate the offset in hours from UTC. TIME_ZONE_OFFSET is formatted as INTERVAL HOUR TO MINUTE (see "Interval Types" on page 68) and can contain the values listed in Table 3.14. Append AT TIME ZONE *time_zone_offset* to the TIME to assign a value to the time zone (22:06:57 AT TIME ZONE -08:00, for example). Alternatively, you can append AT LOCAL to indicate that the time zone is the default for the session (22:06:57 AT LOCAL, for example). If the AT clause is omitted, then all times default to AT LOCAL.
TIMESTAMP WITH TIMEZONE	This data type is the same as TIMESTAMP except that it adds a field, TIME_ZONE_OFFSET, to indicate the offset in hours from UTC. The syntax rules are the same as those of TIME WITH TIME ZONE except that you must include a date (2006-03-17 22:06:57 AT TIME ZONE -08:00, for example).

Table 3.14 Valid Values for Datetime Fields

Field	Valid Values
YEAR	0001 to 9999
MONTH	01 to 12
DAY	01 to 31
HOUR	00 to 23
MINUTE	00 to 59
SECOND	00 to 61.999
TIME_ZONE_OFFSET	-12:59 to +13:00

Table 3.15 DBMS Datetime Types

DBMS	Types
Access	date/time
SQL Server	date, datetime, datetime2, datetimeoffset, smalldatetime, time
Oracle	date, timestamp
Db2	date, time, timestamp
MySQL	date, datetime, timestamp, time, year
PostgreSQL	date, time, timestamp

In **Microsoft Access**, surround datetime literals with # characters instead of quotes and omit the data type name prefix. The standard SQL date DATE '2006-03-17' is equivalent to the Access date #2006-03-17#, for example.

In **Microsoft SQL Server**, omit the data type name prefix from datetime literals. The standard SQL date DATE '2006-03-17' is equivalent to the SQL Server date '2006-03-17', for example.

In **Db2**, omit the data type name prefix from datetime literals. The standard SQL date DATE '2006-03-17' is equivalent to the Db2 date '2006-03-17', for example.

Tips for Datetime Values

- To get your system time, see "Getting the Current Date and Time" on page 142.

- You can compare two datetime values if they have the same fields; see "Filtering Rows with WHERE" on page 89. See also "Performing Datetime and Interval Arithmetic" on page 140.

- The SECOND field in Table 3.14 can accept values up to 61.999... (instead of 59) to allow for the (rare) insertion of **leap seconds** into a particular minute to keep Earth's clocks synchronized with sidereal time.

- A datetime literal is a datetime type name, followed by a space, followed by a datetime value surrounded by single quotes—DATE '*yyyy-mm-dd*', TIME '*hh:mm:ss*', and TIMESTAMP '*yyyy-mm-dd hh:mm:ss*', for example.

- Standard SQL can't handle B.C.E./B.C. (Before the Common Era/Before Christ) dates, but your DBMS might be able to do so.

- Timestamps often are used to mark events associated with the row in which they appear. In **MySQL**, for example, a *timestamp* column is useful for recording the date and time of an UPDATE operation.

- The data type TIME WITH TIME ZONE makes no sense because real-world time zones have no meaning unless they're associated with a date (because the time-zone offset varies throughout the year). Favor TIMESTAMP WITH TIME ZONE.

- **DBMS** Table 3.15 lists datetime and similar types for the DBMSs. See the DBMS documentation for size limits and usage restrictions.

  DBMSs let you enter date values in month-day-year, day-month-year, and other formats and time values based on a 12-hour (a.m./p.m.) clock. The format in which dates and times are displayed can differ from the format in which they're entered.

Interval Types

DBMS DBMS conformance to standard SQL interval types is spotty or nonexistent, so you might not find this section to be useful in practice. DBMSs have their own extended data types and functions that calculate intervals and perform date and time arithmetic.

Use interval data types to represent sets of time values or spans of time. An **interval value** has these characteristics:

- It stores the quantity of time between two datetime values. Between 09:00 and 13:30 is an interval of 04:30 (4 hours and 30 minutes), for example. If you subtract two datetime values, then you get an interval.

- It can be used to increment or decrement a datetime value; see "Performing Datetime and Interval Arithmetic" on page 140.

- It has the same fields as datetime values (YEAR, HOUR, SECOND, and so on), but the number can have a + (forward) or - (backward) sign to indicate a direction in time. The field separators are the same as for datetime values.

- It comes in two categories: year-month intervals and day-time intervals. A **year-month interval** expresses an interval as years and a whole number of months. A **day-time interval** expresses an interval as days, hours, minutes, and seconds.

- It has a single-field or multiple-field qualifier. A single-field qualifier is specified as YEAR, MONTH, DAY, HOUR, MINUTE, or SECOND. A multiple-field qualifier is specified as:

  start_field TO *end_field*

  start_field is YEAR, DAY, HOUR, or MINUTE, and *end_field* is YEAR, MONTH, DAY, HOUR, MINUTE, or SECOND. *end_field* must be a smaller time period than *start_field*.

  A single-field column defined as INTERVAL HOUR could store intervals such as "4 hours" or "25 hours", for example. A multiple-field column defined as INTERVAL DAY TO MINUTE could store intervals such as "2 days, 5 hours, 10 minutes", for example.

- A single-field column can have a precision that specifies the length (number of positions) of the field; INTERVAL HOUR(2), for example. The precision defaults to 2 if omitted. A SECOND field can have an additional fractional precision that specifies the number of digits to the right of the decimal point—INTERVAL SECOND(5,2), for example. The fractional precision defaults to 6 if omitted.

  A multiple-field column can have a precision for *start_field* but not *end_field* (unless *end_field* is SECOND, in which case it can have a fractional precision)—INTERVAL DAY(3) TO MINUTE and INTERVAL MINUTE(2) TO SECOND(4), for example.

- It's one of the types listed in Table 3.16.

Table 3.16 Interval Types

Type	Description
Year-month	These intervals contain only a year value, only a month value, or both. The valid column types are INTERVAL YEAR, INTERVAL YEAR(*precision*), INTERVAL MONTH, INTERVAL MONTH(*precision*), INTERVAL YEAR TO MONTH, or INTERVAL YEAR(*precision*) TO MONTH.
Day-time	These intervals can contain a day value, hour value, minute value, second value, or some combination thereof. Some examples of the valid column types are INTERVAL MINUTE, INTERVAL DAY(*precision*), INTERVAL DAY TO HOUR, INTERVAL DAY(*precision*) TO SECOND, and INTERVAL MINUTE(*precision*) TO SECOND(*frac_precision*).

Table 3.17 DBMS Interval Types

DBMS	Types
Access	Not supported
SQL Server	Not supported
Oracle	interval year to month, interval day to second
Db2	Not supported
MySQL	Not supported
PostgreSQL	interval

Tips for Interval Types

- An interval literal is the word INTERVAL followed by a space, followed by an interval value surrounded by single quotes, followed by the interval qualifier—INTERVAL '15-3' YEAR TO MONTH (15 years and 3 months) and INTERVAL '22:06:5.5' HOUR TO SECOND (22 hours, 6 minutes, and 5.5 seconds), for example.

- See also "Working with Dates" on page 427 Chapter 15.

- DBMS Table 3.17 lists interval and similar types for the DBMSs. See the DBMS documentation for size limits and usage restrictions.

Unique Identifiers

Unique identifiers are used to generate primary-key values to identify rows (see "Primary Keys" on page 26). An identifier can be unique universally (large random numbers unique in any context) or only within a specific table (simple serial numbers 1, 2, 3,…). Table 3.18 lists unique-identifier types and attributes for the DBMSs. See the DBMS documentation for size limits and usage restrictions. The SQL standard calls columns with auto-incrementing values **identity columns**. See also "Generating Sequences" on page 393.

Table 3.18 Unique Identifiers

DBMS	Types or Attributes
Standard SQL	IDENTITY
Access	autonumber, replication id
SQL Server	uniqueidentifier, identity
Oracle	rowid, urowid, sequences
Db2	rowid, identity columns and sequences
MySQL	auto_increment attribute
PostgreSQL	smallserial, serial, bigserial, uuid

UUIDs

A universally unique ID is called a **Universally Unique Identifier (UUID)** or a **Globally Unique Identifier (GUID)**. When you define a column to have a UUID data type, your DBMS will generate a random UUID automatically in each new row, probably according to ISO/IEC 9834-8 (*iso.org*) or IETF RFC 4122 (*ietf.org*).

A UUID in standard form looks like:

a0eebc99-9c0b-4ef8-bb6d-6bb9bd380a11

The letters actually are hexadecimal digits (a–f). Your DBMS might use an alternative form with upper-case hex digits, surrounding braces, or omitted hyphens. UUIDs aren't *technically* guaranteed to be unique, but the probability of generating a duplicate ID is so tiny that they should be considered singular. For more information, read the Wikipedia article "Universally unique identifier" at *wikipedia.org/wiki/Universally_unique_identifier.*

Other Data Types

The SQL standard defines other data types than the ones covered in the preceding sections, but some of them rarely are implemented or used in practice (ARRAY, MULTISET, REF, and ROW, for example). More useful are the extended (nonstandard) data types that are available in various DBMSs. Depending on your DBMS, you can find data types for:

- Time intervals

- Network and internet addresses

- Links to files stored outside the database

- Monetary (currency) amounts

- Geographic and geometric (spatial) coordinates

- Row version-stamping

- Arrays and other collections

- XML

- JSON

- Full text searching

- Enumerated (enum) values from a specified list

- Position in a hierarchy

User-Defined Types

Microsoft SQL Server, Oracle, Db2, and **Post-greSQL** let you create **user-defined types (UDTs)**. The simplest UDT is a standard or built-in data type (CHARACTER, INTEGER, and so on) with additional check and other constraints. You can define the data type *marital_status*, for example, as a single-character CHARACTER data type that allows only the values S, M, W, D, or NULL (for single, married, widowed, divorced, or unknown). More-complex UDTs are similar to classes in object-oriented programming languages such as Java or Python. You can define a UDT once and use it in multiple tables, rather than repeat its definition in each table in which it's used. Search your DBMS documentation for *user-defined type*. UDTs are created in standard SQL with the statement CREATE TYPE.

Nulls

When your data are incomplete, you can use a null to represent a missing or unknown value. A **null** has these characteristics:

- In SQL statements, the keyword NULL represents a null.

- A null is used for a value that might never be known, might be determined later, or is inapplicable. (Think of a null as a marker or flag for a missing value, rather than as a value itself.)

- A null differs from zero, a string that contains only spaces, or an empty string (''). A null in the column *price* doesn't mean that an item has no price or that its price is zero; it means that the price is unknown or has not been set. (**Oracle** is a special case with respect to empty strings; see the DBMS tip in this section.)

- Nulls can appear in columns of any data type that are not restricted by NOT NULL or PRIMARY KEY constraints (Chapter 11). You should not allow nulls in alternate keys.

- To detect nulls, see "Testing for Nulls with IS NULL" on page 112.

- Nulls aren't equal (or unequal) to each other. You can't determine whether a null matches any other value, including another null, so the expressions NULL = *any_value*, NULL <> *any_value*, NULL = NULL, and NULL <> NULL are neither true nor false but unknown; see "Combining and Negating Conditions with AND, OR, and NOT" on page 93.

- Although nulls are never equal to each other, DISTINCT treats all the nulls in a particular column as duplicates; see "Eliminating Duplicate Rows with DISTINCT" on page 81.

- When you sort a column that contains nulls, the nulls will be either greater than or less than all the non-null values, depending on the DBMS; see "Sorting Rows with ORDER BY" on page 83.

- Nulls propagate through computations. The result of any arithmetic expression or operation that involves a null is null: (12*NULL)/4 is null; see Chapter 5.

- Most aggregate functions, such as SUM(), AVG(), and MAX(), ignore nulls. COUNT(*) is an exception. See Chapter 6.

- If the grouping column in a GROUP BY clause contains nulls, then all the nulls are put in a single group; see "Grouping Rows with GROUP BY" on page 169.

- Nulls affect the results of joins; see "Using Joins" on page 184.

- Nulls can cause problems in subqueries; see "Nulls in Subqueries" on page 254.

Tips for Nulls

- Use caution when interpreting results in which nulls are involved. Nulls cause so many problems and complications—some important ones are listed here—that some database experts urge users to minimize their use or not use them at all (and instead use default values or some other missing-data scheme). Nevertheless, you won't become a competent SQL programmer without understanding nulls completely.

- See also "Checking for Nulls with COALESCE()" on page 153 and "Comparing Expressions with NULLIF()" on page 154.

- **Nullable** means that a column is allowed to contain nulls. Use the CREATE TABLE or ALTER TABLE statement (Chapter 11) to set a column's nullability.

- The term *null value* is inaccurate—a null indicates the *lack* of a value.

- Don't place the keyword NULL in quotes; your DBMS will interpret it as the character string 'NULL' rather than as a null.

```
SELECT MAX(au_id)
  FROM authors
  WHERE au_lname = 'XXX';


MAX(au_id)
----------
NULL
```

Figure 3.3 Getting a null from a column that isn't nullable.

employees

emp_id	emp_name	commission
E01	Eli McLemore	NULL
E02	Monty Wendt	0.25
E03	Damien Shaw	NULL
E04	Russell Sager	NULL
E05	Jill Stallworth	NULL
E06	Pamela Gant	0.08

employees

emp_id	emp_name
E01	Eli McLemore
E02	Monty Wendt
E03	Damien Shaw
E04	Russell Sager
E05	Jill Stallworth
E06	Pamela Gant

commissions

emp_id	commission
E02	0.25
E06	0.08

Figure 3.4 Nulls are eliminated by splitting the original table (top) into a one-to-one relationship (bottom).

- You can get a null from a column that doesn't allow nulls. The column *au_id* in the table *authors* doesn't allow nulls, but the SELECT statement in Figure 3.3 returns a null for the maximum *au_id*.

- If nulls appear in a column because actual values are not meaningful (rather than unknown), then you can split the column off into its own table with a one-to-one relationship with the other table. In Figure 3.4, the original table *employees* has the column *commission*, which specifies an employee's sales commission. *commission* contains mostly nulls because most employees aren't salespeople. To avoid the proliferation of nulls, move *commission* to its own table.

- DBMS The display of nulls in results varies by DBMS. A null might appear as NULL, (NULL), <NULL>, -, or empty space, for example.

  Oracle treats an empty string ('') as a null. This treatment might not continue to be true in future releases, however, and Oracle recommends that you do not treat empty strings the same as nulls in your SQL code. This behavior can cause conversion problems among DBMSs. In the sample database, for example, the column *au_fname* in the table *authors* is defined as NOT NULL. In Oracle, the first name of the author Kellsey (author A06) is a space (' '); in the other DBMSs, the first name is an empty string (''). For information about the sample database, see "The Sample Database" on page 39.

CHAPTER 4

Retrieving Data from a Table

This chapter introduces SQL's workhorse—the SELECT statement. Most SQL work involves retrieving and manipulating data by using this one (albeit complex) statement. SELECT retrieves rows, columns, and derived values from one or more tables in a database; its syntax is:

```
SELECT columns
  FROM tables
  [JOIN joins]
  [WHERE search_condition]
  [GROUP BY grouping_columns]
  [HAVING search_condition]
  [ORDER BY sort_columns];
```

SELECT, FROM, ORDER BY, and WHERE are covered in this chapter, GROUP BY and HAVING in Chapter 6, and JOIN in Chapter 7. By convention, I call only a SELECT statement a *query* because it returns a result set. DBMS documentation and other books might refer to *any* SQL statement as a query. Although SELECT is powerful, it's not dangerous: you can't use it to add, change, or delete data or database objects. (The dangerous stuff starts in Chapter 10.)

Tip: Recall that *italic_type* denotes a variable in code that must be replaced with a value, and brackets indicate an optional clause or item; see "About This Book" on page xii for typographic and syntax conventions.

Retrieving Columns with SELECT and FROM

In its simplest form, a SELECT statement retrieves columns from a table; you can retrieve one column, multiple columns, or all columns. The SELECT clause lists the columns to display, and the FROM clause specifies the table from which to draw the columns.

To retrieve a column from a table:

- Type:

  ```
  SELECT column
    FROM table;
  ```

  column is a column name, and *table* is the name of the table that contains *column* (Listing 4.1 and Figure 4.1).

To retrieve multiple columns from a table:

- Type:

  ```
  SELECT columns
    FROM table;
  ```

  columns is two or more comma-separated column names, and *table* is the name of the table that contains *columns* (Listing 4.2 and Figure 4.2).

  Columns are displayed in the same order in which they're listed in *columns*, not the order in which they're defined in *table*.

```
SELECT city
  FROM authors;
```

Listing 4.1 List the cities in which the authors live. See Figure 4.1 for the result.

```
city
-------------
Bronx
Boulder
San Francisco
San Francisco
New York
Palo Alto
Sarasota
```

Figure 4.1 Result of Listing 4.1.

```
SELECT au_fname, au_lname, city, state
  FROM authors;
```

Listing 4.2 List each author's first name, last name, city, and state. See Figure 4.2 for the result.

```
au_fname   au_lname      city           state
---------  -----------   -------------  -----
Sarah      Buchman       Bronx          NY
Wendy      Heydemark     Boulder        CO
Hallie     Hull          San Francisco  CA
Klee       Hull          San Francisco  CA
Christian  Kells         New York       NY
           Kellsey       Palo Alto      CA
Paddy      O'Furniture   Sarasota       FL
```

Figure 4.2 Result of Listing 4.2.

```
SELECT *
  FROM authors;
```

Listing 4.3 List all the columns in the table *authors*. See Figure 4.3 for the result.

To retrieve all columns from a table:

• Type:

```
SELECT *
  FROM table;
```

table is the name of the table (Listing 4.3 and Figure 4.3).

Columns are displayed in the order in which they're defined in *table*.

au_id	au_fname	au_lname	phone	address	city	state	zip
A01	Sarah	Buchman	718-496-7223	75 West 205 St	Bronx	NY	10468
A02	Wendy	Heydemark	303-986-7020	2922 Baseline Rd	Boulder	CO	80303
A03	Hallie	Hull	415-549-4278	3800 Waldo Ave, #14F	San Francisco	CA	94123
A04	Klee	Hull	415-549-4278	3800 Waldo Ave, #14F	San Francisco	CA	94123
A05	Christian	Kells	212-771-4680	114 Horatio St	New York	NY	10014
A06		Kellsey	650-836-7128	390 Serra Mall	Palo Alto	CA	94305
A07	Paddy	O'Furniture	941-925-0752	1442 Main St	Sarasota	FL	34236

Figure 4.3 Result of Listing 4.3.

Tips for Retrieving Columns

- The SELECT and FROM clauses always are required to retrieve columns from tables; all other clauses are optional.

- Closure guarantees that the result of every SELECT statement is a table; see "Tips for Tables, Columns, and Rows" on page 24.

- The result in Figure 4.1 contains duplicate rows because two authors live in San Francisco. To remove duplicates, see "Eliminating Duplicate Rows with DISTINCT" on page 81.

- The rows in your results might be ordered differently from the rows in mine; see "Sorting Rows with ORDER BY" on page 83.

- I use NULL to indicate a null in a table or result; see "Nulls" on page 72 (Listing 4.4 and Figure 4.4).

- Chapters 7, 8, and 9 describe how to retrieve columns from multiple tables.

- SELECT * often is risky because the number or order of a table's columns can change and cause your program to fail. Likewise, SELECT * won't be understood by people unfamiliar with the table's columns. In contrast to queries that name specific columns in the SELECT clause, SELECT * is a resource hog that drags unneeded data across networks. (To see how a table is defined, rather than list its rows, see "Displaying Table Definitions" on page 302.)

- An operation that selects certain columns from a table is called a **projection**.

Results Are Unformatted

All results display raw, unformatted values. Monetary amounts lack currency signs, for example, and numbers might have too many decimal places. Reporting tools—not data-retrieval tools—format data, although DBMSs have non-standard functions that let you format numbers and datetimes in query results. See **Microsoft SQL Server**'s datename() function or **MySQL**'s date_format() function, for example.

```
SELECT city, state, country
  FROM publishers;
```

Listing 4.4 List each publisher's city, state, and country. See Figure 4.4 for the result.

```
city            state country
------------    ----- -------
New York        NY    USA
San Francisco   CA    USA
Hamburg         NULL  Germany
Berkeley        CA    USA
```

Figure 4.4 Result of Listing 4.4. The column *state* doesn't apply to Germany. NULL specifies a null, which is distinct from an "invisible" value such as an empty string or a string of spaces.

Creating Column Aliases with AS

In the query results so far, I've allowed the DBMS to use default values for column headings. (A column's default heading in a result is the source column's name in the table definition.) You can use the AS clause to create a column alias. A **column alias** is an alternative name (identifier) that you specify to control how column headings are displayed in a result. Use column aliases if column names are cryptic, hard to type, too long, or too short.

A column alias immediately follows a column name in the SELECT clause of a SELECT statement. Enclose the alias in single or double quotes if it's a reserved keyword or if it contains spaces, punctuation, or special characters. You can omit the quotes if the alias is a single non-reserved word that contains only letters, digits, or underscores. If you want a particular column to retain its default heading, then omit its AS clause.

To create column aliases:

- Type:

  SELECT
      column1 [AS] *alias1*,
      column2 [AS] *alias2*,
      ...
      columnN [AS] *aliasN*
    FROM *table*;

column1, *column2*,..., *columnN* are column names; *alias1*, *alias2*,..., *aliasN* are their corresponding column aliases; and *table* is the name of the table that contains *column1*, *column2*,....

Listing 4.5 shows the syntactic variations of the AS clause. Figure 4.5 shows the result of Listing 4.5.

```
SELECT
    au_fname AS "First name",
    au_lname AS 'Last name',
    city AS City,
    state,
    zip 'Postal code'
  FROM authors;
```

Listing 4.5 The AS clause specifies a column alias to display in results. This statement shows alternative constructions for AS syntax. In your programs, pick one construction and use it consistently. See Figure 4.5 for the result.

```
First name Last name  City           state Postal code
---------- ---------- -------------- ----- -----------
Sarah      Buchman    Bronx          NY    10468
Wendy      Heydemark  Boulder        CO    80303
Hallie     Hull       San Francisco  CA    94123
Klee       Hull       San Francisco  CA    94123
Christian  Kells      New York       NY    10014
           Kellsey    Palo Alto      CA    94305
Paddy      O'Furniture Sarasota      FL    34236
```

Figure 4.5 Result of Listing 4.5.

In standard SQL and most DBMSs, the keyword AS is optional, but you should include it and surround aliases with double quotes to make your SQL code more portable and readable. With these syntactic conventions, Listing 4.5 is equivalent to:

```
SELECT
    au_fname AS "First name",
    au_lname AS "Last name",
    city     AS "City",
    state,
    zip      AS "Postal code"
  FROM authors;
```

Tips for Column Aliases

- A column alias doesn't change the name of a column in a table.

- To determine a column's name in a table definition, see "Displaying Table Definitions" on page 302.

- You can use a reserved keyword if you quote the alias. The query SELECT SUM(sales) AS "Sum" FROM titles; uses the reserved word SUM as a column alias, for example. For information about keywords, see "SQL Syntax" on page 50 and "Identifiers" on page 54.

- AS also is used to name derived columns (whose values are determined by expressions other than simple column names); see "Creating Derived Columns" on page 116.

- You also can create table aliases with AS; see "Creating Table Aliases with AS" on page 182.

- DBMS **Microsoft Access** and **PostgreSQL** require the AS keyword for column references.

  Oracle and **Db2** display unquoted column names and aliases in uppercase.

  sqlplus (**Oracle**'s command-line processor) truncates column aliases to the number of characters specified in the table's column definitions. The column alias *"Postal code"* displays as *Posta* in a CHAR(5) column, for example.

  DBMSs have restrictions on embedded spaces, punctuation, and special characters in aliases; search your DBMS documentation for *SELECT* or *AS*.

```
SELECT state
  FROM authors;
```

Listing 4.6 List the states in which the authors live. See Figure 4.6 for the result.

```
state
-----
NY
CO
CA
CA
NY
CA
FL
```

Figure 4.6 Result of Listing 4.6. This result contains un-needed duplicates of CA and NY.

```
SELECT DISTINCT state
  FROM authors;
```

Listing 4.7 List the distinct states in which the authors live. The keyword DISTINCT eliminates duplicate rows in the result. See Figure 4.7 for the result.

```
state
-----
NY
CO
CA
FL
```

Figure 4.7 Result of Listing 4.7. This result has no CA or NY duplicates.

Eliminating Duplicate Rows with DISTINCT

Columns often contain duplicate values, and it's common to want a result that lists each duplicate only once. If I type Listing 4.6 to list the states where the authors live, then the result, Figure 4.6, contains unneeded duplicates. The DISTINCT keyword eliminates duplicate rows from a result. Note that the columns of a DISTINCT result form a candidate key (unless they contain nulls).

To eliminate duplicate rows:

• Type:

    SELECT DISTINCT *columns*
      FROM *table*;

  columns is one or more comma-separated column names, and *table* is the name of the table that contains *columns* (Listing 4.7 and Figure 4.7).

If the SELECT DISTINCT clause contains more than one column, then the values of *all* the specified columns combined determine the uniqueness of rows. The result of Listing 4.8 is Figure 4.8, which contains a duplicate row that has two columns. The result of Listing 4.9 is Figure 4.9, which eliminates the two-column duplicate.

Tips for DISTINCT

- Although nulls never equal each other because their values are unknown, DISTINCT considers all nulls to be duplicates of each other. SELECT DISTINCT returns only one null in a result, regardless of how many nulls it encounters; see "Nulls" on page 72.

- The SELECT statement syntax includes the optional ALL keyword. You rarely see ALL in practice because it denotes the default behavior: display all rows, including duplicates.

  SELECT *columns* FROM *table*;

  is equivalent to:

  SELECT ALL *columns* FROM *table*;

  The syntax diagram is:

  SELECT [ALL | DISTINCT] *columns*
    FROM *table*;

- If a table has a properly defined primary key, then SELECT DISTINCT * FROM *table*; and SELECT * FROM *table*; return identical results because all rows are unique.

- See also "Aggregating Distinct Values with DISTINCT" on page 166.

- For DISTINCT operations, the DBMS performs an internal sort to identify and remove duplicate rows. Sorting is computationally expensive—don't use DISTINCT if you don't have to.

```
SELECT city, state
  FROM authors;
```

Listing 4.8 List the cities and states in which the authors live. See Figure 4.8 for the result.

```
city           state
-------------  -----
Bronx          NY
Boulder        CO
New York       NY
Palo Alto      CA
San Francisco  CA
San Francisco  CA
Sarasota       FL
```

Figure 4.8 Result of Listing 4.8. This result contains a duplicate row for San Francisco, California.

```
SELECT DISTINCT city, state
  FROM authors;
```

Listing 4.9 List the distinct cities and states in which the authors live. See Figure 4.9 for the result.

```
city           state
-------------  -----
Bronx          NY
Boulder        CO
New York       NY
Palo Alto      CA
San Francisco  CA
Sarasota       FL
```

Figure 4.9 Result of Listing 4.9. It's the city–state combination that's considered to be unique, not the value in any single column.

```
SELECT au_fname, au_lname, city, state
  FROM authors
  ORDER BY au_lname ASC;
```

Listing 4.10 List the authors' first names, last names, cities, and states, sorted by ascending last name. ORDER BY performs ascending sorts by default, so the ASC keyword is optional. See Figure 4.10 for the result.

```
au_fname    au_lname     city            state
---------   -----------  -------------   -----
Sarah       Buchman      Bronx           NY
Wendy       Heydemark    Boulder         CO
Hallie      Hull         San Francisco   CA
Klee        Hull         San Francisco   CA
Christian   Kells        New York        NY
            Kellsey      Palo Alto       CA
Paddy       O'Furniture  Sarasota        FL
```

Figure 4.10 Result of Listing 4.10. This result is sorted in ascending last-name order.

```
SELECT au_fname, au_lname, city, state
  FROM authors
  ORDER BY au_fname DESC;
```

Listing 4.11 List the authors' first names, last names, cities, and states, sorted by descending first name. The DESC keyword is required. See Figure 4.11 for the result.

```
au_fname    au_lname     city            state
---------   -----------  -------------   -----
Wendy       Heydemark    Boulder         CO
Sarah       Buchman      Bronx           NY
Paddy       O'Furniture  Sarasota        FL
Klee        Hull         San Francisco   CA
Hallie      Hull         San Francisco   CA
Christian   Kells        New York        NY
            Kellsey      Palo Alto       CA
```

Figure 4.11 Result of Listing 4.11. This result is sorted in descending first-name order. The first name of the author Kellsey is an empty string ('') and sorts last (or first in ascending order).

Sorting Rows with ORDER BY

Rows in a query result are unordered, so you should view the order in which rows appear as being arbitrary. This situation arises because the relational model posits that row order is irrelevant for table operations. You can use the ORDER BY clause to sort rows by a specified column or columns in ascending (lowest to highest) or descending (highest to lowest) order; for details, see "Sort Order" on page 84. The ORDER BY clause always is the last clause in a SELECT statement.

To sort by a column:

- Type:

```
SELECT columns
  FROM table
  ORDER BY sort_column [ASC | DESC];
```

columns is one or more comma-separated column names, *sort_column* is the name of the column on which to sort the result, and *table* is the name of the table that contains *columns* and *sort_column*. (*sort_column* doesn't have to be in listed in *columns*.) Specify ASC for an ascending sort or DESC for a descending sort. If no sort direction is specified, then ASC is assumed (Listings 4.10 and 4.11, Figures 4.10 and 4.11).

To sort by multiple columns:

- Type:

```
SELECT columns
  FROM table
  ORDER BY
    sort_column1 [ASC | DESC],
    sort_column2 [ASC | DESC],
    ...
    sort_columnN [ASC | DESC];
```

  columns is one or more comma-separated column names; *sort_column1, sort_column2, ...,* *sort_columnN* are the names of the columns on which to sort the result; and *table* is the name of the table that contains *columns* and the sort columns. (The sort columns don't have to be in listed in *columns*.) Rows are sorted first by *sort_column1*; then rows that have equal values in *sort_column1* are sorted by the values in *sort_column2*, and so on. For each sort column, specify ASC for an ascending sort or DESC for a descending sort. If no sort direction is specified, then ASC is assumed (Listing 4.12 and Figure 4.12).

```
SELECT au_fname, au_lname, city, state
  FROM authors
  ORDER BY
    state ASC,
    city  DESC;
```

Listing 4.12 List the authors' first names, last names, cities, and states, sorted by descending city within ascending state. See Figure 4.12 for the result.

au_fname	au_lname	city	state
Hallie	Hull	San Francisco	CA
Klee	Hull	San Francisco	CA
	Kellsey	Palo Alto	CA
Wendy	Heydemark	Boulder	CO
Paddy	O'Furniture	Sarasota	FL
Christian	Kells	New York	NY
Sarah	Buchman	Bronx	NY

Figure 4.12 Result of Listing 4.12.

Sort Order

Sorting numeric and datetime values is unambiguous; sorting character strings is complex. A DBMS uses a **collating sequence**, or **collation**, to determine the order in which characters are sorted. The collation defines the order of precedence for every character in your character set. Your character set depends on the language that you're using—European languages (a Latin character set), Hebrew (the Hebrew alphabet), or Chinese (ideographs), for example. The collation also determines case sensitivity (is 'A' < 'a'?), accent sensitivity (is 'A' < 'Á'?), width sensitivity (for multibyte or Unicode characters), and other factors such as linguistic practices. The SQL standard doesn't define particular collations and character sets, so each DBMS uses its own sorting strategy and default collation. DBMSs provide commands or tools that display the current collation and character set. Run the command exec sp_helpsort in **Microsoft SQL Server**, for example. Search your DBMS documentation for *collation* or *sort order*.

```
SELECT au_fname, au_lname, city, state
  FROM authors
  ORDER BY 4 ASC, 2 DESC;
```

Listing 4.13 List each author's first name, last name, city, and state, sorted first by ascending state (column 4 in the SELECT clause) and then by descending last name within each state (column 2). See Figure 4.13 for the result.

```
au_fname   au_lname      city            state
---------  -----------   -------------   -----
           Kellsey       Palo Alto       CA
Hallie     Hull          San Francisco   CA
Klee       Hull          San Francisco   CA
Wendy      Heydemark     Boulder         CO
Paddy      O'Furniture   Sarasota        FL
Christian  Kells         New York        NY
Sarah      Buchman       Bronx           NY
```

Figure 4.13 Result of Listing 4.13.

Sorting by Substrings

To sort results by specific parts of a string, use the functions described in "Extracting a Substring with SUBSTRING()" on page 125. For example, this query sorts by the last four characters of *phone*:

```
SELECT au_id, phone
  FROM authors
  ORDER BY substr(phone,
    length(phone)-3);
```

DBMS This query works for **Oracle**, **Db2**, **MySQL**, and **PostgreSQL**. In **Microsoft SQL Server**, use substring(phone, len(phone)-3, 4). In **Microsoft Access**, use Mid(phone, len(phone)-3, 4).

You can specify relative column-position numbers instead of column names in ORDER BY. The position numbers refer to the columns in the result, not the original table. Using column positions saves typing, but the resulting code is unclear and invites mistakes if you reorder the columns in the SELECT clause.

To sort by relative column positions:

- Type:

```
SELECT columns
  FROM table
  ORDER BY
    sort_num1 [ASC | DESC],
    sort_num2 [ASC | DESC],
    ...
    sort_numN [ASC | DESC];
```

columns is one or more comma-separated column names; and *sort_num1*, *sort_num2*,..., *sort_numN* are integers between 1 and the number of columns in *columns*, inclusive. Each integer specifies the relative position of a column in *columns*. *table* is the name of the table that contains *columns*. (The sort numbers can't refer to a column that's not listed in *columns*.) The sort order is the same order described in "To sort by multiple columns" earlier in this section (Listing 4.13 and Figure 4.13).

Sorting and Nulls

Sorting is one of the situations where SQL departs from the idea that a null isn't equal to any other value, including another null. (The logical comparison NULL = NULL is unknown, not true.) When nulls are sorted, they all are considered to be equal to one another. The SQL standard leaves it up to the DBMS to decide whether nulls are either greater than or less than all non-null values. **Microsoft Access**, **Microsoft SQL Server**, and **MySQL** treat nulls as the *lowest* possible values (Listing 4.14 and Figure 4.14). **Oracle**, **Db2**, and **PostgreSQL** treat nulls as the *highest* possible values. See also "Nulls" on page 72.

In **Oracle**, use NULLS FIRST or NULLS LAST with ORDER BY to control null-sorting behavior. For other DBMSs, create a derived column (see Chapter 5) that flags nulls—CASE WHEN *column* IS NULL THEN 0 ELSE 1 END AS is_null, for example—and add it as the first column (with ASC or DESC) in the ORDER BY clause.

```
SELECT pub_id, state, country
  FROM publishers
  ORDER BY state ASC;
```

Listing 4.14 Nulls in a sort column are listed first or last, depending on the DBMS. See Figure 4.14 for the result.

```
pub_id  state  country
------  -----  -------
P03     NULL   Germany
P04     CA     USA
P02     CA     USA
P01     NY     USA
```

Figure 4.14 Result of Listing 4.14. This result is sorted by ascending state. The DBMS in which I ran this query treats nulls as the lowest possible values, so the row with the null state is listed first. A DBMS that treats nulls as the highest possible values would list the same row last.

Sorting Speed

The three factors that most affect sorting speed are, in order of importance:

- The number of rows selected

- The number of columns in the ORDER BY clause

- The length of columns in the ORDER BY clause

Always restrict a sort to the minimum number of rows needed. Running times of sorting routines don't scale linearly with the number of rows sorted—so sorting 10*n* rows takes much more than 10 times longer than sorting *n* rows. Also try to reduce the number of sorted columns and the columns' data-type lengths in the table definition, if possible.

```
SELECT city, state
  FROM authors
  ORDER BY zip ASC;
```

Listing 4.15 *zip* doesn't appear in the list of columns to retrieve. See Figure 4.15 for the result.

```
city           state
-------------  -----
New York       NY
Bronx          NY
Sarasota       FL
Boulder        CO
San Francisco  CA
San Francisco  CA
Palo Alto      CA
```

Figure 4.15 Result of Listing 4.15. This result is sorted by ascending zip code (postal code). Rows might appear to be in random order if you sort by an undisplayed column, confusing your end user.

```
SELECT
    au_fname AS "First Name",
    au_lname AS "Last Name",
    state
  FROM authors
  ORDER BY
    state      ASC,
    "Last Name" ASC,
    "First Name" ASC;
```

Listing 4.16 This query uses column aliases in the ORDER BY clause. See Figure 4.16 for the result.

```
First Name Last Name   state
---------- ----------- -----
Hallie     Hull        CA
Klee       Hull        CA
           Kellsey     CA
Wendy      Heydemark   CO
Paddy      O'Furniture FL
Sarah      Buchman     NY
Christian  Kells       NY
```

Figure 4.16 Result of Listing 4.16.

Tips for ORDER BY

- You can sort by columns that aren't listed in the SELECT clause (Listing 4.15 and Figure 4.15). This technique won't work for relative column positions.

- You can specify column aliases instead of column names in ORDER BY (Listing 4.16 and Figure 4.16). See "Creating Column Aliases with AS" on page 79.

- You can specify the same column multiple times in ORDER BY (but that's silly).

- If the ORDER BY columns don't identify each row uniquely in the result, then rows with duplicate values will be listed in arbitrary order. Although that's the case in some of my examples (refer to Figures 4.10, 4.12, and 4.13), you should include enough ORDER BY columns to identify rows uniquely, particularly if the result is to be displayed to an end user.

- According to the SQL standard, the ORDER BY clause is part of a CURSOR declaration and not the SELECT statement. **Cursors**, which allow result sets to be processed one row at a time, are beyond the scope of this book. All SQL implementations let you to use ORDER BY in a SELECT statement (because the DBMS builds a cursor invisibly). Standard SQL also lets ORDER BY appear in **window functions**; search your DBMS documentation for *window functions*.

- To sort based on conditional logic, add a CASE expression to the ORDER BY clause (see "Evaluating Conditional Values with CASE" on page 149). For example, this query sorts by *price* if *type* is "history"; otherwise, it sorts by *sales*:

```
SELECT title_id, type, price, sales
  FROM titles
  ORDER BY CASE WHEN type = 'history'
    THEN price ELSE sales END;
```

continues on next page

- You can sort by the results of expressions; Chapter 5 describes how to create expressions by using functions and operators (Listing 4.17 and Figure 4.17).

- You can intermingle column names, relative column positions, and expressions in ORDER BY.

- You should create indexes for columns that you sort frequently (see Chapter 12).

- The sequence in which unordered rows appear actually is based on the physical order of rows in the DBMS table. You shouldn't rely on physical order because it changes often, such as when rows are inserted, updated, or deleted or an index is created.

- Sorting by relative column position is useful in UNION queries; see "Combining Rows with UNION" on page 290.

- DBMS DBMSs restrict the columns that can appear in an ORDER BY clause, depending on data type. For example, in **Microsoft SQL Server**, you can't sort by nvarchar(max), varchar(max), and varbinary(max) columns; and in **Oracle**, you can't sort by blob, clob, nclob, and bfile columns. Search your DBMS documentation for *SELECT* or *ORDER BY*.

In **Microsoft Access** you can't use an expression's column alias in ORDER BY. To run Listing 4.17, either retype the expression in the ORDER BY clause:

```
ORDER BY price * sales DESC
```

or use the relative column position:

```
ORDER BY 4 DESC
```

```
SELECT
    title_id,
    price,
    sales,
    price * sales AS "Revenue"
  FROM titles
  ORDER BY "Revenue" DESC;
```

Listing 4.17 This query sorts by an expression. See Figure 4.17 for the result. I've created a column alias for the expression because it would be cumbersome to repeat the expression in the ORDER BY clause and because it creates a more meaningful column label in the result.

```
title_id price sales   Revenue
-------- ----- ------- -----------
T07      23.95 1500200 35929790.00
T05       6.95  201440  1400008.00
T12      12.99  100001  1299012.99
T03      39.95   25667  1025396.65
T11       7.99   94123   752042.77
T13      29.99   10467   313905.33
T06      19.95   11320   225834.00
T02      19.95    9566   190841.70
T04      12.99   13001   168882.99
T09      13.95    5000    69750.00
T08      10.00    4095    40950.00
T01      21.99     566    12446.34
T10       NULL    NULL         NULL
```

Figure 4.17 Result of Listing 4.17. This result lists titles by descending revenue (the product of price and sales).

Filtering Rows with WHERE

The result of each SELECT statement so far has included every row in the table (for the specified columns). You can use the WHERE clause to filter unwanted rows from the result. This filtering capability gives the SELECT statement its real power. In a WHERE clause, you specify a **search condition** that has one or more conditions that need to be satisfied by the rows of a table. A **condition**, or **predicate**, is a logical expression that evaluates to true, false, or unknown. Rows for which the condition is true are included in the result; rows for which the condition is false or unknown are excluded. (An unknown result, which arises from nulls, is described in the next section.) SQL provides operators that express different types of conditions (Table 4.1). Operators are symbols or keywords that specify actions to perform on values or other elements.

SQL's **comparison operators** compare two values and evaluate to true, false, or unknown (Table 4.2). The data type determines how values are compared:

- Character strings are compared lexicographically. < means *precedes*, and > means *follows*. See "Data Types" on page 56 and "Sorting Rows with ORDER BY" on page 83.

- Numbers are compared arithmetically. < means *smaller*, and > means *larger*.

- Datetimes are compared chronologically. < means *earlier*, and > means *later*. Datetimes must have the same fields (year, month, day, hour, and so on) to be compared meaningfully.

Compare only identical or similar data types. If you try to compare values that have different data types, then your DBMS might:

- Return an error

  or

- Compare the values unequally and return a result with no rows

  or

- Attempt to convert the values to a common type and compare them if successful or return an error if unsuccessful

Table 4.1 Types of Conditions

Condition	SQL Operators
Comparison	=, <>, <, <=, >, >=
Pattern matching	LIKE
Range filtering	BETWEEN
List filtering	IN
Null testing	IS NULL

Table 4.2 Comparison Operators

Operator	Description
=	Equal to
<>	Not equal to
<	Less than
<=	Less than or equal to
>	Greater than
>=	Greater than or equal to

To filter rows by making a comparison:

- Type:

  ```
  SELECT columns
    FROM table
    WHERE test_column op value;
  ```

  columns is one or more comma-separated column names, and *table* is the name of the table that contains *columns*.

  In the search condition, *test_column* is the name of a column in *table*. (*test_column* doesn't have to be listed in *columns*.) *op* is one of the comparison operators listed in Table 4.2, and *value* is a value that's compared with the value in *test_column* (Listings 4.18, 4.19, and 4.20, Figures 4.18, 4.19, and 4.20).

  The right and left sides of the comparison can also be complex expressions. The general form of a comparison is:

  expr1 op expr2

  expr1 and *expr2* are expressions. An expression is any valid combination of column names, literals, functions, and operators that resolves to a single value (per row). Chapter 5 covers expressions in more detail (Listing 4.21 and Figure 4.21).

```
SELECT au_id, au_fname, au_lname
  FROM authors
  WHERE au_lname <> 'Hull';
```

Listing 4.18 List the authors whose last name is not Hull. See Figure 4.18 for the result.

```
au_id  au_fname   au_lname
-----  ---------  -----------
A01    Sarah      Buchman
A02    Wendy      Heydemark
A05    Christian  Kells
A06               Kellsey
A07    Paddy      O'Furniture
```

Figure 4.18 Result of Listing 4.18.

```
SELECT title_name, contract
  FROM titles
  WHERE contract = 0;
```

Listing 4.19 List the titles for which there is no signed contract. See Figure 4.19 for the result.

```
title_name                   contract
-------------------------    --------
Not Without My Faberge Egg      0
```

Figure 4.19 Result of Listing 4.19.

```
SELECT title_name, pubdate
  FROM titles
  WHERE pubdate >= DATE '2001-01-01';
```

Listing 4.20 List the titles published in 2001 and later. See Figure 4.20 for the result.

```
title_name                    pubdate
----------------------------  ----------
Exchange of Platitudes        2001-01-01
Just Wait Until After School  2001-06-01
Kiss My Boo-Boo               2002-05-31
```

Figure 4.20 Result of Listing 4.20.

```
SELECT
    title_name,
    price * sales AS "Revenue"
  FROM titles
  WHERE price * sales > 1000000;
```

Listing 4.21 List the titles that generated more than $1 million in revenue. This search condition uses an arithmetic expression. See Figure 4.21 for the result.

```
title_name                    Revenue
----------------------------  ----------
Ask Your System Administrator 1025396.65
Exchange of Platitudes        1400008.00
I Blame My Mother             35929790.00
Spontaneous, Not Annoying     1299012.99
```

Figure 4.21 Result of Listing 4.21.

Tips for WHERE

- Place the WHERE clause before the ORDER BY clause in a SELECT statement in which both appear.

- A null represents the unknown and won't match anything, not even another null. Rows in which nulls are involved in comparisons won't be in the result. To compare nulls, use WHERE *test_column* IS NULL (WHERE *test_column* = NULL is incorrect); see "Testing for Nulls with IS NULL" on page 112. See also "Nulls" on page 72.

- For speed, fold your constants into a minimal number of expressions. For example, change

  WHERE col1 + 2 <= 10

  to

  WHERE col1 <= 8

  The best practice is to put only simple column references to the left of the = and more-complex expressions to the right.

- In general, the fastest comparison is for equality (=), following by the inequalities (<, <=, >, >=). The slowest is not-equal (<>). If possible, express your conditions by using faster comparisons.

- You can't use an aggregate function such as SUM() or COUNT() in a WHERE clause; see Chapter 6.

- An operation that selects certain rows from a table is called a **restriction**.

continues on next page

- Your DBMS's collation determines whether string comparisons are case insensitive ('A' = 'a') or case sensitive ('A' ≠ 'a'). **Microsoft Access**, **Microsoft SQL Server**, **Db2**, and **MySQL** perform case-insensitive comparisons by default. **Oracle** and **PostgreSQL** perform case-sensitive comparisons by default. In general, case-sensitive comparisons are slightly faster than case-insensitive ones. See also "Changing String Case with UPPER() and LOWER()" on page 128.

  Case sensitivity can vary by context. **MySQL** comparisons are case *in*sensitive in WHERE comparisons but are case sensitive in string-related functions, for example.

  In **Microsoft Access** date literals, omit the DATE keyword and surround the literal with # characters instead of quotes. To run Listing 4.20, change the date in the WHERE clause to #2001-01-01#.

  In **Microsoft SQL Server** and **Db2** date literals, omit the DATE keyword. To run Listing 4.20, change the date in the WHERE clause to '2001-01-01'.

  In older **PostgreSQL** versions, to compare a value in a NUMERIC or DECIMAL column with a real (floating-point) number, convert the real number to NUMERIC or DECIMAL explicitly. See "Converting Data Types with CAST()" on page 145.

  Some DBMSs support the comparison operator != as a synonym for <> (not equal). You should use <> to keep your code portable.

Column Aliases and WHERE

If you alias a column in a SELECT clause (see "Creating Column Aliases with AS" on page 79), then you can't reference it in the WHERE clause. The following query fails because the WHERE clause is evaluated before the SELECT clause, so the alias *copies_sold* doesn't yet exist when the WHERE clause is evaluated:

```
-- Wrong
SELECT sales AS copies_sold
  FROM titles
  WHERE copies_sold > 100000;
```

Instead, use a subquery (Chapter 8) in the FROM clause, which is evaluated before the WHERE clause:

```
-- Correct
SELECT *
  FROM (SELECT sales AS copies_sold
        FROM titles) ta
  WHERE copies_sold > 100000;
```

This solution works not only for columns aliases but also for aggregate functions, scalar subqueries, and window functions referenced in WHERE clauses. Note that in the latter query, the subquery is aliased *ta* (a table alias). All DBMSs accept table aliases, but not all require them. See also "Using Subqueries as Column Expressions" on page 256.

Combining and Negating Conditions with AND, OR, and NOT

You can specify multiple conditions in a single WHERE clause to, say, retrieve rows based on the values in multiple columns. You can use the AND and OR operators to combine two or more conditions into a **compound condition**. AND, OR, and a third operator, NOT, are logical operators. **Logical operators**, or **boolean operators**, are operators designed to work with **truth values**: true, false, and unknown.

If you've programmed in other languages (or studied propositional logic), then you're familiar with the two-value logic (2VL) system. In **two-value logic**, the result of a logical expression is either true or false. 2VL assumes perfect knowledge, in which all propositions are known to be true or false. Databases model real data, however, and our knowledge of the world is imperfect—that's why we use nulls to represent unknown values (see "Nulls" on page 72).

2VL is insufficient to represent knowledge gaps, so SQL uses three-value logic (3VL). In **three-value logic**, the result of a logical expression is true, false, or unknown. If the result of a compound condition is false or unknown, then the row is excluded from the result. (To retrieve rows with nulls, see "Testing for Nulls with IS NULL" on page 112.)

The AND Operator

The AND operator's important characteristics are:

- AND connects two conditions and returns true only if *both* conditions are true.

- Table 4.3 shows the possible outcomes when you combine two conditions with AND. The table's left column shows the truth values of the first condition, the top row shows the truth values of the second condition, and each intersection shows the AND outcome. This type of table is called a **truth table**.

- Any number of conditions can be connected with ANDs. All the conditions must be true for the row to be included in the result.

- AND is commutative (independent of order):

  WHERE *condition1* AND *condition2*

  is equivalent to

  WHERE *condition2* AND *condition1*

- You can enclose one or both of the conditions in parentheses. Some compound conditions need parentheses to force the order in which conditions are evaluated.

  See Listings 4.22 and 4.23, and Figures 4.22 and 4.23, for some AND examples.

Table 4.3 AND Truth Table

AND	True	False	Unknown
True	True	False	Unknown
False	False	False	False
Unknown	Unknown	False	Unknown

```
SELECT title_name, type, price
  FROM titles
  WHERE type = 'biography' AND price < 20;
```

Listing 4.22 List the biographies that sell for less than $20. See Figure 4.22 for the result.

```
title_name                    type       price
------------------------- --------- -----
How About Never?              biography 19.95
Spontaneous, Not Annoying biography 12.99
```

Figure 4.22 Result of Listing 4.22.

```
SELECT au_fname, au_lname
  FROM authors
  WHERE au_lname >= 'H'
    AND au_lname <= 'Zz'
    AND state <> 'CA';
```

Listing 4.23 List the authors whose last names begin with one of the letters *H* through *Z* and who don't live in California. See Figure 4.23 for the result.

```
au_fname   au_lname
--------- -----------
Wendy      Heydemark
Christian Kells
Paddy      O'Furniture
```

Figure 4.23 Result of Listing 4.23. Remember that the results of string comparisons depend on the DBMS's collating sequence; see "Sorting Rows with ORDER BY" on page 83.

Table 4.4 OR Truth Table

OR	True	False	Unknown
True	True	True	True
False	True	False	Unknown
Unknown	True	Unknown	Unknown

```
SELECT au_fname, au_lname, city, state
  FROM authors
 WHERE (state = 'NY')
    OR (state = 'CO')
    OR (city  = 'San Francisco');
```

Listing 4.24 List the authors who live in New York State, Colorado, or San Francisco. See Figure 4.24 for the result.

```
au_fname   au_lname   city            state
---------  ---------  --------------  -----
Sarah      Buchman    Bronx           NY
Wendy      Heydemark  Boulder         CO
Hallie     Hull       San Francisco   CA
Klee       Hull       San Francisco   CA
Christian  Kells      New York        NY
```

Figure 4.24 Result of Listing 4.24.

```
SELECT pub_id, pub_name, state, country
  FROM publishers
 WHERE (state =  'CA')
    OR (state <> 'CA');
```

Listing 4.25 List the publishers that are located in California or are not located in California. This example is contrived to show the effect of nulls in conditions. See Figure 4.25 for the result.

```
pub_id pub_name           state country
------ ----------------- ----- -------
P01    Abatis Publishers  NY    USA
P02    Core Dump Books    CA    USA
P04    Tenterhooks Press  CA    USA
```

Figure 4.25 Result of Listing 4.25. Publisher P03 is missing because its *state* is null.

The OR Operator

The OR operator's important characteristics are:

- OR connects two conditions and returns true if *either* condition is true or if *both* conditions are true.

- Table 4.4 shows the OR truth table.

- Any number of conditions can be connected with ORs. OR will retrieve rows that match any condition or all the conditions.

- Like AND, OR is commutative; the order in which you list the conditions doesn't matter.

- You can enclose one or both of the conditions in parentheses.

See Listings 4.24 and 4.25, and Figures 4.24 and 4.25, for some OR examples.

Listing 4.25 shows the effect of nulls in conditions. You might expect the result, Figure 4.25, to display all the rows in the table *publishers*. But the row for publisher P03 (located in Germany) is missing because it contains a null in the column *state*. The null causes the result of both of the OR conditions to be unknown, so the row is excluded from the result. To test for nulls, see "Testing for Nulls with IS NULL" on page 112.

The NOT Operator

The NOT operator's important characteristics are:

- Unlike AND and OR, NOT doesn't connect two conditions. Instead, it negates (reverses) a single condition.

- Table 4.5 shows the NOT truth table.

- In comparisons, place NOT before the column name or expression

  ```
  WHERE NOT state = 'CA'        --Correct
  ```

  and not before the operator (even though it sounds better when read):

  ```
  WHERE state NOT = 'CA'        --Illegal
  ```

- NOT acts on one condition. To negate two or more conditions, repeat the NOT for each condition. To list titles that are not biographies and are not priced less than $20, for example, type

  ```
  SELECT title_id, type, price
    FROM titles
    WHERE NOT type = 'biography'
      AND NOT price < 20;        --Correct
  ```

  and not

  ```
  SELECT title_id, type, price
    FROM titles
    WHERE NOT type = 'biography'
      AND price < 20;            --Wrong
  ```

  The latter clause is legal but returns the wrong result. See "Tips for AND, OR, and NOT" on page 99 to learn ways to express equivalent NOT conditions.

- In comparisons, using NOT often is a matter of style. The following two clauses are equivalent:

  ```
  WHERE NOT state = 'CA'
  ```

  and

  ```
  WHERE state <> 'CA'
  ```

- You can enclose the condition in parentheses.

  See Listings 4.26 and 4.27, and Figures 4.26 and 4.27, for some NOT examples.

Table 4.5 NOT Truth Table

Condition	NOT Condition
True	False
False	True
Unknown	Unknown

```
SELECT au_fname, au_lname, state
  FROM authors
  WHERE NOT (state = 'CA');
```

Listing 4.26 List the authors who don't live in California. See Figure 4.26 for the result.

```
au_fname    au_lname     state
---------   -----------  -----
Sarah       Buchman      NY
Wendy       Heydemark    CO
Christian   Kells        NY
Paddy       O'Furniture  FL
```

Figure 4.26 Result of Listing 4.26.

```
SELECT title_name, sales, price
  FROM titles
  WHERE NOT (price < 20)
    AND (sales > 15000);
```

Listing 4.27 List the titles whose price is not less than $20 and that have sold more than 15000 copies. See Figure 4.27 for the result.

```
title_name                      sales    price
----------------------------    -------  -----
Ask Your System Administrator   25667    39.95
I Blame My Mother               1500200  23.95
```

Figure 4.27 Result of Listing 4.27.

```
SELECT title_id, type, price
  FROM titles
  WHERE type = 'history'
    OR type = 'biography'
    AND price < 20;
```

Listing 4.28 This query won't work if I want to list history and biography titles less than $20 because AND has higher precedence than OR. See Figure 4.28 for the result.

```
title_id type       price
-------- ---------- -----
T01      history    21.99
T02      history    19.95
T06      biography  19.95
T12      biography  12.99
T13      history    29.99
```

Figure 4.28 Result of Listing 4.28. This result contains two history titles priced more than $20, which isn't what I want.

```
SELECT title_id, type, price
  FROM titles
  WHERE (type = 'history'
    OR  type = 'biography')
    AND  price < 20;
```

Listing 4.29 To fix Listing 4.28, add parentheses to force OR to be evaluated before AND. See Figure 4.29 for the result.

```
title_id type       price
-------- ---------- -----
T02      history    19.95
T06      biography  19.95
T12      biography  12.99
```

Figure 4.29 Result of Listing 4.29.

Using AND, OR, and NOT Together

You can combine the three logical operators in a compound condition. Your DBMS uses SQL's precedence rules to determine which operators to evaluate first. Precedence is covered in "Determining the Order of Evaluation" on page 121, but for now you need know only that when you use multiple logical operators in a compound condition, NOT is evaluated first, then AND, and finally OR. You can override this order with parentheses: everything in parentheses is evaluated first. When parenthesized conditions are nested, the innermost condition is evaluated first. Under the default precedence rules, the condition

p AND NOT *q* OR *r*

is equivalent to

(*p* AND (NOT *q*)) OR *r*

It's wise to use parentheses, rather than rely on the default evaluation order, to make the evaluation order clear.

If I want to list history and biography titles priced less than $20, for example, then Listing 4.28 won't work. AND is evaluated before OR, so the query is evaluated as follows:

1. Find all the biography titles less than $20.

2. Find all the history titles (regardless of price).

3. List both sets of titles in the result (Figure 4.28).

To fix this query, add parentheses to force evaluation of OR first. Listing 4.29 is evaluated as follows:

1. Find all the biography and history titles.

2. Of the titles found in step 1, keep the ones priced less than $20.

3. List the subset of titles in the result (Figure 4.29).

Dissecting WHERE Clauses

If your WHERE clause isn't working, then you can debug it by displaying the result of each condition individually. To see the result of each comparison in Listing 4.29, for example, put each comparison expression in the SELECT clause's output column list, along with the values you're comparing:

```
SELECT
    type,
    type = 'history' AS "Hist?",
    type = 'biography' AS "Bio?",
    price,
    price < 20 AS "<20?"
  FROM titles;
```

This query runs on Microsoft Access, MySQL, and PostgreSQL. If your DBMS interprets the = symbol as an assignment operator rather than as a comparison operator, then you must substitute equivalent expressions for the logical comparisons. In Oracle, for example, you can replace type = 'history' with INSTR(type,'history'). The query's result is:

```
type        Hist? Bio?  price  <20?
----------  ----- ----  -----  ----
history         1    0  21.99     0
history         1    0  19.95     1
computer        0    0  39.95     0
psychology      0    0  12.99     1
psychology      0    0   6.95     1
biography       0    1  19.95     1
biography       0    1  23.95     0
children        0    0  10.00     1
children        0    0  13.95     1
biography       0    1   NULL  NULL
psychology      0    0   7.99     1
biography       0    1  12.99     1
history         1    0  29.99     0
```

The comparison columns display zero if the comparison is false, nonzero if it's true, or null if it's unknown.

Tips for AND, OR, and NOT

- The examples in this section show the AND, OR, and NOT operators used with comparison conditions, but these operators can be used with any type of condition.

- If your search condition contains only AND operators, then your query will run faster if you put the conditions *least* likely to be true first. If *col1* = *'A'* is less likely than *col2* = *'B'*, then

  ```
  WHERE col1 = 'A' AND col2 = 'B'
  ```

  is faster than

  ```
  WHERE col2 = 'B' AND col1 = 'A'
  ```

  because the DBMS won't bother to evaluate the second expression if the first is false. For search conditions that contain only OR operators, do the reverse: put the *most* likely conditions first. If the conditions are equally likely, then put the least complex expression first.

  This logic depends on your DBMS's optimizer reading WHERE clauses from left to right, which most do. **Oracle**'s cost-based optimizer (as opposed to its rule-based optimizer), however, reads right to left.

- It's a common error to type

  ```
  WHERE state = 'NY' OR 'CA'  --Illegal
  ```

  instead of

  ```
  WHERE state = 'NY' OR state = 'CA'
  ```

  continues on next page

- It's easy to translate a correctly phrased spoken-language statement into an incorrect SQL statement. If you say, "List the books priced less than $10 and more than $30," then the *and* suggests the use of the AND operator:

```
SELECT title_name, price
  FROM titles
  WHERE price < 10 AND price > 30; --Wrong
```

This query returns no rows, however, because it's impossible for a book to be priced less than $10 and more than $30 simultaneously, as AND logic commands. The logical meaning of OR finds books that meet any of the criteria, not all the criteria at the same time:

```
WHERE price < 10 OR price > 30 --Correct
```

- Table 4.6 shows alternative ways of expressing the same condition. The first equivalency is **double negation**, the second two are **De Morgan's Laws**, and the final two are the **distributive laws**.

- Some DBMSs support the **exclusive-or** (or **xor**) logical operator, which yields true only if exactly one of its operands is true:

  p XOR *q*

  is equivalent to

  (*p* AND (NOT *q*)) OR ((NOT *p*) AND *q*)

- DBMS In **MySQL** 4.0.4 and earlier, false AND unknown evaluates to unknown, not false.

Table 4.6 Equivalent Conditions

This Condition	Is Equivalent To
NOT (NOT *p*)	*p*
NOT (*p* AND *q*)	(NOT *p*) OR (NOT *q*)
NOT (*p* OR *q*)	(NOT *p*) AND (NOT *q*)
p AND (*q* OR *r*)	(*p* AND *q*) OR (*p* AND *r*)
p OR (*q* AND *r*)	(*p* OR *q*) AND (*p* OR *r*)

Re-expressing Conditions

You must master the laws in Table 4.6 to become a competent programmer in SQL (or any language). They're especially useful when you want to re-express conditions to make queries run faster. For example, the statement

```
SELECT * FROM mytable
  WHERE col1 = 1
    AND NOT (col1 = col2 OR col3 = 3);
```

is equivalent to

```
SELECT * FROM mytable
  WHERE col1 = 1
    AND col2 <> 1
    AND col3 <> 3;
```

but the latter one will run faster if your DBMS's optimizer isn't smart enough to re-express the former internally. (The condition *col1 = col2* is more expensive computationally than comparing *col1* and *col2* to literal values.)

You also can use the laws to change a condition into its opposite. For example, the reverse of the condition

```
WHERE (col1 = 'A') AND (col2 = 'B')
```

is

```
WHERE (col1 <> 'A') OR (col2 <> 'B')
```

In this case, it would have easier just to negate the entire original expression with NOT:

```
WHERE NOT ((col1 = 'A') AND (col2 = 'B'))
```

But this simple approach won't work with complex conditions involving multiple ANDs, ORs, and NOTs.

Here's a problem to solve: look at only the first code line below and see whether you can repeatedly apply equivalency rules to push the NOT operators inward until they apply to only the individual expressions *p*, *q*, and *r*:

```
  NOT ((p AND q) OR (NOT p AND r))
= NOT (p AND q) AND NOT (NOT p AND r)
= (NOT p OR NOT q) AND (p OR NOT r)
```

Matching Patterns with LIKE

The preceding examples retrieved rows based on the exact value of a column or columns. You can use LIKE to retrieve rows based on partial information. LIKE is useful if you don't know an exact value ("The author's last name is *Kel*-something") or you want to retrieve rows with similar values ("Which authors live in the San Francisco Bay Area?"). The LIKE condition's important characteristics are:

- LIKE works with only character strings, not numbers or datetimes.

- LIKE uses a pattern that values are matched against. A **pattern** is a quoted string that contains the literal characters to match and any combination of wildcards. **Wildcards** are special characters used to match parts of a value. Table 4.7 lists the wildcard operators, and Table 4.8 lists some example patterns.

- String comparisons are case insensitive or case sensitive, depending on your DBMS; see the DBMS tip in "Tips for WHERE" on page 91.

- You can negate a LIKE condition with NOT LIKE.

- You can combine LIKE conditions and other conditions with AND and OR.

Table 4.7 Wildcard Operators

Operator	Matches
%	A percent sign matches any string of zero or more characters.
_	An underscore matches any one character.

Table 4.8 Examples of % and _ Patterns

Pattern	Matches
'A%'	Matches a string of length ≥ 1 that begins with A, including the single letter A. Matches 'A', 'Anonymous', and 'AC/DC'.
'%s'	Matches a string of length ≥ 1 that ends with s, including the single letter s. A string with trailing spaces (after the s) won't match. Matches 's', 'Victoria Falls', and 'DBMSs'.
'%in%'	Matches a string of length ≥ 2 that contains in anywhere. Matches 'in', 'inch', 'Pine', 'linchpin', and 'lynchpin'.
'____'	Matches any four-character string. Matches 'ABCD', 'I am', and 'Jack'.
'Qua__'	Matches any five-character string that begins with Qua. Matches 'Quack', 'Quaff', and 'Quake'.
'_re_'	Matches any four-character string that has re as its second and third characters. Matches 'Tree', 'area', and 'fret'.
'_re%'	Matches a string of length ≥ 3 that begins with any character and has re as its second and third characters. Matches 'Tree', 'area', 'fret', 'are', and 'fretful'.
'%re_'	Matches a string of length ≥ 3 that has re as the second and third characters from its end and ends with any character. Matches 'Tree', 'area', 'fret', 'red', and 'Blood red'.

```
SELECT au_fname, au_lname
  FROM authors
  WHERE au_lname LIKE 'Kel%';
```

Listing 4.30 List the authors whose last names begin with *Kel.* See Figure 4.30 for the result.

```
au_fname   au_lname
---------  --------
Christian  Kells
           Kellsey
```

Figure 4.30 Result of Listing 4.30.

```
SELECT au_fname, au_lname
  FROM authors
  WHERE au_lname LIKE '__ll%';
```

Listing 4.31 List the authors whose last names have *ll* (el-el) as the third and fourth characters. See Figure 4.31 for the result.

```
au_fname   au_lname
---------  --------
Hallie     Hull
Klee       Hull
Christian  Kells
           Kellsey
```

Figure 4.31 Result of Listing 4.31.

```
SELECT au_fname, au_lname, city, state, zip
  FROM authors
  WHERE zip LIKE '94___';
```

Listing 4.32 List the authors who live in the San Francisco Bay Area (that is, with postal codes that begin with *94*). See Figure 4.32 for the result.

```
au_fname  au_lname  city           state  zip
--------  --------  -------------  -----  -----
Hallie    Hull      San Francisco  CA     94123
Klee      Hull      San Francisco  CA     94123
          Kellsey   Palo Alto      CA     94305
```

Figure 4.32 Result of Listing 4.32.

To filter rows by matching a pattern:

- Type:

  ```
  SELECT columns
    FROM table
    WHERE test_column [NOT] LIKE 'pattern';
  ```

  columns is one or more comma-separated column names, and *table* is the name of the table that contains *columns*.

  In the search condition, *test_column* is the name of a column in *table* (*test_column* doesn't have to be listed in *columns*), and *pattern* is the pattern that's compared with the value in *test_column*. *pattern* is a string like one of the examples listed in Table 4.8. To retrieve rows with values that don't match *pattern*, specify NOT LIKE (Listings 4.30 through 4.33, Figures 4.30 through 4.33).

```
SELECT au_fname, au_lname, phone
  FROM authors
  WHERE phone NOT LIKE '212-___-____'
    AND phone NOT LIKE '415-___-%'
    AND phone NOT LIKE '303-%';
```

Listing 4.33 List the authors who live outside the 212, 415, and 303 area codes. This example shows three alternative patterns for excluding telephone numbers. You should favor the first alternative because single-character matches (_) are faster than multiple-character ones (%). See Figure 4.33 for the result.

```
au_fname  au_lname    phone
--------  ----------  ------------
Sarah     Buchman     718-496-7223
          Kellsey     650-836-7128
Paddy     O'Furniture 941-925-0752
```

Figure 4.33 Result of Listing 4.33.

You can search for values that contain the special wildcard characters. Use the ESCAPE keyword to specify an escape character that you can use to search for a percent sign or underscore as a literal character. Immediately precede a wildcard character with an escape character to strip the wildcard of its special meaning. If the escape character is !, for example, then !% in a pattern searches values for a literal %. (Unescaped wildcards still have their special meaning.) The escape character can't be part of the value that you're trying to retrieve; if you're searching for '50% OFF!', then choose an escape character other than !. Table 4.9 shows some examples of escaped and unescaped patterns; the designated escape character is !.

To match a wildcard character:

- Type:

```
SELECT columns
  FROM table
  WHERE test_column [NOT] LIKE 'pattern'
    ESCAPE 'escape_char';
```

The syntax is the same as the SELECT statement in "To filter rows by matching a pattern" earlier in this section, except for the ESCAPE clause. *escape_char* is a single character. Any character in *pattern* that follows *escape_char* is interpreted literally; *escape_char* itself is not considered to be part of the search pattern (Listing 4.34 and Figure 4.34).

Tips for LIKE

- *test_column* can be an expression.

- The NOT that can precede LIKE is independent of the NOT that can precede *test_column* (see "The NOT Operator" on page 96). The clause

```
WHERE phone NOT LIKE '212-%'
```

is equivalent to

```
WHERE NOT phone LIKE '212-%'
```

You even can write this silly double negation, which retrieves everyone with a 212 area code:

```
WHERE NOT phone NOT LIKE '212-%'
```

Table 4.9 Escaped and Unescaped Patterns

Pattern	Matches
'100%'	Unescaped. Matches *100* followed by a string of zero or more characters.
'100!%'	Escaped. Matches '100%'.
'_op'	Unescaped. Matches 'top', 'hop', 'pop', and so on.
'!_op'	Escaped. Matches '_op'.

```
SELECT title_name
  FROM titles
  WHERE title_name LIKE '%!%%' ESCAPE '!';
```

Listing 4.34 List the titles that contain percent signs. Only the % that follows the escape character ! has its literal meaning; the other two percent signs still act as wildcards. See Figure 4.34 for the result.

```
title_name
-----------------------------------------
```

Figure 4.34 Result of Listing 4.34. An empty result. No title names contain a % character.

Table 4.10 Examples of [] and [^] Patterns

Pattern	Matches
'[a-c]at'	Matches 'bat' and 'cat' but not 'fat'.
'[bcf]at'	Matches 'bat', 'cat', and 'fat' but not 'eat'.
'[^c]at'	Matches 'bat' and 'fat' but not 'cat'.
'se[^n]%'	Matches strings of length ≥ 2 that begin with *se* and whose third character isn't *n*.

- Wildcard searches are time-consuming—particularly if you use % at the start of a pattern. Don't use wildcards if another type of search will do.

- In the simplest case in which a pattern contains no wildcards, LIKE works like an = comparison (and NOT LIKE works like <>). In many cases

  ```
  WHERE city LIKE 'New York'
  ```

  is equivalent to

  ```
  WHERE city = 'New York'
  ```

  But these comparisons will differ if your DBMS takes trailing spaces into account for LIKE but not for =. If that's not important, then the = form is usually faster than LIKE.

- DBMS **Microsoft Access** doesn't support the ESCAPE clause. Instead, surround a wildcard character with brackets to render it a literal character. To run Listing 4.34, replace the WHERE clause with:

  ```
  WHERE title_name LIKE '%[%]%'
  ```

  Some DBMSs let you use **regular expressions** to match patterns. **Microsoft SQL Server**, for example, supports a limited variant of POSIX-style regular expressions. The [] wildcard matches any single character within a range or set, and the [^] wildcard matches any single character *not* within a range or set. Table 4.10 lists some examples. The SQL standard uses the SIMILAR operator for regex matching. Regex support varies by DBMS; search your DBMS documentation for *LIKE*, *regular expressions*, or *pattern matching*.

  Some DBMSs let you use LIKE to search numeric and datetime columns.

Range Filtering with BETWEEN

Use BETWEEN to determine whether a given value falls within a specified range. The BETWEEN condition's important characteristics are:

- BETWEEN works with character strings, numbers, and datetimes.

- The BETWEEN range contains a low value and a high value, separated by AND. The low value must be less than or equal to the high value.

- BETWEEN is a convenient, shorthand clause that you can replicate by using AND.

  ```
  WHERE test_column BETWEEN
      low_value AND high_value
  ```

  is equivalent to:

  ```
  WHERE (test_column >= low_value)
    AND (test_column <= high_value)
  ```

- BETWEEN specifies an **inclusive range**, in which the high value and low value are included in the search. To specify an **exclusive range**, which excludes endpoints, use > and < comparisons instead of BETWEEN:

  ```
  WHERE (test_column > low_value)
    AND (test_column < high_value)
  ```

- String comparisons are case insensitive or case sensitive, depending on your DBMS; see the DBMS tip in "Tips for WHERE" on page 91.

- You can negate a BETWEEN condition with NOT BETWEEN.

- You can combine BETWEEN conditions and other conditions with AND and OR.

```
SELECT au_fname, au_lname, zip
  FROM authors
  WHERE zip NOT BETWEEN '20000' AND '89999';
```

Listing 4.35 List the authors who live outside the postal range 20000–89999. See Figure 4.35 for the result.

```
au_fname   au_lname  zip
---------  --------  -----
Sarah      Buchman   10468
Hallie     Hull      94123
Klee       Hull      94123
Christian  Kells     10014
           Kellsey   94305
```

Figure 4.35 Result of Listing 4.35.

```
SELECT title_id, price
  FROM titles
  WHERE price BETWEEN 10 AND 19.95;
```

Listing 4.36 List the titles priced between $10 and $19.95, inclusive. See Figure 4.36 for the result.

```
title_id price
-------- -----
T02      19.95
T04      12.99
T06      19.95
T08      10.00
T09      13.95
T12      12.99
```

Figure 4.36 Result of Listing 4.36.

```
SELECT title_id, pubdate
  FROM titles
  WHERE
    pubdate BETWEEN DATE '2000-01-01'
                AND DATE '2000-12-31';
```

Listing 4.37 List the titles published in 2000. See Figure 4.37 for the result.

```
title_id pubdate
-------- ----------
T01      2000-08-01
T03      2000-09-01
T06      2000-07-31
T11      2000-11-30
T12      2000-08-31
```

Figure 4.37 Result of Listing 4.37.

To filter rows by using a range:

*   Type:

    ```
    SELECT columns
      FROM table
        WHERE test_column [NOT] BETWEEN
            low_value AND high_value;
    ```

    columns is one or more comma-separated column names, and *table* is the name of the table that contains *columns*.

    In the search condition, *test_column* is the name of a column in *table* (*test_column* doesn't have to be listed in *columns*), and *low_value* and *high_value* specify the endpoints of the range that is compared with the value in *test_column*. *low_value* must be less than or equal to *high_value*, and both values must be the same as or comparable to the data type of *test_column*. To match values that lie outside the range, specify NOT BETWEEN (Listings 4.35, 4.36, and 4.37, Figures 4.35, 4.36, and 4.37).

Tips for BETWEEN

- *test_column* can be an expression.

- The NOT that can precede BETWEEN is independent of the NOT that can precede *test_column*; see "Tips for LIKE" on page 104.

- Listing 4.38 shows how to rewrite Listing 4.36 with an exclusive range, which doesn't include the $10 and $19.95 endpoints. See Figure 4.38 for the result.

- Specifying a character range often needs some thought. Suppose you want to search for last names that begin with the letter *F*. The following clause won't work because it will retrieve someone whose last name is the letter *G* (*is* the letter *G*, not *starts* with the letter *G*):

```
WHERE last_name BETWEEN 'F' AND 'G'
```

This next clause shows the correct way to specify the ending point (in most cases):

```
WHERE last_name BETWEEN 'F' AND 'Fz'
```

- **DBMS** In older **PostgreSQL** versions, convert the floating-point numbers in Listings 4.36 and 4.38 to DECIMAL; see "Converting Data Types with CAST()" on page 145. To run Listings 4.36 and 4.38, change the floating-point literals to:

```
CAST(19.95 AS DECIMAL)
```

In **Microsoft Access** date literals, omit the DATE keyword and surround the literal with # characters instead of quotes. To run Listing 4.37, change the dates in the WHERE clause to #2000-01-01# and #2000-12-31#.

In **Microsoft SQL Server** and **Db2** date literals, omit the DATE keyword. To run Listing 4.37, change the dates in the WHERE clause to '2000-01-01' and '2000-12-31'.

In some DBMSs, *low_value* can exceed *high_value*; search your DBMS documentation for *WHERE* or *BETWEEN*.

```
SELECT title_id, price
  FROM titles
  WHERE (price > 10)
    AND (price < 19.95);
```

Listing 4.38 List the titles priced between $10 and $19.95, exclusive. See Figure 4.38 for the result.

```
title_id price
-------- -----
T04       12.99
T09       13.95
T12       12.99
```

Figure 4.38 Result of Listing 4.38.

List Filtering with IN

Use IN to determine whether a given value matches any value in a specified list. The IN condition's important characteristics are:

- IN works with character strings, numbers, and datetimes.

- The IN list is a parenthesized listing of one or more comma-separated values. The list items needn't be in any particular order.

- IN is a convenient, shorthand clause that you can replicate by using OR.

```
WHERE test_column IN
    (value1, value2, value3)
```

is equivalent to:

```
WHERE (test_column = value1)
  OR (test_column = value2)
  OR (test_column = value3)
```

- String comparisons are case insensitive or case sensitive, depending on your DBMS; see the DBMS tip in "Tips for WHERE" on page 91.

- You can negate an IN condition with NOT IN.

- You can combine IN conditions and other conditions with AND and OR.

To filter rows by using a list:

- Type:

```
SELECT columns
  FROM table
  WHERE test_column [NOT] IN
      (value1, value2,...);
```

columns is one or more comma-separated column names, and *table* is the name of the table that contains *columns*.

In the search condition, *test_column* is the name of a column in *table* (*test_column* doesn't have to be listed in *columns*), and *value1*, *value2*,... are one or more comma-separated values that are compared with the value in *test_column*. The list values can appear in any order and must be the same as or comparable to the data type of *test_column*. To match values that aren't in the list, specify NOT IN (Listings 4.39, 4.40, and 4.41, Figures 4.39, 4.40, and 4.41).

Tips for IN

- *test_column* can be an expression.

- The NOT that can precede IN is independent of the NOT that can precede *test_column*; see "Tips for LIKE" on page 104.

- If your list contains a large number of values, then your code will be easier to read if you use one IN condition instead of many OR conditions. (Also, one IN usually runs faster than multiple ORs.)

- For speed, list the most likely values first. If you're testing U.S. addresses, for example, then list the most populous states first:

```
WHERE state IN ('CA', 'TX', 'NY',
'FL',...,'VT', 'DC', 'WY')
```

- The search condition

```
WHERE col1 BETWEEN 1 AND 5
  AND col1 <> 3
```

usually is faster than

```
WHERE col1 IN (1, 2, 4, 5)
```

```
SELECT au_fname, au_lname, state
  FROM authors
  WHERE state NOT IN ('NY', 'NJ', 'CA');
```

Listing 4.39 List the authors who don't live in New York State, New Jersey, or California. See Figure 4.39 for the result.

```
au_fname  au_lname      state
--------  -----------   -----
Wendy     Heydemark     CO
Paddy     O'Furniture   FL
```

Figure 4.39 Result of Listing 4.39.

```
SELECT title_id, advance
  FROM royalties
  WHERE advance IN (0.00, 1000.00, 5000.00);
```

Listing 4.40 List the titles for which advances of $0, $1000, or $5000 were paid. See Figure 4.40 for the result.

```
title_id advance
-------- -------
T02       1000.00
T08          0.00
T09          0.00
```

Figure 4.40 Result of Listing 4.40.

```
SELECT title_id, pubdate
  FROM titles
  WHERE pubdate IN
    (DATE '2000-01-01',
     DATE '2001-01-01',
     DATE '2002-01-01');
```

Listing 4.41 List the titles published on the first day of the year 2000, 2001, or 2002. See Figure 4.41 for the result.

```
title_id pubdate
-------- ----------
T05      2001-01-01
```

Figure 4.41 Result of Listing 4.41.

- A compound condition's order of evaluation is easier to read and manage if you use IN instead of multiple ORs; see "Combining and Negating Conditions with AND, OR, and NOT" on page 93.

- You also can use IN to determine whether a given value matches any value in a subquery; see Chapter 8.

- NOT IN is equivalent to combining tests for inequality with AND. This statement is equivalent to Listing 4.39:

```
SELECT au_fname, au_lname, state
  FROM authors
  WHERE state <> 'NY'
    AND state <> 'NJ'
    AND state <> 'CA';
```

- **DBMS** In **Microsoft Access** date literals, omit the DATE keyword and surround the literal with # characters instead of quotes. To run Listing 4.41, change the WHERE clause to:

```
WHERE pubdate IN
      (#1/1/2000#,
       #1/1/2001#,
       #1/1/2002#)
```

In **Microsoft SQL Server** and **Db2** date literals, omit the DATE keyword. To run Listing 4.41, change the WHERE clause to:

```
WHERE pubdate IN
      ('2000-01-01',
       '2001-01-01',
       '2002-01-01')
```

In older **PostgreSQL** versions, convert the floating-point number in Listing 4.40 to DECIMAL; see "Converting Data Types with CAST()" on page 145. To run Listing 4.40, change the WHERE clause to:

```
WHERE advance IN
      (CAST(   0.00 AS DECIMAL),
       CAST(1000.00 AS DECIMAL),
       CAST(5000.00 AS DECIMAL))
```

Testing for Nulls with IS NULL

Recall from "Nulls" on page 72 that nulls represent missing or unknown values. This situation causes a problem: LIKE, BETWEEN, IN, and other WHERE-clause conditions can't find nulls because unknown values don't satisfy specific conditions. A null matches no value—not even other nulls. You can't use = or <> to test whether a value is null.

In the table *publishers*, for example, note that publisher P03 has a null in the column *state* because that column doesn't apply to Germany (Listing 4.42 and Figure 4.42). I can't use complementary comparisons to select the null because null is neither California nor not-California; it's undefined (Listings 4.43 and 4.44, Figures 4.43 and 4.44).

To avert disaster, SQL provides IS NULL to determine whether a given value is null. The IS NULL condition's important characteristics are:

- IS NULL works for columns of any data type.

- You can negate an IS NULL condition with IS NOT NULL.

- You can combine IS NULL conditions and other conditions with AND and OR.

```
SELECT pub_id, city, state, country
  FROM publishers;
```

Listing 4.42 List the locations of all the publishers. See Figure 4.42 for the result.

```
pub_id city          state country
------ ------------- ----- -------
P01    New York      NY    USA
P02    San Francisco CA    USA
P03    Hamburg       NULL  Germany
P04    Berkeley      CA    USA
```

Figure 4.42 Result of Listing 4.42. The column *state* doesn't apply to the publisher located in Germany.

```
SELECT pub_id, city, state, country
  FROM publishers
  WHERE state = 'CA';
```

Listing 4.43 List the publishers located in California. See Figure 4.43 for the result.

```
pub_id city          state country
------ ------------- ----- -------
P02    San Francisco CA    USA
P04    Berkeley      CA    USA
```

Figure 4.43 Result of Listing 4.43. This result doesn't include publisher P03.

```
SELECT pub_id, city, state, country
  FROM publishers
  WHERE state <> 'CA';
```

Listing 4.44 List the publishers located outside California (the wrong way—see Listing 4.45 for the correct way). See Figure 4.44 for the result.

```
pub_id city     state country
------ -------- ----- -------
P01    New York NY    USA
```

Figure 4.44 Result of Listing 4.44. This result doesn't include publisher P03 either. The conditions *state = 'CA'* and *state <> 'CA'* aren't complementary after all; nulls don't match any value and so can't be selected by using the types of conditions I've covered so far.

```
SELECT pub_id, city, state, country
  FROM publishers
  WHERE state <> 'CA'
    OR state IS NULL;
```

Listing 4.45 List the publishers located outside California (the correct way). See Figure 4.45 for the result.

```
pub_id city      state country
------ --------  ----- -------
P01    New York  NY    USA
P03    Hamburg   NULL  Germany
```

Figure 4.45 Result of Listing 4.45. Now publisher P03 is in the result.

```
SELECT title_id, type, pubdate
  FROM titles
  WHERE type = 'biography'
    AND pubdate IS NOT NULL;
```

Listing 4.46 List the biographies whose (past or future) publication dates are known. See Figure 4.46 for the result.

```
title_id type      pubdate
-------- --------- ----------
T06      biography 2000-07-31
T07      biography 1999-10-01
T12      biography 2000-08-31
```

Figure 4.46 Result of Listing 4.46. Without the IS NOT NULL condition, this result would have included title T10.

To retrieve rows with nulls or non-null values:

- Type:

  ```
  SELECT columns
    FROM table
    WHERE test_column IS [NOT] NULL;
  ```

  columns is one or more comma-separated column names, and *table* is the name of the table that contains *columns*.

  In the search condition, *test_column* is the name of a column in *table*. (*test_column* doesn't have to be listed in *columns*.) To match non-null values, specify NOT NULL (Listings 4.45 and 4.46, Figures 4.45 and 4.46).

Tips for IS NULL

- *test_column* can be an expression.

- The NOT that can precede NULL is independent of the NOT that can precede *test_column*; see "Tips for LIKE" on page 104.

- Nulls cause rows to be excluded from results only if a column containing nulls is a test column in a WHERE condition. The following query, for example, retrieves all the rows in the table *publishers* (refer to Figure 4.42) because the null in the column *state* isn't compared with anything:

```
SELECT pub_id, city, state, country
  FROM publishers
  WHERE country <> 'Canada';
```

To forbid nulls in a column, see "Forbidding Nulls with NOT NULL" on page 329.

- It bears repeating that a null isn't the same as an empty string (''). In the table *authors*, for example, the column *au_fname* contains an empty string for author A06 (last name of Kellsey). The WHERE condition to find the first name is

```
WHERE au_fname = ''
```

and not

```
WHERE au_fname IS NULL
```

- DBMS **Oracle** treats an empty string ('') as a null; see the DBMS tip in "Tips for Nulls" on page 72.

CHAPTER 5

Operators and Functions

Operators and functions let you calculate results derived from column values, system-determined values, constants, and other data. You can perform:

- Arithmetic operations—Cut everyone's salary by 10 percent.

- String operations—Concatenate personal information into a mailing address.

- Datetime operations—Compute the time interval between two dates.

- System operations—Find out what time your DBMS thinks it is.

An **operator** is a symbol or keyword indicating an operation that acts on one or more elements. The elements, called **operands**, are SQL expressions. Recall from "Tips for SQL Syntax" on page 52 that an expression is any legal combination of symbols and tokens that evaluates to a single value (or null). In the expression *price * 2*, for example, *** is the operator, and *price* and *2* are its operands.

A **function** is a built-in, named routine that performs a specialized task. Most functions take parenthesized **arguments**, which are values you pass to the function that the function then uses to perform its task. Arguments can be column names, literals, nested functions, or more-complex expressions. In *UPPER(au_lname)*, for example, *UPPER* is the function name, and *au_lname* is the argument.

Creating Derived Columns

You can use operators and functions to create derived columns. A **derived column** is the result of a calculation and is created with a SELECT-clause expression that is something other than a simple reference to a column. Derived columns don't become permanent columns in a table; they're for display and reporting purposes.

The values in a derived column are often computed from values in existing columns, but you can also create a derived column by using a constant expression (such as a string, number, or date) or system value (such as the system time). Listing 5.1 shows a SELECT statement that yields a trivial arithmetic calculation; it needs no FROM clause because it doesn't retrieve data from a table. Figure 5.1 shows the result.

Recall from "Tables, Columns, and Rows" on page 22 that closure guarantees that every result is a table, so even this simple result is a table: a 1 × 1 table that contains the value 5. If I retrieve a column along with a constant, then the constant appears in every row of the result (Listing 5.2 and Figure 5.2).

Your DBMS will assign the derived column a default name, typically the expression itself as a quoted identifier. You should name derived columns explicitly with an AS clause because system-assigned names can be long, unwieldy, and inconvenient for database applications to refer to; see "Creating Column Aliases with AS" on page 79 (Listing 5.3 and Figure 5.3).

```
SELECT 2 + 3;
```

Listing 5.1 A constant expression in a SELECT clause. No FROM clause is needed because I'm not retrieving data from a table. See Figure 5.1 for the result.

```
2 + 3
-----
    5
```

Figure 5.1 Result of Listing 5.1. This result is a table with one row and one column.

```
SELECT au_id, 2 + 3
  FROM authors;
```

Listing 5.2 Here, I've retrieved a column and a constant expression. See Figure 5.2 for the result.

```
au_id 2 + 3
----- -----
A01       5
A02       5
A03       5
A04       5
A05       5
A06       5
A07       5
```

Figure 5.2 Result of Listing 5.2. The constant is repeated in each row.

```
SELECT
    title_id,
    price,
    0.10 AS "Discount",
    price * (1 - 0.10) AS "New price"
  FROM titles;
```

Listing 5.3 List the book prices discounted by 10 percent. The derived columns would have DBMS-specific default names if the AS clauses were removed. See Figure 5.3 for the result.

```
title_id price Discount New price
-------- ----- -------- ---------
T01      21.99     0.10     19.79
T02      19.95     0.10     17.95
T03      39.95     0.10     35.96
T04      12.99     0.10     11.69
T05       6.95     0.10      6.25
T06      19.95     0.10     17.95
T07      23.95     0.10     21.56
T08      10.00     0.10      9.00
T09      13.95     0.10     12.56
T10       NULL     0.10      NULL
T11       7.99     0.10      7.19
T12      12.99     0.10     11.69
T13      29.99     0.10     26.99
```

Figure 5.3 Result of Listing 5.3.

Tips for Derived Columns

- DBMS **Oracle** requires a FROM clause in a SELECT statement and so creates the **dummy table** DUAL automatically to be used for SELECTing a constant expression; search Oracle documentation for *DUAL table*. To run Listing 5.1, add a FROM clause that selects the constant value from DUAL:

```
SELECT 2 + 3
  FROM DUAL;
```

Db2 requires a FROM clause in a SELECT statement and so creates the dummy table SYSIBM. SYSDUMMY1 automatically to be used for SELECTing a constant expression; search Db2 documentation for *SYSIBM.SYSDUMMY1*. To run Listing 5.1, add a FROM clause that selects the constant value from SYSIBM.SYSDUMMY1:

```
SELECT 2 + 3
  FROM SYSIBM.SYSDUMMY1;
```

In older **PostgreSQL** versions, convert the floating-point number in Listing 5.3 to DECIMAL; see "Converting Data Types with CAST()" on page 145. To run Listing 5.3, change the *New price* calculation in the SELECT clause to:

```
price * CAST((1 - 0.10) AS DECIMAL)
```

Performing Arithmetic Operations

A **monadic** (or **unary**) **arithmetic operator** performs a mathematical operation on a single numeric operand to produce a result. The - (negation) operator changes the sign of its operand, and the not-very-useful + (identity) operator leaves its operand unchanged. A **dyadic** (or **binary**) **arithmetic operator** performs a mathematical operation on two numeric operands to produce a result. These operators include the usual ones: + (addition), - (subtraction), * (multiplication), and / (division). Table 5.1 lists SQL's arithmetic operators (*expr* is a numeric expression).

To change the sign of a number:

* Type *-expr*

    expr is a numeric expression (Listing 5.4 and Figure 5.4).

Table 5.1 Arithmetic Operators

Operator	What It Does
-expr	Reverses the sign of *expr*
+expr	Leaves *expr* unchanged
expr1 + *expr2*	Sums *expr1* and *expr2*
expr1 - *expr2*	Subtracts *expr2* from *expr1*
expr1 * *expr2*	Multiplies *expr1* and *expr2*
expr1 / *expr2*	Divides *expr1* by *expr2*

```
SELECT
    title_id,
    -advance AS "Advance"
  FROM royalties;
```

Listing 5.4 The negation operator changes the sign of a number. See Figure 5.4 for the result.

```
title_id Advance
-------- -----------
T01         -10000.00
T02          -1000.00
T03         -15000.00
T04         -20000.00
T05        -100000.00
T06         -20000.00
T07       -1000000.00
T08              0.00
T09              0.00
T10              NULL
T11        -100000.00
T12         -50000.00
T13         -20000.00
```

Figure 5.4 Result of Listing 5.4. Note that zero has no sign (is neither positive nor negative).

```
SELECT
    title_id,
    price * sales AS "Revenue"
  FROM titles
  WHERE type = 'biography'
  ORDER BY price * sales DESC;
```

Listing 5.5 List the biographies by descending revenue (= price × sales). See Figure 5.5 for the result.

```
title_id  Revenue
--------  -----------
T07          35929790.00
T12           1299012.99
T06            225834.00
T10                  NULL
```

Figure 5.5 Result of Listing 5.5.

Other Operators and Functions

All DBMSs provide plenty of operators and functions in addition to those defined in the SQL standard (or covered in this book). In fact, the standard is playing catch-up—many of the functions introduced in revised standards have existed for years in DBMSs. The earlier standards were so anemic that they left SQL weaker than a desktop calculator. Search your DBMS documentation for *operators* and *functions* to find mathematical, statistical, financial, scientific, trigonometric, conversion, string, datetime, bitwise, system, metadata, security, and other categories.

To add, subtract, multiply, or divide:

- Type *expr1* + *expr2* to add, *expr1* - *expr2* to subtract, *expr1* * *expr2* to multiply, or *expr1*/*expr2* to divide.

  expr1 and *expr2* are numeric expressions (Listing 5.5 and Figure 5.5).

Tips for Arithmetic Operations

- The result of any arithmetic operation that involves a null is null.

- If you use multiple operators in a single expression, then you might need to use parentheses to control the calculation order; see "Determining the Order of Evaluation" on page 121.

- If you mix numeric data types in an arithmetic expression, then your DBMS converts, or **coerces**, all the numbers to the data type of the expression's most complex operand and returns the result in this type. This conversion process is called **promotion**. If you add an INTEGER and a FLOAT, for example, then the DBMS converts the integer to a float, adds the numbers, and returns the sum as a float. In some cases, you must convert a data type to another data type explicitly; see "Converting Data Types with CAST()" on page 145.

continues on next page

- If you're writing a database application or UPDATEing rows, then note that data types aren't **closed** for some arithmetic operations. If you multiply or add two SMALLINTs, for example, then the result might be greater than a SMALLINT column can hold. Similarly, dividing two INTEGERs doesn't necessarily yield an INTEGER.

- DBMS Sometimes DBMSs force mathematical closure, so be careful when dividing integers by integers. If an integer dividend is divided by an integer divisor, then the result might be an integer that has any fractional part of the result truncated. You might expect the two derived columns in Listing 5.6 to contain the same values because the column *pages* (an INTEGER) is divided by two equal constants: 10 (an integer) and 10.0 (a float). **Microsoft Access, Oracle,** and **MySQL** return the result you'd expect (Figure 5.6a), but **Microsoft SQL Server, Db2,** and **PostgreSQL** truncate the result of an integer division (Figure 5.6b).

```
SELECT
    title_id,
    pages,
    pages/10   AS "pages/10",
    pages/10.0 AS "pages/10.0"
  FROM titles;
```

Listing 5.6 This query's first derived column divides *pages* by the integer constant 10, and the second derived column divides *pages* by the floating-point constant 10.0. In the result, you'd expect identical values to be in both derived columns. See Figures 5.6a and 5.6b for the results.

title_id	pages	pages/10	pages/10.0
T01	107	10.7	10.7
T02	14	1.4	1.4
T03	1226	122.6	122.6
T04	510	51.0	51.0
T05	201	20.1	20.1
T06	473	47.3	47.3
T07	333	33.3	33.3
T08	86	8.6	8.6
T09	22	2.2	2.2
T10	NULL	NULL	NULL
T11	826	82.6	82.6
T12	507	50.7	50.7
T13	802	80.2	80.2

Figure 5.6a Result of Listing 5.6 for Microsoft Access, Oracle, and MySQL. Dividing two integers yields a floating-point number (as you'd expect).

title_id	pages	pages/10	pages/10.0
T01	107	10	10.7
T02	14	1	1.4
T03	1226	122	122.6
T04	510	51	51.0
T05	201	20	20.1
T06	473	47	47.3
T07	333	33	33.3
T08	86	8	8.6
T09	22	2	2.2
T10	NULL	NULL	NULL
T11	826	82	82.6
T12	507	50	50.7
T13	802	80	80.2

Figure 5.6b Result of Listing 5.6 for Microsoft SQL Server, Db2, and PostgreSQL. Dividing two integers yields an integer; the fractional part of the result is discarded (not as you'd expect).

Table 5.2 Order of Evaluation (Highest to Lowest)

Operator	Description
+, -	Monadic identity, monadic negation
*, /	Multiplication, division
+, -	Addition, subtraction
=, <>, <, <=, >, >=	Comparison operators
NOT	Logical NOT
AND	Logical AND
OR	Logical OR

```
SELECT
    2 + 3 * 4    AS "2+3*4",
    (2 + 3) * 4 AS "(2+3)*4",
    6 / 2 * 3    AS "6/2*3",
    6 / (2 * 3) AS "6/(2*3)";
```

Listing 5.7 The first and second columns show how to use parentheses to override precedence rules. The third and fourth columns show how to use parentheses to override associativity rules. See Figure 5.7 for the result.

```
2+3*4  (2+3)*4 6/2*3 6/(2*3)
-----  ------- ----- -------
   14       20     9       1
```

Figure 5.7 Result of Listing 5.7.

Determining the Order of Evaluation

Precedence determines the priority of various operators when more than one operator is used in an expression. Operators with higher precedence are evaluated first. Arithmetic operators (+, -, *, and so on) have higher precedence than comparison operators (<, =, >, and so on), which have higher precedence than logical operators (NOT, AND, OR), so the expression

a or b * c >= d

is equivalent to

a or ((b * c) >= d)

Operators with lower precedence are less **binding** than those with higher precedence. Table 5.2 lists operator precedences from most to least binding. Operators in the same row have equal precedence.

Associativity determines the order of evaluation in an expression when adjacent operators have equal precedence. SQL uses left-to-right associativity.

You don't need to memorize all this information. You can use parentheses to override precedence and associativity rules (Listing 5.7 and Figure 5.7).

Tips for Order of Evaluation

- It's good programming style to add parentheses (even when they're unnecessary) to complex expressions to ensure your intended evaluation order and make code more portable and easier to read.

- DBMS Table 5.2 is incomplete; it omits some standard (such as IN and EXISTS) and nonstandard (DBMS-specific) operators. To determine the complete order of evaluation that your DBMS uses, search your DBMS documentation for *precedence*.

  To run Listing 5.7 in **Oracle**, add the clause FROM DUAL. To run it in **Db2**, add the clause FROM SYSIBM.SYSDUMMY1. See the DBMS tip in "Tips for Derived Columns" on page 117.

Concatenating Strings with ||

Use the operator || to combine, or **concatenate**, strings. The operator's important characteristics are:

- The operator || is two consecutive vertical-bar, or pipe, characters.

- Concatenation doesn't add a space between strings.

- ||, a dyadic (binary) operator, combines two strings into a single string: 'formal' || 'dehyde' is 'formaldehyde'.

- You can chain concatenations to combine multiple strings into a single string: 'a' || 'b' || 'c' || 'd' is 'abcd'.

- Concatenation with an empty string ('') leaves a string unchanged: 'a' || '' || 'b' is 'ab'.

- The result of any concatenation operation that involves a null is null: 'a' || NULL || 'b' is NULL. (But see the **Oracle** exception in the DBMS tip in "Tips for Concatenating Strings".)

- To concatenate a string and a nonstring (such as a numeric or datetime value), you must convert the nonstring to a string if your DBMS doesn't convert it implicitly; see "Converting Data Types with CAST()" on page 145.

```
SELECT au_fname || ' ' || au_lname
    AS "Author name"
  FROM authors
  ORDER BY au_lname ASC, au_fname ASC;
```

Listing 5.8 List the authors' first and last names, concatenated into a single column and sorted by last name/first name. See Figure 5.8 for the result.

```
Author name
-----------------
Sarah Buchman
Wendy Heydemark
Hallie Hull
Klee Hull
Christian Kells
 Kellsey
Paddy O'Furniture
```

Figure 5.8 Result of Listing 5.8.

```
SELECT
    CAST(sales AS CHAR(7))
    || ' copies sold of title '
    || title_id
      AS "Biography sales"
  FROM titles
  WHERE type = 'biography'
    AND sales IS NOT NULL
  ORDER BY sales DESC;
```

Listing 5.9 List biography sales by descending sales order. Here, I need to convert *sales* from an integer to a string. See Figure 5.9 for the result.

```
Biography sales
--------------------------------
1500200 copies sold of title T07
100001  copies sold of title T12
11320   copies sold of title T06
```

Figure 5.9 Result of Listing 5.9.

```
SELECT
    'Title '
    || title_id
    || ' published on '
    || CAST(pubdate AS CHAR(10))
      AS "Biography publication dates"
  FROM titles
 WHERE type = 'biography'
   AND pubdate IS NOT NULL
 ORDER BY pubdate DESC;
```

Listing 5.10 List biographies by descending publication date. Here, I need to convert *pubdate* from a datetime to a string. See Figure 5.10 for the result.

```
Biography publication dates
--------------------------------
Title T12 published on 2000-08-31
Title T06 published on 2000-07-31
Title T07 published on 1999-10-01
```

Figure 5.10 Result of Listing 5.10.

```
SELECT au_id, au_fname, au_lname
  FROM authors
 WHERE au_fname || ' ' || au_lname
       = 'Klee Hull';
```

Listing 5.11 List all the authors named *Klee Hull*. See Figure 5.11 for the result.

```
au_id au_fname au_lname
----- -------- --------
A04   Klee     Hull
```

Figure 5.11 Result of Listing 5.11.

To concatenate strings:

- Type:

  string1 || string2

  string1 and *string2* are the strings to be combined. Each operand is a string expression such as a column that contains character strings, a string literal, or the result of an operation or function that returns a string (Listings 5.8 through 5.11, Figures 5.8 through 5.11).

Tips for Concatenating Strings

- You can use || in SELECT, WHERE, and ORDER BY clauses or anywhere an expression is allowed.

- You can concatenate hex and bit strings: B'0100' || B'1011' is B'01001011'.

- Listing 5.11 shows how to use || in a WHERE clause, but it's actually *bad* SQL. The efficient way to express the clause is:

  ```
  WHERE au_fname = 'Klee'
    AND au_lname = 'Hull'
  ```

- You can use the TRIM() function to remove unwanted spaces from concatenated strings. Recall from "Character String Types" on page 58 that CHAR values are padded with trailing spaces, sometimes creating long, ugly stretches of spaces in concatenated strings. TRIM() will remove the extra space in front of the name *Kellsey* in Figure 5.8, for example; see "Trimming Characters with TRIM()" on page 130.

continues on next page

- **DBMS** In **Microsoft Access**, the concatenation operator is +, and the conversion function is Format(*string*). To run Listings 5.8 through 5.11, change the concatenation and conversion expressions to (Listing 5.8):

```
au_fname + ' ' + au_lname
```

and (Listing 5.9):

```
Format(sales) +
' copies sold of title ' + title_id
```

and (Listing 5.10):

```
'Title ' + title_id +
' published on ' + Format(pubdate)
```

and (Listing 5.11):

```
au_fname + ' ' + au_lname = 'Klee Hull';
```

In **Microsoft SQL Server**, the concatenation operator is +. To run Listings 5.8 through 5.11, change the concatenation expressions to (Listing 5.8):

```
au_fname + ' ' + au_lname
```

and (Listing 5.9):

```
CAST(sales AS CHAR(7)) +
' copies sold of title ' + title_id
```

and (Listing 5.10):

```
'Title ' + title_id + ' published on ' +
CAST(pubdate AS CHAR(10))
```

and (Listing 5.11):

```
au_fname + ' ' + au_lname = 'Klee Hull';
```

In **MySQL**, the concatenation function is CONCAT(). The || operator is legal, but it means logical OR in MySQL by default. (Use PIPES_AS_CONCAT mode to treat || as a string-concatenation operator rather than as a synonym for OR.) CONCAT() takes any number of arguments and converts nonstrings to strings as necessary (so CAST() isn't needed). To run Listings 5.8 through 5.11, change the concatenation expressions to (Listing 5.8):

```
CONCAT(au_fname, ' ', au_lname)
```

and (Listing 5.9):

```
CONCAT(sales, ' copies sold of title ',
title_id)
```

and (Listing 5.10):

```
CONCAT('Title ', title_id,
' published on ', pubdate)
```

and (Listing 5.11):

```
CONCAT(au_fname, ' ', au_lname) =
'Klee Hull';
```

For string operations, **Oracle** treats a null as an empty string: 'a' || NULL || 'b' returns 'ab' (not NULL). See the DBMS tip in "Tips for Nulls" on page 72.

Oracle, MySQL, and **PostgreSQL** convert nonstrings to strings implicitly in concatenations; Listings 5.9 and 5.10 still will run on these DBMSs if you omit CAST(). Search your DBMS documentation for *concatenation* or *conversion*.

Microsoft SQL Server, Oracle, Db2, and **PostgreSQL** also support the CONCAT() function.

```
SELECT
    pub_id,
    SUBSTRING(pub_id FROM 1 FOR 1)
      AS "Alpha part",
    SUBSTRING(pub_id FROM 2)
      AS "Num part"
  FROM publishers;
```

Listing 5.12 Split the publisher IDs into alphabetic and numeric parts. The alphabetic part of a publisher ID is the first character, and the remaining characters are the numeric part. See Figure 5.12 for the result.

```
pub_id Alpha part Num part
------ ---------- --------
P01    P          01
P02    P          02
P03    P          03
P04    P          04
```

Figure 5.12 Result of Listing 5.12.

```
SELECT
    SUBSTRING(au_fname FROM 1 FOR 1)
    || '. '
    || au_lname
      AS "Author name",
    state
  FROM authors
  WHERE state IN ('NY', 'CO');
```

Listing 5.13 List the first initial and last name of the authors from New York State and Colorado. See Figure 5.13 for the result.

```
Author name   state
-----------   -----
S. Buchman    NY
W. Heydemark  CO
C. Kells      NY
```

Figure 5.13 Result of Listing 5.13.

Extracting a Substring with SUBSTRING()

Use the function SUBSTRING() to extract part of a string. The function's important characteristics are:

- A **substring** is any sequence of contiguous characters from the source string, including an empty string or the entire source string itself.

- SUBSTRING() extracts part of a string starting at a specified position and continuing for a specified number of characters.

- A substring of an empty string is an empty string.

- If any argument is null, then SUBSTRING() returns null. (But see the **Oracle** exception in the DBMS tip in "Tips for Substrings".)

To extract a substring:

- Type:

  SUBSTRING(*string* FROM *start* [FOR *length*])

  string is the source string from which to extract the substring. *string* is a string expression such as a column that contains character strings, a string literal, or the result of an operation or function that returns a string. *start* is an integer that specifies where the substring begins, and *length* is an integer that specifies the length of the substring (the number of characters to return). *start* starts counting at 1. If FOR *length* is omitted, then SUBSTRING() returns all the characters from *start* to the end of *string* (Listings 5.12, 5.13, and 5.14, Figures 5.12, 5.13, and 5.14).

Tips for Substrings

- You can use SUBSTRING() in SELECT, WHERE, and ORDER BY clauses or anywhere an expression is allowed.

- You can extract substrings from hex and bit strings: SUBSTRING(B'01001011' FROM 5 FOR 4) returns B'1011'.

- DBMS In **Microsoft Access**, the substring function is Mid(*string*, *start* [,*length*]). Use + to concatenate strings. To run Listings 5.12 through 5.14, change the substring expressions to (Listing 5.12):

Mid(pub_id, 1, 1)

Mid(pub_id, 2)

and (Listing 5.13):

Mid(au_fname, 1, 1) + '. ' + au_lname

and (Listing 5.14):

Mid(phone, 1, 3) = '415'

In **Microsoft SQL Server**, the substring function is SUBSTRING(*string*, *start*, *length*). Use + to concatenate strings. To run Listings 5.12 through 5.14, change the substring expressions to (Listing 5.12):

SUBSTRING(pub_id, 1, 1)

SUBSTRING(pub_id, 2, LEN(pub_id)-1)

and (Listing 5.13):

SUBSTRING(au_fname, 1, 1) + '. ' + au_lname

and (Listing 5.14):

SUBSTRING(phone, 1, 3) = '415'

```
SELECT au_fname, au_lname, phone
  FROM authors
  WHERE SUBSTRING(phone FROM 1 FOR 3) = '415';
```

Listing 5.14 List the authors whose area code is 415. See Figure 5.14 for the result.

```
au_fname  au_lname  phone
--------  --------  ------------
Hallie    Hull      415-549-4278
Klee      Hull      415-549-4278
```

Figure 5.14 Result of Listing 5.14.

In **Oracle** and **Db2**, the substring function is SUBSTR(*string*, *start* [,*length*]). To run Listings 5.12 through 5.14, change the substring expressions to (Listing 5.12):

```
SUBSTR(pub_id, 1, 1)
```

```
SUBSTR(pub_id, 2)
```

and (Listing 5.13):

```
SUBSTR(au_fname, 1, 1) || '. ' || au_lname
```

and (Listing 5.14):

```
SUBSTR(phone, 1, 3) = '415'
```

In **MySQL**, use CONCAT() to run Listing 5.13 (see "Concatenating Strings with ||" on page 122). Change the concatenation expression to:

```
CONCAT(SUBSTRING(au_fname FROM 1 FOR 1),
'. ', au_lname)
```

For string operations, **Oracle** treats a null as an empty string: SUBSTR(NULL, 1, 2) returns '' (not NULL). See the DBMS tip in "Tips for Nulls" on page 72.

Your DBMS implicitly might constrain *start* and *length* arguments that are too small or too large to sensible values. The substring function silently might replace a negative *start* with 1 or a too-long *length* with the length of *string*, for example. Search your DBMS documentation for *substring* or *substr*.

MySQL and **PostgreSQL** also support the SUBSTR(*string*, *start*, *length*) form of the substring function.

Changing String Case with UPPER() and LOWER()

Use the function UPPER() to return a string with lowercase letters converted to uppercase, and use the function LOWER() to return a string with uppercase letters converted to lowercase. The functions' important characteristics are:

- A **cased** character is a letter that can be lowercase (*a*) or uppercase (*A*).

- Case changes affect only letters. Digits, punctuation, and whitespace are left unchanged.

- Case changes have no effect on empty strings ('').

- If its argument is null, then UPPER() and LOWER() return null. (But see the **Oracle** exception in the DBMS tip in "Tips for String Case".)

Case-Insensitive Comparisons

In DBMSs that perform case-sensitive WHERE-clause comparisons by default, UPPER() or LOWER() often is used to make case-insensitive comparisons:

```
WHERE UPPER(au_fname) = 'JOHN'
```

If you're sure that your data are clean, then it's faster to look for only reasonable letter combinations than to use case functions:

```
WHERE au_fname = 'JOHN'
   OR au_fname = 'John'
```

UPPER() and LOWER() affect characters with diacritical marks (such as accents and umlauts): UPPER('ö') is 'Ö', for example. If your data contain such characters and you're making case-insensitive comparisons such as

```
WHERE UPPER(au_fname) = 'JOSÉ'
```

then make sure that your DBMS doesn't lose the marks on conversion. UPPER('José') should be 'JOSÉ', not 'JOSE'. See also "Filtering Rows with WHERE" on page 89.

```
SELECT
    LOWER(au_fname) AS "Lower",
    UPPER(au_lname) AS "Upper"
  FROM authors;
```

Listing 5.15 List the authors' first names in lowercase and last names in uppercase. See Figure 5.15 for the result.

```
Lower      Upper
---------  -----------
sarah      BUCHMAN
wendy      HEYDEMARK
hallie     HULL
klee       HULL
christian  KELLS
           KELLSEY
paddy      O'FURNITURE
```

Figure 5.15 Result of Listing 5.15.

```
SELECT title_name
  FROM titles
  WHERE UPPER(title_name) LIKE '%MO%';
```

Listing 5.16 List the titles that contain the characters *MO*, regardless of case. All the letters in the LIKE pattern must be uppercase for this query to work. See Figure 5.16 for the result.

```
title_name
------------------------
200 Years of German Humor
I Blame My Mother
```

Figure 5.16 Result of Listing 5.16.

To convert a string to uppercase or lowercase:

- To convert a string to uppercase, type:

  UPPER(*string*)

  or

  To convert a string to lowercase, type:

  LOWER(*string*)

  string is a string expression such as a column that contains character strings, a string literal, or the result of an operation or function that returns a string (Listings 5.15 and 5.16, Figures 5.15 and 5.16).

Tips for String Case

- You can use UPPER() and LOWER() in SELECT, WHERE, and ORDER BY clauses or anywhere an expression is allowed.

- UPPER() and LOWER() don't affect character sets with no concept of case (such as Hebrew and Chinese).

- DBMS In **Microsoft Access**, the upper- and lowercase functions are UCase(string) and LCase(string). To run Listings 5.15 and 5.16, change the case expressions to (Listing 5.15):

  LCase(au_fname)

  UCase(au_lname)

  and (Listing 5.16):

  UCase(title_name) LIKE '%MO%'

  For string operations, **Oracle** treats a null as an empty string: UPPER(NULL) and LOWER(NULL) return '' (not NULL). See the DBMS tip in "Tips for Nulls" on page 72.

  Your DBMS might provide other string-casing functions to, say, invert case or convert strings to sentence or title case. Search your DBMS documentation for character *functions* or *string functions*.

Trimming Characters with TRIM()

Use the function TRIM() to remove unwanted characters from the ends of a string. The function's important characteristics are:

- You can trim leading characters, trailing characters, or both. (You can't use TRIM() to remove characters from *within* a string.)

- By default, TRIM() trims spaces, but you can strip off any unwanted characters, such as leading and trailing zeros or asterisks.

- TRIM() typically is used to format results and make comparisons in a WHERE clause.

- TRIM() is useful for trimming trailing spaces from CHAR values. Recall from "Character String Types" on page 58 that DBMSs add spaces automatically to the end of CHAR values to create strings of exactly a specified length.

- Trimming has no effect on empty strings (").

- If any argument is null, then TRIM() returns null. (But see the **Oracle** exception in the DBMS tip in "Tips for Trimming Characters" on page 133.)

```
SELECT
  '<' || '  AAA  ' || '>'
    AS "Untrimmed",
  '<' || TRIM(LEADING FROM '  AAA  ') || '>'
    AS "Leading",
  '<' || TRIM(TRAILING FROM '  AAA  ') || '>'
    AS "Trailing",
  '<' || TRIM('  AAA  ') || '>'
    AS "Both";
```

Listing 5.17 This query strips leading, trailing, and both leading and trailing spaces from the string ' AAA '. The < and > characters show the extent of the trimmed strings. See Figure 5.17 for the result.

```
Untrimmed Leading    Trailing  Both
--------- ---------  --------- -----
<  AAA  > <AAA    >  <   AAA>  <AAA>
```

Figure 5.17 Result of Listing 5.17.

To trim spaces from a string:

* Type:

   TRIM([[LEADING | TRAILING | BOTH] FROM] *string*)

   string is a string expression such as a column that contains character strings, a string literal, or the result of an operation or function that returns a string. Specify LEADING to remove leading spaces, TRAILING to remove trailing spaces, or BOTH to remove leading and trailing spaces. If this specifier is omitted, then BOTH is assumed (Listing 5.17 and Figure 5.17).

To trim characters from a string:

- Type:

TRIM([LEADING | TRAILING | BOTH] 'trim_chars' FROM string)

string is the string to trim, and trim_chars is one or more characters to remove from string. Each argument is a string expression such as a column that contains character strings, a string literal, or the result of an operation or function that returns a string. Specify LEADING to remove leading characters, TRAILING to remove trailing characters, or BOTH to remove leading and trailing characters. If this specifier is omitted, then BOTH is assumed (Listings 5.18 and 5.19, Figures 5.18 and 5.19).

```
SELECT
    au_lname,
    TRIM(LEADING 'H' FROM au_lname)
      AS "Trimmed name"
  FROM authors;
```

Listing 5.18 Strip the leading *H* from the authors' last names that begin with *H*. See Figure 5.18 for the result.

```
au_lname    Trimmed name
----------  ------------
Buchman     Buchman
Heydemark   eydemark
Hull        ull
Hull        ull
Kells       Kells
Kellsey     Kellsey
O'Furniture O'Furniture
```

Figure 5.18 Result of Listing 5.18.

```
SELECT title_id
  FROM titles
   WHERE TRIM(title_id) LIKE 'T1_';
```

Listing 5.19 List the three-character title IDs that start with *T1*, ignoring leading and trailing spaces. See Figure 5.19 for the result.

```
title_id
--------
T10
T11
T12
T13
```

Figure 5.19 Result of Listing 5.19.

Tips for Trimming Characters

- You can use TRIM() in SELECT, WHERE, and ORDER BY clauses or anywhere an expression is allowed.

- In Listing 5.8 earlier in this chapter, I concatenated authors' first and last names into a single column. The result, Figure 5.8, contains a single extra space before the author named Kellsey. This space—which separates the first and last names in the other rows—appears because Kellsey has no first name. You can use TRIM() to remove this leading space. Change the concatenation expression in Listing 5.8 to:

```
TRIM(au_fname || ' ' || au_lname)
```

DBMS In **Microsoft Access**, the trimming functions are LTrim(*string*) to trim leading spaces, RTrim(*string*) to trailing spaces, and Trim(*string*) to trim both leading and trailing spaces. Use the function Replace(*string*, *find*, *replacement* [, *start*[, *count*[, *compare*]]]) to trim nonspace characters (actually, to replace nonspaces with empty strings). Use + to concatenate strings. To run Listings 5.17 and 5.18, change the trim expressions to (Listing 5.17):

```
'<' + '   AAA   ' + '>'

'<' + LTRIM('   AAA   ') + '>'

'<' + RTRIM('   AAA   ') + '>'

'<' + TRIM('   AAA   ') + '>'
```

and (Listing 5.18):

```
Replace(au_lname, 'H', '', 1, 1)
```

continues on next page

In **Microsoft SQL Server**, the trimming functions are LTRIM(*string*) to trim leading spaces and RTRIM(*string*) to trim trailing spaces. Use + to concatenate strings. To run Listing 5.17, change the trim expressions to:

```
'<' + '  AAA  ' + '>'

'<' + LTRIM('  AAA  ') + '>'

'<' + RTRIM('  AAA  ') + '>'

'<' + LTRIM(RTRIM('  AAA  ')) + '>'
```

SQL Server's LTRIM() and RTRIM() functions remove spaces but not arbitrary *trim_chars* characters. You can nest and chain SQL Server's CHARINDEX(), LEN(), PATINDEX(), REPLACE(), STUFF(), SUBSTRING(), and other character functions to replicate arbitrary-character trimming. To run Listing 5.18, change the trim expression to:

```
REPLACE(SUBSTRING(au_lname, 1, 1),'H','')
+ SUBSTRING(au_lname, 2, LEN(au_lname))
```

To run Listing 5.19, change the trim expression to:

```
LTRIM(RTRIM(title_id)) LIKE 'T1_'
```

In **Oracle**, add the clause FROM DUAL to run Listing 5.17; see the DBMS tip in "Tips for Derived Columns" on page 117. Oracle forbids multiple characters in *trim_chars*.

In **Db2**, the trimming functions are LTRIM(*string*) to trim leading spaces and RTRIM(*string*) to trim trailing spaces. To run Listing 5.17, change the trim expressions:

```
'<' || '  AAA  ' || '>'

'<' || LTRIM('  AAA  ') || '>'

'<' || RTRIM('  AAA  ') || '>'

'<' || LTRIM(RTRIM('  AAA  ')) || '>'
```

You also must add the clause FROM SYSIBM. SYSDUMMY1 to Listing 5.17; see the DBMS tip in "Tips for Derived Columns" on page 117.

You can nest and chain Db2's LENGTH(), LOCATE(), POSSTR(), REPLACE(), SUBSTR(), and other character functions to replicate arbitrary-character trimming. To run Listing 5.18, change the trim expression to:

```
REPLACE(SUBSTR(au_lname, 1, 1),'H','')
|| SUBSTR(au_lname, 2, LENGTH(au_lname))
```

To run Listing 5.19, change the trim expression to:

```
LTRIM(RTRIM(title_id)) LIKE 'T1_'
```

In **MySQL**, use CONCAT() to run Listing 5.17 (see "Concatenating Strings with ||" on page 122). Change the concatenation expressions to:

```
CONCAT('<','  AAA  ','>')

CONCAT('<', TRIM(LEADING FROM '  AAA  '),
'>')

CONCAT('<', TRIM(TRAILING FROM
'  AAA  '), '>')

CONCAT('<',TRIM('  AAA  '),'>')
```

For string operations, **Oracle** treats a null as an empty string: TRIM(NULL) returns '' (not NULL). See the DBMS tip in "Tips for Nulls" on page 72.

Your DBMS might provide padding functions to *add* spaces or other characters to strings. The **Oracle** and **PostgreSQL** padding functions are LPAD() and RPAD(), for example. Search your DBMS documentation for *character functions* or *string functions*.

```
SELECT
    au_fname,
    CHARACTER_LENGTH(au_fname) AS "Len"
  FROM authors;
```

Listing 5.20 List the lengths of the authors' first names. See Figure 5.20 for the result.

```
au_fname  Len
--------- ---
Sarah       5
Wendy       5
Hallie      6
Klee        4
Christian   9
            0
Paddy       5
```

Figure 5.20 Result of Listing 5.20.

```
SELECT
    title_name,
    CHARACTER_LENGTH(title_name) AS "Len"
  FROM titles
  WHERE CHARACTER_LENGTH(title_name) < 30
  ORDER BY CHARACTER_LENGTH(title_name) ASC;
```

Listing 5.21 List the books whose titles contain fewer than 30 characters, sorted by ascending title length. See Figure 5.21 for the result.

```
title_name                    Len
----------------------------- ---
1977!                           5
Kiss My Boo-Boo                15
How About Never?               16
I Blame My Mother              17
Exchange of Platitudes         22
200 Years of German Humor      25
Spontaneous, Not Annoying      25
But I Did It Unconsciously     26
Not Without My Faberge Egg     26
Just Wait Until After School   28
Ask Your System Administrator  29
```

Figure 5.21 Result of Listing 5.21.

Finding the Length of a String with CHARACTER_LENGTH()

Use the function CHARACTER_LENGTH() to return the number of characters in a string. The function's important characteristics are:

- CHARACTER_LENGTH() returns an integer greater than or equal to zero.

- CHARACTER_LENGTH() counts characters, not bytes. A multibyte or Unicode character (page 59) represents one character. (To count bytes, see the tips in this section.)

- The length of an empty string (") is zero.

- If its argument is null, then CHARACTER_LENGTH() returns null. (But see the **Oracle** exception in the DBMS tip in "Tips for String Lengths".)

To find the length of a string:

- Type:

  CHARACTER_LENGTH(*string*)

  string is a string expression such as a column that contains character strings, a string literal, or the result of an operation or function that returns a string (Listings 5.20 and 5.21, Figures 5.20 and 5.21).

Tips for String Lengths

- You can use CHARACTER_LENGTH() in SELECT, WHERE, and ORDER BY clauses or anywhere an expression is allowed.

- CHARACTER_LENGTH and CHAR_LENGTH are synonyms.

- SQL also defines the BIT_LENGTH() and OCTET_LENGTH() functions. BIT_LENGTH(*expr*) returns the number of bits in an expression; BIT_LENGTH(B'01001011') returns 8. OCTET_LENGTH(*expr*) returns the number of bytes in an expression; OCTET_LENGTH(B'01001011') returns 1, and OCTET_LENGTH('ABC') returns 3. Octet length equals bit-length ÷ 8 (rounded up to the nearest integer, if necessary). See the DBMS tip in this section for information about DBMS bit- and byte-length functions.

- DBMS In **Microsoft Access** and **Microsoft SQL Server**, the string-length function is LEN(*string*). To run Listings 5.20 and 5.21, change the length expressions to (Listing 5.20):

  LEN(au_fname)

  and (Listing 5.21):

  LEN(title_name)

  In **Oracle** and **Db2**, the string-length function is LENGTH(*string*). To run Listings 5.20 and 5.21, change the length expressions to (Listing 5.20):

  LENGTH(au_fname)

  and (Listing 5.21):

  LENGTH(title_name)

  Bit- and byte-count functions vary by DBMS. **Microsoft Access** has Len(). **Microsoft SQL Server** has DATALENGTH(). **Oracle** has LENGTHB(). **Db2** has LENGTH(). **MySQL** has BIT_COUNT() and OCTET_LENGTH(). **PostgreSQL** has BIT_LENGTH() and OCTET_LENGTH().

  For string operations, **Oracle** treats a null as an empty string: LENGTH('') returns NULL (not 0). Listing 5.20 will show 1 (not 0) in the next-to-last row because the author's first name is ' ' (a space) in the Oracle database. For more information, see the DBMS tip in "Tips for Nulls" on page 72.

Finding Substrings with POSITION()

Use the function POSITION() to locate a particular substring within a given string. The function's important characteristics are:

- POSITION() returns an integer (≥0) that indicates the starting position of a substring's first occurrence within a string.

- If the string doesn't contain the substring, then POSITION() returns zero.

- String comparisons are case insensitive or case sensitive, depending on your DBMS; see the DBMS tip in "Tips for WHERE" on page 91.

- The position of any substring within an empty string (") is zero. (But see the **Oracle** exception in the DBMS tip in "Tips for Finding Substrings".)

- If any argument is null, then POSITION() returns null.

To find a substring:

- Type:

  POSITION(*substring* IN *string*)

  substring is the string to search for, and *string* is the string to search. Each argument is a string expression such as a column that contains character strings, a string literal, or the result of an operation or function that returns a string. POSITION() returns the lowest (integer) position in *string* in which *substring* occurs, or zero if *substring* isn't found (Listings 5.22 and 5.23, Figures 5.22 and 5.23).

```
SELECT
    au_fname,
    POSITION('e' IN au_fname) AS "Pos e",
    au_lname,
    POSITION('ma' IN au_lname) AS "Pos ma"
  FROM authors;
```

Listing 5.22 List the position of the substring *e* in the authors' first names and the position of the substring *ma* in the authors' last names. See Figure 5.22 for the result.

au_fname	Pos e	au_lname	Pos ma
Sarah	0	Buchman	5
Wendy	2	Heydemark	6
Hallie	6	Hull	0
Klee	3	Hull	0
Christian	0	Kells	0
	0	Kellsey	0
Paddy	0	O'Furniture	0

Figure 5.22 Result of Listing 5.22.

```
SELECT
    title_name,
    POSITION('u' IN title_name) AS "Pos"
  FROM titles
  WHERE POSITION('u' IN title_name)
        BETWEEN 1 AND 10
  ORDER BY POSITION('u' IN title_name) DESC;
```

Listing 5.23 List the books whose titles contain the letter *u* somewhere within the first 10 characters, sorted by descending position of the *u*. See Figure 5.23 for the result.

title_name	Pos
Not Without My Faberge Egg	10
Spontaneous, Not Annoying	10
How About Never?	8
Ask Your System Administrator	7
But I Did It Unconsciously	2
Just Wait Until After School	2

Figure 5.23 Result of Listing 5.23.

Tips for Finding Substrings

- You can use POSITION() in SELECT, WHERE, and ORDER BY clauses or anywhere an expression is allowed.

The SQL standard also defines the function OVERLAY() to *replace* substrings. The syntax is:

```
OVERLAY(string PLACING substring FROM
start_position [FOR length])
```

For example, OVERLAY('Txxxxas' PLACING 'hom' FROM 2 FOR 4) is 'Thomas'. The equivalent functions in the DBMSs are REPLACE() (**Microsoft Access**, **Microsoft SQL Server**, **Db2**, and **MySQL**), REGEXP_REPLACE() (**Oracle**), and OVERLAY() (**PostgreSQL**).

- DBMS In **Microsoft Access**, the position function is InStr(*start_position*, *string*, *substring*). To run Listings 5.22 and 5.23, change the position expressions to (Listing 5.22):

```
InStr(1, au_fname, 'e')
```

```
InStr(1, au_lname, 'ma')
```

and (Listing 5.23):

```
InStr(1, title_name, 'u')
```

In **Microsoft SQL Server**, the position function is CHARINDEX(*substring*, *string*). To run Listings 5.22 and 5.23, change the position expressions to (Listing 5.22):

```
CHARINDEX('e', au_fname)
```

```
CHARINDEX('ma', au_lname)
```

and (Listing 5.23):

```
CHARINDEX('u', title_name)
```

In **Oracle**, the position function is INSTR(*string*, *substring*). To run Listings 5.22 and 5.23, change the position expressions to (Listing 5.22):

```
INSTR(au_fname, 'e')
```

```
INSTR(au_lname, 'ma')
```

and (Listing 5.23):

```
INSTR(title_name, 'u')
```

In **Db2**, the position function is POSSTR(*string*, *substring*). To run Listings 5.22 and 5.23, change the position expressions to (Listing 5.22):

```
POSSTR(au_fname, 'e')
```

```
POSSTR(au_lname, 'ma')
```

and (Listing 5.23):

```
POSSTR(title_name, 'u')
```

For string operations, **Oracle** treats a null as an empty string: INSTR('', *substring*) returns NULL (not 0). See the DBMS tip in "Tips for Nulls" on page 72.

You can nest and chain substring and position functions to find substring occurrences beyond the first occurrence, but DBMSs provide enhanced position functions to do that. **Microsoft Access** has InStr(). **Microsoft SQL Server** has CHARINDEX(). **Oracle** has INSTR(). **Db2** has LOCATE(). **MySQL** has LOCATE().

Performing Datetime and Interval Arithmetic

DBMS DBMS compliance with standard SQL datetime and interval operators and functions is spotty because DBMSs usually provide their own extended (nonstandard) operators and functions that perform date and time arithmetic. For information about datetime and interval data types, see "Datetime Types" and "Interval Types" in Chapter 3.

Use the same operators introduced in "Performing Arithmetic Operations" on page 118 to perform datetime and interval arithmetic. The common temporal operations are:

- Subtracting two dates to calculate the interval between them

- Adding or subtracting an interval and a date to calculate a future or past date

- Adding or subtracting two intervals to get a new interval

- Multiplying or dividing an interval by a number to get a new interval

Some operations are undefined; adding two dates makes no sense, for example. Table 5.3 lists the valid SQL operators involving datetimes and intervals. The "Operator Overloading" sidebar explains why you can use the same operator to perform different operations.

The function EXTRACT() isolates a single field of a datetime or interval and returns it as a number. EXTRACT() typically is used in comparison expressions or for formatting results.

Table 5.3 Datetime and Interval Operations

Operation	Result
Datetime – Datetime	Interval
Datetime + Interval	Datetime
Datetime – Interval	Datetime
Interval + Datetime	Datetime
Interval + Interval	Interval
Interval – Interval	Interval
Interval * Numeric	Interval
Interval / Numeric	Interval
Numeric * Interval	Interval

Operator Overloading

Recall that the +, -, *, and / operators also are used for numeric operations and that Microsoft DBMSs use + for string concatenation as well. **Operator overloading** is the assignment of more than one function to a particular operator. The operation performed depends on the data types of the operands involved. Here, the +, -, *, and / operators behave differently with numbers than they do with datetimes and intervals (as well as strings, in the case of **Microsoft Access** and **Microsoft SQL Server**). Your DBMS might overload other operators and functions as well.

Function overloading is the assignment of more than one behavior to a particular function, depending on the data types of the arguments involved. The **MySQL** CONCAT() function (see the DBMS tip in "Tips for Concatenating Strings" on page 123), for example, takes nonstring as well as string arguments. Nonstrings cause CONCAT() to perform additional conversions that it doesn't need to perform on strings.

To extract part of a datetime or interval:

- Type:

  EXTRACT(*field* FROM *datetime_or_interval*)

  field is the part of *datetime_or_interval* to return. *field* is YEAR, MONTH, DAY, HOUR, MINUTE, SECOND, TIMEZONE_HOUR, or TIMEZONE_MINUTE (refer to Table 3.14 on page 67). *datetime_or_interval* is a datetime or interval expression such as a column that contains datetime or interval values, a datetime or interval literal, or the result of an operation or function that returns a datetime or interval. If *field* is SECOND, then EXTRACT() returns a NUMERIC value; otherwise, it returns an INTEGER (Listing 5.24 and Figure 5.24).

```
SELECT
    title_id,
    pubdate
  FROM titles
  WHERE EXTRACT(YEAR FROM pubdate)
        BETWEEN 2001 AND 2002
    AND EXTRACT(MONTH FROM pubdate)
        BETWEEN 1 AND 6
  ORDER BY pubdate DESC;
```

Listing 5.24 List the books published in the first half of the years 2001 and 2002, sorted by descending publication date. See Figure 5.24 for the result.

```
title_id pubdate
-------- ----------
T09      2002-05-31
T08      2001-06-01
T05      2001-01-01
```

Figure 5.24 Result of Listing 5.24.

Tips for Datetime and Interval Arithmetic

- You can use temporal operators and functions in SELECT, WHERE, and ORDER BY clauses or anywhere an expression is allowed.

- If any operand or argument is null, then an expression returns null.

- See also "Working with Dates" on page 427.

- DBMS In **Microsoft Access** and **Microsoft SQL Server**, the extraction function is DATEPART(*datepart*, *date*). To run Listing 5.24, change the extraction expressions to:

  DATEPART("yyyy", pubdate)

  DATEPART("m", pubdate)

  Oracle, **MySQL**, and **PostgreSQL** accept different or additional values for the *field* argument of EXTRACT().

  Instead of EXTRACT(), **Db2** extracts parts by using individual functions such as DAY(), HOUR(), and SECOND(). To run Listing 5.24, change the extraction expressions to:

  YEAR(pubdate)

  MONTH(pubdate)

  In addition to (or instead of) the standard arithmetic operators, DBMSs provide functions that add intervals to dates. Some examples: DATEDIFF() in **Microsoft Access** and **Microsoft SQL Server**, ADD_MONTHS() in **Oracle**, and DATE_ADD() and DATE_SUB() in **MySQL**.

  Complex date and time arithmetic is so common in SQL programming that all DBMSs provide lots of temporal extensions. Search your DBMS documentation for *date and time functions* or *datetime functions*.

Getting the Current Date and Time

Use the functions CURRENT_DATE, CURRENT_TIME, and CURRENT_TIMESTAMP to get the current date and time from the system clock of the particular computer where the DBMS is running.

To get the current date and time:

- To get the current date, type:

  CURRENT_DATE

  or

  To get the current time, type:

  CURRENT_TIME

  or

  To get the current timestamp, type:

  CURRENT_TIMESTAMP

  CURRENT_DATE returns a DATE, CURRENT_TIME returns a TIME, and CURRENT_TIMESTAMP returns a TIMESTAMP; see "Datetime Types" on page 66 (Listings 5.25 and 5.26, Figures 5.25 and 5.26).

```
SELECT
    CURRENT_DATE AS "Date",
    CURRENT_TIME AS "Time",
    CURRENT_TIMESTAMP AS "Timestamp";
```

Listing 5.25 Print the current date, time, and timestamp. See Figure 5.25 for the result.

```
Date        Time      Timestamp
----------  --------  -------------------
2002-03-10  10:09:24  2002-03-10 10:09:24
```

Figure 5.25 Result of Listing 5.25.

```
SELECT title_id, pubdate
  FROM titles
  WHERE pubdate
        BETWEEN CURRENT_TIMESTAMP -
                INTERVAL 90 DAY
            AND CURRENT_TIMESTAMP +
                INTERVAL 90 DAY
     OR pubdate IS NULL
  ORDER BY pubdate DESC;
```

Listing 5.26 List the books whose publication date falls within 90 days of the current date or is unknown, sorted by descending publication date (refer to Figure 5.25 for the "current" date of this query). See Figure 5.26 for the result.

```
title_id pubdate
-------- ----------
T09      2002-05-31
T10      NULL
```

Figure 5.26 Result of Listing 5.26.

Tips for the Current Date and Time

- You can use datetime functions in SELECT, WHERE, and ORDER BY clauses or anywhere an expression is allowed.

- CURRENT_TIME and CURRENT_TIMESTAMP each take a precision argument that specifies the decimal fractions of a second to be included in the time. CURRENT_TIME(6), for example, returns the current time with six digits of precision in the SECOND field. For information about precision, see "Datetime Types" on page 66.

- See also "Working with Dates" on page 427.

- DBMS | In **Microsoft Access**, the datetime system functions are Date(), Time(), and Now(). To run Listing 5.25, change the datetime expressions to:

```
Date() AS "Date"

Time() AS "Time"

Now() AS "Timestamp"
```

To run Listing 5.26, change the BETWEEN clause to:

```
BETWEEN NOW() - 90
    AND NOW() + 90
```

In **Microsoft SQL Server**, the datetime system function is CURRENT_TIMESTAMP (or its synonym, GETDATE()). CURRENT_DATE and CURRENT_TIME aren't supported. To run Listing 5.25, omit the CURRENT_DATE and CURRENT_TIME expressions. To run Listing 5.26, change the BETWEEN clause to:

```
BETWEEN CURRENT_TIMESTAMP - 90
    AND CURRENT_TIMESTAMP + 90
```

In **Oracle**, the datetime system function is SYSDATE. Oracle 9i and later versions support CURRENT_DATE and CURRENT_TIMESTAMP (but not CURRENT_TIME). Listing 5.25 also requires the clause FROM DUAL; see the DBMS tip in "Tips for Derived Columns" on page 117. To run Listing 5.25, change the statement to:

```
SELECT SYSDATE AS "Date"
  FROM DUAL;
```

SYSDATE returns the system date and time but doesn't display the time unless formatted to do so with the function TO_CHAR():

```
SELECT TO_CHAR(SYSDATE,
    'YYYY-MM-DD HH24:MI:SS')
  FROM DUAL;
```

To run Listing 5.26, change the BETWEEN clause to:

```
BETWEEN SYSDATE - 90
    AND SYSDATE + 90
```

To run Listing 5.25 in **Db2**, add the clause FROM SYSIBM.SYSDUMMY1; see the DBMS tip in "Tips for Derived Columns" on page 117. To run Listing 5.26, change the WHERE clause to:

```
BETWEEN CURRENT_DATE - 90 DAYS
    AND CURRENT_DATE + 90 DAYS
```

To run Listing 5.26 in **PostgreSQL**, change the WHERE clause to:

```
BETWEEN CURRENT_TIMESTAMP - 90
    AND CURRENT_TIMESTAMP + 90
```

For information about datetime system functions, search your DBMS documentation for *date and time functions* or *system functions*.

Getting User Information

Use the function CURRENT_USER to identify the active user within the database server.

To get the current user:

*   Type:

    CURRENT_USER

    (Listing 5.27 and Figure 5.27).

Tips for User Information

*   You can use user functions in SELECT, WHERE, and ORDER BY clauses or anywhere an expression is allowed.

*   SQL also defines the SESSION_USER and SYSTEM_USER functions. The **current user** indicates the **authorization identifier** under whose privileges SQL statements currently are run. (The current user might have permission to run, say, only SELECT statements.) The **session user** indicates the authorization ID associated with the current session. The **system user** is the user as identified by the host operating system. The DBMS determines user values, and these three values may or may not be identical. For information about users, sessions, and privileges, search your DBMS documentation for *authorization*, *session*, *user*, or *role*.

*   See also "Retrieving Metadata" on page 424.

*   DBMS To run Listing 5.27 in **Microsoft Access**, change the statement to:

    SELECT CurrentUser AS "User";

    To run Listing 5.27 in **Oracle**, change the statement to:

    SELECT USER AS "User"
      FROM DUAL;

    To run Listing 5.27 in **Db2**, change the statement to:

    SELECT CURRENT_USER AS "User"
      FROM SYSIBM.SYSDUMMY1;

    To run Listing 5.27 in **MySQL**, change the statement to:

    SELECT USER() AS "User";

    Microsoft SQL Server supports SESSION_USER and SYSTEM_USER. **MySQL** supports SESSION_USER() and SYSTEM_USER(). **Oracle**'s SYS_CONTEXT() returns a session's user attributes. **Db2** supports SESSION_USER and SYSTEM_USER. **PostgreSQL** supports SESSION_USER.

    For information about user system functions, search your DBMS documentation for *user* or *system functions*.

```
SELECT CURRENT_USER AS "User";
```

Listing 5.27 Print the current user. See Figure 5.27 for the result.

```
User
------
jsmith
```

Figure 5.27 Result of Listing 5.27.

Converting Data Types with CAST()

In many situations, your DBMS will convert, or **cast**, data types automatically. It might allow you to use numbers and dates in character expressions such as concatenation, for example, or it will promote numbers automatically in mixed arithmetic expressions (see "Tips for Arithmetic Operations" on page 119). Use the function CAST() to convert an expression of one data type to another data type when your DBMS doesn't perform the conversion automatically. For information about data types, see "Data Types" on page 56. The function's important characteristics are:

- **Implicit conversions** (or **coercions**) are those conversions that occur without specifying CAST(). **Explicit conversions** are those conversions that require CAST() to be specified. In some cases, conversion isn't allowed; you can't convert a FLOAT to a TIMESTAMP, for example.

- The data type being converted is the **source data type**, and the result data type is the **target data type**.

- You can convert any numeric or datetime data type to any character data type.

- You can convert any character data type to any other data type if the character string represents a valid literal value of the target data type. (DBMSs remove leading and trailing spaces when converting strings to numeric or datetime values.)

- Some numeric conversions, such as DECIMAL-to-INTEGER, round or truncate values. (Whether the value is rounded or truncated depends on the DBMS.)

- A VARCHAR-to-CHAR conversion can truncate strings.

- Some conversions can cause an error if the new data type doesn't have enough room to display the converted value. A FLOAT-to-SMALLINT conversion will fail if the floating-point number falls outside the range your DBMS allows for SMALLINT values.

- A NUMERIC-to-DECIMAL conversion can require an explicit cast to prevent the loss of precision or scale that might occur in an implicit conversion.

- In a DATE-to-TIMESTAMP conversion, the time part of the result will be 00:00:00 (midnight).

- If any argument is null, then CAST() returns null. (But see the **Oracle** exception in the DBMS tip in "Tips for Converting Data Types".)

To convert one data type to another:

- Type:

  CAST(*expr* AS *data_type*)

  expr is the expression to convert, and *data_type* is the target data type. *data_type* is one of the data types described in Chapter 3 and can include length, precision, or scale arguments where applicable. Acceptable *data_type* values include CHAR(10), VARCHAR(25), NUMERIC(5,2), INTEGER, FLOAT, and DATE, for example. An error occurs if the data type or value of *expr* is incompatible with *data_type* (Listings 5.28 and 5.29, Figures 5.28a, 5.28b, and 5.29).

```
SELECT
    price
      AS "price(DECIMAL)",
    CAST(price AS INTEGER)
      AS "price(INTEGER)",
    '<' || CAST(price AS CHAR(8)) || '>'
      AS "price(CHAR(8))"
  FROM titles;
```

Listing 5.28 Convert the book prices from the DECIMAL data type to INTEGER and CHAR(8) data types. The < and > characters show the extent of the CHAR(8) strings. Your result will be either Figure 5.28a or 5.28b, depending on whether your DBMS truncates or rounds integers.

price(DECIMAL)	price(INTEGER)	price(CHAR(8))
21.99	21	<21.99 >
19.95	19	<19.95 >
39.95	39	<39.95 >
12.99	12	<12.99 >
6.95	6	<6.95 >
19.95	19	<19.95 >
23.95	23	<23.95 >
10.00	10	<10.00 >
13.95	13	<13.95 >
NULL	NULL	NULL
7.99	7	<7.99 >
12.99	12	<12.99 >
29.99	29	<29.99 >

Figure 5.28a Result of Listing 5.28. You'll get this result if your DBMS *truncates* decimal numbers to convert them to integers.

price(DECIMAL)	price(INTEGER)	price(CHAR(8))
21.99	22	<21.99 >
19.95	20	<19.95 >
39.95	40	<39.95 >
12.99	13	<12.99 >
6.95	7	<6.95 >
19.95	20	<19.95 >
23.95	24	<23.95 >
10.00	10	<10.00 >
13.95	14	<13.95 >
NULL	NULL	NULL
7.99	8	<7.99 >
12.99	13	<12.99 >
29.99	30	<29.99 >

Figure 5.28b Result of Listing 5.28. You'll get this result if your DBMS *rounds* decimal numbers to convert them to integers.

```
SELECT
    CAST(sales AS CHAR(8))
    || ' copies sold of '
    || CAST(title_name AS CHAR(20))
      AS "History and biography sales"
  FROM titles
  WHERE sales IS NOT NULL
    AND type IN ('history', 'biography')
  ORDER BY sales DESC;
```

Listing 5.29 List history and biography book sales with a portion of the book title, sorted by descending sales. The CHAR(20) conversion shortens the title to make the result more readable. See Figure 5.29 for the result.

```
History and biography sales
---------------------------------------------
1500200   copies sold of I Blame My Mother
100001    copies sold of Spontaneous, Not Ann
11320     copies sold of How About Never?
10467     copies sold of What Are The Civilia
9566      copies sold of 200 Years of German
566       copies sold of 1977!
```

Figure 5.29 Result of Listing 5.29.

Tips for Converting Data Types

- You can use CAST() in SELECT, WHERE, and ORDER BY clauses or anywhere an expression is allowed.

- **Widening conversions** are those conversions in which there is no possibility of data loss or incorrect results. SMALLINT-to-INTEGER, for example, is a widening conversion because the INTEGER data type can accommodate every possible value of the SMALLINT data type. The reverse operation, called a **narrowing conversion**, can cause data loss because extreme INTEGER values can't be represented by a SMALLINT. Widening conversions are always allowed, but narrowing conversions can cause your DBMS to issue a warning or error.

- DBMS **Microsoft Access** has a family of type-conversion functions rather than a single CAST() function: CStr(*expr*), CInt(*expr*), and CDec(*expr*) convert *expr* to a string, integer, and decimal number, for example. You can use Space(*number*) to add spaces to strings and Left(*string*, *length*) to truncate strings. Use + to concatenate strings. To run Listings 5.28 and 5.29, change the cast expressions to (Listing 5.28):

  CInt(price)

  '<' + CStr(price) + '>'

  and (Listing 5.29):

  CStr(sales) +
  Space(8 - Len(CStr(sales))) +
  ' copies sold of ' +
  Left(title_name, 20)

  continues on next page

In **Microsoft SQL Server**, use + to concatenate strings (Listing 5.28):

```
'<' + CAST(price AS CHAR(8)) + '>'
```

and (Listing 5.29):

```
CAST(sales AS CHAR(8)) +
' copies sold of ' +
CAST(title_name AS CHAR(20))
```

Oracle doesn't allow character conversions to CHAR(*length*) if *length* is shorter than the source string. Instead, use SUBSTR() to truncate strings; see the DBMS tip in "Tips for Substrings" on page 126. To run Listing 5.29, change the CAST() expression to:

```
CAST(sales AS CHAR(8)) ||
' copies sold of ' ||
SUBSTR(title_name, 1, 20)
```

In **MySQL**, use SIGNED instead of INTEGER for *data_type*, and use CONCAT() to concatenate strings. To run Listings 5.28 and 5.29, change the CAST() expressions to (Listing 5.28):

```
CAST(price AS SIGNED)
```

```
CONCAT('<', CAST(price AS CHAR(8)), '>')
```

and (Listing 5.29):

```
CONCAT(CAST(sales AS CHAR(8)),
' copies sold of ',
CAST(title_name AS CHAR(20)))
```

For cast operations, **Oracle** treats an empty string as a null: CAST('' AS CHAR) returns NULL (not ''). See the DBMS tip in "Tips for Nulls" on page 72.

In older **PostgreSQL** versions, to compare a value in a NUMERIC or DECIMAL column with a real (floating-point) number, you must convert the real number to NUMERIC or DECIMAL explicitly. The following statement, for example, fails in older PostgreSQL versions because the data type of the column *price* is DECIMAL(5,2):

```
SELECT price
  FROM titles
  WHERE price < 20.00;
```

This statement fixes the problem:

```
SELECT price
  FROM titles
  WHERE price < CAST(20.00 AS DECIMAL);
```

DBMSs have additional conversion and formatting functions. Some examples: CONVERT() in **Microsoft SQL Server** and **MySQL**; TO_CHAR(), TO_DATE(), TO_TIMESTAMP(), and TO_NUMBER() in **Oracle** and **PostgreSQL**; and TO_CHAR() and TO_DATE() in **Db2**. Search your DBMS documentation for *conversion*, *cast*, or *formatting functions*.

Evaluating Conditional Values with CASE

The CASE expression and its shorthand equivalents, COALESCE() and NULLIF(), let you take actions based on a condition's truth value (true, false, or unknown). The CASE expression's important characteristics are:

- If you've programmed before, then you'll recognize that CASE provides SQL the equivalent of the *if-then-else*, *case*, or *switch* statements used in procedural languages, except that CASE is an expression, not a statement.

- CASE evaluates several conditions and returns a single value for the first true condition.

- CASE lets you display an alternative value to the actual value in a column. CASE makes no changes to the underlying data.

- A common use of CASE is to replace codes or abbreviations with more-readable values. If the column *marital_status* contains the integer codes 1, 2, 3, or 4—meaning single, married, divorced, or widowed— then your human readers will prefer to see explanatory text rather than cryptic codes. (Some database designers prefer to use codes because it's more efficient to store and manage abbreviated codes than explanatory text.)

- CASE has two formats: simple and searched. The **simple CASE** expression compares an expression to a set of simple expressions to determine the result. The **searched CASE** expression evaluates a set of logical (boolean) expressions to determine the result.

- CASE returns an optional ELSE result as the default value if no test condition is true.

To use a simple CASE expression:

- Type:

```
CASE comparison_value
  WHEN value1 THEN result1
  WHEN value2 THEN result2
  ...
  WHEN valueN THEN resultN
  [ELSE default_result]
END
```

value1, *value2*,…, *valueN* are expressions. *result1*, *result2*,…, *resultN* are expressions returned when the corresponding value matches the expression *comparison_value*. All expressions must be of the same type or must be implicitly convertible to the same type.

Each value is compared to *comparison_value* in order. First, *value1* is compared. If it matches *comparison_value*, then *result1* is returned; otherwise, *value2* is compared to *comparison_value*. If *value2* matches *comparison_value*, then *result2* is returned, and so on. If no matches occur, then *default_result* is returned. If ELSE *default_result* is omitted, then ELSE NULL is assumed (Listing 5.30 and Figure 5.30).

```
SELECT
    title_id,
    type,
    price,
    CASE type
      WHEN 'history'
        THEN price * 1.10
      WHEN 'psychology'
        THEN price * 1.20
      ELSE price
    END
      AS "New price"
FROM titles
ORDER BY type ASC, title_id ASC;
```

Listing 5.30 Raise the price of history books by 10 percent and psychology books by 20 percent, and leave the prices of other books unchanged. See Figure 5.30 for the result.

```
title_id type        price New price
-------- ----------  ----- ---------
T06      biography   19.95     19.95
T07      biography   23.95     23.95
T10      biography    NULL      NULL
T12      biography   12.99     12.99
T08      children    10.00     10.00
T09      children    13.95     13.95
T03      computer    39.95     39.95
T01      history     21.99     24.19
T02      history     19.95     21.95
T13      history     29.99     32.99
T04      psychology  12.99     15.59
T05      psychology   6.95      8.34
T11      psychology   7.99      9.59
```

Figure 5.30 Result of Listing 5.30.

```
SELECT
    title_id,
    CASE
      WHEN sales IS NULL
        THEN 'Unknown'
      WHEN sales <= 1000
        THEN 'Not more than 1,000'
      WHEN sales <= 10000
        THEN 'Between 1,001 and 10,000'
      WHEN sales <= 100000
        THEN 'Between 10,001 and 100,000'
      WHEN sales <= 1000000
        THEN 'Between 100,001 and 1,000,000'
      ELSE 'Over 1,000,000'
    END
      AS "Sales category"
  FROM titles
  ORDER BY sales ASC;
```

Listing 5.31 List the books categorized by different sales ranges, sorted by ascending sales. See Figure 5.31 for the result.

```
title_id Sales category
-------- ----------------------------
T10      Unknown
T01      Not more than 1,000
T08      Between 1,001 and 10,000
T09      Between 1,001 and 10,000
T02      Between 1,001 and 10,000
T13      Between 10,001 and 100,000
T06      Between 10,001 and 100,000
T04      Between 10,001 and 100,000
T03      Between 10,001 and 100,000
T11      Between 10,001 and 100,000
T12      Between 100,001 and 1,000,000
T05      Between 100,001 and 1,000,000
T07      Over 1,000,000
```

Figure 5.31 Result of Listing 5.31.

To use a searched CASE expression:

- Type:

  ```
  CASE
    WHEN condition1 THEN result1
    WHEN condition2 THEN result2
    ...
    WHEN conditionN THEN resultN
    [ELSE default_result]
  END
  ```

  condition1, *condition2*,…, *conditionN* are search conditions. (Search conditions have one or more logical expressions, with multiple expressions linked by AND or OR; see "Filtering Rows with WHERE" on page 89.) *result1*, *result2*,…, *resultN* are expressions returned when the corresponding condition evaluates to true. All expressions must be of the same type or must be implicitly convertible to the same type.

  Each condition is evaluated in order. First, *condition1* is evaluated. If it's true, then *result1* is returned; otherwise, *condition2* is evaluated. If *condition2* is true, then *result2* is returned, and so on. If no conditions are true, then *default_result* is returned. If ELSE *default_result* is omitted, then ELSE NULL is assumed (Listing 5.31 and Figure 5.31).

Tips for CASE

- You can use CASE in SELECT, WHERE, and ORDER BY clauses or anywhere an expression is allowed.

- When a result is returned, CASE may or may not evaluate the expressions in any remaining WHEN clauses, depending on the DBMS. For this reason, you should watch for undesirable side effects, such as the evaluation of any expression resulting in a division-by-zero error.

- This CASE expression can help you prevent division-by-zero errors:

```
CASE
  WHEN n <> 0 THEN expr/n
  ELSE NULL
END
```

- You can use CASE to omit identical function calls.

```
WHERE some_function(col1) = 10
  OR some_function(col1) = 20
```

is equivalent to

```
WHERE 1 =
  CASE some_function(col1)
    WHEN 10 THEN 1
    WHEN 20 THEN 1
  END
```

Some DBMS optimizers will run the CASE form faster.

- The simple CASE expression is just shorthand for this searched CASE expression:

```
CASE
  WHEN comparison_value = value1
    THEN result1
  WHEN comparison_value = value2
    THEN result2
  ...
  WHEN comparison_value = valueN
    THEN resultN
  [ELSE default_result]
END
```

- **DBMS** **Microsoft Access** doesn't support CASE; instead, use the function Switch(*condition1, result1, condition2, result2,...*). To run Listings 5.30 and 5.31, change the CASE expressions to (Listing 5.30):

```
Switch(
type IS NULL, NULL,
type = 'history', price * 1.10,
type = 'psychology', price * 1.20,
type IN ('biography',
'children', 'computer'), price)
```

and (Listing 5.31):

```
Switch(
sales IS NULL,
'Unknown',
sales <= 1000,
'Not more than 1,000',
sales <= 10000,
'Between 1,001 and 10,000',
sales <= 100000,
'Between 10,001 and 100,000',
sales <= 1000000,
'Between 100,001 and 1,000,000',
sales > 1000000, 'Over 1,000,000')
```

Oracle 9i and later will run Listings 5.30 and 5.31. To run Listing 5.30 in Oracle 8i and earlier, translate the simple CASE expression to a searched CASE expression, or use the function DECODE(*comparison_value, value1, result1, value2, result2,..., default_result*):

```
DECODE(type,
NULL, NULL,
'history', price * 1.10,
'psychology', price * 1.20,
price)
```

In older **PostgreSQL** versions, convert the floating-point numbers in Listing 5.30 to DECIMAL; see "Converting Data Types with CAST()" on page 145. To run Listing 5.30, change the new-price calculations in the CASE expression to:

```
price * CAST((1.10) AS DECIMAL)
price * CAST((1.20) AS DECIMAL)
```

Checking for Nulls with COALESCE()

The function COALESCE() returns the first non-null expression among its arguments. COALESCE() often is used to display a specific value instead of a null in a result, which is helpful if your users find nulls confusing. COALESCE() is just shorthand for a common form of the searched CASE expression.

```
COALESCE(expr1, expr2, expr3)
```

is equivalent to:

```
CASE
  WHEN expr1 IS NOT NULL THEN expr1
  WHEN expr2 IS NOT NULL THEN expr2
  ELSE expr3
END
```

To return the first non-null value:

- Type:

  ```
  COALESCE(expr1, expr2,...)
  ```

  expr1, *expr2*,..., represent one or more comma-separated expressions. All expressions must be of the same type or must be implicitly convertible to the same type. Each expression is evaluated in order (left to right) until one evaluates to non-null and is returned. If all the expressions are null, then COALESCE() returns null (Listing 5.32 and Figure 5.32).

Tips for COALESCE

- You can use COALESCE() in SELECT, WHERE, and ORDER BY clauses or anywhere an expression is allowed.

- Be aware that you can get a null from a column that doesn't allow nulls; see Figure 3.3 on page 73, for example.

- **DBMS** **Microsoft Access** doesn't support COALESCE(); instead, use the function Switch(). To run Listing 5.32, change the COALESCE() expression to:

  ```
  Switch(
  state IS NOT NULL, state,
  state IS NULL, 'N/A')
  ```

  Oracle 9i and later will run Listing 5.32. Oracle 8i and earlier don't support COALESCE(); instead, use the function NVL(*expr1*, *expr2*). NVL() takes only two expressions; use CASE for three or more expressions. To run Listing 5.32 in Oracle 8i and earlier, change the COALESCE() expression to:

  ```
  NVL(state, 'N/A')
  ```

```
SELECT
    pub_id,
    city,
    COALESCE(state, 'N/A') AS "state",
    country
  FROM publishers;
```

Listing 5.32 List the publishers' locations. If the state is null, then print N/A. See Figure 5.32 for the result.

```
pub_id city            state country
------ ------------- ----- -------
P01    New York        NY    USA
P02    San Francisco CA    USA
P03    Hamburg         N/A   Germany
P04    Berkeley        CA    USA
```

Figure 5.32 Result of Listing 5.32.

Comparing Expressions with NULLIF()

The function NULLIF() compares two expressions and returns null if they are equal or the first expression otherwise. NULLIF() typically is used to convert a user-defined missing, unknown, or inapplicable value to null.

Rather than use a null, some people prefer to represent a missing value with, say, the number −1 or −99, or the string 'N/A', 'Unknown', or 'Missing'. DBMSs have clear rules for operations that involve nulls, so it's sometimes desirable to convert user-defined missing values to nulls. If you want to calculate the average of the values in a column, for example, then you'd get the wrong answer if you had −1 values intermingled with the real, non-missing values. Instead, you can use NULLIF() to convert the −1 values to nulls, which your DBMS will ignore during calculations.

NULLIF() is just shorthand for a common form of the searched CASE expression.

```
NULLIF(expr1, expr2)
```

is equivalent to:

```
CASE
  WHEN expr1 = expr2 THEN NULL
  ELSE expr1
END
```

Avoiding Division by Zero

Suppose you want to calculate the male–female ratios for various school clubs, but you discover that the following query fails and issues a divide-by-zero error when it tries to calculate *ratio* for the Lord of the Rings Club, which has no women:

```
SELECT
    club_id, males, females,
    males/females AS ratio
  FROM school_clubs;
```

You can use NULLIF to avoid division by zero. Rewrite the query as:

```
SELECT
    club_id, males, females,
    males/NULLIF(females,0) AS ratio
  FROM school_clubs;
```

Any number divided by NULL gives NULL, and no error is generated.

```
SELECT
    title_id,
    contract,
    NULLIF(contract, 0) AS "Null contract"
  FROM titles;
```

Listing 5.33 In the table *titles*, the column contract *contains* zero if no book contract exists. This query changes the value zero to null. Nonzero values aren't affected. See Figure 5.33 for the result.

```
title_id contract Null contract
-------- -------- -------------
T01            1             1
T02            1             1
T03            1             1
T04            1             1
T05            1             1
T06            1             1
T07            1             1
T08            1             1
T09            1             1
T10            0          NULL
T11            1             1
T12            1             1
T13            1             1
```

Figure 5.33 Result of Listing 5.33.

To return a null if two expressions are equivalent:

- Type:

  NULLIF(*expr1, expr2*)

  expr1 and *expr2* are expressions. NULLIF() compares *expr1* and *expr2*. If they are equal, then the function returns null. If they're unequal, then the function returns *expr1*. You can't specify the literal NULL for *expr1* (Listing 5.33 and Figure 5.33).

Tips for NULLIF

- You can use NULLIF() in SELECT, WHERE, and ORDER BY clauses or anywhere an expression is allowed.

- **DBMS** **Microsoft Access** doesn't support NULLIF(); instead, use the expression iif(*expr1* = *expr2*, NULL, *expr1*). To run Listing 5.33, change the NULLIF() expression to:

  iif(contract = 0, NULL, contract)

  Oracle 9i and later will run Listing 5.33. Oracle 8i and earlier don't support NULLIF(); instead, use CASE. To run Listing 5.33 in Oracle 8i and earlier, change the NULLIF() expression to:

  ```
  CASE
    WHEN contract = 0 THEN NULL
    ELSE contract
  END
  ```

CHAPTER 6

Summarizing and Grouping Data

The preceding chapter described **scalar functions**, which operate on individual row values. This chapter introduces SQL's **aggregate functions**, or **set functions**, which operate on a group of values to produce a single, summarizing value. You apply an aggregate to a set of rows, which can be:

- All the rows in a table

- Only those rows specified by a WHERE clause

- Those rows created by a GROUP BY clause

A GROUP BY clause, which groups rows, often is used with a HAVING clause, which filters groups. No matter how many rows the input set contains, an aggregate function returns a single statistic: a sum, minimum, or average, for example.

The main difference between queries with and without aggregate functions is that nonaggregate queries process the rows one by one. Each row is processed independently and put into the result. (ORDER BY and DISTINCT make the DBMS look at all the rows, but they're essentially postprocessing operations.) Aggregate queries do something completely different: they take a table as a whole and construct new rows from it.

Using Aggregate Functions

Table 6.1 lists SQL's standard aggregate functions. The important characteristics of the aggregate functions are:

- In Table 6.1, the expression *expr* often is a column name, but it also can be a literal, function, or any combination of chained or nested column names, literals, and functions.

- SUM() and AVG() work with only numeric data types. MIN() and MAX() work with character, numeric, and datetime data types. COUNT(*expr*) and COUNT(*) work with all data types.

- All aggregate functions except COUNT(*) ignore nulls. (You can use COALESCE() in an aggregate function argument to substitute a value for a null; see "Checking for Nulls with COALESCE()" on page 153.)

- COUNT(*expr*) and COUNT(*) never return null but return either a positive integer or zero. The other aggregate functions return null if the set contains no rows or contains rows with only nulls.

- Default column headings for aggregate expressions vary by DBMS; use AS to name the result column. See "Creating Column Aliases with AS" on page 79.

Tips for Aggregate Functions

- [DBMS] DBMSs provide additional aggregate functions to calculate other statistics, such as the standard deviation; search your DBMS documentation for *aggregate functions* or *group functions*.

Table 6.1 Aggregate Functions

Function	Returns
MIN(*expr*)	Minimum value in *expr*
MAX(*expr*)	Maximum value in *expr*
SUM(*expr*)	Sum of the values in *expr*
AVG(*expr*)	Average (arithmetic mean) of the values in *expr*
COUNT(*expr*)	The number of non-null values in *expr*
COUNT(*)	The number of rows in a table or set

Creating Aggregate Expressions

Aggregate functions can be tricky to use. This section explains what's legal and what's not.

- An aggregate expression *can't* appear in a WHERE clause. If you want to find the title of the book with the highest sales, then you *can't* use:

```
SELECT title_id
  FROM titles
  WHERE sales = MAX(sales);   --Illegal
```

- You *can't* mix nonaggregate (row-by-row) and aggregate expressions in a SELECT clause. A SELECT clause must contain either all nonaggregate expressions or all aggregate expressions. If you want to find the title of the book with the highest sales, then you *can't* use:

```
SELECT title_id, MAX(sales)
  FROM titles;                --Illegal
```

The one exception to this rule is that you *can* mix nonaggregate and aggregate expressions for grouping columns (see "Grouping Rows with GROUP BY" on page 169):

```
SELECT type, SUM(sales)
  FROM titles
  GROUP BY type;              --Legal
```

- You *can* use more than one aggregate expression in a SELECT clause:

```
SELECT MIN(sales), MAX(sales)
  FROM titles;                --Legal
```

- You *can't* nest aggregate functions:

```
SELECT SUM(AVG(sales))
  FROM titles;                --Illegal
```

- You *can* use aggregate expressions in subqueries (see Chapter 8). This statement finds the title of the book with the highest sales:

```
SELECT title_id, price        --Legal
  FROM titles
  WHERE sales =
    (SELECT MAX(sales) FROM titles);
```

- You *can't* use subqueries in aggregate expressions:

```
AVG(SELECT price FROM titles)  --Illegal
```

Tips for Aggregate Expressions

- DBMS **Oracle** lets you nest aggregate expressions in GROUP BY queries. The following example calculates the average of the maximum sales of all book types. Oracle evaluates the inner aggregate MAX(sales) for the grouping column type and then aggregates the results again:

```
SELECT AVG(MAX(sales))
  FROM titles
  GROUP BY type;      --Legal in Oracle
```

To replicate this query in standard SQL, use a subquery in the FROM clause:

```
SELECT AVG(s.max_sales)
  FROM (SELECT MAX(sales) AS max_sales
          FROM titles
          GROUP BY type) s;
```

Finding a Minimum with MIN()

Use the aggregate function MIN() to find the minimum of a set of values.

To find the minimum of a set of values:

- Type:

  MIN(*expr*)

  expr is a column name, literal, or expression. The result has the same data type as *expr*.

  Listing 6.1 and Figure 6.1 show some queries that involve MIN(). The first query returns the price of the lowest-priced book. The second query returns the earliest publication date. The third query returns the number of pages in the shortest history book.

Tips for MIN

- MIN() works with character, numeric, and date-time data types.

- With character data columns, MIN() finds the value that is lowest in the sort sequence; see "Sorting Rows with ORDER BY" on page 83.

- DISTINCT isn't meaningful with MIN(); see "Aggregating Distinct Values with DISTINCT" on page 166.

- **DBMS** String comparisons are case insensitive or case sensitive, depending on your DBMS; see the DBMS tip in "Tips for WHERE" on page 91.

  When comparing two VARCHAR strings for equality, your DBMS might right-pad the shorter string with spaces and compare the strings position by position. In this case, the strings 'John' and 'John ' are equal. Refer to your DBMS documentation (or experiment) to determine which string MIN() returns.

```
SELECT MIN(price) AS "Min price"
  FROM titles;

SELECT MIN(pubdate) AS "Earliest pubdate"
  FROM titles;

SELECT MIN(pages) AS "Min history pages"
  FROM titles
  WHERE type = 'history';
```

Listing 6.1 Some MIN() queries. See Figure 6.1 for the result.

```
Min price
---------
     6.95


Earliest pubdate
----------------
1998-04-01


Min history pages
-----------------
               14
```

Figure 6.1 Result of Listing 6.1.

```
SELECT MAX(au_lname) AS "Max last name"
  FROM authors;

SELECT
    MIN(price) AS "Min price",
    MAX(price) AS "Max price",
    MAX(price) - MIN(price) AS "Range"
  FROM titles;

SELECT MAX(price * sales)
        AS "Max history revenue"
  FROM titles
  WHERE type = 'history';
```

Listing 6.2 Some MAX() queries. See Figure 6.2 for the result.

```
Max last name
-------------
O'Furniture

Min price Max price Range
--------- --------- -----
     6.95     39.95 33.00

Max history revenue
-------------------
         313905.33
```

Figure 6.2 Result of Listing 6.2.

Finding a Maximum with MAX()

Use the aggregate function MAX() to find the maximum of a set of values.

To find the maximum of a set of values:

*   Type:

    MAX(*expr*)

    expr is a column name, literal, or expression. The result has the same data type as *expr*.

Listing 6.2 and Figure 6.2 show some queries that involve MAX(). The first query returns the author's last name that is last alphabetically. The second query returns the prices of the cheapest and most expensive books, as well as the price range. The third query returns the highest revenue (= price × sales) among the history books.

Tips for MAX

*   MAX() works with character, numeric, and datetime data types.

*   With character data columns, MAX() finds the value that is highest in the sort sequence; see "Sorting Rows with ORDER BY" on page 83.

*   DISTINCT isn't meaningful with MAX(); see "Aggregating Distinct Values with DISTINCT" on page 166.

*   **DBMS** String comparisons are case insensitive or case sensitive, depending on your DBMS; see the DBMS tip in "Tips for WHERE" on page 91.

    When comparing two VARCHAR strings for equality, your DBMS might right-pad the shorter string with spaces and compare the strings position by position. In this case, the strings 'John' and 'John ' are equal. Refer to your DBMS documentation (or experiment) to determine which string MAX() returns.

Calculating a Sum with SUM()

Use the aggregate function SUM() to find the sum (total) of a set of values.

To calculate the sum of a set of values:

* Type:

  SUM(*expr*)

  expr is a column name, literal, or numeric expression. The result's data type is at least as precise as the most precise data type used in *expr*.

Listing 6.3 and Figure 6.3 show some queries that involve SUM(). The first query returns the total advances paid to all authors. The second query returns the total sales of books published in 2000. The third query returns the total price, sales, and revenue (= price × sales) of all books. Note a mathematical rule in action here: "The sum of the products doesn't (necessarily) equal the product of the sums."

Tips for SUM

* SUM() works with only numeric data types.

* The sum of no rows is null—not zero, as you might expect.

* ┌─────────┐
  │ **DBMS** │ In **Microsoft Access** date literals, omit
  └─────────┘ the DATE keyword and surround the
  literal with # characters instead of quotes. To run Listing 6.3, change the date literals in the second query to #2000-01-01# and #2000-12-31#.

  In **Microsoft SQL Server** and **Db2** date literals, omit the DATE keyword. To run Listing 6.3, change the date literals to '2000-01-01' and '2000-12-31'.

```
SELECT
    SUM(advance) AS "Total advances"
  FROM royalties;

SELECT
    SUM(sales)
      AS "Total sales (2000 books)"
  FROM titles
  WHERE pubdate
    BETWEEN DATE '2000-01-01'
        AND DATE '2000-12-31';

SELECT
    SUM(price) AS "Total price",
    SUM(sales) AS "Total sales",
    SUM(price * sales) AS "Total revenue"
  FROM titles;
```

Listing 6.3 Some SUM() queries. See Figure 6.3 for the result.

```
Total advances
--------------
   1336000.00


Total sales (2000 books)
------------------------
                  231677


Total price Total sales Total revenue
----------- ----------- -------------
     220.65     1975446   41428860.77
```

Figure 6.3 Result of Listing 6.3.

```
SELECT
    AVG(price * 2) AS "AVG(price * 2)"
  FROM titles;

SELECT
    AVG(sales) AS "AVG(sales)",
    SUM(sales) AS "SUM(sales)"
  FROM titles
  WHERE type = 'business';

SELECT title_id, sales
  FROM titles
  WHERE sales >
        (SELECT AVG(sales) FROM titles)
  ORDER BY sales DESC;
```

Listing 6.4 Some AVG() queries. See Figure 6.4 for the result.

```
AVG(price * 2)
--------------
     36.775000

AVG(sales) SUM(sales)
---------- ----------
NULL       NULL

title_id sales
-------- -------
T07       1500200
T05        201440
```

Figure 6.4 Result of Listing 6.4.

Calculating an Average with AVG()

Use the aggregate function AVG() to find the average, or arithmetic mean, of a set of values. The **arithmetic mean** is the sum of a set of quantities divided by the number of quantities in the set.

To calculate the average of a set of values:

*   Type:

    AVG(*expr*)

    expr is a column name, literal, or numeric expression. The result's data type is at least as precise as the most precise data type used in *expr*.

Listing 6.4 and Figure 6.4 shows some queries that involve AVG(). The first query returns the average price of all books if prices were doubled. The second query returns the average and total sales for business books; both calculations are null (not zero) because the table contains no business books. The third query uses a subquery (see Chapter 8) to list the books with above-average sales.

Tips for AVG

*   AVG() works with only numeric data types.

*   The average of no rows is null—not zero, as you might expect.

*   If you've used, say, 0 or −1 instead of null to represent missing values, then the inclusion of those numbers in AVG() calculations yields an incorrect result. Use NULLIF() to convert the missing-value numbers to nulls so they'll be excluded from calculations; see "Comparing Expressions with NULLIF()" on page 154.

*   DBMS **MySQL** 4.0 and earlier lack subquery support and won't run the third query in Listing 6.4.

Aggregating and Nulls

Aggregate functions (except COUNT(*)) ignore nulls. If an aggregation requires that you account for nulls, then you can replace each null with a specified value by using COALESCE() (see "Checking for Nulls with COALESCE()" on page 153). For example, the following query returns the average sales of biographies by including nulls (replaced by zeroes) in the calculation:

```
SELECT AVG(COALESCE(sales,0)) AS AvgSales
  FROM titles
  WHERE type = 'biography';
```

Statistics in SQL

SQL isn't a statistical programming language, but you can use built-in functions and a few tricks to calculate simple descriptive statistics such as the sum, mean, and standard deviation. For more-sophisticated analyses you should use your DBMS's statistics, data science, or machine learning components or export your data to a dedicated statistical environment such as Excel, R, Python, SAS, or SPSS.

What you should *not* do is write statistical routines yourself in SQL or a host language. Implementing statistical algorithms correctly—even simple ones—means understanding trade-offs in efficiency (the space needed for arithmetic operations), stability (cancellation of significant digits), and accuracy (handling pathologic sets of values). See, for example, Ronald Thisted's *Elements of Statistical Computing* or John Monahan's *Numerical Methods of Statistics*.

You *can* get away with using small combinations of built-in SQL functions, such as STDEV()/(SQRT(COUNT()) for the standard error of the mean, but don't use complex SQL expressions for correlations, regression, ANOVA (analysis of variance), or matrix arithmetic, for example. Check your DBMS's documentation to see which functions and packages it offers. Built-in functions aren't portable, but they run far faster and more accurately than equivalent query expressions.

The functions MIN() and MAX() calculate **order statistics**, which are values derived from a dataset that's been sorted (ordered) by size. Well-known order statistics include the trimmed mean, rank, range, mode, and median. Chapter 15 covers the trimmed mean, rank, and median. The **range** is the difference between the largest and smallest values: MAX(*expr*)−MIN(*expr*). The **mode** is the value that appears most frequently. A dataset can have more than one mode. The mode is a weak descriptive statistic because it's not **robust**, meaning that it can be affected by adding a small number or unusual or incorrect values to the dataset. This query finds the mode of book prices in the sample database:

```
SELECT price, COUNT(*) AS frequency
  FROM titles
  GROUP BY price
  HAVING COUNT(*) >= ALL(SELECT COUNT(*) FROM titles GROUP BY price);
```

price has two modes:

price	frequency
12.99	2
19.95	2

```
SELECT
    COUNT(title_id) AS "COUNT(title_id)",
    COUNT(price) AS "COUNT(price)",
    COUNT(*) AS "COUNT(*)"
  FROM titles;

SELECT
    COUNT(title_id) AS "COUNT(title_id)",
    COUNT(price) AS "COUNT(price)",
    COUNT(*) AS "COUNT(*)"
  FROM titles
  WHERE price IS NOT NULL;

SELECT
    COUNT(title_id) AS "COUNT(title_id)",
    COUNT(price) AS "COUNT(price)",
    COUNT(*) AS "COUNT(*)"
  FROM titles
  WHERE price IS NULL;
```

Listing 6.5 Some COUNT() queries. See Figure 6.5 for the result.

```
COUNT(title_id)  COUNT(price)  COUNT(*)
---------------  ------------  --------
             13            12        13

COUNT(title_id)  COUNT(price)  COUNT(*)
---------------  ------------  --------
             12            12        12

COUNT(title_id)  COUNT(price)  COUNT(*)
---------------  ------------  --------
              1             0         1
```

Figure 6.5 Result of Listing 6.5.

Counting Rows with COUNT()

Use the aggregate function COUNT() to count the number of rows in a set of values. COUNT() has two forms:

- COUNT(*expr*) returns the number of rows in which *expr* is not null.

- COUNT(*) returns the count of all rows in a set, including nulls and duplicates.

To count non-null rows:

- Type:

  COUNT(*expr*)

  expr is a column name, literal, or expression. The result is an integer greater than or equal to zero.

To count all rows, including nulls:

- Type:

  COUNT(*)

  The result is an integer greater than or equal to zero.

Listing 6.5 and Figure 6.5 show some queries that involve COUNT(*expr*) and COUNT(*). The three queries count rows in the table *titles* and are identical except for the WHERE clause. The row counts in the first query differ because the column *price* contains a null. In the second query, the row counts are identical because the WHERE clause eliminates the row with the null price before the count. The third query shows the row-count differences between the results of the first two queries.

Tips for COUNT

- COUNT(*expr*) and COUNT(*) work with all data types and never return null.

- DISTINCT isn't meaningful with COUNT(*); see "Aggregating Distinct Values with DISTINCT" on page 166.

- COUNT(*) - COUNT(*expr*) returns the number of nulls, and ((COUNT(*) - COUNT(*expr*))*100)/ COUNT(*) returns the percentage of nulls.

Aggregating Distinct Values with DISTINCT

You can use DISTINCT to eliminate duplicate values in aggregate function calculations; see "Eliminating Duplicate Rows with DISTINCT" on page 81. The general syntax of an aggregate function is:

agg_func([ALL | DISTINCT] *expr*)

agg_func is MIN, MAX, SUM, AVG, or COUNT. *expr* is a column name, literal, or expression. ALL applies the aggregate function to all values, and DISTINCT specifies that each unique value is considered. ALL is the default and is usually omitted in practice.

With SUM(), AVG(), and COUNT(*expr*), DISTINCT eliminates duplicate values before the sum, average, or count is calculated. DISTINCT isn't meaningful with MIN() and MAX(); you can use it, but it won't change the result. You can't use DISTINCT with COUNT(*).

To calculate the sum of a set of distinct values:

* Type:

  SUM(DISTINCT *expr*)

  expr is a column name, literal, or numeric expression. The result's data type is at least as precise as the most precise data type used in *expr*.

To calculate the average of a set of distinct values:

* Type:

  AVG(DISTINCT *expr*)

  expr is a column name, literal, or numeric expression. The result's data type is at least as precise as the most precise data type used in *expr*.

To count distinct non-null rows:

* Type:

  COUNT(DISTINCT *expr*)

  expr is a column name, literal, or expression. The result is an integer greater than or equal to zero.

The queries in Listing 6.6 return the count, sum, and average of book prices. The non-DISTINCT and DISTINCT results in Figure 6.6 differ because the DISTINCT results eliminate the duplicates of prices $12.99 and $19.95 from calculations.

```
SELECT
    COUNT(*) AS "COUNT(*)"
  FROM titles;

SELECT
    COUNT(price) AS "COUNT(price)",
    SUM(price)   AS "SUM(price)",
    AVG(price)   AS "AVG(price)"
  FROM titles;

SELECT
    COUNT(DISTINCT price)
      AS "COUNT(DISTINCT)",
    SUM(DISTINCT price)
      AS "SUM(DISTINCT)",
    AVG(DISTINCT price)
      AS "AVG(DISTINCT)"
  FROM titles;
```

Listing 6.6 Some DISTINCT aggregate queries. See Figure 6.6 for the result.

```
COUNT(*)
--------
      13

COUNT(price) SUM(price) AVG(price)
------------ ---------- ----------
          12     220.65    18.3875

COUNT(DISTINCT) SUM(DISTINCT) AVG(DISTINCT)
--------------- ------------- -------------
             10        187.71       18.7710
```

Figure 6.6 Result of Listing 6.6.

```
SELECT
    COUNT(au_id)
        AS "COUNT(au_id)"
  FROM title_authors;

SELECT
    DISTINCT COUNT(au_id)
        AS "DISTINCT COUNT(au_id)"
  FROM title_authors;

SELECT
    COUNT(DISTINCT au_id)
        AS "COUNT(DISTINCT au_id)"
  FROM title_authors;
```

Listing 6.7 DISTINCT in a SELECT clause and DISTINCT in an aggregate function differ in meaning. See Figure 6.7 for the result.

```
COUNT(au_id)
------------
          17

DISTINCT COUNT(au_id)
---------------------
                   17

COUNT(DISTINCT au_id)
---------------------
                    6
```

Figure 6.7 Result of Listing 6.7.

DISTINCT in a SELECT clause (Chapter 4) and DISTINCT in an aggregate function don't return the same result.

The three queries in Listing 6.7 count the author IDs in the table *title_authors*. Figure 6.7 shows the results. The first query counts all the author IDs in the table. The second query returns the same result as the first query because COUNT() already has done its work and returned a value in a single row before DISTINCT is applied. In the third query, DISTINCT is applied to the author IDs before COUNT() starts counting.

Mixing non-DISTINCT and DISTINCT aggregates in the same SELECT clause can produce misleading results.

The four queries in Listing 6.8 show the four combinations of non-DISTINCT and DISTINCT sums and counts. Of the four results in Figure 6.8, only the first result (no DISTINCTs) and final result (all DISTINCTs) are consistent mathematically, which you can verify with AVG(price) and AVG(DISTINCT price). In the second and third queries (mixed non-DISTINCTs and DISTINCTs), you can't calculate a valid average by dividing the sum by the count.

Tips for DISTINCT

• The ratio COUNT(DISTINCT)/COUNT() tells you how repetitive a set of values is. A ratio of one or close to it means that the set contains many unique values. The closer the ratio is to zero, the more repeats the set has.

• **DBMS** **Microsoft Access** doesn't support DISTINCT aggregate functions. This statement, for example, is illegal in Access:

```
SELECT SUM(DISTINCT price)
  FROM titles;      --Illegal in Access
```

But you can replicate it with this subquery (see "Using Subqueries as Column Expressions" on page 256):

```
SELECT SUM(price)
  FROM (SELECT DISTINCT price
          FROM titles);
```

This Access workaround won't let you mix non-DISTINCT and DISTINCT aggregates, however, as in the second and third queries in Listing 6.8.

MySQL 4.1 and earlier support COUNT(DISTINCT *expr*) but not SUM(DISTINCT *expr*) and AVG(DISTINCT *expr*) and so won't run Listings 6.6 and 6.8. MySQL 5.0 and later support all DISTINCT aggregates.

```
SELECT
    COUNT(price)
      AS "COUNT(price)",
    SUM(price)
      AS "SUM(price)"
  FROM titles;


SELECT
    COUNT(price)
      AS "COUNT(price)",
    SUM(DISTINCT price)
      AS "SUM(DISTINCT price)"
  FROM titles;


SELECT
    COUNT(DISTINCT price)
      AS "COUNT(DISTINCT price)",
    SUM(price)
      AS "SUM(price)"
  FROM titles;


SELECT
    COUNT(DISTINCT price)
      AS "COUNT(DISTINCT price)",
    SUM(DISTINCT price)
      AS "SUM(DISTINCT price)"
  FROM titles;
```

Listing 6.8 Combining non-DISTINCT and DISTINCT aggregates gives inconsistent results. See Figure 6.8 for the result.

```
COUNT(price) SUM(price)
------------ ----------
          12     220.65


COUNT(price) SUM(DISTINCT price)
------------ -------------------
          12              187.71


COUNT(DISTINCT price) SUM(price)
--------------------- ----------
                   10     220.65


COUNT(DISTINCT price) SUM(DISTINCT price)
--------------------- -------------------
                   10              187.71
```

Figure 6.8 Result of Listing 6.8. The differences in the counts and sums indicate duplicate prices. Averages (sum/count) obtained from the second (187.71/12) or third query (220.65/10) are incorrect. The first (220.65/12) and fourth (187.71/10) queries produce consistent averages.

```
SELECT
    au_id,
    COUNT(*) AS "num_books"
  FROM title_authors
  GROUP BY au_id;
```

Listing 6.9 List the number of books each author wrote (or cowrote). See Figure 6.9 for the result.

```
au_id  num_books
-----  ---------
A01            3
A02            4
A03            2
A04            4
A05            1
A06            3
```

Figure 6.9 Result of Listing 6.9.

Grouping Rows with GROUP BY

To this point, I've used aggregate functions to summarize all the values in a column or just those values that matched a WHERE search condition. You can use the GROUP BY clause to divide a table into logical **groups** (categories) and calculate aggregate statistics for each group.

An example will clarify the concept. Listing 6.9 uses GROUP BY to count the number of books that each author wrote (or cowrote). In the SELECT clause, the column *au_id* identifies each author, and the derived column *num_books* counts each author's books. The GROUP BY clause causes *num_books* to be calculated for every unique *au_id* instead of only once for the entire table. Figure 6.9 shows the result. In this example, *au_id* is called the **grouping column**.

The GROUP BY clause's important characteristics are:

- The GROUP BY clause comes after the WHERE clause and before the ORDER BY clause.

- Grouping columns can be column names or derived columns.

- No columns from the input table can appear in an aggregate query's SELECT clause unless they're also included in the GROUP BY clause. A column has (or can have) different values in different rows, so there's no way to decide which of these values to include in the result if you're generating a single new row from the table as a whole. The following statement is illegal because GROUP BY returns only one row for each value of *type*; the query can't return the multiple values of *pub_id* that are associated with each value of *type*:

```
SELECT type, pub_id, COUNT(*)
  FROM titles
  GROUP BY type;              --Illegal
```

- If the SELECT clause contains a complex non-aggregate expression (more than just a simple column name), then the GROUP BY expression must match the SELECT expression exactly.

- To nest groups, specify multiple, comma-separated grouping columns in the GROUP BY clause. Data are summarized at the final specified group.

- If a grouping column contains a null, then that row becomes a group in the result. If a grouping column contains more than one null, then the nulls are put into a single group. A group that contains multiple nulls doesn't imply that the nulls equal one another.

- To eliminate rows before grouping occurs, use a WHERE clause in a query containing a GROUP BY clause.

- You can't use a column alias (page 79) in the GROUP BY clause, although table aliases are allowed as qualifiers; see "Creating Table Aliases with AS" on page 182.

- Without an ORDER BY clause, groups returned by GROUP BY aren't in any particular order. To sort the result of Listing 6.9 by the descending number of books, for example, add the clause ORDER BY "num_books" DESC.

To group rows:

- Type:

```
SELECT columns
  FROM table
  [WHERE search_condition]
  GROUP BY grouping_columns
  [HAVING search_condition]
  [ORDER BY sort_columns];
```

columns and grouping_columns are one or more comma-separated column names, and table is the name of the table that contains columns and grouping_columns. The nonaggregate columns that appear in columns also must appear in grouping_columns. The order of the column names in grouping_columns determines the grouping levels, from the highest to the lowest level of grouping.

The GROUP BY clause restricts the rows of the result; only one row appears for each distinct value in the grouping column or columns. Each row in the result contains summary data related to the specific value in its grouping columns.

If the statement includes a WHERE clause, then the DBMS groups values after it applies search_condition to the rows in table. If the statement includes an ORDER BY clause, then the columns in sort_columns must be drawn from those in columns. The WHERE and ORDER BY clauses are covered in "Filtering Rows with WHERE" on page 89 and "Sorting Rows with ORDER BY" on page 83. HAVING, which filters grouped rows, is covered in the next section.

Listing 6.10 and Figure 6.10 show the difference between COUNT(*expr*) and COUNT(*) in a query that contains GROUP BY. The table *publishers* contains one null in the column *state* (for publisher P03 in Germany). Recall from "Counting Rows with COUNT()" on page 165 that COUNT(*expr*) counts non-null values and COUNT(*) counts all values, including nulls. In the result, GROUP BY recognizes the null and creates a null group for it. COUNT(*) finds (and counts) the one null in the column *state*. But COUNT(state) contains a zero for the null group because COUNT(state) finds only a null in the null group, which it excludes from the count—that's why you have the zero.

If a nonaggregate column contains nulls, then using COUNT(*) rather than COUNT(*expr*) can produce misleading results. Listing 6.11 and Figure 6.11 show summary sales statistics for each type of book. The sales value for one of the biographies is null, so COUNT(sales) and COUNT(*) differ by 1. The average calculation in the fifth column, SUM/COUNT(sales), is consistent mathematically, whereas the sixth-column average, SUM/COUNT(*), is not. I've verified the inconsistency with AVG(sales) in the final column. (Recall a similar situation in Listing 6.8 in "Aggregating Distinct Values with DISTINCT" on page 166.)

```
SELECT
    state,
    COUNT(state) AS "COUNT(state)",
    COUNT(*)     AS "COUNT(*)"
 FROM publishers
 GROUP BY state;
```

Listing 6.10 This query illustrates the difference between COUNT(*expr*) and COUNT(*) in a GROUP BY query. See Figure 6.10 for the result.

```
state COUNT(state) COUNT(*)
----- ------------ --------
NULL            0        1
CA              2        2
NY              1        1
```

Figure 6.10 Result of Listing 6.10.

```
SELECT
    type,
    SUM(sales)   AS "SUM(sales)",
    COUNT(sales) AS "COUNT(sales)",
    COUNT(*)     AS "COUNT(*)",
    SUM(sales)/COUNT(sales)
      AS "SUM/COUNT(sales)",
    SUM(sales)/COUNT(*)
      AS "SUM/COUNT(*)",
    AVG(sales)   AS "AVG(sales)"
 FROM titles
 GROUP BY type;
```

Listing 6.11 For mathematically consistent results, use COUNT(*expr*), rather than COUNT(*), if *expr* contains nulls. See Figure 6.11 for the result.

type	SUM(sales)	COUNT(sales)	COUNT(*)	SUM/COUNT(sales)	SUM/COUNT(*)	AVG(sales)
biography	1611521	3	4	537173.67	402880.25	537173.67
children	9095	2	2	4547.50	4547.50	4547.50
computer	25667	1	1	25667.00	25667.00	25667.00
history	20599	3	3	6866.33	6866.33	6866.33
psychology	308564	3	3	102854.67	102854.67	102854.67

Figure 6.11 Result of Listing 6.11.

Listing 6.12 and Figure 6.12 show a simple GROUP BY query that calculates the total sales, average sales, and number of titles for each type of book. In Listing 6.13 and Figure 6.13, I've added a WHERE clause to eliminate books priced less than $13 before grouping. I've also added an ORDER BY clause to sort the result by descending total sales of each book type.

Listing 6.14 and Figure 6.14 use multiple grouping columns to count the number of titles of each type that each publisher publishes.

In Listing 6.15 and Figure 6.15, I revisit Listing 5.31 in "Evaluating Conditional Values with CASE" on page 149. But instead of listing each book categorized by its sales range, I use GROUP BY to list the number of books in each sales range.

```
SELECT
    type,
    SUM(sales)   AS "SUM(sales)",
    AVG(sales)   AS "AVG(sales)",
    COUNT(sales) AS "COUNT(sales)"
  FROM titles
  GROUP BY type;
```

Listing 6.12 This simple GROUP BY query calculates a few summary statistics for each type of book. See Figure 6.12 for the result.

```
TYPE        SUM(sales) AVG(sales) COUNT(sales)
----------  ---------- ---------- ------------
biography    1611521   537173.67            3
children        9095     4547.50            2
computer       25667    25667.00            1
history        20599     6866.33            3
psychology    308564   102854.67            3
```

Figure 6.12 Result of Listing 6.12.

```
SELECT
    type,
    SUM(sales)   AS "SUM(sales)",
    AVG(sales)   AS "AVG(sales)",
    COUNT(sales) AS "COUNT(sales)"
  FROM titles
  WHERE price >= 13
  GROUP BY type
  ORDER BY "SUM(sales)" DESC;
```

Listing 6.13 Here, I've added WHERE and ORDER BY clauses to Listing 6.12 to cull books priced less than $13 and sort the result by descending total sales. See Figure 6.13 for the result.

```
type        SUM(sales) AVG(sales) COUNT(sales)
----------  ---------- ---------- ------------
biography    1511520   755760.00            2
computer       25667    25667.00            1
history        20599     6866.33            3
children        5000     5000.00            1
```

Figure 6.13 Result of Listing 6.13.

```
SELECT
    pub_id,
    type,
    COUNT(*) AS "COUNT(*)"
  FROM titles
  GROUP BY pub_id, type
  ORDER BY pub_id ASC, "COUNT(*)" DESC;
```

Listing 6.14 List the number of books of each type for each publisher, sorted by descending count within ascending publisher ID. See Figure 6.14 for the result.

```
pub_id  type        COUNT(*)
------  ----------  --------
P01     biography          3
P01     history            1
P02     computer           1
P03     history            2
P03     biography          1
P04     psychology         3
P04     children           2
```

Figure 6.14 Result of Listing 6.14.

```
SELECT
    CASE
      WHEN sales IS NULL
        THEN 'Unknown'
      WHEN sales <= 1000
        THEN 'Not more than 1,000'
      WHEN sales <= 10000
        THEN 'Between 1,001 and 10,000'
      WHEN sales <= 100000
        THEN 'Between 10,001 and 100,000'
      WHEN sales <= 1000000
        THEN 'Between 100,001 and 1,000,000'
      ELSE 'Over 1,000,000'
    END
      AS "Sales category",
    COUNT(*) AS "Num titles"
  FROM titles
  GROUP BY
    CASE
      WHEN sales IS NULL
        THEN 'Unknown'
      WHEN sales <= 1000
        THEN 'Not more than 1,000'
      WHEN sales <= 10000
        THEN 'Between 1,001 and 10,000'
      WHEN sales <= 100000
        THEN 'Between 10,001 and 100,000'
      WHEN sales <= 1000000
        THEN 'Between 100,001 and 1,000,000'
      ELSE 'Over 1,000,000'
    END
  ORDER BY MIN(sales) ASC;
```

Listing 6.15 List the number of books in each calculated sales range, sorted by ascending sales. See Figure 6.15 for the result.

```
Sales category                  Num titles
------------------------------  ----------
Unknown                                  1
Not more than 1,000                      1
Between 1,001 and 10,000                 3
Between 10,001 and 100,000               5
Between 100,001 and 1,000,000            2
Over 1,000,000                           1
```

Figure 6.15 Result of Listing 6.15.

When used without an aggregate function, GROUP BY acts like DISTINCT (Listing 6.16 and Figure 6.16). For information about DISTINCT, see "Eliminating Duplicate Rows with DISTINCT" on page 81.

You can use GROUP BY to look for patterns in your data. In Listing 6.17 and Figure 6.17, I'm looking for a relationship between price categories and average sales.

```
SELECT type
  FROM titles
  GROUP BY type;

SELECT DISTINCT type
  FROM titles;
```

Listing 6.16 Both of these queries return the same result. The bottom form is preferred. See Figure 6.16 for the result.

```
type
----------
biography
children
computer
history
psychology
```

Figure 6.16 Either statement in Listing 6.16 returns this result.

```
SELECT price, AVG(sales) AS "AVG(sales)"
  FROM titles
  WHERE price IS NOT NULL
  GROUP BY price
  ORDER BY price ASC;
```

Listing 6.17 List the average sales for each price, sorted by ascending price. See Figure 6.17 for the result.

```
price    AVG(sales)
-------  ----------
  6.95    201440.0
  7.99     94123.0
 10.00      4095.0
 12.99     56501.0
 13.95      5000.0
 19.95     10443.0
 21.99       566.0
 23.95   1500200.0
 29.99     10467.0
 39.95     25667.0
```

Figure 6.17 Result of Listing 6.17. Ignoring the statistical outlier at $23.95, a weak inverse relationship between price and sales is apparent.

Categorizing Numeric Values

You can use the function FLOOR(*x*) to categorize numeric values. FLOOR(*x*) returns the greatest integer that is lower than *x*. This query groups books in $10 price intervals:

```
SELECT
    FLOOR(price/10)*10 AS "Category",
    COUNT(*) AS "Count"
  FROM titles
  GROUP BY FLOOR(price/10)*10;
```

The result is:

```
Category Count
-------- -----
0        2
10       6
20       3
30       1
NULL     1
```

Category 0 counts prices between $0.00 and $9.99; category 10 counts prices between $10.00 and $19.99; and so on. (The analogous function CEILING(*x*) returns the smallest integer that is higher than *x*.)

Tips for GROUP BY

- Use the WHERE clause to exclude rows that you don't want grouped and use the HAVING clause to filter rows after they have been grouped. The next section covers HAVING.

- Don't rely on GROUP BY to sort your result. Include ORDER BY whenever you use GROUP BY (even though I've omitted ORDER BY in some examples). In some DBMSs, a GROUP BY implies an ORDER BY.

- The multiple values returned by an aggregate function in a GROUP BY query are called **vector aggregates**. In a query that lacks a GROUP BY clause, the single value returned by an aggregate function is a **scalar aggregate**.

- You should create indexes for columns that you group frequently (see Chapter 12).

- DBMS In **Microsoft Access**, use the Switch() function instead of the CASE expression in Listing 6.15. See the DBMS tip in "Tips for CASE" on page 152.

  MySQL 4.1 and earlier don't allow CASE in a GROUP BY clause and so won't run Listing 6.15. MySQL 5.0 and later will run it.

Filtering Groups with HAVING

The HAVING clause sets conditions on the GROUP BY clause similar to the way that WHERE interacts with SELECT. The HAVING clause's important characteristics are:

- The HAVING clause comes after the GROUP BY clause and before the ORDER BY clause.

- Just as WHERE limits the number of rows displayed by SELECT, HAVING limits the number of groups displayed by GROUP BY.

- The WHERE search condition is applied *before* grouping occurs, and the HAVING search condition is applied *after*.

- HAVING syntax is similar to the WHERE syntax, except that HAVING can contain aggregate functions.

- A HAVING clause can reference any of the items that appear in the SELECT list.

The sequence in which the WHERE, GROUP BY, and HAVING clauses are applied is:

1. The WHERE clause filters the rows that result from the operations specified in the FROM and JOIN clauses.

2. The GROUP BY clause groups the output of the WHERE clause.

3. The HAVING clause filters rows from the grouped result.

```
SELECT
    au_id,
    COUNT(*) AS "num_books"
  FROM title_authors
  GROUP BY au_id
  HAVING COUNT(*) >= 3;
```

Listing 6.18 List the number of books written (or cowritten) by each author who has written three or more books. See Figure 6.18 for the result.

```
au_id  num_books
-----  ---------
A01            3
A02            4
A04            4
A06            3
```

Figure 6.18 Result of Listing 6.18.

```
SELECT
    type,
    COUNT(price) AS "COUNT(price)",
    AVG(price * sales) AS "AVG revenue"
  FROM titles
  GROUP BY type
  HAVING AVG(price * sales) > 1000000;
```

Listing 6.19 List the number of titles and average revenue for the types with average revenue more than $1 million. See Figure 6.19 for the result.

```
type       COUNT(price) AVG revenue
---------- ------------ -----------
biography             3 12484878.00
computer              1  1025396.65
```

Figure 6.19 Result of Listing 6.19.

```
SELECT
    type,
    COUNT(price) AS "COUNT(price)"
  FROM titles
  GROUP BY type
  HAVING AVG(price * sales) > 1000000;
```

Listing 6.20 Listing 6.19 still works without AVG(price * sales) in the SELECT list. See Figure 6.20 for the result.

```
type       COUNT(price)
---------- ------------
biography             3
computer              1
```

Figure 6.20 Result of Listing 6.20.

To filter groups:

- Following the GROUP BY clause, type:

  HAVING *search_condition*

  search_condition is a search condition used to filter groups. *search_condition* can contain aggregate functions but otherwise is identical to the WHERE search condition, described in "Filtering Rows with WHERE" and subsequent sections in Chapter 4. You can combine and negate multiple HAVING conditions with the logical operators AND, OR, and NOT.

  The HAVING search condition is applied to the rows in the output produced by grouping. Only the groups that meet the search condition appear in the result. You can apply a HAVING clause only to columns that appear in the GROUP BY clause or in an aggregate function.

  In Listing 6.18 and Figure 6.18, I revisit Listing 6.9 earlier in this chapter, but instead of listing the number of books that each author wrote (or cowrote), I use HAVING to list only the authors who have written three or more books.

  In Listing 6.19 and Figure 6.19, the HAVING condition also is an aggregate expression in the SELECT clause. This query still works if you remove the AVG() expression from the SELECT list (Listing 6.20 and Figure 6.20).

In Listing 6.21 and Figure 6.21, multiple grouping columns count the number of titles of each type that each publisher publishes. The HAVING condition removes groups in which the publisher has one or fewer titles of a particular type. This query retrieves a subset of the result of Listing 6.14 earlier in this chapter.

In Listing 6.22 and Figure 6.22, the WHERE clause first removes all rows except for books from only publishers P03 and P04. Then the GROUP BY clause groups the output of the WHERE clause by *type*. Finally, the HAVING clause filters rows from the grouped result.

Tips for HAVING

- Generally, a HAVING clause should involve only aggregates. The only conditions that you specify in the HAVING clause are those conditions that must be applied *after* the grouping operation has been performed. It's more efficient to specify conditions that can be applied before the grouping operation in the WHERE clause. The following statements, for example, are equivalent, but the first statement is preferable because it reduces the number of rows that have to be grouped:

```
SELECT pub_id, SUM(sales)      --Faster
  FROM titles
  WHERE pub_id IN ('P03', 'P04')
  GROUP BY pub_id
  HAVING SUM(sales) > 10000;
```

```
SELECT pub_id, SUM(sales)      --Slower
  FROM titles
  GROUP BY pub_id
  HAVING SUM(sales) > 10000
    AND pub_id IN ('P03', 'P04');
```

```
SELECT
    pub_id,
    type,
    COUNT(*) AS "COUNT(*)"
  FROM titles
  GROUP BY pub_id, type
  HAVING COUNT(*) > 1
  ORDER BY pub_id ASC, "COUNT(*)" DESC;
```

Listing 6.21 List the number of books of each type for each publisher, for publishers with more than one title of a type. See Figure 6.21 for the result.

pub_id	type	COUNT(*)
P01	biography	3
P03	history	2
P04	psychology	3
P04	children	2

Figure 6.21 Result of Listing 6.21.

```
SELECT
    type,
    SUM(sales) AS "SUM(sales)",
    AVG(price) AS "AVG(price)"
  FROM titles
  WHERE pub_id IN ('P03', 'P04')
  GROUP BY type
  HAVING SUM(sales) > 10000
    AND AVG(price) < 20;
```

Listing 6.22 For books from only publishers P03 and P04, list the total sales and average price by type, for types with more than $10000 total sales and less than $20 average price. See Figure 6.22 for the result.

type	SUM(sales)	AVG(price)
psychology	308564	9.31

Figure 6.22 Result of Listing 6.22

CHAPTER 7

Joins

All the queries so far have retrieved rows from a single table. This chapter explains how to use joins to retrieve rows from multiple tables simultaneously. Recall from "Relationships" on page 30 that a relationship is an association established between common columns in two tables. A **join** is a table operation that uses related columns to combine rows from two input tables into one result table. You can chain joins to retrieve rows from an unlimited number of tables.

Why do joins matter? The most important database information isn't so much stored in the rows of individual tables; rather, it's the implied relationships between sets of related rows. In the sample database, for example, the individual rows of the tables *authors*, *publishers*, and *titles* contain important values, of course, but it's the implied relationships that let you understand and analyze your data in its entirety: Who wrote what? Who published what? To whom do we send royalty checks? For how much? And so on.

This chapter explains the different types of joins, why they're used, and how to create a SELECT statement that uses them.

Qualifying Column Names

Recall from "Tables, Columns, and Rows" on page 22 that column names must be unique within a table but can be reused in other tables. The tables *authors* and *publishers* in the sample database both contain a column named *city*, for example.

To identify an otherwise-ambiguous column uniquely in a query that involves multiple tables, use its qualified name. A **qualified name** is a table name followed by a dot and the name of the column in the table. Because tables must have different names within a database, a qualified name identifies a single column uniquely within the entire database.

To qualify a column name:

*   Type:

    table.column

    column is a column name, and *table* is name of the table that contains *column* (Listing 7.1 and Figure 7.1).

```
SELECT au_id, authors.city
  FROM authors
  INNER JOIN publishers
    ON authors.city = publishers.city;
```

Listing 7.1 Here, the qualified names resolve otherwise-ambiguous references to the column *city* in the tables *authors* and *publishers*. See Figure 7.1 for the result.

```
au_id city
----- -------------
A03   San Francisco
A04   San Francisco
A05   New York
```

Figure 7.1 Result of Listing 7.1. This result lists authors who live in the same city as some publisher; the join syntax is explained later in this chapter.

Tips for Qualified Column Names

- You can mix qualified and unqualified names within the same statement.

- Qualified names aren't required if there's no chance of ambiguity—that is, if the query's tables have no column names in common. To improve system performance, however, qualify *all* columns in a query with joins.

- Another good reason to use qualified names is to ensure that changes to a table's structure don't introduce ambiguities. If someone adds the column *zip* to the table *publishers*, then any unqualified references to *zip* in a query that selects from the tables *authors* (which already contains a column *zip*) and *publishers* would be ambiguous.

- Qualification still works in queries that involve a single table. In fact, every column has an implicit qualifier. The following two statements are equivalent:

```
SELECT
    au_fname,
    au_lname
  FROM authors;
```

and

```
SELECT
    authors.au_fname,
    authors.au_lname
  FROM authors;
```

- DBMS Your query might require still more qualifiers, depending on where it resides in the DBMS hierarchy. You might need to qualify a table with a server, database, or schema name, for example (see Table 2.2 on page 25). Table aliases, described in the next section, are useful in SQL statements that require lengthy qualified names. A fully qualified table name in **Microsoft SQL Server**, for example, is:

`server.database.owner.table`

Oracle 8i and earlier require WHERE join syntax; see "Creating Joins with JOIN or WHERE" on page 186. To run Listing 7.1, type:

```
SELECT au_id, authors.city
  FROM authors, publishers
  WHERE authors.city =
      publishers.city;
```

Creating Table Aliases with AS

You can create table aliases by using AS just as you can create column aliases; see "Creating Column Aliases with AS" on page 79. Table aliases:

- Save typing

- Reduce statement clutter

- Exist only for the duration of a statement

- Don't appear in the result (unlike column aliases)

- Don't change the name of a table in the database

- Also are called **correlation names** in the context of subqueries (see Chapter 8)

To create a table alias:

- In a FROM clause or JOIN clause, type:

  table [AS] *alias*

  table is a table name, and *alias* is its alias name. *alias* is a single, unquoted word that contains only letters, digits, or underscores; don't use spaces, punctuation, or special characters. The AS keyword is optional (Listing 7.2 and Figure 7.2).

```
SELECT au_fname, au_lname, a.city
  FROM authors a
  INNER JOIN publishers p
    ON a.city = p.city;
```

Listing 7.2 Tables aliases make queries shorter and easier to read. Note that you can use an alias in the SELECT clause before it's actually defined later in the statement. See Figure 7.2 for the result.

```
au_fname   au_lname  city
---------  --------  -------------
Hallie     Hull      San Francisco
Klee       Hull      San Francisco
Christian  Kells     New York
```

Figure 7.2 Result of Listing 7.2.

Tips for AS

- In this book, I omit the keyword AS for DBMS portability (see the DBMS tip in this section).

- In practice, table aliases are short (typically, one or two characters), but long names are valid.

- If you want to use the actual name of any particular table, then omit its alias.

- An alias name hides a table name. If you alias a table, then you must use its alias in all qualified references. The following statement is illegal because the alias *a* occludes the table name *authors*:

```
SELECT authors.au_id
   FROM authors a;            --Illegal
```

- Each table's alias must be unique within the same SQL statement.

- Table aliases are required to refer to the same table more than once in a self-join; see "Creating a Self-Join" on page 233.

- You also can use AS to assign aliases to views; see Chapter 13.

- You can't use keywords as table aliases; see "SQL Syntax" on page 50.

- Using WHERE join syntax (page 186), Listing 7.2 is equivalent to:

```
SELECT a.au_fname, a.au_lname, a.city
   FROM authors a, publishers p
   WHERE a.city = p.city;
```

- DBMS In **Oracle**, you must omit the keyword AS when you create a table alias.

  PostgreSQL implicitly adds table name(s) that appear in the SELECT clause to the FROM clause, which can cause unexpected cross joins. The query SELECT titles.title_id FROM titles t;, for example, cross-joins the table *titles*, returning 169 (13^2) rows instead of an error. To turn off this behavior, use SET ADD_MISSING_FROM TO FALSE;.

Using Joins

You can use a join to extract data from more than one table. The rest of this chapter explains the different types of joins (Table 7.1), why they're used, and how to create SELECT statements that use them.

The important characteristics of joins are:

- The two join **operands** (input tables) usually are called the first table and the second table, but they are called the left table and the right table in outer joins, in which table order matters.

- Tables are joined row by row and side by side by satisfying whatever join condition(s) you specify in the query.

- Rows that don't match are included or excluded, depending on the type of join.

- A **theta join** uses a comparison operator (=, <>, <, <=, >, or >=) to compare values in joined columns. An **equijoin**, the most common type of join, is a theta join that compares values for equality.

- A join's connecting columns often are associated key columns, but you can join any columns with compatible data types (except for cross joins, which require no specific join columns).

- To ensure that a join is meaningful, compare values in columns defined over the same domain. It's possible to join the columns *titles.price* and *royalties.advance*, for example, but the result will be meaningless. A typical join condition specifies a foreign key in one table and the associated primary key in the other table (see "Primary Keys" on page 26 and "Foreign Keys" on page 28).

- If a key is composite (has multiple columns), then you can (and normally should) join all the key's columns.

- Joined columns needn't have the same column name (except for natural joins).

Table 7.1 Types of Joins

Join	Description
Cross join	Returns all rows from the first table in which each row from the first table is combined with all rows from the second table.
Natural join	A join that compares, for equality, all the columns in the first table with corresponding columns that have the same name in the second table.
Inner join	A join that uses a comparison operator to match rows from two tables based on the values in common columns from each table. Inner joins are the most common type of join.
Left outer join	Returns *all* the rows from the left table, not just the ones in which the joined columns match. If a row in the left table has no matching rows in the right table, then the associated result row contains nulls for all SELECT-clause columns coming from the right table.
Right outer join	The reverse of a left outer join. All rows from the right table are returned. Nulls are returned for the left table if a right-table row has no matching left-table row.
Full outer join	Returns all rows in both the left and right tables. If a row has no match in the other table, then the SELECT-clause columns from the other table contain nulls. If there is a match between the tables, then the entire result row contains values from both tables.
Self- join	A join of a table to itself.

- You can nest and chain joins to join more than two tables, but understand that the DBMS works its way through your query by executing joins on exactly two tables at a time. The two tables in each join can be two base tables from the database, a base table and a table that is the result of a previous join, or two tables that are the results of previous joins.

- The SQL standard doesn't limit the number of tables (or joins) that can appear in a query, but your DBMS will have built-in limits, or your database administrator might set limits that are lower than the built-in limits. A small, routine query might involve five or fewer joined tables.

- If a join's connecting columns contain nulls, then the nulls never join. Nulls represent unknown values that aren't considered to be equal (or unequal) to one another. Nulls in a column from one of the joined tables can be returned only by using a cross join or an outer join (unless a WHERE clause excludes null values explicitly). For information about nulls, see "Nulls" on page 72.

- Joins exist only for the duration of a query and aren't part of the database or DBMS.

- The data types of the join columns must be compatible, meaning that the DBMS can convert values to a common type for comparisons. For most DBMSs, numeric data types (INTEGER, FLOAT, and NUMERIC, for example), character data types (CHAR, VARCHAR), and datetime data types (DATE, TIMESTAMP) are compatible. You can't join binary objects.

  Conversions require computational overhead. For the best performance, the join columns should have *identical* data types (page 56) and constraints (page 325), including whether nulls are allowed.

- For faster queries, index the join columns (see Chapter 12).

- You can join views to tables or to other views (see Chapter 13).

- You can use either JOIN syntax or WHERE syntax to create a join; see "Creating Joins with JOIN or WHERE" on page 186.

Domains and Comparisons

The values that you compare in joins and WHERE clauses must be *meaningfully* comparable—that is, have the same data type *and* the same meaning. The sample-database columns *au_id* and *pub_id*, for example, have the same data type—both are CHAR(3), a letter followed by two digits—but mean different things, so they can't be compared sensibly.

Recall from "Tables, Columns, and Rows" on page 22 that a domain is the set of permissible values for a column. To prevent meaningless comparisons, the relational model requires that comparable columns draw from domains that have the same meaning. Unfortunately, SQL and DBMSs stray from the model and have no intrinsic mechanism that prevents users from comparing, say, IQ and shoe size. If you're building a database application, then it's up to you to stop (or warn) users from making meaningless comparisons that waste processing time or, worse, yield results that might be interpreted as valid.

Creating Joins with JOIN or WHERE

You have two alternative ways of specifying a join: by using JOIN syntax or WHERE syntax. SQL-92 and later standards prescribe JOIN syntax, but older standards prescribe WHERE; hence, both JOIN and WHERE are used widely.

This section explains the general syntax for JOIN and WHERE joins that involve two tables. The actual syntax that you'll use in real queries will vary by the join type, the number of columns joined, the number of tables joined, and the syntax requirements of your DBMS. The syntax diagrams and examples in the following sections show you how to create specific joins.

To create a join by using JOIN:

* Type:

```
SELECT columns
  FROM table1 join_type table2
    ON join_conditions
  [WHERE search_condition]
  [GROUP BY grouping_columns]
  [HAVING search_condition]
  [ORDER BY sort_columns];
```

columns is one or more comma-separated expressions or column names from *table1* or *table2*. If *table1* and *table2* have a column name in common, then you must qualify all references to these columns throughout the query to prevent ambiguity; see "Qualifying Column Names" on page 180.

table1 and *table2* are the names of the joined tables. You can alias the table names; see "Creating Table Aliases with AS" on page 182.

join_type specifies what kind of join is performed: CROSS JOIN, NATURAL JOIN, INNER JOIN, LEFT OUTER JOIN, RIGHT OUTER JOIN, or FULL OUTER JOIN.

join_conditions specifies one or more join conditions to be evaluated for each pair of joined rows. (The ON clause isn't allowed in cross joins and natural joins.) A join condition takes this form:

```
[table1.]column op [table2.]column
```

op usually is = but can be any comparison operator: =, <>, <, <=, >, or >= (refer to Table 4.2 on page 89). You can combine multiple join conditions with AND or OR; see "Combining and Negating Conditions with AND, OR, and NOT" on page 93.

The WHERE and ORDER BY clauses are covered in Chapter 4; GROUP BY and HAVING are covered in Chapter 6.

```
SELECT au_fname, au_lname, a.city
  FROM authors a
  INNER JOIN publishers p
    ON a.city = p.city;
```

Listing 7.3a A join that uses JOIN syntax. See Figure 7.3 for the result.

```
SELECT au_fname, au_lname, a.city
  FROM authors a, publishers p
  WHERE a.city = p.city;
```

Listing 7.3b The same join, using WHERE syntax. See Figure 7.3 for the result.

```
au_fname   au_lname city
---------  -------- -------------
Hallie     Hull     San Francisco
Klee       Hull     San Francisco
Christian  Kells    New York
```

Figure 7.3 Result of Listings 7.3a and 7.3b.

To create a join by using WHERE:

- Type:

```
SELECT columns
  FROM table1, table2
  WHERE join_conditions
  [GROUP BY grouping_columns]
  [HAVING search_condition]
  [ORDER BY sort_columns];
```

columns, *table1*, and *table2* have the same meaning as in "To create a join by using JOIN" earlier in this section.

join_conditions also has the same meaning as in "To create a join by using JOIN" earlier in this section, except that *op* can be a special symbol that indicates the join type. The WHERE clause also can include (nonjoin) search conditions to filter rows; see "Filtering Rows with WHERE" on page 89.

The ORDER BY clause is covered in Chapter 4; GROUP BY and HAVING are covered in Chapter 6.

Listings 7.3a and 7.3b show equivalent queries that use JOIN and WHERE syntax. See Figure 7.3 for the result.

Query Execution Sequence

When your DBMS processes joins, it uses a logical sequence to execute the entire query. The DBMS:

1. Applies the join conditions in the JOIN clause.

2. Applies the join conditions and search conditions in the WHERE clause.

3. Groups rows according to the GROUP BY clause.

4. Applies the search conditions in the HAVING clause to the groups.

5. Sorts the result according to the ORDER BY clause.

Tips for JOIN and WHERE

- It might seem odd to use a WHERE clause to specify join conditions, but the join condition *does* act as a filter. When you join two tables, the DBMS internally pairs every row in the left table with every row in the right table, forming a cross join (see the next section). The DBMS then uses the join condition to filter rows from the cross join (conceptually, anyway; DBMS optimizers don't actually create enormous cross-joined tables for every join).

- The compelling reason to prefer JOIN to WHERE syntax is that JOIN makes the join type explicit. A LEFT OUTER JOIN B is clearer than, say, A *= B. For the most common type of joins— simple inner joins—I think that WHERE syntax is easier to understand, however. Both JOIN and WHERE syntax are popular, so you'll have to learn both to read queries created by other people.

- In a three-table join, only one table can be used to bridge from one of the other tables to the third table.

- The SELECT-clause list for a join can reference all the columns in the joined tables or any subset of the columns. The list isn't required to contain columns from every table in the join. In a three-table join, for example, none of the columns from the middle table needs to be in the list.

- Joined columns don't need to have the same data type. If the data types aren't identical, then they must be compatible or must be data types that your DBMS can convert implicitly to a common type. If the data types can't be converted implicitly, then the join condition must convert the data type explicitly by using the CAST() function. For information about implicit and explicit conversions, see "Converting Data Types with CAST()" on page 145.

- If you're using WHERE syntax with two or more join conditions, then you'll almost always want to combine all the join conditions with AND. Combining join conditions with OR is legal, but the result is hard to interpret. For more information about AND and OR, see "Combining and Negating Conditions with AND, OR, and NOT" on page 93.

- Most queries that use joins can be rewritten by using a subquery (a query nested within another query), and most subqueries can be rewritten as joins. For information about subqueries, see Chapter 8.

- **DBMS** **Oracle** 8i and earlier don't support JOIN syntax; use WHERE joins instead. Oracle 9i and later support JOIN syntax.

  Your DBMS might prohibit joins on columns with particular data types (especially binary and long-text data types). **Microsoft SQL Server** prohibits joins on nvarchar(max), varchar(max), and varbinary(max) columns, and **Oracle** prohibits joins on LOB columns, for example. Search your DBMS documentation for *joins*.

The USING Clause

For JOIN syntax, the SQL standard also defines a USING clause that can be used instead of the ON clause if the joined columns have the same name and are compared for equality:

```
FROM table1 join_type table2
  USING (columns)
```

columns is a comma-separated list of one or more column names. The parentheses are required. The query performs an equijoin on the named pair(s) of columns. The type of join is called a **named columns join**. Rewriting Listing 7.3a with USING:

```
SELECT au_fname, au_lname, city
  FROM authors
  INNER JOIN publishers
    USING (city);
```

The USING clause acts like a natural join, except that you can use it if you don't want to join *all* pairs of columns with the same name in both tables. Note that the preceding USING example joins only on the column *city* in both tables, whereas a natural join would join on both the columns *city* and *state* common to the tables. See "Creating a Natural Join with NATURAL JOIN" on page 192.

USING is a syntactic convenience that doesn't add extra functionality to SQL. A USING clause always can be replicated with an ON clause in JOIN syntax or with a WHERE clause in WHERE syntax.

DBMS   **Microsoft Access**, **Microsoft SQL Server**, and **Db2** don't support USING. **MySQL** requires the SELECT clause's common column names to be qualified in USING queries. To run the preceding example, change *city* to *authors.city* in the SELECT clause.

Creating a Cross Join with CROSS JOIN

A **cross join**:

- Returns all possible combinations of rows of two tables. The result contains all rows from the first table; *each* row from the first table is combined with *all* rows from the second table.

- Doesn't use a join condition. To create a cross join, omit the ON clause if you're using JOIN syntax, or omit the WHERE clause if you're using WHERE syntax.

- Seldom is used alone because the result is cumbersome and hard to interpret but does appear in some types of queries as an intermediate result. For example, see "Calculating Running Statistics" on page 390 and "Generating Sequences" on page 393.

- Can produce a huge result, even with small tables. If one table has m rows and the other has n rows, then the result contains $m \times n$ rows.

- Is a computationally expensive and time-consuming query.

- Also is called a **Cartesian product** or **cross product**.

To create a cross join:

- Type:

```
SELECT columns
  FROM table1
  CROSS JOIN table2
```

columns is one or more comma-separated expressions or column names from *table1* or *table2*. *table1* and *table2* are the names of the joined tables. If the tables have some column names in common, then qualify those column names with the names of the tables (Listing 7.4 and Figure 7.4).

```
SELECT
    au_id,
    pub_id,
    a.state AS "au_state",
    p.state AS "pub_state"
  FROM authors a
  CROSS JOIN publishers p;
```

Listing 7.4 A cross join displays all possible combinations of rows from two tables. See Figure 7.4 for the result.

au_id	pub_id	au_state	pub_state
A01	P01	NY	NY
A02	P01	CO	NY
A03	P01	CA	NY
A04	P01	CA	NY
A05	P01	NY	NY
A06	P01	CA	NY
A07	P01	FL	NY
A01	P02	NY	CA
A02	P02	CO	CA
A03	P02	CA	CA
A04	P02	CA	CA
A05	P02	NY	CA
A06	P02	CA	CA
A07	P02	FL	CA
A01	P03	NY	NULL
A02	P03	CO	NULL
A03	P03	CA	NULL
A04	P03	CA	NULL
A05	P03	NY	NULL
A06	P03	CA	NULL
A07	P03	FL	NULL
A01	P04	NY	CA
A02	P04	CO	CA
A03	P04	CA	CA
A04	P04	CA	CA
A05	P04	NY	CA
A06	P04	CA	CA
A07	P04	FL	CA

Figure 7.4 Result of Listing 7.4.

Tips for CROSS JOIN

- Using WHERE syntax, Listing 7.4 is equivalent to:

```
SELECT au_id, pub_id,
    a.state AS "au_state",
    p.state AS "pub_state"
  FROM authors a, publishers p;
```

- Use SELECT * to retrieve all columns from both tables. This query retrieves all columns from the tables *authors* and *publishers*:

```
SELECT *
  FROM authors
  CROSS JOIN publishers;
```

Equivalently, using WHERE syntax:

```
SELECT *
  FROM authors, publishers;
```

- Use SELECT *table.** to retrieve all columns from just one of the tables. The following query retrieves all columns from the table *authors* and only the column *pub_id* from the table *publishers*:

```
SELECT authors.*, p.pub_id
  FROM authors
  CROSS JOIN publishers p;
```

Equivalently, using WHERE syntax:

```
SELECT authors.*, p.pub_id
  FROM authors, publishers p;
```

- To find the cross product of *n* tables by using JOIN syntax, type:

```
SELECT columns
  FROM table1
  CROSS JOIN table2
  ...
  CROSS JOIN tableN
```

Equivalently, using WHERE syntax:

```
SELECT columns
  FROM table1, table2,..., tableN
```

- Cross products often are produced mistakenly. If your result contains an unexpectedly large number of rows, then you might have omitted a join condition from your query accidentally.

- Although a cross product rarely is the result you want in practice, your DBMS (theoretically) generates a cross product internally as the first step in processing every join. After the DBMS has the cross product, it uses the SELECT-clause list to delete columns and the join and search conditions to delete rows.

- The join

  t1 CROSS JOIN *t2*

  is equivalent to any of the following joins:

  t1 INNER JOIN *t2* ON 1 = 1

  t1 LEFT OUTER JOIN *t2* ON 1 = 1

  t1 RIGHT OUTER JOIN *t2* ON 1 = 1

  t1 FULL OUTER JOIN *t2* ON 1 = 1

  t1 and *t2* are tables, and *1 = 1* represents any condition that's always true. Inner and outer joins are covered later in this chapter.

- One practical use of cross joins is to produce datasets for testing software. Suppose that you have a function that takes *n* arguments, and each argument assumes *m* representative test values. You can generate all $m \times n$ test cases by finding the cross product of *n* tables (one table for each argument), in which each table has one column and *m* rows (one row that contains each test value). This method still works if *m* differs for each argument.

- **DBMS** **Microsoft Access** supports only WHERE syntax for cross joins. To run Listing 7.4, use the SQL statement given in the first tip in this section.

  Oracle 8i and earlier don't support JOIN syntax; use WHERE joins instead.

Creating a Natural Join with NATURAL JOIN

A **natural join**:

- Is a special case of an equijoin; it compares all the columns in one table with corresponding columns that have the *same name* in the other table for equality.

- Works only if the input tables have one or more pairs of meaningfully comparable, identically named columns.

- Performs joins implicitly. Don't specify an ON or USING clause in a natural join.

- Is a syntactic convenience that can be replicated explicitly with an ON clause in JOIN syntax or a WHERE clause in WHERE syntax.

To create a natural join:

- Type:

```
SELECT columns
  FROM table1
  NATURAL JOIN table2
```

columns is one or more comma-separated expressions or column names from *table1* or *table2*. Your DBMS might require identical column names to be qualified with the names of the tables (see the DBMS tip in "Tips for NATURAL JOIN"). *table1* and *table2* are the names of the joined tables.

The columns in *table1* are joined with the identically named columns in *table2* and compared for equality. NATURAL JOIN creates natural inner joins; to create natural outer joins, see "Tips for NATURAL JOIN".

```
SELECT
    title_id,
    pub_id,
    pub_name
  FROM publishers
  NATURAL JOIN titles;
```

Listing 7.5 List each book's publisher. See Figure 7.5 for the result.

title_id	pub_id	pub_name
T01	P01	Abatis Publishers
T02	P03	Schadenfreude Press
T03	P02	Core Dump Books
T04	P04	Tenterhooks Press
T05	P04	Tenterhooks Press
T06	P01	Abatis Publishers
T07	P03	Schadenfreude Press
T08	P04	Tenterhooks Press
T09	P04	Tenterhooks Press
T10	P01	Abatis Publishers
T11	P04	Tenterhooks Press
T12	P01	Abatis Publishers
T13	P03	Schadenfreude Press

Figure 7.5 Result of Listing 7.5.

```
SELECT
    title_id,
    pub_id,
    pub_name,
    advance
  FROM publishers
  NATURAL JOIN titles
  NATURAL JOIN royalties
  WHERE advance < 20000;
```

Listing 7.6 List each book's publisher and advance for books with advances less than $20000. See Figure 7.6 for the result.

```
title_id  pub_id  pub_name              advance
--------  ------  --------------------  -------
T01       P01     Abatis Publishers       10000
T02       P03     Schadenfreude Press      1000
T03       P02     Core Dump Books         15000
T08       P04     Tenterhooks Press           0
T09       P04     Tenterhooks Press           0
```

Figure 7.6 Result of Listing 7.6.

When your DBMS runs Listing 7.5, it will join rows in the table *publishers* with rows in the table *titles* that have equal values in the columns *publishers.pub_id* and *titles.pub_id*—the two columns that have the same name in both tables. See Figure 7.5 for the result.

In Listing 7.6, I've added another join to Listing 7.5 to retrieve the advance for each book. The WHERE condition retrieves books with advances less than $20000. When your DBMS runs Listing 7.6, it will join the *pub_id* columns in the tables *publishers* and *titles*, *and* it will join the *title_id* columns in the tables *titles* and *royalties*. See Figure 7.6 for the result.

Tips for NATURAL JOIN

- To replicate a natural join by using WHERE syntax, use an equijoin with a WHERE clause that uses AND operators to combine join conditions. Each join condition equates each pair of columns with the same name in the input tables. The equivalent WHERE queries are (Listing 7.5):

```
SELECT t.title_id, t.pub_id,
    p.pub_name
  FROM publishers p, titles t
  WHERE p.pub_id = t.pub_id;
```

and (Listing 7.6):

```
SELECT t.title_id, t.pub_id,
    p.pub_name, r.advance
  FROM publishers p, titles t,
    royalties r
  WHERE p.pub_id = t.pub_id
    AND t.title_id = r.title_id
    AND r.advance < 20000;
```

- To replicate a natural join by using inner or outer JOIN syntax, use an equijoin with an ON clause that uses AND operators to combine join conditions. Each join condition equates each pair of columns with the same name in both input tables. The equivalent JOIN queries are (Listing 7.5):

```
SELECT t.title_id, t.pub_id,
    p.pub_name
  FROM publishers p
  INNER JOIN titles t
    ON p.pub_id = t.pub_id;
```

and (Listing 7.6):

```
SELECT t.title_id, t.pub_id,
    p.pub_name, r.advance
  FROM publishers p
  INNER JOIN titles t
    ON p.pub_id = t.pub_id
  INNER JOIN royalties r
    ON t.title_id = r.title_id
  WHERE r.advance < 20000;
```

- You also can replicate a natural join by using JOIN syntax with a USING clause (see "The USING Clause" on page 189). NATURAL JOIN is a shorthand form of USING; it forms a USING list consisting of exactly those column names that appear in both tables. The equivalent USING queries are (Listing 7.5):

```
SELECT title_id, pub_id,
    pub_name
  FROM publishers
  INNER JOIN titles
    USING (pub_id);
```

and (Listing 7.6):

```
SELECT title_id, pub_id,
    pub_name, advance
  FROM publishers
  INNER JOIN titles
    USING (pub_id)
  INNER JOIN royalties
    USING (title_id)
  WHERE advance < 20000;
```

- The syntax NATURAL JOIN actually creates an inner join: NATURAL JOIN is equivalent to NATURAL INNER JOIN. You can create natural outer joins with:

  `NATURAL LEFT [OUTER] JOIN`

  `NATURAL RIGHT [OUTER] JOIN`

  `NATURAL FULL [OUTER] JOIN`

- If you use a natural join, then be certain that all related (joinable) columns have the same name in both tables and that all unrelated columns have unique names.

- Natural joins make some queries shorter and easier to understand, but be wary of them. They will return different results unexpectedly if the columns involved in the join are added, deleted, or renamed without your knowledge.

- The meaning of *natural join* differs slightly in the relational model (Chapter 2) and the SQL standard. In the model, a natural join always is a join from a foreign key to its parent key. In SQL, a natural join is a join of two tables over *all* columns that have the same name (not just key columns). See Listing 7.9 later in this chapter for an example of a natural join that doesn't involve key columns.

  To make the model and the SQL definitions of a natural join agree, a database designer will ensure that all the foreign keys have the same names as their parent keys and that all other columns have unique names.

- DBMS **Microsoft Access**, **Microsoft SQL Server**, and **Db2** don't support NATURAL JOIN syntax. To run Listings 7.5 and 7.6, use either WHERE syntax (given in the first tip in this section) or equivalent JOIN syntax (given in the second tip in this section).

  Oracle 8i and earlier don't support JOIN syntax; use WHERE joins instead.

  MySQL 4.1 and earlier require common column names to be qualified in natural joins. To run Listings 7.5 and 7.6, add qualifiers (Listing 7.5):

```
SELECT
    t.title_id,
    t.pub_id,
    p.pub_name
  FROM publishers p
  NATURAL JOIN titles t;
```

  and (Listing 7.6):

```
SELECT
    t.title_id,
    t.pub_id,
    p.pub_name,
    r.advance
  FROM publishers p
  NATURAL JOIN titles t
  NATURAL JOIN royalties r
  WHERE r.advance < 20000;
```

Creating an Inner Join with INNER JOIN

An **inner join**:

- Uses a comparison operator (=, <>, <, <=, >, or >=) to match rows from two tables based on the values in common columns from each table. You can retrieve all rows in which the author identifier (the column *au_id*) is the same in both the tables *authors* and *title_authors*, for example.

- Returns a result that contains only joined rows that satisfy the join condition(s).

- Is the most common type of join.

To create an inner join:

- Type:

```
SELECT columns
  FROM table1
  INNER JOIN table2
    ON join_conditions
```

columns is one or more comma-separated expressions or column names from *table1* or *table2*. *table1* and *table2* are the names of the joined tables. If the tables have some column names in common, then qualify those column names with the names of the tables.

join_conditions specifies one or more join conditions to be evaluated for each pair of joined rows. A join condition takes this form:

```
[table1.]column op [table2.]column
```

op usually is = but can be any comparison operator: =, <>, <, <=, >, or >= (refer to Table 4.2 on page 89). You can combine multiple join conditions with AND or OR; see "Combining and Negating Conditions with AND, OR, and NOT" on page 93.

Tips for INNER JOIN

- To create an inner join of three or more tables by using JOIN syntax, type:

```
SELECT columns
  FROM table1
  INNER JOIN table2
    ON join_condition1
  INNER JOIN table3
    ON join_condition2
...
```

Using WHERE syntax, type:

```
SELECT columns
  FROM table1, table2,...
  WHERE join_condition1
  AND join_condition2
...
```

- If you're using WHERE syntax and you omit a join condition accidentally, then you'll create a cross join. If the affected tables are large production tables, then you'll have a "runaway query" that you might have to ask your database administrator to kill.

- JOIN (without CROSS, NATURAL, OUTER, or any other modifiers) is equivalent to INNER JOIN.

- | DBMS | You can use WHERE syntax or JOIN syntax in **Microsoft Access**, but if you use JOIN syntax in joins that involve three or more tables, then Access requires you to nest joins by using the following general syntax:

```
SELECT columns
  FROM table1
  INNER JOIN (table2 INNER JOIN [(]table3
  [INNER JOIN [(]tableN [INNER JOIN ...)]
  ON table3.column3 op tableN.columnN)]
  ON table2.column2 op table3.column3)
  ON table1.column1 op table2.column2;
```

(Other DBMSs also let you nest joins by using parentheses, but Access requires it.)

Oracle 8i and earlier don't support JOIN syntax; use WHERE joins instead. Oracle 9i and later support JOIN syntax.

```
SELECT
    a.au_id,
    a.au_fname,
    a.au_lname,
    ta.title_id
FROM authors a
INNER JOIN title_authors ta
    ON a.au_id = ta.au_id
ORDER BY a.au_id ASC, ta.title_id ASC;
```

Listing 7.7 List the books that each author wrote (or cowrote). See Figure 7.7 for the result.

au_id	au_fname	au_lname	title_id
A01	Sarah	Buchman	T01
A01	Sarah	Buchman	T02
A01	Sarah	Buchman	T13
A02	Wendy	Heydemark	T06
A02	Wendy	Heydemark	T07
A02	Wendy	Heydemark	T10
A02	Wendy	Heydemark	T12
A03	Hallie	Hull	T04
A03	Hallie	Hull	T11
A04	Klee	Hull	T04
A04	Klee	Hull	T05
A04	Klee	Hull	T07
A04	Klee	Hull	T11
A05	Christian	Kells	T03
A06		Kellsey	T08
A06		Kellsey	T09
A06		Kellsey	T11

Figure 7.7 Result of Listing 7.7.

Listing 7.7 joins two tables on the column *au_id* to list the books that each author wrote (or cowrote). Each author's *au_id* in the table *authors* matches zero or more rows in the table *title_authors*. See Figure 7.7 for the result. Note that author A07 (Paddy O'Furniture) is omitted from the result because he has written no books and so has no matching rows in *title_authors*.

Tips for Listing 7.7

- Using WHERE syntax, Listing 7.7 is equivalent to:

```
SELECT a.au_id, a.au_fname,
    a.au_lname, ta.title_id
  FROM authors a, title_authors ta
  WHERE a.au_id = ta.au_id
  ORDER BY a.au_id ASC,
    ta.title_id ASC;
```

Listing 7.8 joins two tables on the column *pub_id* to list each book's title name and ID, and each book's publisher name and ID. Note that the join is necessary to retrieve only the publisher name (the fourth column in the result); all the other three columns are available in the table *titles*. See Figure 7.8 for the result.

Tips for Listing 7.8

- Using WHERE syntax, Listing 7.8 is equivalent to:

```
SELECT t.title_id, t.title_name,
    t.pub_id, p.pub_name
  FROM titles t, publishers p
  WHERE p.pub_id = t.pub_id
  ORDER BY t.title_name ASC;
```

```
SELECT
    t.title_id,
    t.title_name,
    t.pub_id,
    p.pub_name
  FROM titles t
  INNER JOIN publishers p
    ON p.pub_id = t.pub_id
  ORDER BY t.title_name ASC;
```

Listing 7.8 List each book's title name and ID and each book's publisher name and ID. See Figure 7.8 for the result.

title_id	title_name	pub_id	pub_name
T01	1977!	P01	Abatis Publishers
T02	200 Years of German Humor	P03	Schadenfreude Press
T03	Ask Your System Administrator	P02	Core Dump Books
T04	But I Did It Unconsciously	P04	Tenterhooks Press
T05	Exchange of Platitudes	P04	Tenterhooks Press
T06	How About Never?	P01	Abatis Publishers
T07	I Blame My Mother	P03	Schadenfreude Press
T08	Just Wait Until After School	P04	Tenterhooks Press
T09	Kiss My Boo-Boo	P04	Tenterhooks Press
T10	Not Without My Faberge Egg	P01	Abatis Publishers
T11	Perhaps It's a Glandular Problem	P04	Tenterhooks Press
T12	Spontaneous, Not Annoying	P01	Abatis Publishers
T13	What Are The Civilian Applications?	P03	Schadenfreude Press

Figure 7.8 Result of Listing 7.8.

```
SELECT
    a.au_id,
    a.au_fname,
    a.au_lname,
    a.city,
    a.state
FROM authors a
INNER JOIN publishers p
  ON a.city = p.city
  AND a.state = p.state
ORDER BY a.au_id;
```

Listing 7.9 List the authors who live in the same city and state in which a publisher is located. See Figure 7.9 for the result.

```
au_id au_fname   au_lname city          state
----- ---------- -------- ------------- -----
A03   Hallie     Hull     San Francisco CA
A04   Klee       Hull     San Francisco CA
A05   Christian  Kells    New York      NY
```

Figure 7.9 Result of Listing 7.9.

Listing 7.9 uses two join conditions to list the authors who live in the same city and state as some publisher (any publisher). See Figure 7.9 for the result. Note that this query is a natural join on the identically named, nonkey columns *city* and *state* in the two tables (see "Creating a Natural Join with NATURAL JOIN" on page 192). An equivalent query is:

```
SELECT a.au_id, a.au_fname,
    a.au_lname, a.city, a.state
  FROM authors a
  NATURAL JOIN publishers p
  ORDER BY a.au_id ASC;
```

Tips for Listing 7.9

- Using WHERE syntax, Listing 7.9 is equivalent to:

  ```
  SELECT a.au_id, a.au_fname,
      a.au_lname, a.city, a.state
    FROM authors a, publishers p
    WHERE a.city = p.city
      AND a.state = p.state
    ORDER BY a.au_id ASC;
  ```

Listing 7.10 combines an inner join with WHERE conditions to list books published in California or outside the large North American countries; see "Filtering Rows with WHERE" on page 89. See Figure 7.10 for the result.

Tips for Listing 7.10

*   Using WHERE syntax, Listing 7.10 is equivalent to:

```
SELECT t.title_id, t.title_name,
    p.state, p.country
  FROM titles t, publishers p
  WHERE t.pub_id = p.pub_id
    AND (p.state = 'CA'
    OR p.country NOT IN
      ('USA', 'Canada', 'Mexico'))
  ORDER BY t.title_id ASC;
```

```
SELECT
    t.title_id,
    t.title_name,
    p.state,
    p.country
  FROM titles t
  INNER JOIN publishers p
    ON t.pub_id = p.pub_id
  WHERE p.state = 'CA'
    OR p.country NOT IN
      ('USA', 'Canada', 'Mexico')
  ORDER BY t.title_id ASC;
```

Listing 7.10 List the books published in California or outside the large North American countries. See Figure 7.10 for the result.

```
title_id title_name                          state country
-------- ----------------------------------- ----- -------
T02      200 Years of German Humor           NULL  Germany
T03      Ask Your System Administrator       CA    USA
T04      But I Did It Unconsciously          CA    USA
T05      Exchange of Platitudes              CA    USA
T07      I Blame My Mother                   NULL  Germany
T08      Just Wait Until After School        CA    USA
T09      Kiss My Boo-Boo                     CA    USA
T11      Perhaps It's a Glandular Problem    CA    USA
T13      What Are The Civilian Applications? NULL  Germany
```

Figure 7.10 Result of Listing 7.10.

```
SELECT
    a.au_id,
    COUNT(ta.title_id) AS "Num books"
  FROM authors a
  INNER JOIN title_authors ta
    ON a.au_id = ta.au_id
  GROUP BY a.au_id
  ORDER BY a.au_id ASC;
```

Listing 7.11 List the number of books that each author wrote (or cowrote). See Figure 7.11 for the result.

```
au_id Num books
----- ---------
A01           3
A02           4
A03           2
A04           4
A05           1
A06           3
```

Figure 7.11 Result of Listing 7.11.

Listing 7.11 combines an inner join with the aggregate function COUNT() and a GROUP BY clause to list the number of books that each author wrote (or cowrote). For information about aggregate functions and GROUP BY, see Chapter 6. See Figure 7.11 for the result. Note that, as in Figure 7.7, author A07 (Paddy O'Furniture) is omitted from the result because he has written no books and so has no matching rows in *title_authors*. See Listing 7.30 in "Creating Outer Joins with OUTER JOIN" later in this chapter for an example that lists authors who have written no books.

Tips for Listing 7.11

- Using WHERE syntax, Listing 7.11 is equivalent to:

```
SELECT a.au_id,
    COUNT(ta.title_id)
        AS "Num books"
  FROM authors a, title_authors ta
  WHERE a.au_id = ta.au_id
  GROUP BY a.au_id
  ORDER BY a.au_id ASC;
```

Listing 7.12 uses WHERE conditions to list the advance paid for each biography. See Figure 7.12 for the result.

Tips for Listing 7.12

- Using WHERE syntax, Listing 7.12 is equivalent to:

```
SELECT t.title_id, t.title_name,
    r.advance
  FROM royalties r, titles t
  WHERE r.title_id = t.title_id
    AND t.type = 'biography'
    AND r.advance IS NOT NULL
  ORDER BY r.advance DESC;
```

```
SELECT
    t.title_id,
    t.title_name,
    r.advance
  FROM royalties r
  INNER JOIN titles t
    ON r.title_id = t.title_id
  WHERE t.type = 'biography'
    AND r.advance IS NOT NULL
  ORDER BY r.advance DESC;
```

Listing 7.12 List the advance paid for each biography. See Figure 7.12 for the result.

```
title_id title_name                  advance
-------- --------------------------- -----------
T07      I Blame My Mother           1000000.00
T12      Spontaneous, Not Annoying     50000.00
T06      How About Never?              20000.00
```

Figure 7.12 Result of Listing 7.12.

```
SELECT
    t.type,
    COUNT(r.advance)
      AS "COUNT(r.advance)",
    SUM(r.advance)
      AS "SUM(r.advance)"
  FROM royalties r
  INNER JOIN titles t
    ON r.title_id = t.title_id
  WHERE r.advance IS NOT NULL
  GROUP BY t.type
  ORDER BY t.type ASC;
```

Listing 7.13 List the count and total advance paid for each type of book. See Figure 7.13 for the result.

```
type         COUNT(r.advance) SUM(r.advance)
----------   ---------------- --------------
biography                   3     1070000.00
children                    2           0.00
computer                    1       15000.00
history                     3       31000.00
psychology                  3      220000.00
```

Figure 7.13 Result of Listing 7.13.

Listing 7.13 uses aggregate functions and a GROUP BY clause to list the count and total advance paid for each type of book. See Figure 7.13 for the result.

Tips for Listing 7.13

- Using WHERE syntax, Listing 7.13 is equivalent to:

```
SELECT t.type,
    COUNT(r.advance)
      AS "COUNT(r.advance)",
    SUM(r.advance)
      AS "SUM(r.advance)"
  FROM royalties r, titles t
  WHERE r.title_id = t.title_id
    AND r.advance IS NOT NULL
  GROUP BY t.type
  ORDER BY t.type ASC;
```

Listing 7.14 is similar to Listing 7.13, except that it uses an additional grouping column to list the count and total advance paid for each type of book by publisher. See Figure 7.14 for the result.

Tips for Listing 7.14

- Using WHERE syntax, Listing 7.14 is equivalent to:

```
SELECT t.type, t.pub_id,
    COUNT(r.advance)
      AS "COUNT(r.advance)",
    SUM(r.advance)
      AS "SUM(r.advance)"
  FROM royalties r, titles t
  WHERE r.title_id = t.title_id
    AND r.advance IS NOT NULL
  GROUP BY t.type, t.pub_id
  ORDER BY t.type ASC, t.pub_id ASC;
```

```
SELECT
    t.type,
    t.pub_id,
    COUNT(r.advance) AS "COUNT(r.advance)",
    SUM(r.advance) AS "SUM(r.advance)"
  FROM royalties r
  INNER JOIN titles t
    ON r.title_id = t.title_id
  WHERE r.advance IS NOT NULL
  GROUP BY t.type, t.pub_id
  ORDER BY t.type ASC, t.pub_id ASC;
```

Listing 7.14 List the count and total advance paid for each type of book, by publisher. See Figure 7.14 for the result.

type	pub_id	COUNT(r.advance)	SUM(r.advance)
biography	P01	2	70000.00
biography	P03	1	1000000.00
children	P04	2	0.00
computer	P02	1	15000.00
history	P01	1	10000.00
history	P03	2	21000.00
psychology	P04	3	220000.00

Figure 7.14 Result of Listing 7.14.

```
SELECT
    ta.title_id,
    COUNT(ta.au_id) AS "Num authors"
FROM authors a
INNER JOIN title_authors ta
    ON a.au_id = ta.au_id
GROUP BY ta.title_id
HAVING COUNT(ta.au_id) > 1
ORDER BY ta.title_id ASC;
```

Listing 7.15 List the number of coauthors of each book written by two or more authors. See Figure 7.15 for the result.

```
title_id Num authors
-------- -----------
T04                2
T07                2
T11                3
```

Figure 7.15 Result of Listing 7.15.

Listing 7.15 uses a HAVING clause to list the number of coauthors of each book written by two or more authors. For information about HAVING, see "Filtering Groups with HAVING" on page 176. See Figure 7.15 for the result.

Tips for Listing 7.15

Using WHERE syntax, Listing 7.15 is equivalent to:

```
SELECT ta.title_id,
    COUNT(ta.au_id) AS "Num authors"
  FROM authors a, title_authors ta
  WHERE a.au_id = ta.au_id
  GROUP BY ta.title_id
  HAVING COUNT(ta.au_id) > 1
  ORDER BY ta.title_id ASC;
```

You also can join values in two columns that aren't equal. Listing 7.16 uses greater-than (>) join to find each book whose revenue (= price × sales) is at least 10 times greater than the advance paid to the author(s). See Figure 7.16 for the result. The use of <, <=, >, and >= joins is common, but not-equal joins (<>) are used rarely. Generally, not-equal joins make sense only when used with a self-join; see "Creating a Self-Join" on page 233.

Tips for Listing 7.16

- Using WHERE syntax, Listing 7.16 is equivalent to:

```
SELECT t.title_id, t.title_name,
    r.advance,
    t.price * t.sales AS "Revenue"
  FROM titles t, royalties r
  WHERE t.price * t.sales >
        r.advance * 10
    AND t.title_id = r.title_id
  ORDER BY t.price * t.sales DESC;
```

```
SELECT
    t.title_id,
    t.title_name,
    r.advance,
    t.price * t.sales AS "Revenue"
  FROM titles t
  INNER JOIN royalties r
    ON t.price * t.sales > r.advance * 10
    AND t.title_id = r.title_id
  ORDER BY t.price * t.sales DESC;
```

Listing 7.16 List each book whose revenue (= price × sales) is at least 10 times greater than its advance. See Figure 7.16 for the result.

```
title_id title_name                          advance     Revenue
-------- ----------------------------------- ----------- -----------
T07      I Blame My Mother                   1000000.00  35929790.00
T05      Exchange of Platitudes               100000.00   1400008.00
T12      Spontaneous, Not Annoying             50000.00   1299012.99
T03      Ask Your System Administrator         15000.00   1025396.65
T13      What Are The Civilian Applications?   20000.00    313905.33
T06      How About Never?                      20000.00    225834.00
T02      200 Years of German Humor              1000.00    190841.70
T09      Kiss My Boo-Boo                            .00     69750.00
T08      Just Wait Until After School               .00     40950.00
```

Figure 7.16 Result of Listing 7.16.

```
SELECT
    a.au_fname,
    a.au_lname,
    t.title_name
  FROM authors a
  INNER JOIN title_authors ta
    ON a.au_id = ta.au_id
  INNER JOIN titles t
    ON t.title_id = ta.title_id
  ORDER BY a.au_lname ASC,
    a.au_fname ASC, t.title_name ASC;
```

Listing 7.17 List the author names and the names of the books that each author wrote (or cowrote). See Figure 7.17 for the result.

Complicated queries can arise from simple questions. In Listing 7.17, I must join three tables to list the author names and the names of the books that each author wrote (or cowrote). See Figure 7.17 for the result.

```
au_fname   au_lname   title_name
---------  ---------  ------------------------------------
Sarah      Buchman    1977!
Sarah      Buchman    200 Years of German Humor
Sarah      Buchman    What Are The Civilian Applications?
Wendy      Heydemark  How About Never?
Wendy      Heydemark  I Blame My Mother
Wendy      Heydemark  Not Without My Faberge Egg
Wendy      Heydemark  Spontaneous, Not Annoying
Hallie     Hull       But I Did It Unconsciously
Hallie     Hull       Perhaps It's a Glandular Problem
Klee       Hull       But I Did It Unconsciously
Klee       Hull       Exchange of Platitudes
Klee       Hull       I Blame My Mother
Klee       Hull       Perhaps It's a Glandular Problem
Christian  Kells      Ask Your System Administrator
           Kellsey    Just Wait Until After School
           Kellsey    Kiss My Boo-Boo
           Kellsey    Perhaps It's a Glandular Problem
```

Figure 7.17 Result of Listing 7.17.

Tips for Listing 7.17

- Using WHERE syntax, Listing 7.17 is equivalent to:

```
SELECT a.au_fname, a.au_lname,
    t.title_name
  FROM authors a, title_authors ta,
    titles t
  WHERE a.au_id = ta.au_id
    AND t.title_id = ta.title_id
  ORDER BY a.au_lname ASC,
    a.au_fname ASC,
    t.title_name ASC;
```

- **DBMS** To run Listing 7.17 in **Microsoft Access**, type:

```
SELECT a.au_fname, a.au_lname,
    t.title_name
  FROM titles AS t
  INNER JOIN (authors AS a
    INNER JOIN title_authors AS ta
      ON a.au_id = ta.au_id)
    ON t.title_id = ta.title_id
  ORDER BY a.au_lname ASC,
    a.au_fname ASC,
    t.title_name ASC;
```

```
SELECT
    a.au_fname,
    a.au_lname,
    t.title_name,
    p.pub_name
 FROM authors a
 INNER JOIN title_authors ta
   ON a.au_id = ta.au_id
 INNER JOIN titles t
   ON t.title_id = ta.title_id
 INNER JOIN publishers p
   ON p.pub_id = t.pub_id
 ORDER BY a.au_lname ASC, a.au_fname ASC,
    t.title_name ASC;
```

Listing 7.18 List the author names, the names of the books that each author wrote (or cowrote), and the publisher names. See Figure 7.18 for the result.

Expanding on Listing 7.17, Listing 7.18 requires a four-table join to list the publisher names along with the names of the authors and books. See Figure 7.18 for the result.

```
au_fname  au_lname  title_name                            pub_name
--------- --------- ------------------------------------- -------------------
Sarah     Buchman   1977!                                 Abatis Publishers
Sarah     Buchman   200 Years of German Humor             Schadenfreude Press
Sarah     Buchman   What Are The Civilian Applications?   Schadenfreude Press
Wendy     Heydemark How About Never?                      Abatis Publishers
Wendy     Heydemark I Blame My Mother                     Schadenfreude Press
Wendy     Heydemark Not Without My Faberge Egg            Abatis Publishers
Wendy     Heydemark Spontaneous, Not Annoying             Abatis Publishers
Hallie    Hull      But I Did It Unconsciously            Tenterhooks Press
Hallie    Hull      Perhaps It's a Glandular Problem      Tenterhooks Press
Klee      Hull      But I Did It Unconsciously            Tenterhooks Press
Klee      Hull      Exchange of Platitudes                Tenterhooks Press
Klee      Hull      I Blame My Mother                     Schadenfreude Press
Klee      Hull      Perhaps It's a Glandular Problem      Tenterhooks Press
Christian Kells     Ask Your System Administrator         Core Dump Books
          Kellsey   Just Wait Until After School          Tenterhooks Press
          Kellsey   Kiss My Boo-Boo                       Tenterhooks Press
          Kellsey   Perhaps It's a Glandular Problem      Tenterhooks Press
```

Figure 7.18 Result of Listing 7.18.

Tips for Listing 7.18

- Using WHERE syntax, Listing 7.18 is equivalent to:

```
SELECT a.au_fname, a.au_lname,
    t.title_name, p.pub_name
  FROM authors a, title_authors ta,
    titles t, publishers p
  WHERE a.au_id = ta.au_id
    AND t.title_id = ta.title_id
    AND p.pub_id = t.pub_id
  ORDER BY a.au_lname ASC,
    a.au_fname ASC,
    t.title_name ASC;
```

- **DBMS** To run Listing 7.18 in **Microsoft Access**, type:

```
SELECT a.au_fname, a.au_lname,
    t.title_name, p.pub_name
  FROM (publishers AS p
    INNER JOIN titles AS t
      ON p.pub_id = t.pub_id)
  INNER JOIN (authors AS a
    INNER JOIN title_authors AS ta
      ON a.au_id = ta.au_id)
    ON t.title_id = ta.title_id
  ORDER BY a.au_lname ASC,
    a.au_fname ASC,
    t.title_name ASC;
```

Listing 7.19 calculates the total royalties for all books. The gross royalty of a book is the book's revenue (= sales × price) times the royalty rate (the fraction of revenue paid to the author). In most cases, the author receives an initial advance against royalties. The publisher deducts the advance from the gross royalty to get the net royalty. If the net royalty is positive, then the publisher must pay the author; if the net royalty is negative or zero, then the author gets nothing because he or she still hasn't "earned out" the advance. See Figure 7.19 for the result. Gross royalties are labeled "Total royalties", gross advances are labeled "Total advances", and net royalties are labeled "Total due to authors".

Listing 7.19 calculates total royalties for all books; the subsequent examples in this section will show you how to break down royalties by author, book, publisher, and other groups.

Tips for Listing 7.19

- Using WHERE syntax, Listing 7.19 is equivalent to:

```
SELECT
    SUM(t.sales * t.price *
      r.royalty_rate)
      AS "Total royalties",
    SUM(r.advance)
      AS "Total advances",
    SUM((t.sales * t.price *
      r.royalty_rate) - r.advance)
      AS "Total due to authors"
  FROM titles t, royalties r
 WHERE r.title_id = t.title_id
   AND t.sales IS NOT NULL;
```

```
SELECT
    SUM(t.sales * t.price * r.royalty_rate) AS "Total royalties",
    SUM(r.advance) AS "Total advances",
    SUM((t.sales * t.price * r.royalty_rate) - r.advance) AS "Total due to authors"
  FROM titles t
  INNER JOIN royalties r
    ON r.title_id = t.title_id
  WHERE t.sales IS NOT NULL;
```

Listing 7.19 Calculate the total royalties for all books. See Figure 7.19 for the result.

```
Total royalties Total advances Total due to authors
--------------- -------------- --------------------
   4387219.55     1336000.00            3051219.55
```

Figure 7.19 Result of Listing 7.19.

Listing 7.20 uses a three-table join to calculate the royalty earned by each author for each book that the author wrote (or cowrote). Because a book can have multiple authors, per-author royalty calculations involve each author's share of a book's royalty (and advance). The author's royalty share for each book is given in the table *title_authors* in the column *royalty_share*. For a book with a sole author, *royalty_share* is 1.0 (100 percent). For a book with multiple authors, the *royalty_share* of each author is a fractional amount between 0 and 1 (inclusive); all the *royalty_share* values for a particular book must sum to 1.0 (100 percent). See Figure 7.20 for the result. The sum of the values in each of the last three columns in the result equals the corresponding total in Figure 7.19.

Tips for Listing 7.20

* Using WHERE syntax, Listing 7.20 is equivalent to:

```
SELECT ta.au_id, t.title_id, t.pub_id,
    t.sales * t.price *
      r.royalty_rate * ta.royalty_share
      AS "Royalty share",
    r.advance * ta.royalty_share
      AS "Advance share",
    (t.sales * t.price *
     r.royalty_rate * ta.royalty_share) -
     (r.advance * ta.royalty_share)
      AS "Due to author"
  FROM title_authors ta,
    titles t, royalties r
  WHERE t.title_id = ta.title_id
    AND r.title_id = t.title_id
    AND t.sales IS NOT NULL
  ORDER BY ta.au_id ASC,
    t.title_id ASC;
```

* DBMS To run Listing 7.20 in **Microsoft Access**, type:

```
SELECT ta.au_id, t.title_id, t.pub_id,
    t.sales * t.price *
      r.royalty_rate * ta.royalty_share
      AS "Royalty share",
    r.advance * ta.royalty_share
      AS "Advance share",
    (t.sales * t.price *
     r.royalty_rate * ta.royalty_share) -
     (r.advance * ta.royalty_share)
      AS "Due to author"
  FROM (titles AS t
  INNER JOIN royalties AS r
    ON t.title_id = r.title_id)
  INNER JOIN title_authors AS ta
    ON t.title_id = ta.title_id
  WHERE t.sales IS NOT NULL
  ORDER BY ta.au_id ASC,
    t.title_id ASC;
```

```
SELECT
    ta.au_id,
    t.title_id,
    t.pub_id,
    t.sales * t.price * r.royalty_rate * ta.royalty_share AS "Royalty share",
    r.advance * ta.royalty_share AS "Advance share",
    (t.sales * t.price * r.royalty_rate * ta.royalty_share) -
      (r.advance * ta.royalty_share) AS "Due to author"
  FROM title_authors ta
  INNER JOIN titles t
    ON t.title_id = ta.title_id
  INNER JOIN royalties r
    ON r.title_id = t.title_id
  WHERE t.sales IS NOT NULL
  ORDER BY ta.au_id ASC, t.title_id ASC;
```

Listing 7.20 Calculate the royalty earned by each author for each book that the author wrote (or cowrote). See Figure 7.20 for the result.

```
au_id title_id pub_id Royalty share Advance share Due to author
----- -------- ------ ------------- ------------- -------------
A01   T01      P01          622.32      10000.00      -9377.68
A01   T02      P03        11450.50       1000.00      10450.50
A01   T13      P03        18834.32      20000.00      -1165.68
A02   T06      P01        18066.72      20000.00      -1933.28
A02   T07      P03      1976138.45     500000.00    1476138.45
A02   T12      P01       116911.17      50000.00      66911.17
A03   T04      P04         8106.38      12000.00      -3893.62
A03   T11      P04        15792.90      30000.00     -14207.10
A04   T04      P04         5404.26       8000.00      -2595.74
A04   T05      P04       126000.72     100000.00      26000.72
A04   T07      P03      1976138.45     500000.00    1476138.45
A04   T11      P04        15792.90      30000.00     -14207.10
A05   T03      P02        71777.77      15000.00      56777.77
A06   T08      P04         1638.00           .00       1638.00
A06   T09      P04         3487.50           .00       3487.50
A06   T11      P04        21057.20      40000.00     -18942.80
```

Figure 7.20 Result of Listing 7.20.

Listing 7.21 is similar to Listing 7.20 except that it adds a join to the table *authors* to print the author names and includes a WHERE condition to retrieve rows with only positive royalties. See Figure 7.21 for the result.

Tips for Listing 7.21

- Using WHERE syntax, Listing 7.21 is equivalent to:

```
SELECT a.au_id, a.au_fname,
    a.au_lname, t.title_name,
    (t.sales * t.price *
    r.royalty_rate * ta.royalty_share) -
    (r.advance * ta.royalty_share)
    AS "Due to author"
  FROM authors a, title_authors ta,
    titles t, royalties r
  WHERE a.au_id = ta.au_id
    AND t.title_id = ta.title_id
    AND r.title_id = t.title_id
    AND t.sales IS NOT NULL
    AND (t.sales * t.price *
    r.royalty_rate * ta.royalty_share) -
    (r.advance * ta.royalty_share) > 0
  ORDER BY a.au_id ASC,
    t.title_id ASC;
```

- DBMS To run Listing 7.21 in **Microsoft Access**, type:

```
SELECT a.au_id, a.au_fname,
    a.au_lname, t.title_name,
    (t.sales * t.price *
    r.royalty_rate * ta.royalty_share) -
    (r.advance * ta.royalty_share)
    AS "Due to author"
  FROM (titles AS t
    INNER JOIN royalties AS r
    ON t.title_id = r.title_id)
  INNER JOIN (authors AS a
    INNER JOIN title_authors AS ta
    ON a.au_id = ta.au_id)
    ON t.title_id = ta.title_id
  WHERE t.sales IS NOT NULL
    AND (t.sales * t.price *
    r.royalty_rate * ta.royalty_share) -
    (r.advance * ta.royalty_share) > 0
  ORDER BY a.au_id ASC,
    t.title_id ASC;
```

```
SELECT
    a.au_id,
    a.au_fname,
    a.au_lname,
    t.title_name,
    (t.sales * t.price * r.royalty_rate * ta.royalty_share) -
      (r.advance * ta.royalty_share) AS "Due to author"
  FROM authors a
  INNER JOIN title_authors ta
    ON a.au_id = ta.au_id
  INNER JOIN titles t
    ON t.title_id = ta.title_id
  INNER JOIN royalties r
    ON r.title_id = t.title_id
  WHERE t.sales IS NOT NULL
    AND (t.sales * t.price * r.royalty_rate * ta.royalty_share) -
      (r.advance * ta.royalty_share) > 0
  ORDER BY a.au_id ASC, t.title_id ASC;
```

Listing 7.21 List only positive royalties earned by each author for each book that the author wrote (or cowrote). See Figure 7.21 for the result.

```
au_id au_fname  au_lname  title_name                    Due to author
----- --------- --------- ----------------------------- -------------
A01   Sarah     Buchman   200 Years of German Humor        10450.50
A02   Wendy     Heydemark I Blame My Mother              1476138.45
A02   Wendy     Heydemark Spontaneous, Not Annoying        66911.17
A04   Klee      Hull      Exchange of Platitudes           26000.72
A04   Klee      Hull      I Blame My Mother              1476138.45
A05   Christian Kells     Ask Your System Administrator    56777.77
A06             Kellsey   Just Wait Until After School       1638.00
A06             Kellsey   Kiss My Boo-Boo                    3487.50
```

Figure 7.21 Result of Listing 7.21.

Listing 7.22 uses a GROUP BY clause to calculate the total royalties paid by each publisher. The aggregate function COUNT() computes the total number of books for which each publisher pays royalties. Note that each author's royalty share is unnecessary here because no per-author calculations are involved. See Figure 7.22 for the result. The sum of the values in each of the last three columns in the result equals the corresponding total in Figure 7.19.

Tips for Listing 7.22

- Using WHERE syntax, Listing 7.22 is equivalent to :

```
SELECT t.pub_id,
    COUNT(t.sales)
      AS "Num books",
    SUM(t.sales * t.price *
      r.royalty_rate)
      AS "Total royalties",
    SUM(r.advance)
      AS "Total advances",
    SUM((t.sales * t.price *
      r.royalty_rate) -
      r.advance)
      AS "Total due to authors"
  FROM titles t, royalties r
WHERE r.title_id = t.title_id
    AND t.sales IS NOT NULL
  GROUP BY t.pub_id
  ORDER BY t.pub_id ASC;
```

```
SELECT
    t.pub_id,
    COUNT(t.sales) AS "Num books",
    SUM(t.sales * t.price * r.royalty_rate) AS "Total royalties",
    SUM(r.advance) AS "Total advances",
    SUM((t.sales * t.price * r.royalty_rate) - r.advance) AS "Total due to authors"
  FROM titles t
  INNER JOIN royalties r
    ON r.title_id = t.title_id
  WHERE t.sales IS NOT NULL
  GROUP BY t.pub_id
  ORDER BY t.pub_id ASC;
```

Listing 7.22 Calculate the total royalties paid by each publisher. See Figure 7.22 for the result.

```
pub_id Num books Total royalties Total advances Total due to authors
------ --------- --------------- -------------- --------------------
P01            3       135600.21       80000.00             55600.21
P02            1        71777.77       15000.00             56777.77
P03            3      3982561.72     1021000.00           2961561.72
P04            5       197279.85      220000.00            -22720.15
```

Figure 7.22 Result of Listing 7.22.

Listing 7.23 is similar to Listing 7.22 except that it calculates the total royalties earned by each author for all books written (or cowritten). See Figure 7.23 for the result. The sum of the values in each of the last three columns in the result equals the corresponding total in Figure 7.19.

```
SELECT
    ta.au_id,
    COUNT(sales) AS "Num books",
    SUM(t.sales * t.price * r.royalty_rate * ta.royalty_share) AS "Total royalties share",
    SUM(r.advance * ta.royalty_share) AS "Total advances share",
    SUM((t.sales * t.price * r.royalty_rate * ta.royalty_share) - (r.advance * ta.royalty_share))
      AS "Total due to author"
  FROM title_authors ta
  INNER JOIN titles t
    ON t.title_id = ta.title_id
  INNER JOIN royalties r
    ON r.title_id = t.title_id
  WHERE t.sales IS NOT NULL
  GROUP BY ta.au_id
  ORDER BY ta.au_id ASC;
```

Listing 7.23 Calculate the total royalties earned by each author for all books written (or cowritten). See Figure 7.23 for the result.

au_id	Num books	Total royalties share	Total advances share	Total due to author
A01	3	30907.14	31000.00	-92.86
A02	3	2111116.34	570000.00	1541116.34
A03	2	23899.28	42000.00	-18100.72
A04	4	2123336.32	638000.00	1485336.32
A05	1	71777.77	15000.00	56777.77
A06	3	26182.70	40000.00	-13817.30

Figure 7.23 Result of Listing 7.23.

Tips for Listing 7.23

- Using WHERE syntax, Listing 7.23 is equivalent to:

```
SELECT ta.au_id,
   COUNT(sales)
     AS "Num books",
   SUM(t.sales * t.price *
     r.royalty_rate * ta.royalty_share)
     AS "Total royalties share",
   SUM(r.advance * ta.royalty_share)
     AS "Total advances share",
   SUM((t.sales * t.price *
     r.royalty_rate * ta.royalty_share) -
     (r.advance * ta.royalty_share))
     AS "Total due to author"
  FROM title_authors ta, titles t,
    royalties r
  WHERE t.title_id = ta.title_id
    AND r.title_id = t.title_id
    AND t.sales IS NOT NULL
  GROUP BY ta.au_id
  ORDER BY ta.au_id ASC;
```

- **DBMS** To run Listing 7.23 in **Microsoft Access**, type:

```
SELECT ta.au_id,
   COUNT(sales)
     AS "Num books",
   SUM(t.sales * t.price *
     r.royalty_rate * ta.royalty_share)
     AS "Total royalties share",
   SUM(r.advance * ta.royalty_share)
     AS "Total advances share",
   SUM((t.sales * t.price *
     r.royalty_rate * ta.royalty_share) -
     (r.advance * ta.royalty_share))
     AS "Total due to author"
  FROM (title_authors AS ta
    INNER JOIN titles AS t
      ON t.title_id = ta.title_id)
  INNER JOIN royalties AS r
    ON r.title_id = t.title_id
  WHERE t.sales IS NOT NULL
  GROUP BY ta.au_id
  ORDER BY ta.au_id ASC;
```

Listing 7.24 uses two grouping columns to calculate the total royalties to be paid by each U.S. publisher to each author for all books written (or cowritten) by the author. The HAVING condition returns retrieve rows with only positive net royalties, and the WHERE condition retrieves only U.S. publishers. See Figure 7.24 for the result.

```
SELECT
    t.pub_id,
    ta.au_id,
    COUNT(*) AS "Num books",
    SUM(t.sales * t.price * r.royalty_rate * ta.royalty_share) AS "Total royalties share",
    SUM(r.advance * ta.royalty_share) AS "Total advances share",
    SUM((t.sales * t.price * r.royalty_rate * ta.royalty_share) - (r.advance * ta.royalty_share))
      AS "Total due to author"
  FROM title_authors ta
  INNER JOIN titles t
    ON t.title_id = ta.title_id
  INNER JOIN royalties r
    ON r.title_id = t.title_id
  INNER JOIN publishers p
    ON p.pub_id = t.pub_id
  WHERE t.sales IS NOT NULL
    AND p.country IN ('USA')
  GROUP BY t.pub_id, ta.au_id
  HAVING SUM((t.sales * t.price * r.royalty_rate * ta.royalty_share) -
    (r.advance * ta.royalty_share)) > 0
  ORDER BY t.pub_id ASC, ta.au_id ASC;
```

Listing 7.24 Calculate the positive net royalties to be paid by each U.S. publisher to each author for all books written (or cowritten) by the author. See Figure 7.24 for the result.

pub_id	au_id	Num books	Total royalties share	Total advances share	Total due to author
P01	A02	2	134977.89	70000.00	64977.89
P02	A05	1	71777.77	15000.00	56777.77
P04	A04	3	147197.87	138000.00	9197.87

Figure 7.24 Result of Listing 7.24.

Tips for Listing 7.24

- Using WHERE syntax, Listing 7.24 is equivalent to:

```
SELECT t.pub_id, ta.au_id,
    COUNT(*)
      AS "Num books",
    SUM(t.sales * t.price *
      r.royalty_rate * ta.royalty_share)
      AS "Total royalties share",
    SUM(r.advance * ta.royalty_share)
      AS "Total advances share",
    SUM((t.sales * t.price *
      r.royalty_rate * ta.royalty_share) -
      (r.advance * ta.royalty_share))
      AS "Total due to author"
  FROM title_authors ta, titles t,
    royalties r, publishers p
  WHERE t.title_id = ta.title_id
    AND r.title_id = t.title_id
    AND p.pub_id = t.pub_id
    AND t.sales IS NOT NULL
    AND p.country IN ('USA')
  GROUP BY t.pub_id, ta.au_id
  HAVING SUM((t.sales * t.price *
    r.royalty_rate * ta.royalty_share) -
    (r.advance * ta.royalty_share)) > 0
  ORDER BY t.pub_id ASC,
    ta.au_id ASC;
```

- **DBMS** To run Listing 7.24 in **Microsoft Access**, type:

```
SELECT t.pub_id, ta.au_id,
    COUNT(*)
      AS "Num books",
    SUM(t.sales * t.price *
      r.royalty_rate * ta.royalty_share)
      AS "Total royalties share",
    SUM(r.advance * ta.royalty_share)
      AS "Total advances share",
    SUM((t.sales * t.price *
      r.royalty_rate * ta.royalty_share) -
      (r.advance * ta.royalty_share))
      AS "Total due to author"
  FROM ((publishers AS p
    INNER JOIN titles AS t
      ON p.pub_id = t.pub_id)
      INNER JOIN royalties AS r
        ON t.title_id = r.title_id)
  INNER JOIN title_authors AS ta
    ON t.title_id = ta.title_id
  WHERE t.sales IS NOT NULL
    AND p.country IN ('USA')
  GROUP BY t.pub_id, ta.au_id
  HAVING SUM((t.sales * t.price *
    r.royalty_rate * ta.royalty_share) -
    (r.advance * ta.royalty_share)) > 0
  ORDER BY t.pub_id ASC,
    ta.au_id ASC;
```

Creating Outer Joins with OUTER JOIN

In the preceding section, you learned that inner joins return rows only if at least one row from both tables satisfies the join condition(s). An inner join eliminates the rows that don't match with a row from the other table, whereas an **outer join** returns *all* rows from at least one of the tables (provided that those rows meet any WHERE or HAVING search conditions).

Outer joins are useful for answering questions that involve missing quantities: authors who have written no books or classes with no enrolled students, for example. Outer joins also are helpful for creating reports in which you want to list all the rows of one table along with matching rows from another table: all authors and any books that sold more than a given number of copies, for example, or all products with order quantities, including products that no one ordered.

Unlike other joins, the order in which you specify the tables in outer joins is important, so the two join operands are called the **left table** and the **right table**. Outer joins come in three flavors:

- **Left outer join.** The result of a left outer join includes all the rows from the left table specified in the LEFT OUTER JOIN clause, not just the rows in which the joined columns match. If a row in the left table has no matching rows in the right table, then the associated row in the result contains nulls for all SELECT-clause columns coming from the right table.

- **Right outer join.** A right outer join is the reverse of a left outer join. All rows from the right table are returned. Nulls are returned for the left table if a right-table row has no matching row in the left table.

- **Full outer join.** A full outer join, which is a combination of left and right outer joins, returns all rows in both the left and right tables. If a row has no match in the other table, then the SELECT-clause columns from the other table contain nulls. If a match occurs between the tables, then the entire row in the result contains data values from both tables.

To summarize, all rows are retrieved from the left table referenced in a left outer join, all rows are retrieved from the right table referenced in a right outer join, and all rows from both tables are retrieved in a full outer join. In all cases, unmatched rows are padded with nulls. In the result, you can't distinguish the nulls (if any) that were in the input tables originally from the nulls inserted by the outer-join operation. Remember that the conditions NULL = NULL and NULL = *any_value* are unknown and not matches; see "Nulls" on page 72.

To create a left outer join:

- Type:

```
SELECT columns
  FROM left_table
  LEFT [OUTER] JOIN right_table
    ON join_conditions
```

columns is one or more comma-separated expressions or column names from *left_table* or *right_table*. *left_table* and *right_table* are the names of the joined tables. If the tables have some column names in common, then qualify those column names with the names of the tables.

join_conditions specifies one or more join conditions to be evaluated for each pair of joined rows. A join condition takes this form:

```
[left_table.]column op
  [right_table.]column
```

op usually is = but can be any comparison operator: =, <>, <, <=, >, or >= (refer to Table 4.2 on page 89). You can combine multiple join conditions with **AND** or **OR**; see "Combining and Negating Conditions with AND, OR, and NOT" on page 93.

The keyword OUTER is optional.

To create a right outer join:

- Type:

```
SELECT columns
  FROM left_table
  RIGHT [OUTER] JOIN right_table
    ON join_conditions
```

columns, *left_table*, *right_table*, and *join_conditions* have the same meanings as in "To create a left outer join" earlier in this section.

The keyword OUTER is optional.

To create a full outer join:

- Type:

```
SELECT columns
  FROM left_table
  FULL [OUTER] JOIN right_table
    ON join_conditions
```

columns, *left_table*, *right_table*, and *join_conditions* have the same meanings as in "To create a left outer join" earlier in this section.

The keyword OUTER is optional.

Tips for OUTER JOIN

- For outer joins, you should use JOIN syntax instead of WHERE syntax when possible because JOIN syntax is more precise. SQL lacks standardized WHERE syntax for outer joins, so syntax varies by DBMS. A DBMS also might place restrictions on WHERE outer joins that don't exist for JOIN outer joins. See the DBMS tip later in this section for specific information.

- Be wary of the order in which tables appear in outer joins. Unlike other joins, outer joins aren't **associative**—that is, the result of a query that involves an outer join depends on the order in which the tables are grouped and joined (associated). The following two three-table inner joins are equivalent (except for the column order in the result):

```
SELECT * FROM table1
   INNER JOIN table2
   INNER JOIN table3
```

and:

```
SELECT * FROM table2
   INNER JOIN table3
   INNER JOIN table1
```

But the following three-table outer joins yield different results:

```
SELECT * FROM table1
   LEFT OUTER JOIN table2
   LEFT OUTER JOIN table3
```

and:

```
SELECT * FROM table2
   LEFT OUTER JOIN table3
   LEFT OUTER JOIN table1
```

- Prior to the SQL:2003 standard, SQL had a **union join**, which doesn't actually match rows from two tables but returns a full outer join with matching rows removed. Every row in a union join has the columns of one table joined with nulls for the columns of the other table. The result of the statement t1 UNION JOIN t2 looks like this table:

All rows of *t1*	Nulls
Nulls	All rows of *t2*

A UNION JOIN has few practical uses, and not many DBMSs support it. You can simulate a union join by using a full outer join.

t1 UNION JOIN *t2*

is equivalent to:

t1 FULL OUTER JOIN *t2* ON 1 = 2

t1 and *t2* are tables, and *1 = 2* represents any condition that's always false. Note that UNION JOIN differs from UNION, which is a set operation and not a join; see "Combining Rows with UNION" on page 290.

- DBMS **Microsoft SQL Server** supports the standard OUTER JOIN syntax but older versions use the (nonstandard) outer join operator * in WHERE syntax to create outer joins. Attach * to the left or right of the comparison operator to create a left or right outer join. For outer joins, WHERE syntax is less precise than OUTER JOIN syntax and can yield an ambiguous query. The *= and =* outer-join operators are deprecated (slated for extinction) in newer versions of SQL Server.

  Oracle 8i and earlier don't support JOIN syntax; use WHERE joins instead. Oracle 9i and later support the standard OUTER JOIN syntax. In WHERE syntax, Oracle uses the (nonstandard) outer join operator (+) to create outer joins. Add (+) after the table that must be expanded (filled with nulls). See the examples later in this section.

For reference in the following four examples, Listing 7.25 and Figure 7.25 show the city for each author and publisher.

Listing 7.26 performs an inner join of the tables *authors* and *publishers* on their *city* columns. The result, Figure 7.26, lists only the authors who live in cities in which a publisher is located. You can compare the result of this inner join with the results of the outer joins in the following three examples.

Tips for Listing 7.26

- Using WHERE syntax, Listing 7.26 is equivalent to:

```
SELECT a.au_fname, a.au_lname, p.pub_name
  FROM authors a, publishers p
  WHERE a.city = p.city;
```

```
SELECT a.au_fname, a.au_lname, a.city
  FROM authors a;

SELECT p.pub_name, p.city
  FROM publishers p;
```

Listing 7.25 List the cities of the authors and the cities of the publishers. See Figure 7.25 for the result.

```
SELECT a.au_fname, a.au_lname, p.pub_name
  FROM authors a
  INNER JOIN publishers p
  ON a.city = p.city;
```

Listing 7.26 List the authors who live in cities in which a publisher is located. See Figure 7.26 for the result.

au_fname	au_lname	pub_name
Hallie	Hull	Core Dump Books
Klee	Hull	Core Dump Books
Christian	Kells	Abatis Publishers

Figure 7.26 Result of Listing 7.26.

au_fname	au_lname	city
Sarah	Buchman	Bronx
Wendy	Heydemark	Boulder
Hallie	Hull	San Francisco
Klee	Hull	San Francisco
Christian	Kells	New York
	Kellsey	Palo Alto
Paddy	O'Furniture	Sarasota

pub_name	city
Abatis Publishers	New York
Core Dump Books	San Francisco
Schadenfreude Press	Hamburg
Tenterhooks Press	Berkeley

Figure 7.25 Result of Listing 7.25.

```
SELECT a.au_fname, a.au_lname, p.pub_name
  FROM authors a
  LEFT OUTER JOIN publishers p
    ON a.city = p.city
  ORDER BY p.pub_name ASC,
    a.au_lname ASC, a.au_fname ASC;
```

Listing 7.27 This left outer join includes all rows in the table *authors* in the result, whether or not there's a match in the column *city* in the table *publishers*. See Figure 7.27 for the result.

```
au_fname   au_lname     pub_name
---------  -----------  ------------------
Sarah      Buchman      NULL
Wendy      Heydemark    NULL
           Kellsey      NULL
Paddy      O'Furniture  NULL
Christian  Kells        Abatis Publishers
Hallie     Hull         Core Dump Books
Klee       Hull         Core Dump Books
```

Figure 7.27 Result of Listing 7.27. Note that there's no matching data for four of the listed authors, so these rows contain null in the column *pub_name*.

Listing 7.27 uses a left outer join to include all authors in the result, regardless of whether a publisher is located in the same city. See Figure 7.27 for the result.

Tips for Listing 7.27

- DBMS To run Listing 7.27 in older versions of **Microsoft SQL Server** by using WHERE syntax, type:

```
SELECT a.au_fname, a.au_lname, p.pub_name
  FROM authors a, publishers p
  WHERE a.city *= p.city
  ORDER BY p.pub_name ASC,
    a.au_lname ASC, a.au_fname ASC;
```

To run Listing 7.27 in **Oracle** 8i or earlier, type:

```
SELECT a.au_fname, a.au_lname, p.pub_name
  FROM authors a, publishers p
  WHERE a.city = p.city (+)
  ORDER BY p.pub_name ASC,
    a.au_lname ASC, a.au_fname ASC;
```

Listing 7.28 uses a right outer join to include all publishers in the result, regardless of whether an author lives in the publisher's city. See Figure 7.28 for the result.

Tips for Listing 7.28

- **DBMS** To run Listing 7.28 in older versions of **Microsoft SQL Server** by using WHERE syntax, type:

```
SELECT a.au_fname, a.au_lname, p.pub_name
  FROM authors a, publishers p
  WHERE a.city =* p.city
  ORDER BY p.pub_name ASC,
    a.au_lname ASC, a.au_fname ASC;
```

To run Listing 7.28 in **Oracle** 8i or earlier, type:

```
SELECT a.au_fname, a.au_lname, p.pub_name
  FROM authors a, publishers p
  WHERE a.city (+) = p.city
  ORDER BY p.pub_name ASC,
    a.au_lname ASC, a.au_fname ASC;
```

```
SELECT a.au_fname, a.au_lname, p.pub_name
  FROM authors a
  RIGHT OUTER JOIN publishers p
  ON a.city = p.city
  ORDER BY p.pub_name ASC,
    a.au_lname ASC, a.au_fname ASC;
```

Listing 7.28 This right outer join includes all rows in the table *publishers* in the result, whether or not there's a match in the column *city* in the table *authors*. See Figure 7.28 for the result.

au_fname	au_lname	pub_name
Christian	Kells	Abatis Publishers
Hallie	Hull	Core Dump Books
Klee	Hull	Core Dump Books
NULL	NULL	Schadenfreude Press
NULL	NULL	Tenterhooks Press

Figure 7.28 Result of Listing 7.28. Note that there's no matching data for two of the listed publishers, so these rows contain nulls in the columns *au_fname* and *au_lname*.

```
SELECT a.au_fname, a.au_lname, p.pub_name
  FROM authors a
  FULL OUTER JOIN publishers p
    ON a.city = p.city
  ORDER BY p.pub_name ASC,
    a.au_lname ASC, a.au_fname ASC;
```

Listing 7.29 This full outer join includes all rows in the tables *authors* and *publishers* in the result, whether or not there's a match in the *city* columns. See Figure 7.29 for the result.

```
au_fname    au_lname     pub_name
---------   -----------  --------------------

Sarah       Buchman      NULL
Wendy       Heydemark    NULL
            Kellsey      NULL
Paddy       O'Furniture  NULL
Christian   Kells        Abatis Publishers
Hallie      Hull         Core Dump Books
Klee        Hull         Core Dump Books
NULL        NULL         Schadenfreude Press
NULL        NULL         Tenterhooks Press
```

Figure 7.29 Result of Listing 7.29. This result contains nine rows: four rows for authors who have no matching rows in the table *publishers*, three rows in which the author and publisher coexist in the same city, and two rows for publishers who have no matching city in the table *authors*.

Listing 7.29 uses a full outer join to include all publishers and all authors in the result, regardless of whether a publisher and author are located in the same city. See Figure 7.29 for the result.

Tips for Listing 7.29

- **DBMS** In older versions of **Microsoft SQL Server**, you can't place the * operator on both sides of the comparison operator to form a full outer join. Instead, form the union of a left and right outer join; see "Combining Rows with UNION" on page 290. To run Listing 7.29 by using WHERE syntax, type:

```
SELECT a.au_fname, a.au_lname, p.pub_name
  FROM authors a, publishers p
  WHERE a.city *= p.city
UNION ALL
SELECT a.au_fname, a.au_lname, p.pub_name
  FROM authors a, publishers p
  WHERE a.city =* p.city
    AND a.city IS NULL;
```

In **Oracle**, you can't place the (+) operator on both sides of the comparison operator to form a full outer join. Instead, form the union of a left and right outer join; see "Combining Rows with UNION" on page 290. To run Listing 7.29 in Oracle 8i or earlier, type:

```
SELECT a.au_fname, a.au_lname, p.pub_name
  FROM authors a, publishers p
  WHERE a.city = p.city (+)
UNION ALL
SELECT a.au_fname, a.au_lname, p.pub_name
  FROM authors a, publishers p
  WHERE a.city (+) = p.city
    AND a.city IS NULL;
```

Microsoft Access and **MySQL** don't support full outer joins, but you can replicate one by taking the union of left and right outer joins; see "Combining Rows with UNION" on page 290. In the following example, the first UNION table is a left outer join restricted to return all the rows in *authors* as well as the matched rows in *publishers* based on *city*. The second UNION table is a right outer join restricted to return only the unmatched rows in *publishers*. To run Listing 7.29, type:

```
SELECT a.au_fname, a.au_lname, p.pub_name
  FROM authors a
  LEFT OUTER JOIN publishers p
    ON a.city = p.city
UNION ALL
SELECT a.au_fname, a.au_lname, p.pub_name
  FROM authors a
  RIGHT OUTER JOIN publishers p
    ON a.city = p.city
  WHERE a.city IS NULL;
```

```
SELECT
    a.au_id,
    COUNT(ta.title_id) AS "Num books"
  FROM authors a
  LEFT OUTER JOIN title_authors ta
    ON a.au_id = ta.au_id
  GROUP BY a.au_id
  ORDER BY a.au_id ASC;
```

Listing 7.30 List the number of books that each author wrote (or cowrote), including authors who have written no books. See Figure 7.30 for the result.

```
au_id Num books
----- ---------
A01          3
A02          4
A03          2
A04          4
A05          1
A06          3
A07          0
```

Figure 7.30 Result of Listing 7.30.

Listing 7.30 uses a left outer join to list the number of books that each author wrote (or cowrote). See Figure 7.30 for the result. Note that in contrast to Listing 7.11 in "Creating an Inner Join with INNER JOIN" earlier in this chapter, the author A07 (Paddy O'Furniture) appears in the result even though he has written no books.

Tips for Listing 7.30

- DBMS To run Listing 7.30 in **Oracle** 8i or earlier, type:

```
SELECT a.au_id,
    COUNT(ta.title_id) AS "Num books"
  FROM authors a, title_authors ta
  WHERE a.au_id = ta.au_id (+)
  GROUP BY a.au_id
  ORDER BY a.au_id ASC;
```

Listing 7.31 uses a WHERE condition to test for null and list *only* the authors who haven't written a book. See Figure 7.31 for the result.

Tips for Listing 7.31

- DBMS To run Listing 7.31 in **Oracle** 8i or earlier, type:

```
SELECT a.au_id, a.au_fname, a.au_lname
  FROM authors a, title_authors ta
  WHERE a.au_id = ta.au_id (+)
    AND ta.au_id IS NULL;
```

```
SELECT a.au_id, a.au_fname, a.au_lname
  FROM authors a
  LEFT OUTER JOIN title_authors ta
    ON a.au_id = ta.au_id
  WHERE ta.au_id IS NULL;
```

Listing 7.31 List the authors who haven't written (or co-written) a book. See Figure 7.31 for the result.

```
au_id au_fname au_lname
----- -------- -----------
A07   Paddy    O'Furniture
```

Figure 7.31 Result of Listing 7.31.

```
SELECT a.au_id, a.au_fname, a.au_lname,
    tta.title_id, tta.title_name, tta.sales
  FROM authors a
  LEFT OUTER JOIN
  (SELECT ta.au_id, t.title_id,
      t.title_name, t.sales
    FROM title_authors ta
    INNER JOIN titles t
      ON t.title_id = ta.title_id
    WHERE sales > 100000) tta
    ON a.au_id = tta.au_id
  ORDER BY a.au_id ASC, tta.title_id ASC;
```

Listing 7.32 List all authors and any books written (or cowritten) that sold more than 100,000 copies. See Figure 7.32 for the result.

Listing 7.32 combines an inner join and a left outer join to list all authors and any books they wrote (or cowrote) that sold more than 100,000 copies. In this example, first I created a filtered INNER JOIN result and then OUTER JOINed it with the table authors, from which I wanted all rows. See Figure 7.32 for the result.

au_id	au_fname	au_lname	title_id	title_name	sales
A01	Sarah	Buchman	NULL	NULL	NULL
A02	Wendy	Heydemark	T07	I Blame My Mother	1500200
A02	Wendy	Heydemark	T12	Spontaneous, Not Annoying	100001
A03	Hallie	Hull	NULL	NULL	NULL
A04	Klee	Hull	T05	Exchange of Platitudes	201440
A04	Klee	Hull	T07	I Blame My Mother	1500200
A05	Christian	Kells	NULL	NULL	NULL
A06		Kellsey	NULL	NULL	NULL
A07	Paddy	O'Furniture	NULL	NULL	NULL

Figure 7.32 Result of Listing 7.32.

Tips for Listing 7.32

- DBMS To run Listing 7.32 in **Oracle** 8i or earlier, type:

```
SELECT a.au_id, a.au_fname, a.au_lname,
    tta.title_id, tta.title_name,
    tta.sales
  FROM authors a,
    (SELECT ta.au_id, t.title_id,
        t.title_name, t.sales
      FROM title_authors ta, titles t
      WHERE t.title_id = ta.title_id
        AND sales > 100000) tta
  WHERE a.au_id = tta.au_id (+)
  ORDER BY a.au_id ASC, tta.title_id ASC;
```

MySQL 4.1 and later will run Listing 7.32, but earlier versions don't support subqueries; see the DBMS tip in "Tips for Subqueries" on page 241. For complicated queries, you often can create a temporary table to hold the subquery; see "Creating a Temporary Table with CREATE TEMPORARY TABLE" on page 352. To run Listing 7.32 in MySQL 4.0 and earlier, type:

```
CREATE TEMPORARY TABLE tta
  SELECT ta.au_id, t.title_id,
      t.title_name, t.sales
  FROM title_authors ta
  INNER JOIN titles t
    ON t.title_id = ta.title_id
  WHERE sales > 100000;

SELECT a.au_id, a.au_fname,
    a.au_lname, tta.title_id,
    tta.title_name, tta.sales
  FROM authors a
  LEFT OUTER JOIN tta
    ON a.au_id = tta.au_id
  ORDER BY a.au_id ASC, tta.title_id ASC;

DROP TABLE tta;
```

Creating a Self-Join

A **self-join** is a normal SQL join that joins a table to itself and retrieves rows from a table by comparing values in one or more columns in the same table. Self-joins often are used in tables with a **reflexive relationship**, which is a primary-key/foreign-key relationship from a column or combination of columns in a table to other columns in that same table. For information about keys, see "Primary Keys" on page 26 and "Foreign Keys" on page 28.

Suppose that you have the following table, named *employees*:

```
emp_id  emp_name          boss_id
------  ----------------  -------

E01     Lord Copper       NULL
E02     Jocelyn Hitchcock E01
E03     Mr. Salter        E01
E04     William Boot      E03
E05     Mr. Corker        E03
```

emp_id is a primary key that uniquely identifies the employee, and *boss_id* is an employee ID that identifies the employee's manager. Each manager also is an employee, so to ensure that each manager ID that is added to the table matches an existing employee ID, *boss_id* is defined as a foreign key of *emp_id*. Listing 7.33 uses this reflexive relationship to compare rows within the table and retrieve the *name* of the manager of each employee. (You wouldn't need a join at all to get just the manager's ID.) See Figure 7.33 for the result.

The same table (*employees*) appears twice in Listing 7.33 with two different aliases (*e1* and *e2*) that are used to qualify column names in the join condition:

```
e1.boss_id = e2.emp_id
```

As with any join, a self-join requires two tables, but instead of adding a second table to the join, you add a second **instance** of the same table. That way, you can compare a column in the first instance of the table to a column in the second instance. As with all joins, the DBMS combines and returns rows of the table that satisfy the join condition. You actually aren't creating another copy of the table—you're joining the table to itself—but the effect might be easier to understand if you think about it as being two tables.

```
SELECT
    e1.emp_name AS "Employee name",
    e2.emp_name AS "Boss name"
  FROM employees e1
  INNER JOIN employees e2
    ON e1.boss_id = e2.emp_id;
```

Listing 7.33 List the name of each employee and the name of his or her manager. See Figure 7.33 for the result.

```
Employee name      Boss name
-----------------  -----------

Jocelyn Hitchcock  Lord Copper
Mr. Salter         Lord Copper
William Boot       Mr. Salter
Mr. Corker         Mr. Salter
```

Figure 7.33 Result of Listing 7.33. Note that Lord Copper, who has no boss, is excluded from the result because his null *boss_id* doesn't satisfy the join condition.

To create a self-join:

- Type:

```
SELECT columns
  FROM table [AS] alias1
  INNER JOIN table [AS] alias2
    ON join_conditions
```

columns is one or more comma-separated expressions or column names from *table*. *alias1* and *alias2* are different alias names that are used to refer to *table* in *join_conditions*. See "Creating Table Aliases with AS" on page 182.

join_conditions specifies one or more join conditions to be evaluated for each pair of joined rows. A join condition takes this form:

```
alias1.column op alias2.column
```

op can be any comparison operator: =, <>, <, <=, >, or >= (refer to Table 4.2 on page 89). You can combine multiple join conditions with AND or OR; see "Combining and Negating Conditions with AND, OR, and NOT" on page 93.

Tips for Self Joins

- You can join a table to itself even if no reflexive relationship exists. A common type of self-join compares a column in the first instance of the table to the *same* column in the second instance. This join condition lets you compare the values in a column to one another, as shown in the subsequent examples in this section.

- See also "Working with Hierarchies" on page 440.

- DBMS **Oracle** 8i and earlier don't support JOIN syntax; use WHERE joins instead. Oracle 9i and later support JOIN syntax.

```
SELECT a1.au_id, a1.au_fname,
    a1.au_lname, a1.state
  FROM authors a1
  INNER JOIN authors a2
    ON a1.state = a2.state
  WHERE a2.au_id = 'A04';
```

Listing 7.34 List the authors who live in the same state as author A04 (Klee Hull). See Figure 7.34 for the result.

```
au_id au_fname au_lname state
----- -------- -------- -----
A03   Hallie   Hull     CA
A04   Klee     Hull     CA
A06            Kellsey  CA
```

Figure 7.34 Result of Listing 7.34.

Listing 7.34 uses a WHERE search condition and self-join from the column *state* to itself to find all authors who live in the same state as author A04 (Klee Hull). See Figure 7.34 for the result.

Tips for Listing 7.34

- Using WHERE syntax, Listing 7.34 is equivalent to:

```
SELECT a1.au_id, a1.au_fname,
    a1.au_lname, a1.state
  FROM authors a1, authors a2
  WHERE a1.state = a2.state
 AND a2.au_id = 'A04';
```

- Self-joins can often be restated as subqueries (see Chapter 8). Using a subquery, Listing 7.34 is equivalent to:

```
SELECT au_id, au_fname,
    au_lname, state
  FROM authors
  WHERE state IN
    (SELECT state
       FROM authors
     WHERE au_id = 'A04');
```

For every biography, Listing 7.35 lists the other biographies that outsold it. Note that the WHERE search condition requires *type = 'biography'* for both tables *t1* and *t2* because the join condition considers the column *type* to be two separate columns. See Figure 7.35 for the result.

Tips for Listing 7.35

- Using WHERE syntax, Listing 7.35 is equivalent to:

```
SELECT t1.title_id, t1.sales,
    t2.title_id AS "Better seller",
    t2.sales AS "Higher sales"
  FROM titles t1, titles t2
  WHERE t1.sales < t2.sales
    AND t1.type = 'biography'
    AND t2.type = 'biography'
  ORDER BY t1.title_id ASC, t2.sales ASC;
```

```
SELECT t1.title_id, t1.sales,
    t2.title_id AS "Better seller",
    t2.sales AS "Higher sales"
  FROM titles t1
  INNER JOIN titles t2
    ON t1.sales < t2.sales
  WHERE t1.type = 'biography'
    AND t2.type = 'biography'
  ORDER BY t1.title_id ASC, t2.sales ASC;
```

Listing 7.35 For every biography, list the title ID and sales of the other biographies that outsold it. See Figure 7.35 for the result.

```
title_id sales  Better seller Higher sales
-------- ------ ------------- ------------
T06       11320 T12                 100001
T06       11320 T07                1500200
T12      100001 T07                1500200
```

Figure 7.35 Result of Listing 7.35.

```
SELECT
    a1.au_fname, a1.au_lname,
    a2.au_fname, a2.au_lname
  FROM authors a1
  INNER JOIN authors a2
    ON a1.state = a2.state
  WHERE a1.state = 'NY'
  ORDER BY a1.au_id ASC, a2.au_id ASC;
```

Listing 7.36 List all pairs of authors who live in New York state. See Figure 7.36 for the result.

au_fname	au_lname	au_fname	au_lname
Sarah	Buchman	Sarah	Buchman
Sarah	Buchman	Christian	Kells
Christian	Kells	Sarah	Buchman
Christian	Kells	Christian	Kells

Figure 7.36 Result of Listing 7.36.

Listing 7.36 is a self-join to find all pairs of authors within New York state. See Figure 7.36 for the result.

Tips for Listing 7.36

- Using WHERE syntax, Listing 7.36 is equivalent to:

```
SELECT
    a1.au_fname, a1.au_lname,
    a2.au_fname, a2.au_lname
  FROM authors a1, authors a2
  WHERE a1.state = a2.state
    AND a1.state = 'NY'
  ORDER BY a1.au_id ASC, a2.au_id ASC;
```

The first and fourth rows of Figure 7.36 are unnecessary because they indicate that Sarah Buchman lives in the same state as Sarah Buchman, and likewise for Christian Kells. Adding a join condition retains only those rows in which the two authors differ (Listing 7.37 and Figure 7.37).

Tips for Listing 7.37

- Using WHERE syntax, Listing 7.37 is equivalent to:

```
SELECT
    a1.au_fname, a1.au_lname,
    a2.au_fname, a2.au_lname
  FROM authors a1, authors a2
  WHERE a1.state = a2.state
    AND a1.au_id <> a2.au_id
    AND a1.state = 'NY'
  ORDER BY a1.au_id ASC, a2.au_id ASC;
```

Listing 7.37 still isn't quite what I want because the two result rows are redundant. The first row states that Sarah Buchman lives in the same state as Christian Kells, and the second row gives the same information. To eliminate this redundancy, I'll change the second join condition's comparison operator from not-equal to less-than (Listing 7.38 and Figure 7.38).

Tips for Listing 7.38

- Using WHERE syntax, Listing 7.38 is equivalent to:

```
SELECT
    a1.au_fname, a1.au_lname,
    a2.au_fname, a2.au_lname
  FROM authors a1, authors a2
  WHERE a1.state = a2.state
    AND a1.au_id < a2.au_id
    AND a1.state = 'NY'
  ORDER BY a1.au_id ASC, a2.au_id ASC;
```

```
SELECT
    a1.au_fname, a1.au_lname,
    a2.au_fname, a2.au_lname
  FROM authors a1
  INNER JOIN authors a2
    ON a1.state = a2.state
    AND a1.au_id <> a2.au_id
  WHERE a1.state = 'NY'
  ORDER BY a1.au_id ASC, a2.au_id ASC;
```

Listing 7.37 List all different pairs of authors who live in New York state. See Figure 7.37 for the result.

```
au_fname   au_lname au_fname   au_lname
---------  -------- ---------  --------
Sarah      Buchman  Christian  Kells
Christian  Kells    Sarah      Buchman
```

Figure 7.37 Result of Listing 7.37.

```
SELECT
    a1.au_fname, a1.au_lname,
    a2.au_fname, a2.au_lname
  FROM authors a1
  INNER JOIN authors a2
    ON a1.state = a2.state
    AND a1.au_id < a2.au_id
  WHERE a1.state = 'NY'
  ORDER BY a1.au_id ASC, a2.au_id ASC;
```

Listing 7.38 List all different pairs of authors who live in New York state, with no redundancies. See Figure 7.38 for the result.

```
au_fname  au_lname au_fname   au_lname
--------  -------- ---------  --------
Sarah     Buchman  Christian  Kells
```

Figure 7.38 Result of Listing 7.38.

CHAPTER 8

Subqueries

To this point, I've used a single SELECT statement to retrieve data from one or more tables. This chapter describes nested queries, which let you retrieve or modify data based on another query's result.

A **subquery**, or **subselect**, is a SELECT statement embedded in another SQL statement. You can nest a subquery in:

- The SELECT, FROM, WHERE, or HAVING clause of a SELECT statement

- Another subquery

- An INSERT, UPDATE, or DELETE statement

In general, you can use a subquery anywhere an expression is allowed, but your DBMS might restrict where they can appear. This chapter covers subqueries nested in a SELECT statement or another subquery; Chapter 10 covers subqueries embedded in INSERT, UPDATE, and DELETE statements.

Understanding Subqueries

This section defines some terms and introduces subqueries by giving an example of a SELECT statement that contains a simple subquery. Subsequent sections explain the types of subqueries and their syntax and semantics.

Suppose that you want to list the names of the publishers of biographies. The naive approach is to write two queries: one query to retrieve the IDs of all the biography publishers (Listing 8.1 and Figure 8.1) and a second query that uses the first query's result to list the publisher names (Listing 8.2 and Figure 8.2).

A better way is to use an inner join (Listing 8.3 and Figure 8.3); see "Creating an Inner Join with INNER JOIN" on page 196.

Another alternative is to use a subquery (Listing 8.4 and Figure 8.4). The subquery in Listing 8.4 is highlighted. A subquery also is called an **inner query**, and the statement containing a subquery is called an **outer query**. In other words, an enclosed subquery is an inner query of an outer query. Remember that a subquery can be nested in another subquery, so *inner* and *outer* are relative terms in statements with multiple nested subqueries.

I'll explain how a DBMS executes subqueries in "Simple and Correlated Subqueries" on page 248, but for now, all that you need to know is that in Listing 8.4, the DBMS processes the inner query (highlighted text) first and then uses its interim result to run the outer query (plain text) and get the final result. The IN keyword that introduces the subquery tests for list membership and works like IN in "List Filtering with IN" on page 109. Note that the inner query in Listing 8.4 is the same query as Listing 8.1, and the outer query is the same query as Listing 8.2.

```
SELECT pub_id
  FROM titles
  WHERE type = 'biography';
```

Listing 8.1 List the biography publishers. See Figure 8.1 for the result.

```
pub_id
------
P01
P03
P01
P01
```

Figure 8.1 Result of Listing 8.1. You can add DISTINCT to the SELECT clause of Listing 8.1 to list the publishers only once; see "Eliminating Duplicate Rows with DISTINCT" on page 81.

```
SELECT pub_name
  FROM publishers
  WHERE pub_id IN ('P01', 'P03');
```

Listing 8.2 This query uses the result of Listing 8.1 to list the names of the biography publishers. See Figure 8.2 for the result.

```
pub_name
------------------
Abatis Publishers
Schadenfreude Press
```

Figure 8.2 Result of Listing 8.2.

```
SELECT DISTINCT pub_name
  FROM publishers p
  INNER JOIN titles t
    ON p.pub_id = t.pub_id
  WHERE t.type = 'biography';
```

Listing 8.3 List the names of the biography publishers by using an inner join. See Figure 8.3 for the result.

```
pub_name
-------------------
Abatis Publishers
Schadenfreude Press
```

Figure 8.3 Result of Listing 8.3.

```
SELECT pub_name
  FROM publishers
  WHERE pub_id IN
    (SELECT pub_id
      FROM titles
      WHERE type = 'biography');
```

Listing 8.4 List the names of the biography publishers by using a subquery. See Figure 8.4 for the result.

```
pub_name
-------------------
Abatis Publishers
Schadenfreude Press
```

Figure 8.4 Result of Listing 8.4.

Tips for Subqueries

- Sometimes you'll see the term *subquery* used to refer to an *entire* SQL statement that contains one or more subqueries. To prevent confusion, I don't use that terminology in this book.

- **DBMS** **MySQL** 4.1 and later support subqueries, but earlier versions don't. You can't run the examples in this chapter if you're using MySQL 4.0 or earlier, but you have a few choices, in order of preference:

  ▸ Upgrade to the latest version of MySQL (*mysql.com*).

  ▸ Recast the subquery as a join (see "Subqueries vs. Joins" on page 243).

  ▸ Create a temporary table to hold the result of a subquery (see "Creating a Temporary Table with CREATE TEMPORARY TABLE" on page 352 and the temporary-table example in the DBMS tip in "Tips for Listing 7.32" on page 232).

  ▸ Simulate the subquery in a procedural host language such as PHP or Java.

Subquery Syntax

The syntax of a subquery is the same as that of a normal SELECT statement (see Chapters 4 through 7) except for the following differences:

- You can nest a subquery in a SELECT, FROM, WHERE, or HAVING clause or in another subquery.

- Always enclose a subquery in parentheses.

- Don't terminate a subquery with a semicolon. (You still must terminate the statement that contains the subquery with a semicolon.)

- Don't put an ORDER BY clause in a subquery. (A subquery returns an intermediate result that you never see, so sorting a subquery makes no sense.)

- A subquery is a single SELECT statement. (You can't use, say, a UNION of multiple SELECT statements as a subquery.)

- A subquery can use columns in the tables listed in its own FROM clause or in the outer query's FROM clause.

- If a table appears in an inner query but not in the outer query, then you can't include that table's columns in the final result (that is, in the outer query's SELECT clause).

- Depending on the context in which it's used, a subquery might be required to return a limited number of rows or columns. The SQL standard categorizes a subquery by the number of rows and columns it returns (Table 8.1). In all cases, the subquery also can return an empty table (zero rows).

In practice, a subquery usually appears in a WHERE clause that takes one of these forms:

- `WHERE test_expr op (subquery)`
- `WHERE test_expr [NOT] IN (subquery)`
- `WHERE test_expr op ALL (subquery)`
- `WHERE test_expr op ANY (subquery)`
- `WHERE [NOT] EXISTS (subquery)`

test_expr is a literal value, a column name, an expression, or a scalar subquery; *op* is a comparison operator (=, <>, <, <=, >, or >=); and *subquery* is a simple or correlated subquery. I'll cover each of these forms later in this chapter. You can use these subquery forms in a HAVING clause, too.

Tips for Subquery Syntax

- DBMS The SQL standard doesn't specify a maximum number of subquery nesting levels, so your DBMS will set its own upper limit. This built-in limit typically exceeds the limit of human comprehension. **Microsoft SQL Server**, for example, allows 32 levels of nesting.

Table 8.1 Size of Subquery Results

Subquery	Rows	Columns
Scalar subquery	1	1
Row subquery	1	≥ 1
Table subquery	≥ 1	≥ 1

Subqueries vs. Joins

In "Understanding Subqueries" on page 240, Listings 8.3 and 8.4 showed two equivalent queries: one used a join, and the other used a subquery. Many subqueries can be formulated alternatively as joins. In fact, a subquery is a way to relate one table to another without actually doing a join.

Because subqueries can be hard to use and debug, you might prefer to use joins, but you can pose some questions only as subqueries. In cases where you can use subqueries and joins interchangeably, you should test queries on your DBMS to see whether a performance difference exists between a statement that uses a subquery and a semantically equivalent statement that uses a join. For example, the query

```
SELECT MAX(table1.col1)
  FROM table1
  WHERE table1.col1 IN
    (SELECT table2.col1
       FROM table2);
```

usually will run faster than

```
SELECT MAX(table1.col1)
  FROM table1
  INNER JOIN table2
    ON table1.col1 = table2.col1;
```

For more information, see "Comparing Equivalent Queries" on page 287.

The following syntax diagrams show some equivalent statements that use subqueries and joins. These two statements are equivalent (IN subquery):

```
SELECT *
  FROM table1
  WHERE id IN
    (SELECT id FROM table2);
```

and (inner join):

```
SELECT DISTINCT table1.*
  FROM table1
  INNER JOIN table2
  ON table1.id = table2.id;
```

See Listings 8.5a and 8.5b and Figure 8.5 for an example.

```
SELECT au_id, city
  FROM authors
  WHERE city IN
    (SELECT city FROM publishers);
```

Listing 8.5a This statement uses a subquery to list the authors who live in the same city in which a publisher is located. See Figure 8.5 for the result.

```
SELECT DISTINCT a.au_id, a.city
  FROM authors a
  INNER JOIN publishers p
  ON a.city = p.city;
```

Listing 8.5b This statement is equivalent to Listing 8.5a but uses an inner join instead of a subquery. See Figure 8.5 for the result.

```
au_id city
----- ------------
A03   San Francisco
A04   San Francisco
A05   New York
```

Figure 8.5 Result of Listings 8.5a and 8.5b.

```
SELECT au_id, au_fname, au_lname
  FROM authors
  WHERE au_id NOT IN
    (SELECT au_id FROM title_authors);
```

Listing 8.6a This statement uses an IN subquery to list the authors who haven't written (or cowritten) a book. See Figure 8.6 for the result.

```
SELECT au_id, au_fname, au_lname
FROM authors a
  WHERE NOT EXISTS
    (SELECT *
       FROM title_authors ta
       WHERE a.au_id = ta.au_id);
```

Listing 8.6b This statement is equivalent to Listing 8.6a but uses an EXISTS subquery instead of an IN subquery. See Figure 8.6 for the result.

```
SELECT a.au_id, a.au_fname, a.au_lname
  FROM authors a
  LEFT OUTER JOIN title_authors ta
    ON a.au_id = ta.au_id
  WHERE ta.au_id IS NULL;
```

Listing 8.6c This statement is equivalent to Listings 8.6a and 8.6b but uses a left outer join instead of a subquery. See Figure 8.6 for the result.

```
au_id au_fname au_lname
----- -------- -----------
A07   Paddy    O'Furniture
```

Figure 8.6 Result of Listings 8.6a, 8.6b, and 8.6c.

These three statements are equivalent (NOT IN subquery):

```
SELECT *
  FROM table1
  WHERE id NOT IN
    (SELECT id FROM table2);
```

and (NOT EXISTS subquery):

```
SELECT *
  FROM table1
  WHERE NOT EXISTS
    (SELECT *
       FROM table2
       WHERE table1.id = table2.id);
```

and (left outer join):

```
SELECT table1.*
  FROM table1
  LEFT OUTER JOIN table2
    ON table1.id = table2.id
  WHERE table2.id IS NULL;
```

See Listings 8.6a, 8.6b, and 8.6c and Figure 8.6 for an example. IN and EXISTS subqueries are covered later in this chapter.

You also can write a self-join as a subquery (Listings 8.7a and 8.7b and Figure 8.7). For information about self-joins, see "Creating a Self-Join" on page 233.

```
SELECT au_id, au_fname, au_lname, state
  FROM authors
  WHERE state IN
    (SELECT state
       FROM authors
       WHERE au_id = 'A04');
```

Listing 8.7a This statement uses a subquery to list the authors who live in the same state as author A04 (Klee Hull). See Figure 8.7 for the result.

```
SELECT a1.au_id, a1.au_fname,
    a1.au_lname, a1.state
  FROM authors a1
  INNER JOIN authors a2
    ON a1.state = a2.state
  WHERE a2.au_id = 'A04';
```

Listing 8.7b This statement is equivalent to Listing 8.7a but uses an inner join instead of a subquery. See Figure 8.7 for the result.

```
au_id au_fname au_lname state
----- -------- -------- -----
A03   Hallie   Hull     CA
A04   Klee     Hull     CA
A06            Kellsey  CA
```

Figure 8.7 Result of Listings 8.7a and 8.7b.

```
SELECT title_id, price
  FROM titles
  WHERE price =
    (SELECT MAX(price)
       FROM titles);
```

Listing 8.8 List all books whose price equals the highest book price. See Figure 8.8 for the result.

```
title_id price
-------- -----
T03       39.95
```

Figure 8.8 Result of Listing 8.8.

```
SELECT a.au_id, a.city, p.pub_id
  FROM authors a
  INNER JOIN publishers p
    ON a.city = p.city;
```

Listing 8.9 List the authors who live in the same city in which a publisher is located, and include the publisher in the result. See Figure 8.9 for the result.

```
au_id city           pub_id
----- ------------- ------
A03   San Francisco P02
A04   San Francisco P02
A05   New York      P01
```

Figure 8.9 Result of Listing 8.9.

Favor subqueries if you're comparing an aggregate value to other values (Listing 8.8 and Figure 8.8). Without a subquery, you'd need two SELECT statements to list all the books with the highest price: one query to find the highest price and a second query to list all the books selling for that price. For information about aggregate functions, see Chapter 6.

Use joins when you include columns from multiple tables in the result. Listing 8.5b uses a join to retrieve authors who live in the same city in which a publisher is located. To include the publisher ID in the result, simply add the column *pub_id* to the SELECT-clause list (Listing 8.9 and Figure 8.9).

You can't accomplish this same task with a subquery because it's illegal to include a column in the outer query's SELECT-clause list from a table that appears in only the inner query:

```
SELECT a.au_id, a.city, p.pub_id
  FROM authors a
  WHERE a.city IN
    (SELECT p.city
       FROM publishers p);     --Illegal
```

Tips for Subqueries vs. Joins

- You always can express an inner join as a subquery, but not vice versa. This asymmetry occurs because inner joins are commutative; you can join tables A to B in either order and get the same answer. Subqueries lack this property. (You always can express an outer join as a subquery, too, even though outer joins aren't commutative.)

- DBMS **MySQL** 4.0 and earlier don't support subqueries; see the DBMS tip in "Tips for Subqueries" on page 241.

Simple and Correlated Subqueries

You can use two types of subqueries:

- Simple subqueries

- Correlated subqueries

A **simple subquery**, or **noncorrelated subquery**, is a subquery that can be evaluated independently of its outer query and is processed only once for the entire statement. All the subqueries in this chapter's examples so far have been simple subqueries (except Listing 8.6b).

A **correlated subquery** can't be evaluated independently of its outer query; it's an inner query that depends on data from the outer query. A correlated subquery is used if a statement needs to process a table in the inner query for *each row* in the outer query.

Correlated subqueries have more-complicated syntax and a knottier execution sequence than simple subqueries, but you can use them to solve problems that you can't solve with simple subqueries or joins. This section gives an example of a simple subquery and a correlated subquery and then describes how a DBMS executes each one. Subsequent sections in this chapter contain more examples of each type of subquery.

```
SELECT au_id, city
  FROM authors
  WHERE city IN
    (SELECT city
      FROM publishers);
```

Listing 8.10 List the authors who live in the same city in which a publisher is located. See Figure 8.10 for the result.

```
au_id city
----- -------------
A03    San Francisco
A04    San Francisco
A05    New York
```

Figure 8.10 Result of Listing 8.10.

```
SELECT city
  FROM publishers;
```

Listing 8.11 List the cities in which the publishers are located. See Figure 8.11 for the result.

```
city
------------
New York
San Francisco
Hamburg
Berkeley
```

Figure 8.11 Result of Listing 8.11.

```
SELECT au_id, city
  FROM authors
  WHERE city IN
    ('New York', 'San Francisco',
     'Hamburg', 'Berkeley');
```

Listing 8.12 List the authors who live in one of the cities returned by Listing 8.11. See Figure 8.12 for the result.

```
au_id city
----- ------------
A03   San Francisco
A04   San Francisco
A05   New York
```

Figure 8.12 Result of Listing 8.12.

Simple Subqueries

A DBMS evaluates a simple subquery by evaluating the inner query once and substituting its result into the outer query. A simple subquery executes prior to, and independent of, its outer query.

Let's revisit Listing 8.5a from earlier in this chapter. Listing 8.10 (which is identical to Listing 8.5a) uses a simple subquery to list the authors who live in the same city in which a publisher is located; see Figure 8.10 for the result. Conceptually, a DBMS processes this query in two steps as two separate SELECT statements:

1. The inner query (a simple subquery) returns the cities of all the publishers (Listing 8.11 and Figure 8.11).

2. The DBMS substitutes the values returned by the inner query in step 1 into the outer query, which finds the author IDs corresponding to the publishers' cities (Listing 8.12 and Figure 8.12).

Correlated Subqueries

Correlated subqueries offer a more powerful data-retrieval mechanism than simple subqueries do. A correlated subquery's important characteristics are:

- It differs from a simple query in its order of execution and in the number of times that it's executed.

- It can't be executed independently of its outer query because it depends on the outer query for its values.

- It's executed repeatedly—once for each candidate row selected by the outer query.

- It always refers to the table mentioned in the FROM clause of the outer query.

- It uses qualified column names to refer to values specified in the outer query. In the context of correlated subqueries, these qualified named are called **correlation variables**. For information about qualified names and table aliases, see "Qualifying Column Names" on page 180 and "Creating Table Aliases with AS" on page 182.

- The basic syntax of a query that contains a correlated subquery is:

```
SELECT outer_columns
  FROM outer_table
  WHERE outer_column_value IN
    (SELECT inner_column
        FROM inner_table
      WHERE inner_column = outer_column)
```

Execution always starts with the outer query
(plain text). The outer query selects each individual row of *outer_table* as a candidate row.
For each candidate row, the DBMS executes the
correlated inner query (highlighted text) once
and flags the *inner_table* rows that satisfy the
inner WHERE condition for the value *outer_col-
umn_value*. The DBMS tests the outer WHERE
condition against the flagged *inner_table* rows
and displays the flagged rows that satisfy this
condition. This process continues until all the
candidate rows have been processed.

Listing 8.13 uses a correlated subquery to list
the books that have sales better than the average
sales of books of its type; see Figure 8.13 for the
result. *candidate* (following *titles* in the outer query)
and *average* (following *titles* in the inner query) are
alias table names for the table *titles*, so that the
information can be evaluated as though it comes
from two different tables (see "Creating a Self-Join"
on page 233).

```
SELECT
    candidate.title_id,
    candidate.type,
    candidate.sales
  FROM titles candidate
  WHERE sales >=
    (SELECT AVG(sales)
        FROM titles average
      WHERE average.type = candidate.type);
```

Listing 8.13 List the books that have sales greater than
or equal to the average sales of books of its type. The
correlation variable *candidate.type* defines the *initial*
condition to be met by the rows of the inner table *average*.
The outer WHERE condition (*sales >=*) defines the *final* test
that the rows of the inner table *average* must satisfy. See
Figure 8.13 for the result.

```
title_id type          sales

--------  ----------   -------
T02       history          9566
T03       computer        25667
T05       psychology     201440
T07       biography     1500200
T09       children         5000
T13       history         10467
```

Figure 8.13 Result of Listing 8.13.

In Listing 8.13, the subquery can't be resolved independently of the outer query. It needs a value for *candidate.type*, but this value is a correlation variable that changes as the DBMS examines different rows in the table *candidate*. The column *average. type* is said to **correlate** with *candidate.type* in the outer query. The average sales for a book type are calculated in the subquery by using the type of each book from the table in the outer query (*candidate*). The subquery computes the average sales for this type and then compares it with a row in the table *candidate*. If the sales in the table *candidate* are greater than or equal to average sales for the type, then that book is displayed in the result. A DBMS processes this query as follows:

1. The book type in the first row of *candidate* is used in the subquery to compute average sales.

   Take the row for book T01, whose type is history, so the value in the column *type* in the first row of the table *candidate* is history. In effect, the subquery becomes:

   ```
   SELECT AVG(sales)
     FROM titles average
     WHERE average.type = 'history';
   ```

   This pass through the subquery yields a value of 6866—the average sales of history books. In the outer query, book T01's sales of 566 are compared to the average sales of history books. T01's sales are lower than average, so T01 isn't displayed in the result.

2. Next, book T02's row in *candidate* is evaluated.

   T02 also is a history book, so the evaluated subquery is the same as in step 1:

   ```
   SELECT AVG(sales)
     FROM titles average
     WHERE average.type = 'history';
   ```

   This pass through the subquery again yields 6866 for the average sales of history books. Book T02's sales of 9566 are higher than average, so T02 is displayed in the result.

3. Next, book T03's row in *candidate* is evaluated.

   T03 is a computer book, so this time, the evaluated subquery is:

   ```
   SELECT AVG(sales)
     FROM titles average
     WHERE average.type = 'computer';
   ```

   The result of this pass through the subquery is average sales of 25667 for computer books. Because book T03's sales of 25667 equals the average (it's the only computer book), T03 is displayed in the result.

4. The DBMS repeats this process until every row in the outer table *candidate* has been tested.

If you can get the same result by using a simple subquery or a correlated subquery, then use the simple subquery because it probably will run faster. Listings 8.14a and 8.14b show two equivalent queries that list all authors who earn 100 percent (1.0) of the royalty share on a book. Listing 8.14a, which uses a simple subquery, is more efficient than Listing 8.14b, which uses a correlated subquery. In the simple subquery, the DBMS reads the inner table *title_authors* once. In the correlated subquery, the DBMS must loop through *title_authors* five times—once for each qualifying row in the outer table *authors*. See Figure 8.14 for the result.

Why do I say that a statement that uses a simple subquery *probably* will run faster than an equivalent statement that uses a correlated subquery when a correlated subquery clearly requires more work? Because your DBMS's optimizer might be clever enough to recognize and reformulate a correlated subquery as a semantically equivalent simple subquery internally before executing the statement. For more information, see "Comparing Equivalent Queries" on page 287.

Tips for Simple and Correlated Subqueries

- DBMS **MySQL** 4.0 and earlier don't support subqueries; see the DBMS tip in "Tips for Subqueries" on page 241 earlier in this chapter.

  In older **PostgreSQL** versions, convert the floating-point numbers in Listings 8.14a and 8.14b to DECIMAL; see "Converting Data Types with CAST()" on page 145. To run Listings 8.14a and 8.14b, change the floating-point literal in each listing to:

  ```
  CAST(1.0 AS DECIMAL)
  ```

```
SELECT au_id, au_fname, au_lname
  FROM authors
  WHERE au_id IN
    (SELECT au_id
       FROM title_authors
       WHERE royalty_share = 1.0);
```

Listing 8.14a This statement uses a simple subquery to list all authors who earn 100 percent (1.0) royalty on a book. See Figure 8.14 for the result.

```
SELECT au_id, au_fname, au_lname
  FROM authors
  WHERE 1.0 IN
    (SELECT royalty_share
       FROM title_authors
       WHERE title_authors.au_id =
             authors.au_id);
```

Listing 8.14b This statement is equivalent to Listing 8.14a but uses a correlated subquery instead of a simple subquery. This query probably will run slower than Listing 8.14a. See Figure 8.14 for the result.

```
au_id  au_fname   au_lname
-----  ---------  ---------
A01    Sarah      Buchman
A02    Wendy      Heydemark
A04    Klee       Hull
A05    Christian  Kells
A06               Kellsey
```

Figure 8.14 Result of Listings 8.14a and 8.14b.

```
SELECT pub_name
  FROM publishers
  WHERE pub_id IN
    (SELECT pub_id
       FROM titles
       WHERE type = 'biography');
```

Listing 8.15a The tables *publishers* and *titles* both contain a column named *pub_id*, but you don't have to qualify *pub_id* in this query because of the implicit assumptions about table names that SQL makes. See Figure 8.15 for the result.

```
SELECT pub_name
  FROM publishers
  WHERE publishers.pub_id IN
    (SELECT titles.pub_id
       FROM titles
       WHERE type = 'biography');
```

Listing 8.15b This query is equivalent to Listing 8.15a, but with explicit qualification of *pub_id*. See Figure 8.15 for the result.

```
pub_name
-------------------
Abatis Publishers
Schadenfreude Press
```

Figure 8.15 Result of Listings 8.15a and 8.15b.

Qualifying Column Names in Subqueries

Recall from "Qualifying Column Names" on page 180 that you can qualify a column name explicitly with a table name to identify the column unambiguously. In statements that contain subqueries, column names are qualified implicitly by the table referenced in the FROM clause at the same nesting level.

In Listing 8.15a, which lists the names of biography publishers, the column names are qualified implicitly, meaning:

- The column *pub_id* in the outer query's WHERE clause is qualified implicitly by the table *publishers* in the outer query's FROM clause.

- The column *pub_id* in the subquery's SELECT clause is qualified implicitly by the table *titles* in the subquery's FROM clause.

Listing 8.15b shows Listing 8.15a with explicit qualifiers. See Figure 8.15 for the result.

Tips for Qualified Column Names in Subqueries

- It's never wrong to state a table name explicitly.

- You can use explicit qualifiers to override SQL's default assumptions about table names and specify that a column is to match a table at a nesting level outside the column's own level.

- If a column name can match more than one table at the same nesting level, then the column name is ambiguous, and you must qualify it with a table name (or table alias).

- DBMS **MySQL** 4.0 and earlier don't support subqueries; see the DBMS tip in "Tips for Subqueries" on page 241.

Nulls in Subqueries

Beware of nulls; their presence complicates subqueries. If you don't eliminate them when they're present, then you might get an unexpected answer.

A subquery can hide a comparison to a null. Recall from "Nulls" on page 72 that nulls don't equal each other and that you can't determine whether a null matches any other value. The following example involves a NOT IN subquery (see "Testing Set Membership with IN" on page 267). Consider the following two tables, each with one column. The first table is named *table1*:

```
col
----
   1
   2
```

The second table is named *table2*:

```
col
----
   1
   2
   3
```

If I run Listing 8.16 to list the values in *table2* that aren't in *table1*, then I get Figure 8.16a, as expected.

```
SELECT col
  FROM table2
  WHERE col NOT IN
    (SELECT col
       FROM table1);
```

Listing 8.16 List the values in *table2* that aren't in *table1*. See Figures 8.16a and 8.16b for the result.

```
col
----
   3
```

Figure 8.16a Result of Listing 8.16 when table1 doesn't contain a null.

```
col
----
```

Listing 8.16b Result of Listing 8.16 when *table1* contains a null. This result is an empty table, which is correct logically but not what I expected.

Now add a null to *table1*:

```
col
----
   1
   2
NULL
```

If I rerun Listing 8.16, then I get Figure 8.16b (an empty table), which is correct logically but not what I expected. Why is the result empty this time? The solution requires some algebra. I can move the NOT outside the subquery condition without changing the meaning of Listing 8.16:

```
SELECT col
  FROM table2
  WHERE NOT col IN
    (SELECT col FROM table1);
```

The IN clause determines whether a value in *table2* matches *any* value in *table1*, so I can rewrite the subquery as a compound condition:

```
SELECT col
  FROM table2
  WHERE NOT ((col = 1)
        OR  (col = 2)
        OR  (col = NULL));
```

If I apply De Morgan's Laws (refer to Table 4.6 on page 100), then this query becomes:

```
SELECT col
  FROM table2
  WHERE (col <> 1)
    AND (col <> 2)
    AND (col <> NULL);
```

The final expression, *col <> NULL*, always is unknown. Refer to the AND truth table (Table 4.3 on page 94), and you'll see that the entire WHERE search condition reduces to unknown, which always is rejected by WHERE.

To fix Listing 8.16 so that it doesn't examine the null in *table1*, add an IS NOT NULL condition to the subquery (see "Testing for Nulls with IS NULL" on page 112):

```
SELECT col
  FROM table2
  WHERE col NOT IN
    (SELECT col
        FROM table1
        WHERE col IS NOT NULL);
```

Tips for Nulls in Subqueries

- DBMS **MySQL** 4.0 and earlier don't support subqueries; see the DBMS tip in "Tips for Subqueries" on page 241.

Using Subqueries as Column Expressions

In Chapters 4, 5, and 6, you learned that the items in a SELECT-clause list can be literals, column names, or more-complex expressions. SQL also lets you to embed a subquery in a SELECT-clause list.

A subquery that's used as a column expression must be a scalar subquery. Recall from Table 8.1 on page 242 that a scalar subquery returns a single value (that is, a one-row, one-column result). In most cases, you'll have to use an aggregate function or restrictive WHERE conditions in the subquery to guarantee that the subquery returns only one row.

The syntax for the SELECT-clause list is the same as you've been using all along, except that you can specify a parenthesized subquery as one of the column expressions in the list, as the following examples show.

Listing 8.17 uses two simple subqueries as column expressions to list each biography, its price, the average price of all books (not just biographies), and the difference between the price of the biography and the average price of all books. The aggregate function AVG() guarantees that each subquery returns a single value. See Figure 8.17 for the result. Remember that AVG() ignores nulls when computing an average; see "Calculating an Average with AVG()" on page 163.

```sql
SELECT title_id, price,
    (SELECT AVG(price) FROM titles)
      AS "AVG(price)",
    price - (SELECT AVG(price) FROM titles)
      AS "Difference"
  FROM titles
  WHERE type='biography';
```

Listing 8.17 List each biography, its price, the average price of all books, and the difference between the price of the biography and the average price of all books. See Figure 8.17 for the result.

```
title_id price   AVG(price) Difference
-------- ------- ---------- ----------
T06        19.95   18.3875      1.5625
T07        23.95   18.3875      5.5625
T10        NULL    18.3875      NULL
T12        12.99   18.3875     -5.3975
```

Figure 8.17 Result of Listing 8.17.

```
SELECT title_id,
    (SELECT au_id
      FROM title_authors ta
      WHERE au_order = 1
        AND title_id = t.title_id)
      AS "Author 1",
    (SELECT au_id
      FROM title_authors ta
      WHERE au_order = 2
        AND title_id = t.title_id)
      AS "Author 2",
    (SELECT au_id
      FROM title_authors ta
      WHERE au_order = 3
        AND title_id = t.title_id)
      AS "Author 3"
  FROM titles t;
```

Listing 8.18 List all the authors of each book in one row.
See Figure 8.18 for the result.

Listing 8.18 uses correlated subqueries to list all the authors of each book in one row, as you'd view them in a report or spreadsheet. See Figure 8.18 for the result. Note that in each WHERE clause, SQL qualifies *title_id* implicitly with the table alias *ta* referenced in the subquery's FROM clause; see "Qualifying Column Names in Subqueries" on page 253. For a more efficient way to implement this query, see "Tips for Column Expressions" later in this section. See Listing 15.8 on page 398 for the *reverse* of this query.

```
title_id Author 1 Author 2 Author 3
-------- -------- -------- --------
T01      A01      NULL     NULL
T02      A01      NULL     NULL
T03      A05      NULL     NULL
T04      A03      A04      NULL
T05      A04      NULL     NULL
T06      A02      NULL     NULL
T07      A02      A04      NULL
T08      A06      NULL     NULL
T09      A06      NULL     NULL
T10      A02      NULL     NULL
T11      A06      A03      A04
T12      A02      NULL     NULL
T13      A01      NULL     NULL
```

Figure 8.18 Result of Listing 8.18.

In Listing 8.19, I revisit Listing 7.30 in "Creating Outer Joins with OUTER JOIN" on page 221, but this time, I'm using a correlated subquery instead of an outer join to list the number of books that each author wrote (or cowrote). See Figure 8.19 for the result.

Listing 8.20 uses a correlated subquery to list each author and the latest date on which he or she published a book. You should qualify every column name explicitly in a subquery that contains a join to make it clear which table is referenced (even when qualifiers are unnecessary). See Figure 8.20 for the result.

```
SELECT au_id,
    (SELECT COUNT(*)
        FROM title_authors ta
        WHERE ta.au_id = a.au_id)
      AS "Num books"
  FROM authors a
  ORDER BY au_id;
```

Listing 8.19 List the number of books that each author wrote (or cowrote), including authors who have written no books. See Figure 8.19 for the result.

```
SELECT au_id,
    (SELECT MAX(pubdate)
        FROM titles t
        INNER JOIN title_authors ta
          ON ta.title_id = t.title_id
        WHERE ta.au_id = a.au_id)
      AS "Latest pub date"
  FROM authors a;
```

Listing 8.20 List each author and the latest date on which he or she published a book. See Figure 8.20 for the result.

```
au_id Num books
----- ----------
A01           3
A02           4
A03           2
A04           4
A05           1
A06           3
A07           0
```

Figure 8.19 Result of Listing 8.19.

```
au_id Latest pub date
----- ---------------
A01   2000-08-01
A02   2000-08-31
A03   2000-11-30
A04   2001-01-01
A05   2000-09-01
A06   2002-05-31
A07   NULL
```

Figure 8.20 Result of Listing 8.20.

Listing 8.21 uses a correlated subquery to compute the running total of all book sales. A running total, or running sum, is a common calculation: For each book, I want to compute the sum of all sales of the books that precede the book. Here, I'm defining *precede* to mean those books whose *title_id* comes before the current book's *title_id* alphabetically. Note the use of table aliases to refer to the same table in two contexts. The subquery returns the sum of sales for all books preceding the current book, which is denoted by *t1.title_id*. See Figure 8.21 for the result. See also "Calculating Running Statistics" on page 390.

You also can use a subquery in a FROM clause. In "Tips for DISTINCT" on page 168, I used a FROM subquery to replicate a distinct aggregate function. Listing 8.22 uses a FROM subquery to calculate the greatest number of titles written (or cowritten) by any author. See Figure 8.22 for the result. Note that the outer query uses a table alias (*ta*) and column alias (*count_titles*) to reference the inner query's result. See also "Column Aliases and WHERE" on page 92.

```
SELECT t1.title_id, t1.sales,
    (SELECT SUM(t2.sales)
       FROM titles t2
       WHERE t2.title_id <= t1.title_id)
     AS "Running total"
  FROM titles t1;
```

Listing 8.21 Compute the running sum of all book sales. See Figure 8.21 for the result.

title_id	sales	Running total
T01	566	566
T02	9566	10132
T03	25667	35799
T04	13001	48800
T05	201440	250240
T06	11320	261560
T07	1500200	1761760
T08	4095	1765855
T09	5000	1770855
T10	NULL	1770855
T11	94123	1864978
T12	100001	1964979
T13	10467	1975446

Figure 8.21 Result of Listing 8.21.

```
SELECT MAX(ta.count_titles) AS "Max titles"
  FROM (SELECT COUNT(*) AS count_titles
          FROM title_authors
          GROUP BY au_id) ta;
```

Listing 8.22 Calculate the greatest number of titles written (or cowritten) by any author. See Figure 8.22 for the result.

```
Max titles
----------
         4
```

Figure 8.22 Result of Listing 8.22.

Tips for Column Expressions

- You also can use a subquery as a column expression in UPDATE, INSERT, and DELETE statements (see Chapter 10) but not in an ORDER BY list.

- Use CASE expressions instead of correlated subqueries to implement Listing 8.18 more efficiently (see "Evaluating Conditional Values with CASE" on page 149):

```
SELECT title_id,
    MIN(CASE au_order WHEN 1
            THEN au_id END)
      AS "Author 1",
    MIN(CASE au_order WHEN 2
            THEN au_id END)
      AS "Author 2",
    MIN(CASE au_order WHEN 3
            THEN au_id END)
      AS "Author 3"
  FROM title_authors
  GROUP BY title_id
  ORDER BY title_id ASC;
```

- **DBMS** **MySQL** 4.0 and earlier don't support subqueries; see the DBMS tip in "Tips for Subqueries" on page 241 earlier in this chapter.

  In **Microsoft Access**, you must increase the precision of the average-price calculation in Listing 8.17. Use the type-conversion function CDbl() to coerce the average price to a double-precision floating-point number; see the DBMS tip in "Tips for Converting Data Types" on page 147. To run Listing 8.17, change both occurrences of AVG(price) to CDbl(AVG(price)).

Comparing a Subquery Value by Using a Comparison Operator

You can use a subquery as a filter in a WHERE clause or HAVING clause by using one of the comparison operators (=, <>, <, <=, >, or >=).

The important characteristics of a subquery comparison test are:

- The comparison operators work the same way as they do in other comparisons (refer to Table 4.2 on page 89).

- The subquery can be simple or correlated (see "Simple and Correlated Subqueries" on page 248).

- The subquery's SELECT-clause list can include only one expression or column name.

- The compared values must have the same data type or must be implicitly convertible to the same type (see "Converting Data Types with CAST()" on page 145).

- String comparisons are case insensitive or case sensitive, depending on your DBMS; see the DBMS tip in "Tips for WHERE" on page 91.

- The subquery must return a single value (a one-row, one-column result). A subquery that returns more than one value will cause an error.

- If the subquery result contains zero rows, then the comparison test will evaluate to false.

The hard part of writing these statements is getting the subquery to return one value, which you can guarantee several ways:

- Using an aggregate function on an ungrouped table always returns a single value (see Chapter 6).

- Using a join with the outer query based on a key always returns a single value.

To compare a subquery value:

- In the WHERE clause of a SELECT statement, type:

  WHERE *test_expr op* (*subquery*)

  test_expr is a literal value, a column name, an expression, or a subquery that returns a single value; *op* is a comparison operator (=, <>, <, <=, >, or >=); and *subquery* is a scalar subquery that returns exactly one column and zero or one rows.

  If the value returned by *subquery* satisfies the comparison to *test_expr*, then the comparison condition evaluates to true. The comparison condition is false if the subquery value doesn't satisfy the condition, the subquery value is null, or the subquery result is empty (has zero rows). The same syntax applies to a HAVING clause:

  HAVING *test_expr op* (*subquery*)

  Listing 8.23 tests the result of a simple subquery for equality to list the authors who live in the state in which Tenterhooks Press is located. Only one publisher is named Tenterhooks Press, so the inner WHERE condition guarantees that the inner query returns a single-valued result. See Figure 8.23 for the result.

  Listing 8.24 is the same as Listing 8.23 except for the name of the publisher. No publisher named XXX exists, so the subquery returns an empty table (zero rows). The comparison evaluates to null, so the final result is empty. See Figure 8.24 for the result.

```
SELECT au_id, au_fname, au_lname, state
  FROM authors
  WHERE state =
    (SELECT state
        FROM publishers
        WHERE pub_name = 'Tenterhooks Press');
```

Listing 8.23 List the authors who live in the state in which the publisher Tenterhooks Press is located. See Figure 8.23 for the result.

```
au_id au_fname au_lname state
----- -------- -------- -----
A03   Hallie   Hull     CA
A04   Klee     Hull     CA
A06            Kellsey  CA
```

Figure 8.23 Result of Listing 8.23.

```
SELECT au_id, au_fname, au_lname, state
  FROM authors
  WHERE state =
    (SELECT state
        FROM publishers
        WHERE pub_name = 'XXX');
```

Listing 8.24 List the authors who live in the state in which the publisher XXX is located. See Figure 8.24 for the result.

```
au_id au_fname au_lname state
----- -------- -------- -----
```

Figure 8.24 Result of Listing 8.24 (an empty table).

```
SELECT title_id, sales
  FROM titles
  WHERE sales >
    (SELECT AVG(sales)
      FROM titles);
```

Listing 8.25 List the books with above-average sales. See Figure 8.25 for the result.

```
title_id sales
-------- -------
T05        201440
T07       1500200
```

Figure 8.25 Result of Listing 8.25.

```
SELECT ta.au_id, ta.title_id
  FROM titles t
  INNER JOIN title_authors ta
    ON ta.title_id = t.title_id
  WHERE sales >
    (SELECT AVG(sales)
      FROM titles)
  ORDER BY ta.au_id ASC, ta.title_id ASC;
```

Listing 8.26 List the authors of the books with above-average sales by using a join and a subquery. See Figure 8.26 for the result.

```
au_id title_id
----- --------
A02   T07
A04   T05
A04   T07
```

Figure 8.26 Result of Listing 8.26.

Listing 8.25 lists the books with above-average sales. Subqueries introduced with comparison operators often use aggregate functions to return a single value. See Figure 8.25 for the result.

To list the authors of the books with above-average sales, I've added an inner join to Listing 8.25 (Listing 8.26 and Figure 8.26).

Recall from the introduction to this chapter that you can use a subquery almost anywhere an expression is allowed, so this syntax is valid:

WHERE (*subquery*) *op* (*subquery*)

The left subquery must return a single value. Listing 8.27 is equivalent to Listing 8.26, but I've removed the inner join and instead placed a correlated subquery to the left of the comparison operator. See Figure 8.27 for the result.

You can include GROUP BY or HAVING clauses in a subquery if you know that the GROUP BY or HAVING clause itself returns a single value. Listing 8.28 lists the books priced higher than the highest-priced biography. See Figure 8.28 for the result.

```
SELECT au_id, title_id
  FROM title_authors ta
  WHERE
    (SELECT AVG(sales)
       FROM titles t
       WHERE ta.title_id = t.title_id)
    >
    (SELECT AVG(sales)
       FROM titles)
  ORDER BY au_id ASC, title_id ASC;
```

Listing 8.27 List the authors of the books with above-average sales by using two subqueries. See Figure 8.27 for the result.

```
au_id title_id
----- --------
A02    T07
A04    T05
A04    T07
```

Figure 8.27 Result of Listing 8.27.

```
SELECT title_id, price
  FROM titles
  WHERE price >
    (SELECT MAX(price)
       FROM titles
       GROUP BY type
       HAVING type = 'biography');
```

Listing 8.28 List the books priced higher than the highest-priced biography. See Figure 8.28 for the result.

```
title_id price
-------- -----
T03       39.95
T13       29.99
```

Figure 8.28 Result of Listing 8.28.

```
SELECT pub_id, AVG(sales) AS "AVG(sales)"
  FROM titles
  GROUP BY pub_id
  HAVING AVG(sales) >
    (SELECT AVG(sales)
        FROM titles);
```

Listing 8.29 List the publishers whose average sales exceed the overall average sales. See Figure 8.29 for the result.

```
pub_id AVG(sales)
------ ----------
P03       506744.33
```

Figure 8.29 Result of Listing 8.29.

```
SELECT ta1.au_id, ta1.title_id,
    ta1.royalty_share
  FROM title_authors ta1
  WHERE ta1.royalty_share <
    (SELECT MAX(ta2.royalty_share)
        FROM title_authors ta2
        WHERE ta1.title_id = ta2.title_id);
```

Listing 8.30 List authors whose royalty share is less than the highest royalty share of any coauthor of a book. See Figure 8.30 for the result.

```
au_id title_id royalty_share
----- -------- -------------
A04    T04             0.40
A03    T11             0.30
A04    T11             0.30
```

Figure 8.30 Result of Listing 8.30.

Listing 8.29 uses a subquery in a HAVING clause to list the publishers whose average sales exceed overall average sales. Again, the subquery returns a single value (the average of all sales). See Figure 8.29 for the result.

Listing 8.30 uses a correlated subquery to list authors whose royalty share is less than the highest royalty share of any coauthor of a book. The outer query selects the rows of *title_authors* (that is, of *ta1*) one by one. The subquery calculates the highest royalty share for each book being considered for selection in the outer query. For each possible value of *ta1*, the DBMS evaluates the subquery and puts the row being considered in the result if the royalty share is less than the calculated maximum. See Figure 8.30 for the result.

Listing 8.31 uses a correlated subquery to imitate a GROUP BY clause and list all books that have a price greater than the average for books of its type. For each possible value of *t1*, the DBMS evaluates the subquery and includes the row in the result if the price value in that row exceeds the calculated average. It's unnecessary to group by type explicitly because the rows for which the average price is calculated are restricted by the subquery's WHERE clause. See Figure 8.31 for the result.

Listing 8.32 uses the same structure as Listing 8.31 to list all the books whose sales are less than the best-selling books of their types. See Figure 8.32 for the result.

Tips for Subquery Comparison Operators

- If a subquery returns more than one row, then you can use ALL or ANY to modify the comparison operator, or you can introduce the subquery with IN. (ALL, ANY, and IN are covered later in this chapter.)

- DBMS MySQL 4.0 and earlier don't support subqueries; see the DBMS tip in "Tips for Subqueries" on page 241.

```
SELECT type, title_id, price
  FROM titles t1
  WHERE price >
    (SELECT AVG(t2.price)
       FROM titles t2
       WHERE t1.type = t2.type)
  ORDER BY type ASC, title_id ASC;
```

Listing 8.31 List all books that have a price greater than the average for books of its type. See Figure 8.31 for the result.

```
type        title_id price
----------  -------- -----
biography   T06        19.95
biography   T07        23.95
children    T09        13.95
history     T13        29.99
psychology  T04        12.99
```

Figure 8.31 Result of Listing 8.31.

```
SELECT type, title_id, sales
  FROM titles t1
  WHERE sales <
    (SELECT MAX(sales)
       FROM titles t2
       WHERE t1.type = t2.type
         AND sales IS NOT NULL)
  ORDER BY type ASC, title_id ASC;
```

Listing 8.32 List all the books whose sales are less than the best-selling books of their types. See Figure 8.32 for the result.

```
type        title_id sales
----------  -------- ------
biography   T06         11320
biography   T12        100001
children    T08          4095
history     T01           566
history     T02          9566
psychology  T04         13001
psychology  T11         94123
```

Figure 8.32 Result of Listing 8.32.

Testing Set Membership with IN

"List Filtering with IN" on page 109 describes how to use the IN keyword in a WHERE clause to compare a literal, column value, or more-complex expression to a list of values. You also can use a subquery to generate the list.

The important characteristics of a subquery set membership test are:

- IN works the same way with the values in a subquery result as it does with a parenthesized list of values (see "List Filtering with IN" on page 109).

- The subquery can be simple or correlated (see "Simple and Correlated Subqueries" on page 248).

- The subquery's SELECT-clause list can include only one expression or column name.

- The compared values must have the same data type or must be implicitly convertible to the same type (see "Converting Data Types with CAST()" on page 145).

- String comparisons are case insensitive or case sensitive, depending on your DBMS; see the DBMS tip in "Tips for WHERE" on page 91.

- The subquery must return exactly one column and zero or more rows. A subquery that returns more than one column will cause an error.

- You can use NOT IN to reverse the effect of the IN test. If you specify NOT IN, then the DBMS takes the action specified by the SQL statement if there is no matching value in the subquery's result.

To test set membership:

- In the WHERE clause of a SELECT statement, type:

  ```
  WHERE test_expr [NOT] IN (subquery)
  ```

  test_expr is a literal value, a column name, an expression, or a subquery that returns a single value; and *subquery* is a subquery that returns one column and zero or more rows.

  If the value of *test_expr* equals any value returned by *subquery*, then the IN condition evaluates to true. The IN condition is false if the subquery result is empty, if no row in the subquery result matches *test_expr*, or if all the values in the subquery result are null. Specify NOT to negate the condition's result.

  The same syntax applies to a HAVING clause:

  ```
  HAVING test_expr [NOT] IN (subquery)
  ```

Listing 8.33 lists the names of the publishers that have published biographies. The DBMS evaluates this statement in two steps. First, the inner query returns the IDs of the publishers that have published biographies (P01 and P03). Second, the DBMS substitutes these values into the outer query, which finds the names that go with the IDs in the table *publishers*. See Figure 8.33 for the result.

Here's the join version of Listing 8.33:

```
SELECT DISTINCT pub_name
  FROM publishers p
  INNER JOIN titles t
    ON p.pub_id = t.pub_id
  AND type = 'biography';
```

Listing 8.34 is the same as Listing 8.33, except that it uses NOT IN to list the names of the publishers that haven't published biographies. See Figure 8.34 for the result. This statement can't be converted to a join. The analogous not-equal join has a different meaning: It lists the names of publishers that have published *some* book that isn't a biography.

```
SELECT pub_name
  FROM publishers
  WHERE pub_id IN
    (SELECT pub_id
       FROM titles
       WHERE type = 'biography');
```

Listing 8.33 List the names of the publishers that have published biographies. See Figure 8.33 for the result.

```
pub_name
------------------
Abatis Publishers
Schadenfreude Press
```

Figure 8.33 Result of Listing 8.33.

```
SELECT pub_name
  FROM publishers
  WHERE pub_id NOT IN
    (SELECT pub_id
       FROM titles
       WHERE type = 'biography');
```

Listing 8.34 List the names of the publishers that haven't published biographies. See Figure 8.34 for the result.

```
pub_name
------------------
Core Dump Books
Tenterhooks Press
```

Figure 8.34 Result of Listing 8.34.

```
SELECT au_id, au_fname, au_lname
  FROM authors
  WHERE au_id NOT IN
    (SELECT au_id
       FROM title_authors);
```

Listing 8.35 List the authors who haven't written (or cowritten) a book. See Figure 8.35 for the result.

```
au_id au_fname au_lname
----- -------- -----------
A07    Paddy    O'Furniture
```

Figure 8.35 Result of Listing 8.35.

```
SELECT DISTINCT a.au_id, au_fname, au_lname
  FROM title_authors ta
  INNER JOIN authors a
    ON ta.au_id = a.au_id
  WHERE title_id IN
    (SELECT title_id
       FROM titles
       WHERE pub_id = 'P03');
```

Listing 8.36 List the names of the authors who have published a book with publisher P03. See Figure 8.36 for the result.

```
au_id au_fname au_lname
----- -------- ---------
A01    Sarah    Buchman
A02    Wendy    Heydemark
A04    Klee     Hull
```

Figure 8.36 Result of Listing 8.36.

Listing 8.35 is equivalent to Listing 7.31 in Chapter 7, except that it uses a subquery instead of an outer join to list the authors who haven't written (or cowritten) a book. See Figure 8.35 for the result.

Listing 8.36 lists the names of the authors who have published a book with publisher P03 (Schadenfreude Press). The join to the table *authors* is necessary to include the authors' names (not just their IDs) in the result. See Figure 8.36 for the result.

A subquery can itself include one or more subqueries. Listing 8.37 lists the names of authors who have participated in writing at least one biography. The innermost query returns the title IDs T06, T07, T10, and T12. The DBMS evaluates the subquery at the next higher level by using these title IDs and returns the author IDs. Finally, the outermost query uses the author IDs to find the names of the authors. See Figure 8.37 for the result.

Excessive subquery nesting makes a statement hard to read; often, it's easier to restate the query as a join. Here's the join version of Listing 8.37:

```
SELECT DISTINCT a.au_id, au_fname, au_lname
  FROM authors a
  INNER JOIN title_authors ta
    ON a.au_id = ta.au_id
  INNER JOIN titles t
    ON t.title_id = ta.title_id
  WHERE type = 'biography';
```

Listing 8.38 lists the names of all non-lead authors (*au_order > 1*) who live in California and who receive less than 50 percent of the royalties for a book. See Figure 8.38 for the result.

Here's the join version of Listing 8.38:

```
SELECT DISTINCT a.au_id, au_fname, au_lname
  FROM authors a
  INNER JOIN title_authors ta
    ON a.au_id = ta.au_id
  WHERE state = 'CA'
    AND royalty_share < 0.5
    AND au_order > 1;
```

```
SELECT au_id, au_fname, au_lname
  FROM authors
  WHERE au_id IN
    (SELECT au_id
       FROM title_authors
       WHERE title_id IN
         (SELECT title_id
            FROM titles
            WHERE type = 'biography'));
```

Listing 8.37 List the names of authors who have participated in writing at least one biography. See Figure 8.37 for the result.

au_id	au_fname	au_lname
A02	Wendy	Heydemark
A04	Klee	Hull

Figure 8.37 Result of Listing 8.37.

```
SELECT au_id, au_fname, au_lname
  FROM authors
  WHERE state = 'CA'
    AND au_id IN
      (SELECT au_id
         FROM title_authors
         WHERE royalty_share < 0.5
           AND au_order > 1);
```

Listing 8.38 List the names of all ancillary authors who live in California and who receive less than 50 percent of the royalties for a book. See Figure 8.38 for the result.

au_id	au_fname	au_lname
A03	Hallie	Hull
A04	Klee	Hull

Figure 8.38 Result of Listing 8.38.

```
SELECT au_id, au_fname, au_lname
  FROM authors a
  WHERE au_id IN
    (SELECT au_id
       FROM title_authors
       WHERE royalty_share < 1.0);
```

Listing 8.39 List the names of authors who are coauthors of a book. See Figure 8.39 for the result.

```
au_id au_fname au_lname
----- -------- ---------
A02   Wendy    Heydemark
A03   Hallie   Hull
A04   Klee     Hull
A06            Kellsey
```

Figure 8.39 Result of Listing 8.39.

```
SELECT a.au_id, au_fname, au_lname
  FROM authors a
  WHERE 1.0 IN
    (SELECT royalty_share
       FROM title_authors ta
       WHERE ta.au_id = a.au_id);
```

Listing 8.40 List the names of authors who are sole authors of a book. See Figure 8.40 for the result.

```
au_id au_fname  au_lname
----- --------- ---------
A01   Sarah     Buchman
A02   Wendy     Heydemark
A04   Klee      Hull
A05   Christian Kells
A06             Kellsey
```

Figure 8.40 Result of Listing 8.40.

Listing 8.39 lists the names of authors who are coauthors of a book. To determine whether an author is a coauthor or the sole author of a book, examine his or her royalty share for the book. If the royalty share is less than 100 percent (1.0), then the author is a coauthor; otherwise, he or she is the sole author. See Figure 8.39 for the result.

Listing 8.40 uses a correlated subquery to list the names of authors who are sole authors of a book—that is, authors who earn 100 percent (1.0) of the royalty on a book. See Figure 8.40 for the result. The DBMS considers each row in the outer-query table *authors* to be a candidate for inclusion in the result. When the DBMS examines the first candidate row in *authors*, it sets the correlation variable *a.au_id* equal to A01 (Sarah Buchman), which it substitutes into the inner query:

```
SELECT royalty_share
  FROM title_authors ta
  WHERE ta.au_id = 'A01';
```

The inner query returns 1.0, so the outer query evaluates to:

```
SELECT a.au_id, au_fname, au_lname
  FROM authors a
  WHERE 1.0 IN (1.0)
```

The WHERE condition is true, so author A01 is included in the result. The DBMS repeats this procedure for every author; see "Simple and Correlated Subqueries" on page 248.

Listing 8.41 lists the names of authors who are both coauthors and sole authors. The inner query returns the author IDs of sole authors, and the outer query compares these IDs with the IDs of the coauthors. See Figure 8.41 for the result.

You can rewrite Listing 8.41 as a join or as an intersection. Here's the join version of Listing 8.41:

```
SELECT DISTINCT a.au_id, au_fname, au_lname
  FROM authors a
  INNER JOIN title_authors ta1
    ON a.au_id = ta1.au_id
  INNER JOIN title_authors ta2
    ON a.au_id = ta2.au_id
  WHERE ta1.royalty_share < 1.0
    AND ta2.royalty_share = 1.0;
```

Here's the intersection version of Listing 8.41 (see "Finding Common Rows with INTERSECT" on page 296):

```
SELECT DISTINCT a.au_id, au_fname, au_lname
  FROM authors a
  INNER JOIN title_authors ta
    ON a.au_id = ta.au_id
  WHERE ta.royalty_share < 1.0
INTERSECT
SELECT DISTINCT a.au_id, au_fname, au_lname
  FROM authors a
  INNER JOIN title_authors ta
    ON a.au_id = ta.au_id
  WHERE ta.royalty_share = 1.0;
```

Listing 8.42 uses a correlated subquery to list the types of books published by more than one publisher. See Figure 8.42 for the result.

Here's the self-join version of Listing 8.42:

```
SELECT DISTINCT t1.type
  FROM titles t1
  INNER JOIN titles t2
    ON t1.type = t2.type
    AND t1.pub_id <> t2.pub_id;
```

```
SELECT DISTINCT a.au_id, au_fname, au_lname
  FROM authors a
  INNER JOIN title_authors ta
    ON a.au_id = ta.au_id
  WHERE ta.royalty_share < 1.0
    AND a.au_id IN
      (SELECT a.au_id
         FROM authors a
         INNER JOIN title_authors ta
           ON a.au_id = ta.au_id
         AND ta.royalty_share = 1.0);
```

Listing 8.41 List the names of authors who are both coauthors and sole authors. See Figure 8.41 for the result.

```
au_id  au_fname  au_lname
-----  --------  ---------
A02    Wendy     Heydemark
A04    Klee      Hull
A06              Kellsey
```

Figure 8.41 Result of Listing 8.41.

```
SELECT DISTINCT t1.type
  FROM titles t1
  WHERE t1.type IN
    (SELECT t2.type
       FROM titles t2
       WHERE t1.pub_id <> t2.pub_id);
```

Listing 8.42 List the types of books common to more than one publisher. See Figure 8.42 for the result.

```
type
---------
biography
history
```

Figure 8.42 Result of Listing 8.42.

Tips for IN

- IN is equivalent to =ANY; see "Comparing Some Subquery Values with ANY" on page 277.

- NOT IN is equivalent to <>ALL (*not* <>ANY); see "Comparing All Subquery Values with ALL" on page 274.

- DBMS To run Listing 8.41 in **Microsoft Access**, type:

```
SELECT DISTINCT a.au_id, au_fname,
    au_lname
  FROM (authors AS a
    INNER JOIN title_authors AS ta1
      ON a.au_id = ta1.au_id)
  INNER JOIN title_authors AS ta2
    ON a.au_id = ta2.au_id
  WHERE ta1.royalty_share < 1.0
    AND ta2.royalty_share = 1.0;
```

MySQL 4.0 and earlier don't support subqueries; see the DBMS tip in "Tips for Subqueries" on page 241.

In older **PostgreSQL** versions, convert the floating-point numbers in Listings 8.38 through 8.41 to DECIMAL; see "Converting Data Types with CAST()" on page 145. To run Listings 8.38 through 8.41, change the floating-point literals to (Listing 8.38):

```
CAST(0.5 AS DECIMAL)
```

and (Listing 8.39):

```
CAST(1.0 AS DECIMAL)
```

and (Listing 8.40):

```
CAST(1.0 AS DECIMAL)
```

and (Listing 8.41):

```
CAST(1.0 AS DECIMAL) (in two places)
```

Some DBMSs let you test multiple values simultaneously by using this syntax:

```
SELECT columns
  FROM table1
  WHERE (col1, col2,..., colN) IN
    (SELECT colA, colB,..., colN
       FROM table2);
```

The test expression (left of IN) is a parenthesized list of *table1* columns. The subquery returns the same number of columns as there are in the list. The DBMS compares the values in corresponding columns. The following query, for example, works in **Oracle**, **Db2**, **MySQL**, and **PostgreSQL**:

```
SELECT au_id, city, state
  FROM authors
  WHERE (city, state) IN
    (SELECT city, state
       FROM publishers);
```

The result lists the authors who live in the same city and state as some publisher:

```
au_id city          state
----- ------------- -----
A03   San Francisco CA
A04   San Francisco CA
A05   New York      NY
```

Comparing All Subquery Values with ALL

You can use the ALL keyword to determine whether a value is less than or greater than *all* the values in a subquery result.

The important characteristics of subquery comparisons that use ALL are:

- ALL modifies a comparison operator in a subquery comparison test and follows =, <>, <, <=, >, or >=; see "Comparing a Subquery Value by Using a Comparison Operator" on page 261.

- The combination of a comparison operator and ALL tells the DBMS how to apply the comparison test to the values returned by a subquery. <ALL, for example, means less than every value in the subquery result, and >ALL means greater than every value in the subquery result.

- When ALL is used with <, <=, >, or >=, the comparison is equivalent to evaluating the subquery result's minimum or maximum value. <ALL means less than every subquery value—in other words, less than the minimum value. >ALL means greater than every subquery value—that is, greater than the maximum value. Table 8.2 shows equivalent ALL expressions and column functions. Listing 8.45 later in this section shows how to replicate a >ALL query by using MAX().

- Semantic equivalence doesn't mean that two queries will *run* at the same speed. For example, the query

```
SELECT * FROM table1
  WHERE col1 > ANY
    (SELECT MAX(col1) FROM table2);
```

usually is faster than

```
SELECT * FROM table1
  WHERE col1 > ALL
    (SELECT col1 FROM table2);
```

For more information, see "Comparing Equivalent Queries" on page 287 later in this chapter.

- The comparison =ALL is valid but isn't often used. =ALL always will be false unless all the values returned by the subquery are identical (and equal to the test value).

- The subquery can be simple or correlated (see "Simple and Correlated Subqueries" on page 248).

- The subquery's SELECT-clause list can include only one expression or column name.

- The compared values must have the same data type or must be implicitly convertible to the same type (see "Converting Data Types with CAST()" on page 145).

- String comparisons are case insensitive or case sensitive, depending on your DBMS; see the DBMS tip in "Tips for WHERE" on page 91.

- The subquery must return exactly one column and zero or more rows. A subquery that returns more than one column will cause an error.

- If the subquery returns no rows, then the ALL condition is true. (You might find this result to be counterintuitive.)

Table 8.2 ALL Equivalencies

ALL Expression	Column Function
< ALL(*subquery*)	< MIN(*subquery* values)
> ALL(*subquery*)	> MAX(*subquery* values)

```
SELECT au_id, au_lname, au_fname, city
  FROM authors
  WHERE city <> ALL
    (SELECT city
       FROM publishers);
```

Listing 8.43 List the authors who live in a city in which no publisher is located. See Figure 8.43 for the result.

```
au_id au_lname     au_fname city
----- -----------  -------- ---------
A01   Buchman      Sarah    Bronx
A02   Heydemark    Wendy    Boulder
A06   Kellsey               Palo Alto
A07   O'Furniture  Paddy    Sarasota
```

Figure 8.43 Result of Listing 8.43.

```
SELECT title_id, title_name
  FROM titles
  WHERE type <> 'biography'
    AND price < ALL
    (SELECT price
       FROM titles
       WHERE type = 'biography'
         AND price IS NOT NULL);
```

Listing 8.44 List the nonbiographies that are cheaper than all the biographies. See Figure 8.44 for the result.

```
title_id title_name
-------- --------------------------------
T05      Exchange of Platitudes
T08      Just Wait Until After School
T11      Perhaps It's a Glandular Problem
```

Figure 8.44 Result of Listing 8.44.

To compare all subquery values:

- In the WHERE clause of a SELECT statement, type:

  WHERE *test_expr* *op* ALL (*subquery*)

  test_expr is a literal value, a column name, an expression, or a subquery that returns a single value; *op* is a comparison operator (=, <>, <, <=, >, or >=); and *subquery* is a subquery that returns one column and zero or more rows.

  The ALL condition evaluates to true if all values in *subquery* satisfy the ALL condition or if the *subquery* result is empty (has zero rows). The ALL condition is false if any (at least one) value in *subquery* doesn't satisfy the ALL condition or if any value is null.

  The same syntax applies to a HAVING clause:

  HAVING *test_expr* *op* ALL (*subquery*)

Listing 8.43 lists the authors who live in a city in which no publisher is located. The inner query finds all the cities in which publishers are located, and the outer query compares each author's city to all the publishers' cities. See Figure 8.43 for the result.

You can use NOT IN to replicate Listing 8.43:

```
SELECT au_id, au_lname, au_fname, city
  FROM authors
  WHERE city NOT IN
    (SELECT city FROM publishers);
```

Listing 8.44 lists the nonbiographies that are priced less than all the biographies. The inner query finds all the biography prices. The outer query inspects the lowest price in the list and determines whether each non-biography is cheaper. See Figure 8.44 for the result. The *price IS NOT NULL* condition is required because the price of biography T10 is null. Without this condition, the entire query would return zero rows because it's impossible to determine whether a price is less than null (see "Nulls" on page 72).

Listing 8.45 lists the books that outsold all the books that author A06 wrote (or cowrote). The inner query uses a join to find the sales of each book by author A06. The outer query inspects the highest sales figure in the list and determines whether each book sold more copies. See Figure 8.45 for the result. Again, the IS NOT NULL condition is needed in case *sales* is null for a book by author A06.

I can replicate Listing 8.45 by using GROUP BY, HAVING, and MAX() (instead of ALL):

```
SELECT title_id
  FROM titles
  GROUP BY title_id
  HAVING MAX(sales) >
    (SELECT MAX(sales)
       FROM title_authors ta
       INNER JOIN titles t
         ON t.title_id = ta.title_id
       WHERE ta.au_id = 'A06');
```

Listing 8.46 uses a correlated subquery in the HAVING clause of the outer query to list the types of books for which the highest sales figure is more than twice the average sales for that type. The inner query is evaluated once for each group defined in the outer query (once for each type of book). See Figure 8.46 for the result.

Tips for ALL

- <>ALL is equivalent to NOT IN; see "Testing Set Membership with IN" on page 267.

- **DBMS** **MySQL** 4.0 and earlier don't support subqueries; see the DBMS tip in "Tips for Subqueries" on page 241.

  In older **PostgreSQL** versions, convert the floating-point numbers in Listing 8.46 to DECIMAL; see "Converting Data Types with CAST()" on page 145. To run Listing 8.46, change the floating-point literal to:

  ```
  CAST(2.0 AS DECIMAL)
  ```

```
SELECT title_id, title_name
  FROM titles
  WHERE sales > ALL
    (SELECT sales
       FROM title_authors ta
       INNER JOIN titles t
         ON t.title_id = ta.title_id
       WHERE ta.au_id = 'A06'
         AND sales IS NOT NULL);
```

Listing 8.45 List the books that outsold all the books that author A06 wrote (or cowrote). See Figure 8.45 for the result.

```
title_id title_name
-------- ---------------------------
T05      Exchange of Platitudes
T07      I Blame My Mother
T12      Spontaneous, Not Annoying
```

Figure 8.45 Result of Listing 8.45.

```
SELECT t1.type
  FROM titles t1
  GROUP BY t1.type
  HAVING MAX(t1.sales) >= ALL
    (SELECT 2.0 * AVG(t2.sales)
       FROM titles t2
       WHERE t1.type = t2.type);
```

Listing 8.46 List the types of books for which the highest sales figure is more than twice the average sales for that type. See Figure 8.46 for the result.

```
type
---------
biography
```

Figure 8.46 Result of Listing 8.46.

Comparing Some Subquery Values with ANY

ANY works like ALL (see the preceding section) but instead determines whether a value is equal to, less than, or greater than *any* (at least one) of the values in a subquery result.

The important characteristics of subquery comparisons that use ANY are:

- ANY modifies a comparison operator in a subquery comparison test and follows =, <>, <, <=, >, or >=; see "Comparing a Subquery Value by Using a Comparison Operator" on page 261.

- The combination of a comparison operator and ANY tells the DBMS how to apply the comparison test to the values returned by a subquery. <ANY, for example, means less than at least one value in the subquery result, and >ANY means greater than at least one value in the subquery result.

- When ANY is used with <, <=, >, or >=, the comparison is equivalent to evaluating the subquery result's maximum or minimum value. <ANY means less than at least one subquery value—in other words, less than the maximum value. >ANY means greater than at least one subquery value—that is, greater than the minimum value. Table 8.3 shows equivalent ANY expressions and column functions. Listing 8.49 later in this section shows how to replicate a >ANY query by using MIN().

- The comparison =ANY is equivalent to IN; see "Testing Set Membership with IN" on page 267.

- The subquery can be simple or correlated (see "Simple and Correlated Subqueries" on page 248).

- The subquery's SELECT-clause list can include only one expression or column name.

- The compared values must have the same data type or must be implicitly convertible to the same type (see "Converting Data Types with CAST()" on page 145).

- String comparisons are case insensitive or case sensitive, depending on your DBMS; see the DBMS tip in "Tips for WHERE" on page 91.

- The subquery must return exactly one column and zero or more rows. A subquery that returns more than one column will cause an error.

- If the subquery returns no rows, then the ANY condition is false.

Table 8.3 ANY Equivalencies

ANY Expression	Column Function
< ANY(*subquery*)	< MAX(*subquery* values)
> ANY(*subquery*)	> MIN(*subquery* values)

To compare some subquery values:

- In the WHERE clause of a SELECT statement, type:

  WHERE *test_expr op* ANY (*subquery*)

  test_expr is a literal value, a column name, an expression, or a subquery that returns a single value; *op* is a comparison operator (=, <>, <, <=, >, or >=); and *subquery* is a subquery that returns one column and zero or more rows.

  If any (at least one) value in *subquery* satisfies the ANY condition, then the condition evaluates to true. The ANY condition is false if no value in *subquery* satisfies the condition or if *subquery* is empty (has zero rows) or contains all nulls.

  The same syntax applies to a HAVING clause:

  HAVING *test_expr op* ANY (*subquery*)

Listing 8.47 lists the authors who live in a city in which a publisher is located. The inner query finds all the cities in which publishers are located, and the outer query compares each author's city to all the publishers' cities. See Figure 8.47 for the result.

You can use IN to replicate Listing 8.47:

```
SELECT au_id, au_lname, au_fname, city
FROM authors
  WHERE city IN
    (SELECT city FROM publishers);
```

Listing 8.48 lists the nonbiographies that are priced less than at least one biography. The inner query finds all the biography prices. The outer query inspects the highest price in the list and determines whether each nonbiography is cheaper. See Figure 8.48 for the result.

Unlike the ALL comparison in Listing 8.44 in the preceding section, the *price IS NOT NULL* condition isn't required here, even though the price of biography T10 is null. The DBMS doesn't determine whether all the price comparisons are true—just whether at least one is true—so the null comparison is ignored.

```
SELECT au_id, au_lname, au_fname, city
  FROM authors
  WHERE city = ANY
    (SELECT city
       FROM publishers);
```

Listing 8.47 List the authors who live in a city in which a publisher is located. See Figure 8.47 for the result.

```
au_id au_lname au_fname  city
----- -------- --------- -------------
A03   Hull     Hallie    San Francisco
A04   Hull     Klee      San Francisco
A05   Kells    Christian New York
```

Figure 8.47 Result of Listing 8.47.

```
SELECT title_id, title_name
  FROM titles
  WHERE type <> 'biography'
    AND price < ANY
      (SELECT price
         FROM titles
         WHERE type = 'biography');
```

Listing 8.48 List the nonbiographies that are cheaper than at least one biography. See Figure 8.48 for the result.

```
title_id title_name
-------- --------------------------------
T01      1977!
T02      200 Years of German Humor
T04      But I Did It Unconsciously
T05      Exchange of Platitudes
T08      Just Wait Until After School
T09      Kiss My Boo-Boo
T11      Perhaps It's a Glandular Problem
```

Figure 8.48 Result of Listing 8.48.

```
SELECT title_id, title_name
  FROM titles
  WHERE sales > ANY
    (SELECT sales
       FROM title_authors ta
       INNER JOIN titles t
         ON t.title_id = ta.title_id
       WHERE ta.au_id = 'A06');
```

Listing 8.49 List the books that outsold at least one of the books that author A06 wrote (or cowrote). See Figure 8.49 for the result.

```
title_id  title_name
--------  -----------------------------------
T02       200 Years of German Humor
T03       Ask Your System Administrator
T04       But I Did It Unconsciously
T05       Exchange of Platitudes
T06       How About Never?
T07       I Blame My Mother
T09       Kiss My Boo-Boo
T11       Perhaps It's a Glandular Problem
T12       Spontaneous, Not Annoying
T13       What Are The Civilian Applications?
```

Figure 8.49 Result of Listing 8.49.

Listing 8.49 lists the books that outsold at least one of the books that author A06 wrote (or cowrote). The inner query uses a join to find the sales of each book by author A06. The outer query inspects the lowest sales figure in the list and determines whether each book sold more copies. See Figure 8.49 for the result. Again, unlike the ALL comparison in Listing 8.45 in the preceding section, the IS NOT NULL condition isn't needed here.

I can replicate Listing 8.49 by using GROUP BY, HAVING, and MIN() (instead of ANY):

```
SELECT title_id
  FROM titles
  GROUP BY title_id
  HAVING MIN(sales) >
    (SELECT MIN(sales)
       FROM title_authors ta
       INNER JOIN titles t
         ON t.title_id = ta.title_id
       WHERE ta.au_id = 'A06');
```

Tips for ANY

- =ANY is equivalent to IN, but <>ANY isn't equivalent to NOT IN. If *subquery* returns the values *x*, *y*, and *z*, then

  test_expr <> ANY (*subquery*)

  is equivalent to:

  test_expr <> *x* OR
  test_expr <> *y* OR
  test_expr <> *z*

  But

  test_expr NOT IN (*subquery*)

  is equivalent to:

  test_expr <> *x* AND
  test_expr <> *y* AND
  test_expr <> *z*

  (NOT IN actually is equivalent to <>ALL.)

- In the SQL standard, the keywords ANY and SOME are synonyms. In some DBMSs, you can use SOME in place of ANY.

- DBMS **MySQL** 4.0 and earlier don't support subqueries; see the DBMS tip in "Tips for Subqueries" on page 241.

Testing Existence with EXISTS

So far in this chapter, I've been using the comparison operators IN, ALL, and ANY to compare a specific test value to values in a subquery result. EXISTS and NOT EXISTS don't compare values; rather, they simply look for the existence or nonexistence of rows in a subquery result.

The important characteristics of an existence test are:

- An existence test doesn't compare values, so it isn't preceded by a test expression.

- The subquery can be simple or correlated but usually is correlated (see "Simple and Correlated Subqueries" on page 248).

- The subquery can return any number of columns and rows.

- By convention, the SELECT clause in the subquery is SELECT * to retrieve all columns. Listing specific column names is unnecessary because EXISTS simply tests for the *existence* of rows that satisfy the subquery conditions; the actual values in the rows are irrelevant.

- All IN, ALL, and ANY queries can be expressed with EXISTS or NOT EXISTS. I'll give equivalent queries in some of the examples later in this section.

- If the subquery returns at least one row, then an EXISTS test is true, and a NOT EXISTS test is false.

- If the subquery returns no rows, then an EXISTS test is false, and a NOT EXISTS test is true.

- A subquery row that contains only nulls counts as a row. (An EXISTS test is true, and a NOT EXISTS test is false.)

- Because an EXISTS test performs no comparisons, it's not subject to the same problems with nulls as tests that use IN, ALL, or ANY; see "Nulls in Subqueries" on page 254.

```
SELECT pub_name
  FROM publishers p
  WHERE EXISTS
    (SELECT *
       FROM titles t
       WHERE t.pub_id = p.pub_id
         AND type = 'biography');
```

Listing 8.50 List the names of the publishers that have published biographies. See Figure 8.50 for the result.

```
pub_name
-------------------
Abatis Publishers
Schadenfreude Press
```

Figure 8.50 Result of Listing 8.50.

```
SELECT au_id, au_fname, au_lname
  FROM authors a
  WHERE NOT EXISTS
    (SELECT *
       FROM title_authors ta
       WHERE ta.au_id = a.au_id);
```

Listing 8.51 List the authors who haven't written (or cowritten) a book. See Figure 8.51 for the result.

```
au_id  au_fname   au_lname
-----  ---------  -----------
A07    Paddy      O'Furniture
```

Figure 8.51 Result of Listing 8.51.

To test existence:

- In the WHERE clause of a SELECT statement, type:

  WHERE [NOT] EXISTS (*subquery*)

  subquery is a subquery that returns any number of columns and rows.

  If *subquery* returns one or more rows, then the EXISTS test evaluates to true. If *subquery* returns zero rows, then the EXISTS test evaluates to false. Specify NOT to negate the test's result.

  The same syntax applies to a HAVING clause:

  HAVING [NOT] EXISTS (*subquery*)

Listing 8.50 lists the names of the publishers that have published biographies. This query considers each publisher's ID in turn and determines whether it causes the existence test to evaluate to true. Here, the first publisher is P01 (Abatis Publishers). The DBMS ascertains whether any rows exist in the table *titles* in which *pub_id* is P01 and *type* is biography. If so, then Abatis Publishers is included in the final result. The DBMS repeats the same process for each of the other publisher IDs. See Figure 8.50 for the result. If I wanted to list the names of publishers that *haven't* published biographies, then I'd change EXISTS to NOT EXISTS. See Listing 8.33 earlier in this chapter for an equivalent query that uses IN.

Listing 8.51 lists the authors who haven't written (or cowritten) a book. See Figure 8.51 for the result. See Listing 8.35 earlier in this chapter for an equivalent query that uses NOT IN.

Listing 8.52 lists the authors who live in a city in which a publisher is located. See Figure 8.52 for the result. See Listing 8.47 earlier in this chapter for an equivalent query that uses =ANY.

"Finding Common Rows with INTERSECT" on page 296 describes how to use INTERSECT to retrieve the rows that two tables have in common. You also can use EXISTS to find an intersection. Listing 8.53 lists the cities in which both an author and publisher are located. See Figure 8.53 for the result. See Listing 9.8 in Chapter 9 for an equivalent query that uses INTERSECT.

You also can replicate this query with an inner join:

```
SELECT DISTINCT a.city
  FROM authors a
  INNER JOIN publishers p
    ON a.city = p.city;
```

```
SELECT au_id, au_lname, au_fname, city
  FROM authors a
  WHERE EXISTS
    (SELECT *
       FROM publishers p
       WHERE p.city = a.city);
```

Listing 8.52 List the authors who live in a city in which a publisher is located. See Figure 8.52 for the result.

```
au_id  au_lname  au_fname   city
-----  --------  ---------  -------------
A03    Hull      Hallie     San Francisco
A04    Hull      Klee       San Francisco
A05    Kells     Christian  New York
```

Figure 8.52 Result of Listing 8.52.

```
SELECT DISTINCT city
  FROM authors a
  WHERE EXISTS
    (SELECT *
       FROM publishers p
       WHERE p.city = a.city);
```

Listing 8.53 List the cities in which both an author and publisher are located. See Figure 8.53 for the result.

```
city
------------
New York
San Francisco
```

Figure 8.53 Result of Listing 8.53.

```
SELECT DISTINCT city
  FROM authors a
  WHERE NOT EXISTS
    (SELECT *
       FROM publishers p
       WHERE p.city = a.city);
```

Listing 8.54 List the cities in which an author lives but a publisher isn't located. See Figure 8.54 for the result.

```
city
---------
Boulder
Bronx
Palo Alto
Sarasota
```

Figure 8.54 Result of Listing 8.54.

```
SELECT au_id, au_fname, au_lname
  FROM authors a
  WHERE EXISTS
    (SELECT *
       FROM title_authors ta
       WHERE ta.au_id = a.au_id
       HAVING COUNT(*) >= 3);
```

Listing 8.55 List the authors who wrote (or cowrote) three or more books. See Figure 8.55 for the result.

au_id	au_fname	au_lname
A01	Sarah	Buchman
A02	Wendy	Heydemark
A04	Klee	Hull
A06		Kellsey

Figure 8.55 Result of Listing 8.55.

"Finding Different Rows with EXCEPT" on page 298 describes how to use EXCEPT to retrieve the rows in one table that aren't also in another table. You also can use NOT EXISTS to find a difference. Listing 8.54 lists the cities in which an author lives but a publisher isn't located. See Figure 8.54 for the result. See Listing 9.9 in Chapter 9 for an equivalent query that uses EXCEPT.

You also can replicate this query with NOT IN:

```
SELECT DISTINCT city
  FROM authors
  WHERE city NOT IN
    (SELECT city
       FROM publishers);
```

Or with an outer join:

```
SELECT DISTINCT a.city
  FROM authors a
  LEFT OUTER JOIN publishers p
    ON a.city = p.city
  WHERE p.city IS NULL;
```

Listing 8.55 lists the authors who wrote (or cowrote) three or more books. See Figure 8.55 for the result.

Listing 8.56 uses two existence tests to list the authors who wrote (or cowrote) both children's and psychology books. See Figure 8.56 for the result.

Listing 8.57 performs a uniqueness test to determine whether duplicates occur in the column *au_id* in the table *authors*. The query prints *Yes* if duplicate values exist in the column *au_id*; otherwise, it returns an empty result. See Figure 8.57 for the result. *au_id* is the primary key of *authors*, so of course it contains no duplicates.

```sql
SELECT au_id, au_fname, au_lname
  FROM authors a
  WHERE EXISTS
    (SELECT *
       FROM title_authors ta
       INNER JOIN titles t
         ON t.title_id = ta.title_id
       WHERE ta.au_id = a.au_id
         AND t.type = 'children')
  AND EXISTS
    (SELECT *
       FROM title_authors ta
       INNER JOIN titles t
         ON t.title_id = ta.title_id
       WHERE ta.au_id = a.au_id
         AND t.type = 'psychology');
```

Listing 8.56 List the authors who wrote (or cowrote) a children's book and also wrote (or cowrote) a psychology book. See Figure 8.56 for the result.

```
au_id au_fname au_lname
----- -------- --------
A06            Kellsey
```

Figure 8.56 Result of Listing 8.56.

```sql
SELECT DISTINCT 'Yes' AS "Duplicates?"
  WHERE EXISTS
    (SELECT *
       FROM authors
       GROUP BY au_id
       HAVING COUNT(*) > 1);
```

Listing 8.57 Does the column *au_id* in the table *authors* contain duplicate values? See Figure 8.57 for the result.

```
Duplicates?
-----------
```

Figure 8.57 Result of Listing 8.57.

```
SELECT DISTINCT 'Yes' AS "Duplicates?"
  WHERE EXISTS
    (SELECT *
       FROM title_authors
       GROUP BY au_id
       HAVING COUNT(*) > 1);
```

Listing 8.58 Does the column *au_id* in the table *title_authors* contain duplicate values? See Figure 8.58 for the result.

```
Duplicates?
-----------
Yes
```

Figure 8.58 Result of Listing 8.58.

```
SELECT pub_id
  FROM publishers
  WHERE EXISTS
    (SELECT COUNT(*)
       FROM titles
       WHERE pub_id = 'XXX');
```

Listing 8.59 Be careful when using aggregate functions in a subquery SELECT clause. See Figure 8.59 for the result.

```
pub_id
------
P01
P02
P03
P04
```

Figure 8.59 Result of Listing 8.59.

Listing 8.58 shows the same query for the table *title_authors*, which does contain duplicate *au_id* values. See Figure 8.58 for the result. You can add grouping columns to the GROUP BY clause to determine whether multiple-column duplicates exist.

Tips for EXISTS

- You also can use COUNT(*) to determine whether a subquery returns at least one row, but COUNT(*) (usually) is less efficient than EXISTS. The DBMS quits processing an EXISTS subquery as soon as it determines whether the subquery returns a row, whereas COUNT(*) forces the DBMS to process the entire subquery. This query is equivalent to Listing 8.52 but runs slower:

```
SELECT au_id, au_lname, au_fname, city
  FROM authors a
  WHERE
  (SELECT COUNT(*)
     FROM publishers p
     WHERE p.city = a.city) > 0;
```

- Although SELECT * is the most common form of the SELECT clause in an EXISTS subquery, you can use SELECT *column* or SELECT *constant_value* to speed queries if your DBMS's optimizer isn't bright enough to figure out that it doesn't need to construct an *entire* interim table for an EXISTS subquery. For more information, see "Comparing Equivalent Queries" on page 287.

- Although I use SELECT COUNT(*) in some of the DBMS-specific subqueries in the DBMS tip in this section, you should be wary of using an aggregate function in a subquery's SELECT clause. The existence test in Listing 8.59, for example, *always* is true because COUNT(*) always will return a row (with the value zero here). I could argue that the result, Figure 8.59, is flawed logically because no publisher ID XXX exists.

- **DBMS** To run Listings 8.55, 8.57, and 8.58 in **Microsoft Access**, change SELECT * to SELECT 1. Additionally, in Listing 8.57 add the clause FROM authors to the outer query, and in Listing 8.58 add the clause FROM title_authors to the outer query.

  To run Listings 8.57 and 8.58 in **Oracle**, add the clause FROM DUAL to the outer query; see the DBMS tip in "Tips for Derived Columns" on page 117.

  To run Listings 8.55, 8.57, and 8.58 in **Db2**, change SELECT * to SELECT 1. Additionally, in Listings 8.57 and 8.58, add the clause FROM SYSIBM.SYSDUMMY1 to the outer query; see the DBMS tip in "Tips for Derived Columns" on page 117. For example, change Listing 8.57 to:

  ```
  SELECT DISTINCT 'Yes' AS "Duplicates?"
    FROM SYSIBM.SYSDUMMY1
    WHERE EXISTS
      (SELECT 1
         FROM authors
         GROUP BY au_id
         HAVING COUNT(*) > 1);
  ```

  In **MySQL**, to run Listing 8.57 add the clause FROM authors to the outer query, and in Listing 8.58 add the clause FROM title_authors to the outer query. MySQL 4.0 and earlier don't support subqueries; see the DBMS tip in "Tips for Subqueries" on page 241.

  To run Listings 8.55, 8.57, and 8.58 in **PostgreSQL**, change SELECT * to SELECT 1.

```
SELECT DISTINCT a.au_id
  FROM authors a
  INNER JOIN title_authors ta
    ON a.au_id = ta.au_id;

SELECT DISTINCT a.au_id
  FROM authors a, title_authors ta
  WHERE a.au_id = ta.au_id;

SELECT au_id
  FROM authors a
  WHERE au_id IN
    (SELECT au_id
       FROM title_authors);

SELECT au_id
  FROM authors a
  WHERE au_id = ANY
    (SELECT au_id
       FROM title_authors);

SELECT au_id
  FROM authors a
  WHERE EXISTS
    (SELECT *
       FROM title_authors ta
       WHERE a.au_id = ta.au_id);

SELECT au_id
  FROM authors a
  WHERE 0 <
    (SELECT COUNT(*)
       FROM title_authors ta
       WHERE a.au_id = ta.au_id);
```

Listing 8.60 These six queries are equivalent semantically; they all list the authors who have written (or cowritten) at least one book. See Figure 8.60 for the result.

```
au_id
-----
A01
A02
A03
A04
A05
A06
```

Figure 8.60 Each of the six statements in Listing 8.60 returns this result.

Comparing Equivalent Queries

As you've seen in this chapter and the preceding one, you can express the same query in different ways (different syntax, same semantics). To expand on this point, I've written the same query six semantically equivalent ways. Each of the statements in Listing 8.60 lists the authors who have written (or cowritten) at least one book. See Figure 8.60 for the result.

The first two queries (inner joins) will run at the same speed as one another. Of the third through sixth queries (which use subqueries), the last one probably is the worst performer. The DBMS will stop processing the other subqueries as soon as it encounters a single matching value. But the subquery in the last statement has to count all the matching rows before it returns either true or false. Your DBMS's optimizer should run the inner joins at about the same speed as the fastest subquery statement.

You might find this programming flexibility to be attractive, but people who design DBMS optimizers don't, because they're tasked with considering all the possible ways to express a query, figuring out which one performs best, and reformulating your query internally to its optimal form. (Entire careers are devoted to solving these types of optimization problems.) If your DBMS has a flawless optimizer, then it will run all six of the queries in Listing 8.60 at the same speed. But that situation is unlikely, so you'll have to experiment with your DBMS to see which version runs fastest.

Tips for Comparing Equivalent Queries

- You should compare queries against large test tables (more than 10000 or even 100000 rows) so that speed and memory differences will be obvious.

- DBMS DBMSs provide tools to let you measure the efficiency of queries. Tables 8.4 and 8.5 list the commands that time queries and show their **execution plans**.

Table 8.4 Timing Queries

DBMS	Command
Access	Not available
SQL Server	SET STATISTICS TIME ON
Oracle	SET TIMING ON
Db2	db2batch
MySQL	The mysql command-line utility prints execution times by default.
PostgreSQL	\timing

Table 8.5 Showing Query Execution Plans

DBMS	Command
Access	Not available
SQL Server	SET SHOWPLAN_TEXT ON
Oracle	EXPLAIN PLAN
Db2	EXPLAIN or db2expln
MySQL	EXPLAIN
PostgreSQL	EXPLAIN

SQL Tuning

After you learn the basics of SQL, your next step is to tune your SQL statements so that they run efficiently, which means learning about your DBMS's optimizer. Performance tuning involves some platform-independent general principles, but the most effective tuning relies on the idiosyncrasies of the specific DBMS. Tuning is beyond the scope of this book, but the internet has plenty of discussion groups and articles—search for *tuning* (or *performance* or *optimization*) together with the name of your DBMS.

A good book to get started with is Peter Gulutzan and Trudy Pelzer's *SQL Performance Tuning*, which covers eight DBMSs, or Dan Tow's *SQL Tuning*, which covers Microsoft SQL Server, Oracle, and Db2. If you look up one of these books on Amazon.com, then you can find other tuning books in the "customers also viewed" list.

CHAPTER 9

Set Operations

Recall from Chapter 2 that set theory is fundamental to the relational model. But whereas mathematical sets are unchanging, database sets are dynamic—they grow, shrink, and otherwise change over time. This chapter covers the following SQL set operators, which combine the results of two SELECT statements into one result:

- UNION returns all the rows returned by both queries, with duplicates removed.

- INTERSECT returns all rows common to both queries (that is, all distinct rows retrieved by both queries).

- EXCEPT returns all rows from the first query without the rows that appear in the second query, with duplicates removed.

These set operations aren't joins, but you can mix and chain them to combine two or more tables.

Combining Rows with UNION

A UNION operation combines the results of two queries into a single result that has the rows returned by both queries. (This operation differs from a join, which combines columns from two tables.) A UNION expression removes duplicate rows from the result; a UNION ALL expression doesn't remove duplicates.

Unions are simple, but they have some restrictions:

- The SELECT-clause lists in the two queries must have the same number of columns (column names, arithmetic expressions, aggregate functions, and so on).

- The corresponding columns in the two queries must be listed in the same order in the two queries.

- The corresponding columns must have the same data type or must be implicitly convertible to the same type.

- If the names of corresponding columns match, then that column name is used in the result. If the corresponding column names differ, then it's up to the DBMS to determine the column name in the result. Most DBMSs take the result's column names from the first SELECT query in the union. If you want to rename a column in the result, then use an AS clause in the first query; see "Creating Column Aliases with AS" on page 79.

- An ORDER BY clause can appear in only the final SELECT query in the union. The sort is applied to the final, combined result. Because the result's column names depend on the DBMS, it's often easiest to use relative column positions to specify the sort order; see "Sorting Rows with ORDER BY" on page 83.

- GROUP BY and HAVING can be specified in the individual queries only; they can't be used to affect the final result.

```
SELECT state FROM authors
UNION
SELECT state FROM publishers;
```

Listing 9.1 List the states where authors and publishers are located. See Figure 9.1 for the result.

```
state
-----
NULL
CA
CO
FL
NY
```

Figure 9.1 Result of Listing 9.1.

```
SELECT state FROM authors
UNION ALL
SELECT state FROM publishers;
```

Listing 9.2 List the states where authors and publishers are located, including duplicates. See Figure 9.2 for the result.

```
state
-----
NY
CO
CA
CA
NY
CA
FL
NY
CA
NULL
CA
```

Figure 9.2 Result of Listing 9.2.

```
SELECT au_fname || ' ' || au_lname AS "Name"
   FROM authors
UNION
SELECT pub_name
   FROM publishers
   ORDER BY 1 ASC;
```

Listing 9.3 List the names of all the authors and publishers. See Figure 9.3 for the result.

```
Name
-------------------
 Kellsey
Abatis Publishers
Christian Kells
Core Dump Books
Hallie Hull
Klee Hull
Paddy O'Furniture
Sarah Buchman
Schadenfreude Press
Tenterhooks Press
Wendy Heydemark
```

Figure 9.3 Result of Listing 9.3.

To combine rows:

- Type:

  select_query1
  UNION [ALL]
  select_query2;

  select_query1 and *select_query2* are SELECT queries. The number and the order of the columns must be identical in both queries, and the data types of corresponding columns must be compatible. Duplicate rows are eliminated from the result unless ALL is specified.

  Listing 9.1 lists the states where authors and publishers are located. By default, UNION removes duplicate rows from the result. See Figure 9.1 for the result.
  Listing 9.2 is the same as Listing 9.1 except that it includes the ALL keyword, so all rows are included in the results, and duplicates aren't removed. See Figure 9.2 for the result.
  Listing 9.3 lists the names of all the authors and publishers. The AS clause in the first query names the column in the result. The ORDER BY clause uses a relative column position instead of a column name to sort the result. See Figure 9.3 for the result.

Listing 9.4 expands on Listing 9.3 and defines the extra column *Type* to identify which table each row came from. The WHERE conditions retrieve the authors and publishers from New York state only. See Figure 9.4 for the result.

Listing 9.5 adds a third query to Listing 9.4 to retrieve the titles of books published in New York state also. See Figure 9.5 for the result.

Listing 9.6 is similar to Listing 9.5 except that it lists the counts of each author, publisher, and book, instead of their names. See Figure 9.6 for the result.

```
SELECT
    'author' AS "Type",
    au_fname || ' ' || au_lname AS "Name",
    state
  FROM authors
  WHERE state = 'NY'
UNION
SELECT
    'publisher',
    pub_name,
    state
  FROM publishers
  WHERE state = 'NY'
  ORDER BY 1 ASC, 2 ASC;
```

Listing 9.4 List the names of all the authors and publishers located in New York state, sorted by type and then by name. See Figure 9.4 for the result.

```
Type       Name               state
---------  -----------------  -----
author     Christian Kells    NY
author     Sarah Buchman      NY
publisher  Abatis Publishers  NY
```

Figure 9.4 Result of Listing 9.4.

```
SELECT
    'author' AS "Type",
    au_fname || ' ' || au_lname AS "Name"
  FROM authors
  WHERE state = 'NY'
UNION
SELECT
    'publisher',
    pub_name
  FROM publishers
  WHERE state = 'NY'
UNION
SELECT
    'title',
    title_name
  FROM titles t
  INNER JOIN publishers p
    ON t.pub_id = p.pub_id
  WHERE p.state = 'NY'
  ORDER BY 1 ASC, 2 ASC;
```

Listing 9.5 List the names of all the authors and publishers located in New York state and the titles of books published in New York state, sorted by type and then by name. See Figure 9.5 for the result.

```
Type        Name
---------   --------------------------
author      Christian Kells
author      Sarah Buchman
publisher   Abatis Publishers
title       1977!
title       How About Never?
title       Not Without My Faberge Egg
title       Spontaneous, Not Annoying
```

Figure 9.5 Result of Listing 9.5.

```
SELECT
    'author' AS "Type",
    COUNT(au_id) AS "Count"
  FROM authors
  WHERE state = 'NY'
UNION
SELECT
    'publisher',
    COUNT(pub_id)
  FROM publishers
  WHERE state = 'NY'
UNION
SELECT
    'title',
    COUNT(title_id)
  FROM titles t
  INNER JOIN publishers p
    ON t.pub_id = p.pub_id
  WHERE p.state = 'NY'
  ORDER BY 1 ASC;
```

Listing 9.6 List the counts of all the authors and publishers located in New York state and the titles of books published in New York state, sorted by type. See Figure 9.6 for the result.

```
Type        Count
---------   -----
author      2
publisher   1
title       4
```

Figure 9.6 Result of Listing 9.6.

In Listing 9.7, I revisit Listing 5.30 in "Evaluating Conditional Values with CASE" on page 149. But instead of using CASE to change book prices and simulate if-then logic, I use multiple UNION queries. See Figure 9.7 for the result.

```
SELECT title_id, type, price,
    price * 1.10 AS "New price"
  FROM titles
  WHERE type = 'history'
UNION
SELECT title_id, type, price, price * 1.20
  FROM titles
  WHERE type = 'psychology'
UNION
SELECT title_id, type, price, price
  FROM titles
  WHERE type NOT IN ('psychology','history')
  ORDER BY type ASC, title_id ASC;
```

Listing 9.7 Raise the price of history books by 10 percent and psychology books by 20 percent, and leave the prices of other books unchanged. See Figure 9.7 for the result.

title_id	type	price	New price
T06	biography	19.95	19.95
T07	biography	23.95	23.95
T10	biography	NULL	NULL
T12	biography	12.99	12.99
T08	children	10.00	10.00
T09	children	13.95	13.95
T03	computer	39.95	39.95
T01	history	21.99	24.19
T02	history	19.95	21.95
T13	history	29.99	32.99
T04	psychology	12.99	15.59
T05	psychology	6.95	8.34
T11	psychology	7.99	9.59

Figure 9.7 Result of Listing 9.7.

UNION Commutativity

In theory, the order in which the SELECT queries (tables) occur in a union should make no speed difference. But in practice your DBMS might run

```
small_table1
UNION
small_table2
UNION
big_table;
```

faster than

```
small_table1
UNION
big_table
UNION
small_table2;
```

because of the way the optimizer merges intermediate results and removes duplicate rows. Experiment.

Tips for UNION

- UNION is commutative: A UNION B is the same as B UNION A.

- The SQL standard gives INTERSECT higher precedence than UNION and EXCEPT, but your DBMS might use a different order. Use parentheses to specify order of evaluation in queries with mixed set operators; see "Determining the Order of Evaluation" on page 121.

- Don't use UNION where a compound condition will suffice:

```
SELECT DISTINCT * FROM mytable
  WHERE col1 = 1 AND col2 = 2;
```

usually is faster than

```
SELECT * FROM mytable
  WHERE col1 = 1;
UNION
SELECT * FROM mytable
  WHERE col2 = 2;
```

- If you mix UNION and UNION ALL in a single statement, then use parentheses to specify order of evaluation. Take these two statements, for example:

```
SELECT * FROM table1
UNION ALL
(SELECT * FROM table2
UNION
SELECT * FROM table3);
```

and:

```
(SELECT * FROM table1
UNION ALL
SELECT * FROM table2)
UNION
SELECT * FROM table3;
```

The first statement eliminates duplicates in the union of *table2* and *table3* but doesn't eliminate duplicates in the union of that result and *table1*. The second statement includes duplicates in the union of *table1* and *table2* but eliminates duplicates in the subsequent union with *table3*, so ALL has no effect on the final result of this statement.

- For UNION operations, the DBMS performs an internal sort to identify and remove duplicate rows; hence, the result of a UNION might be sorted even if you don't specify an ORDER BY clause. UNION ALL doesn't sort because it doesn't need to remove duplicates. Sorting is computationally expensive—don't use UNION when UNION ALL will suffice.

- `DBMS` In **Microsoft Access** and **Microsoft SQL Server**, use + to concatenate strings (see "Concatenating Strings with ||" on page 122). To run Listings 9.3 through 9.5, change the concatenation expressions to:

```
au_fname + ' ' + au_lname
```

In **MySQL**, use CONCAT() to concatenate strings (see "Concatenating Strings with ||" on page 122). To run Listings 9.3 through 9.5, change the concatenation expressions to:

```
CONCAT(au_fname, ' ', au_lname)
```

In older **PostgreSQL** versions, convert the floating-point numbers in Listing 9.7 to DECIMAL; see "Converting Data Types with CAST()" on page 145. To run Listing 9.7, change new-price calculations to:

```
price * CAST((1.10) AS DECIMAL)

price * CAST((1.20) AS DECIMAL)
```

Finding Common Rows with INTERSECT

An INTERSECT operation combines the results of two queries into a single result that has all the rows common to both queries. Intersections have the same restrictions as unions; see "Combining Rows with UNION" on page 290.

To find common rows:

* Type:

  select_query1
  INTERSECT
  select_query2;

  select_query1 and *select_query2* are SELECT queries. The number and the order of the columns must be identical in both queries, and the data types of corresponding columns must be compatible. Duplicate rows are eliminated from the result.

  Listing 9.8 uses INTERSECT to list the cities in which both an author and a publisher are located. See Figure 9.8 for the result.

```
SELECT city
  FROM authors
INTERSECT
SELECT city
  FROM publishers;
```

Listing 9.8 List the cities in which both an author and a publisher are located. See Figure 9.8 for the result.

```
city
-------------
New York
San Francisco
```

Figure 9.8 Result of Listing 9.8.

Tips for INTERSECT

- INTERSECT is commutative: A INTERSECT B is the same as B INTERSECT A.

- The SQL standard gives INTERSECT higher precedence than UNION and EXCEPT, but your DBMS might use a different order. Use parentheses to specify order of evaluation in queries with mixed set operators; see "Determining the Order of Evaluation" on page 121.

- It's helpful to think of UNION as logical OR and INTERSECTION as logical AND; see "Combining and Negating Conditions with AND, OR, and NOT" on page 93. If you want to know, for example, which products are supplied by vendor A *or* vendor B, then type:

```
SELECT product_id
  FROM vendor_a_product_list
UNION
SELECT product_id
  FROM vendor_b_product_list;
```

If you want to know which products are supplied by vendor A *and* vendor B, then type:

```
SELECT product_id
  FROM vendor_a_product_list
INTERSECT
SELECT product_id
  FROM vendor_b_product_list;
```

- If your DBMS doesn't support INTERSECT, then you can replicate it with an INNER JOIN or an EXISTS subquery. Each of the following statements is equivalent to Listing 9.8 (inner join):

```
SELECT DISTINCT authors.city
  FROM authors
  INNER JOIN publishers
    ON authors.city = publishers.city;
```

or (EXISTS subquery):

```
SELECT DISTINCT city
  FROM authors
  WHERE EXISTS
    (SELECT *
       FROM publishers
       WHERE authors.city =
             publishers.city;)
```

- **DBMS** **Microsoft Access** and **MySQL** don't support INTERSECT. To run Listing 9.8, use one of the equivalent queries given in the preceding tip.

Finding Different Rows with EXCEPT

An EXCEPT operation, also called a **difference**, combines the results of two queries into a single result that has the rows that belong to only the first query. To contrast INTERSECT and EXCEPT, A INTERSECT B contains rows from table A that are duplicated in table B, whereas A EXCEPT B contains rows from table A that *aren't* duplicated in table B. Differences have the same restrictions as unions; see "Combining Rows with UNION" on page 290.

To find different rows:

* Type:

  select_query1
  EXCEPT
  select_query2;

  select_query1 and *select_query2* are SELECT queries. The number and the order of the columns must be identical in both queries, and the data types of corresponding columns must be compatible. Duplicate rows are eliminated from the result.

  Listing 9.9 uses EXCEPT to list the cities in which an author lives but a publisher isn't located. See Figure 9.9 for the result.

```
SELECT city
  FROM authors
EXCEPT
SELECT city
  FROM publishers;
```

Listing 9.9 List the cities in which an author lives but a publisher isn't located. See Figure 9.9 for the result.

```
city
---------
Boulder
Bronx
Palo Alto
Sarasota
```

Figure 9.9 Result of Listing 9.9.

Tips for EXCEPT

- Unlike UNION and INTERSECT, EXCEPT is not commutative: A EXCEPT B isn't the same as B EXCEPT A.

- The SQL standard gives INTERSECT higher precedence than UNION and EXCEPT, but your DBMS might use a different order. Use parentheses to specify order of evaluation in queries with mixed set operators; see "Determining the Order of Evaluation" on page 121.

- Don't use EXCEPT where a compound condition will suffice.

```
SELECT * FROM mytable
  WHERE col1 = 1 AND NOT col2 = 2;
```

usually is faster than

```
SELECT * FROM mytable
  WHERE col1 = 1;
EXCEPT
SELECT * FROM mytable
  WHERE col2 = 2;
```

- If your DBMS doesn't support EXCEPT, then you can replicate it with an outer join, a NOT EXISTS subquery, or a NOT IN subquery. Each of the following statements is equivalent to Listing 9.9 (outer join):

```
SELECT DISTINCT a.city
  FROM authors a
  LEFT OUTER JOIN publishers p
    ON a.city = p.city
  WHERE p.city IS NULL;
```

or (NOT EXISTS subquery):

```
SELECT DISTINCT city
  FROM authors
  WHERE NOT EXISTS
    (SELECT *
       FROM publishers
       WHERE authors.city =
             publishers.city);
```

or (NOT IN subquery):

```
SELECT DISTINCT city
  FROM authors
  WHERE city NOT IN
    (SELECT city
       FROM publishers);
```

- **DBMS** **Microsoft Access** and **MySQL** don't support EXCEPT. To run Listing 9.9, use one of the equivalent queries given in the preceding tip.

  In **Oracle**, the EXCEPT operator is called MINUS. To run Listing 9.9, type:

```
SELECT city FROM authors
MINUS
SELECT city FROM publishers;
```

CHAPTER 10

Inserting, Updating, and Deleting Rows

To this point, I've explained how to use SELECT to retrieve and analyze the data in tables. In this chapter, I'll explain how to use SQL statements to *modify* table data:

- The INSERT statement adds new rows to a table.

- The UPDATE statement changes the values in a table's existing rows.

- The DELETE statement removes rows from a table.

These statements don't return a result, but your DBMS normally will print a message indicating whether the statement ran successfully and, if so, the number of rows affected by the change. To see the actual effect the statement had on a table, use a SELECT statement.

Unlike SELECT, which only accesses data, these statements change data, so your database administrator might need to grant you permission to run them.

Displaying Table Definitions

To use INSERT, UPDATE, or DELETE, you must know about the columns of the table whose data you're modifying, including:

- The order of the columns in the table

- Each column's name

- Each column's data type

- Whether a column is a key (or part of a key)

- Whether a column's values must be unique within that column

- Whether a column allows nulls

- Each column's default value (if any)

- Table and column constraints (Chapter 11)

    Table definitions of the sample-database tables are given in "The Sample Database" in Chapter 2, but you can get the same information by using DBMS tools that describe database objects. This section explains how to use those tools to display table definitions for the current database.

To display table definitions in Microsoft Access:

- Press F11 to show the Navigation pane (on the left), right-click the table name, and then choose Design View in the context menu (Figure 10.1).

    If tables aren't visible in the Navigation pane, then click the menu at the top of the pane, choose Object Type, click the menu again, and then choose Tables.

Figure 10.1 Displaying a table definition in Microsoft Access.

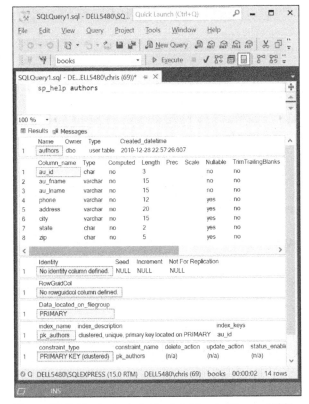

Figure 10.2 Displaying a table definition in Microsoft SQL Server.

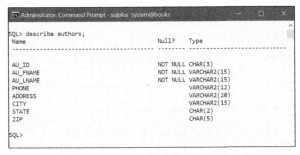

Figure 10.3 Displaying a table definition in Oracle.

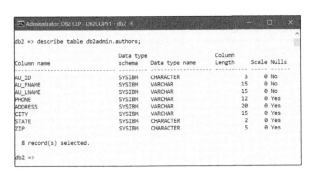

Figure 10.4 Displaying a table definition in IBM Db2.

To display table definitions in Microsoft SQL Server:

1. Start SQL Server Management Studio or the interactive sqlcmd command-line tool (see "Microsoft SQL Server" on page 6).

   The sqlcmd command displays pages that speed by. It's easier to use the graphical tools and choose Query > Results to Grid.

2. Type sp_help *table*.

   table is a table name.

3. In SQL Server Management Studio, choose Query > Execute or press F5 (Figure 10.2).

   or

   In sqlcmd, press Enter, type go, and then press Enter.

To display table definitions in Oracle Database:

1. Start the interactive sqlplus command-line tool (see "Oracle Database" on page 9).

2. Type describe *table*; and then press Enter (Figure 10.3).

   table is a table name.

To display table definitions in IBM Db2 Database:

1. Start the db2 command-line processor (see "IBM Db2 Database" on page 11).

2. Type describe table *table*; and then press Enter (Figure 10.4).

   table is a table name.

To display table definitions in MySQL:

1. Start the interactive mysql command-line tool (see "MySQL" on page 16).

2. Type describe *table*; and then press Enter (Figure 10.5).

   table is a table name.

To display table definitions in PostgreSQL:

1. Start the interactive psql command-line tool (see "PostgreSQL" on page 18).

2. Type \d *table* and then press Enter (Figure 10.6).

   table is a table name. Note that you don't terminate this command with a semicolon.

Tips for Table Definitions

- To list a table's column names and the order in which they appear without listing any of the table's data, type:

  SELECT * FROM *table* WHERE 1 = 2;

  table is a table name, and *1 = 2* represents any condition that's always false.

- For general information about columns, see "Tables, Columns, and Rows" on page 22.

  For information about keys, see "Primary Keys" on page 26 and "Foreign Keys" on page 28.

  For information about data types, see "Data Types" on page 56.

  To modify table definitions, see Chapter 11.

- **DBMS** Table 10.1 shows the commands and queries that list the tables in the current database.

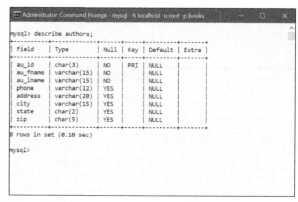

Figure 10.5 Displaying a table definition in MySQL.

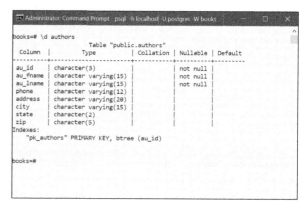

Figure 10.6 Displaying a table definition in PostgreSQL.

Table 10.1 Listing Database Tables

DBMS	Command or Query
Access	Navigation pane (press F11)
SQL Server	sp_tables
Oracle	SELECT * FROM TAB;
Db2	LIST TABLES;
MySQL	SHOW TABLES;
PostgreSQL	\d

Inserting Rows with INSERT

The INSERT statement adds new rows to a table. This section explains how to use several variations of INSERT to:

- Insert a row by using column positions (INSERT VALUES)

- Insert a row by using column names (INSERT VALUES)

- Insert rows from one table into another table (INSERT SELECT)

The important characteristics of INSERT are:

- In a positional insert, you insert ordered values into a new row in the same sequence as the columns appear in a table (see "To insert a row by using column positions" later in this section). In a named-column insert, you name the specific column into which each value is inserted in the new row (see "To insert a row by using column names" later in this section).

  You always should use a named-column insert so your SQL code still will work if someone re-orders the table's columns or adds new columns.

- With INSERT VALUES, you specify explicit values to insert into a table. With INSERT SELECT, you choose rows from another table to insert into a table.

- INSERT VALUES adds one row to a table. INSERT SELECT adds zero or more rows to a table.

- Each inserted value must have the same data type or must be implicitly convertible to the same type as its corresponding column (see "Converting Data Types with CAST()" on page 145).

- To preserve referential integrity, an inserted foreign-key value must contain either null (if allowed) or an existing key value from the primary or unique key column referenced by the foreign key; see "Primary Keys" on page 26 and "Foreign Keys" on page 28.

- An inserted value can't violate a check constraint; see "Adding a Check Constraint with CHECK" on page 349.

- No expression can cause an arithmetic error (an overflow or divide-by-zero error, for example).

- Recall from "Tables, Columns, and Rows" on page 22 that the order of rows in a table is unimportant and that you have no control over the physical location of rows, so new rows can appear anywhere among a table's existing rows.

To insert a row by using column positions:

- Type:

  ```
  INSERT INTO table
    VALUES(value1, value2,..., valueN);
  ```

  table is the name of a table to insert the row into. *value1, value2,..., valueN* is a parenthesized list of comma-separated literals or expressions that provides a value to every column in the new row.

  The number of values must equal the number of columns in *table*, and the values must be listed in the same sequence as the columns in *table*. The DBMS inserts each value into the column that corresponds to the value's position in *table*. *value1* is inserted into the first column of *table* in the new row, *value2* into the second column, and so on.

  This statement adds one row to *table* (Listing 10.1).

```
INSERT INTO authors
  VALUES(
    'A08',
    'Michael',
    'Polk',
    '512-953-1231',
    '4028 Guadalupe St',
    'Austin',
    'TX',
    '78701');
```

Listing 10.1 This INSERT statement adds a new row to the table *authors* by listing values in the same order in which columns are defined in *authors*. See Figure 10.7 for the result.

```
INSERT INTO authors(
    au_id,
    au_fname,
    au_lname,
    phone,
    address,
    city,
    state,
    zip)
  VALUES(
    'A09',
    'Irene',
    'Bell',
    '415-225-4689',
    '810 Throckmorton Ave',
    'Mill Valley',
    'CA',
    '94941');
```

Listing 10.2 This INSERT statement adds a new row to the table *authors* by listing column names and values in the same order in which columns are defined in *authors*. See Figure 10.7 for the result.

```
INSERT INTO authors(
    zip,
    phone,
    address,
    au_lname,
    au_fname,
    state,
    au_id,
    city)
  VALUES(
    '60614',
    '312-998-0020',
    '1937 N. Clark St',
    'Weston',
    'Dianne',
    'IL',
    'A10',
    'Chicago');
```

Listing 10.3 You don't have to list column names in the same order in which they're defined in the table. Here, I've rearranged the column names and their corresponding values. See Figure 10.7 for the result.

To insert a row by using column names:

- Type:

  ```
  INSERT INTO table
    (column1, column2,..., columnN)
    VALUES(value1, value2,..., valueN);
  ```

  table is the name of the table to insert the row into. *column1, column2,…, columnN* is a parenthesized list of comma-separated names of columns in *table*. *value1, value2,…, valueN* is a parenthesized list of comma-separated literals or expressions that provides values to the named columns in the new row.

  The number of values must equal the number of columns in the column list, and the values must be listed in the same sequence as the column names. The DBMS inserts each value into a column by using corresponding list positions. *value1* is inserted into *column1* in the new row, *value2* into *column2*, and so on. An omitted column is assigned its default value or null.

  This statement adds one row to *table*.

  It's clearer to list column names in the same order as they appear in the table (Listing 10.2), but you can list them in any order (Listing 10.3). In either case, the values in the VALUES clause must match the sequence in which you list the column names.

You can omit column names if you want to provide values for only some columns explicitly (Listing 10.4). If you omit a column, then the DBMS must be able to provide a value based on the column's definition. The DBMS will insert the column's default value (if defined) or null (if allowed). If you omit a column that doesn't have a default value or allow nulls, then the DBMS will display an error message and won't insert the row. In this case, the VALUES clause is equivalent to VALUES('A11', 'Max', 'Allard', '212-502-0955', NULL, NULL, NULL, NULL). For information about specifying a default value and allowing nulls, see "Specifying a Default Value with DEFAULT" on page 332 and "Forbidding Nulls with NOT NULL" on page 329.

Figure 10.7 shows the new rows in table *authors* after Listings 10.1 through 10.4 have run.

```
INSERT INTO authors(
    au_id,
    au_fname,
    au_lname,
    phone)
VALUES(
    'A11',
    'Max',
    'Allard',
    '212-502-0955');
```

Listing 10.4 Here, I've added a row for a new author but omitted column names and values for the author's address information. The DBMS inserts nulls into the omitted columns automatically. See Figure 10.7 for the result.

au_id	au_fname	au_lname	phone	address	city	state	zip
A01	Sarah	Buchman	718-496-7223	75 West 205 St	Bronx	NY	10468
A02	Wendy	Heydemark	303-986-7020	2922 Baseline Rd	Boulder	CO	80303
A03	Hallie	Hull	415-549-4278	3800 Waldo Ave, #14F	San Francisco	CA	94123
A04	Klee	Hull	415-549-4278	3800 Waldo Ave, #14F	San Francisco	CA	94123
A05	Christian	Kells	212-771-4680	114 Horatio St	New York	NY	10014
A06		Kellsey	650-836-7128	390 Serra Mall	Palo Alto	CA	94305
A07	Paddy	O'Furniture	941-925-0752	1442 Main St	Sarasota	FL	34236
A08	Michael	Polk	512-953-1231	4028 Guadalupe St	Austin	TX	78701
A09	Irene	Bell	415-225-4689	810 Throckmorton Ave	Mill Valley	CA	94941
A10	Dianne	Weston	312-998-0020	1937 N. Clark St	Chicago	IL	60614
A11	Max	Allard	212-502-0955	NULL	NULL	NULL	NULL

Figure 10.7 The table *authors* has four new rows after I run Listings 10.1 through 10.4.

To insert rows from one table into another table:

- Type:

  ```
  INSERT INTO table
    [(column1, column2,..., columnN)]
    subquery;
  ```

  table is the name of table to insert the rows into. *column1, column2,..., columnN* is an optional parenthesized list of comma-separated names of columns in *table*. *subquery* is a SELECT query that returns rows to insert into *table*.

  The number of columns in the *subquery* result must equal the number of columns in *table* or in the column list. The DBMS ignores the column names in the *subquery* result and uses column position instead. The first column in the *subquery* result is used to populate the first column in *table* or *column1*, and so on. An omitted column is assigned its default value or null.

  This statement adds zero or more rows to *table*.

  The remaining examples in this section use the table *new_publishers* (Figure 10.8), which I created to show how INSERT SELECT works. *new_publishers* has the same structure as the table *publishers* and acts only as the source of new rows; it isn't itself changed by the INSERT operations.

```
pub_id pub_name              city        state country
------ --------------------- ----------- ----- -------------
P05    This is Pizza? Press  New York    NY    USA
P06    This is Beer? Press   Toronto     ON    Canada
P07    This is Irony? Press  London      NULL  United Kindom
P08    This is Fame? Press   Los Angeles CA    USA
```

Figure 10.8 This table, named *new_publishers*, is used in Listings 10.5 through 10.7. *new_publishers* has the same structure as *publishers*.

Listing 10.5 inserts the rows for Los Angeles-based publishers from *new_publishers* into *publishers*. Here, I've omitted the column list, so the DBMS uses the column positions in *publishers* rather than column names to insert values. This statement inserts one row into *publishers*; see Figure 10.9 for the result.

Listing 10.6 inserts the rows for non-U.S. publishers from *new_publishers* into *publishers*. Here, the column names are the same in both the INSERT and SELECT clauses, but they don't have to match because the DBMS disregards the names of the columns returned by SELECT and uses their positions instead. This statement inserts two rows into *publishers*; see Figure 10.9 for the result.

```
INSERT INTO publishers
  SELECT
    pub_id,
    pub_name,
    city,
    state,
    country
  FROM new_publishers
  WHERE city = 'Los Angeles';
```

Listing 10.5 Insert the rows for Los Angeles-based publishers from *new_publishers* into *publishers*. See Figure 10.9 for the result.

```
INSERT INTO publishers(
    pub_id,
    pub_name,
    city,
    state,
    country)
  SELECT
    pub_id,
    pub_name,
    city,
    state,
    country
  FROM new_publishers
  WHERE country <> 'USA';
```

Listing 10.6 Insert the rows for non-U.S. publishers from *new_publishers* into *publishers*. See Figure 10.9 for the result.

```
INSERT INTO publishers(
    pub_id,
    pub_name,
    city,
    state,
    country)
  SELECT *
    FROM new_publishers
    WHERE pub_name = 'XXX';
```

Listing 10.7 Insert the rows for publishers named XXX from *new_publishers* into *publishers*. This statement has no effect on the target table. See Figure 10.9 for the result.

It's legal for the SELECT query to return an empty result (zero rows). Listing 10.7 inserts the rows for publishers named XXX from *new_publishers* into *publishers*. I can use SELECT * instead of listing column names because *new_publishers* and *publishers* have the same structure. This statement inserts no rows into *publishers* because no publisher is named XXX; see Figure 10.9 for the result.

Figure 10.9 shows the table *publishers* after Listings 10.5 through 10.7 are run.

```
pub_id pub_name                city          state country
------ ------------------- ------------- ----- -------------
P01    Abatis Publishers   New York      NY    USA
P02    Core Dump Books     San Francisco CA    USA
P03    Schadenfreude Press Hamburg       NULL  Germany
P04    Tenterhooks Press   Berkeley      CA    USA
P06    This is Beer? Press Toronto       ON    Canada
P07    This is Irony? Press London       NULL  United Kindom
P08    This is Fame? Press  Los Angeles  CA    USA
```

Figure 10.9 The table *publishers* has three new rows after I run Listings 10.5 through 10.7.

Tips for INSERT

- The process of adding rows to a table for the first time is called **populating the table**.

- If you want to be extra-careful before you insert rows, then you can test your INSERT statement on a temporary copy of the target table; see "Creating a Temporary Table with CREATE TEMPORARY TABLE" on page 352 and "Creating a New Table from an Existing One with CREATE TABLE AS" on page 355.

- You also can INSERT rows through a view; see "Updating Data Through a View" on page 378.

- If you're using transactions, then you must use a COMMIT statement after your final INSERT statement to make the changes to the table permanent. For information about transactions, see Chapter 14.

- If *table1* and *table2* have compatible structures, then you can insert all the rows from *table2* into *table1* with:

```
INSERT INTO table1
  SELECT * FROM table2;
```

- DBMS In some DBMSs, the INTO keyword is optional in an INSERT statement, but you should always include it for portability.

By default, **MySQL** (unfortunately) converts some invalid INSERT or UPDATE values and issues a warning instead of triggering an error, which is useless unless you're using transactions and can roll back the operation. If you insert 9/0, for example, then MySQL will try to insert a null rather than return a division-by-zero error and complain only if the column forbids nulls. If you insert the out-of-range value 999999 into a SMALLINT column, then MySQL will insert 32767 (the largest SMALLINT value) and issue a warning. MySQL provides ERROR_FOR_DIVISION_BY_ZERO, STRICT_ALL_TABLES, STRICT_TRANS_TABLES, and other modes to handle invalid or missing values properly.

For **all DBMSs**, check the documentation to see how your DBMS handles the insertion of values into columns whose data type generates a unique row identifier automatically (see "Unique Identifiers" on page 70).

Updating Rows with UPDATE

The UPDATE statement changes the values in a table's existing rows. You can use UPDATE to change:

- All rows in a table
- Specific rows in a table

To update rows, you specify:

- The table to update
- The names of the columns to update and their new values
- An optional search condition that specifies which rows to update

The important characteristics of UPDATE are:

- UPDATE takes an optional WHERE clause that specifies which rows to update. Without a WHERE clause, UPDATE changes *all* the rows in the table.

- UPDATE is dangerous because it's easy to omit the WHERE clause mistakenly (and update all rows) or misspecify the WHERE search condition (and update the wrong rows). It's wise to run a SELECT statement that uses the same WHERE clause before running the actual UPDATE statement. Use SELECT * to display all rows that the DBMS will change when you run UPDATE, or use SELECT COUNT(*) to display only the number of rows that will change.

- Each updated value must have the same data type or must be implicitly convertible to the same type as its column; see "Converting Data Types with CAST()" on page 145.

- To preserve referential integrity, you can define the action that the DBMS takes automatically when you try to UPDATE a key value to which foreign-key values point; see "Tips for FOREIGN KEY" on page 343.

- An updated value can't violate a check constraint; see "Adding a Check Constraint with CHECK" on page 349.

- No expression can cause an arithmetic error (an overflow or divide-by-zero error, for example).

- Recall from "Tables, Columns, and Rows" on page 22 that the order of rows in a table is unimportant and that you have no control over the physical location of rows, so an updated row can change position in a table.

To update rows:

- Type:

  ```
  UPDATE table
    SET column = expr
    [WHERE search_condition];
  ```

  table is the name of a table to update.

  column is the name of the column in *table* that contains the rows to change. *expr* is a literal, an expression, or a parenthesized subquery that returns a single value. The value returned by *expr* replaces the existing value in *column*. To change the values in multiple columns, type a list of comma-separated *column* = *expr* expressions in the SET clause. You can list the *column* = *expr* expressions in any order.

  search_condition specifies the conditions that rows have to meet to be updated. The *search_condition* conditions can be WHERE conditions (comparison operators, LIKE, BETWEEN, IN, or IS NULL; see Chapter 4) or subquery conditions (comparison operators, IN, ALL, ANY, or EXISTS; see Chapter 8), combined with AND, OR, or NOT. If the WHERE clause is omitted, then every row in *table* is updated.

Listing 10.8 changes the value of *contract* to zero in every row of *titles*. The lack of a WHERE clause tells the DBMS to update all the rows in the column *contract*. This statement updates 13 rows; see Figure 10.10 for the result.

Listing 10.9 uses an arithmetic expression and a WHERE condition to double the price of history books. This statement updates three rows; see Figure 10.10 for the result.

Here's a tricky way to change prices with CASE:

```
UPDATE titles
  SET price = price * CASE type
    WHEN 'history' THEN 1.10
    WHEN 'psychology' THEN 1.20
    ELSE 1
  END;
```

```
UPDATE titles
  SET contract = 0;
```

Listing 10.8 Change the value of *contract* to zero in every row. See Figure 10.10 for the result.

```
UPDATE titles
  SET price = price * 2.0
  WHERE type = 'history';
```

Listing 10.9 Double the price of history books. See Figure 10.10 for the result.

```
UPDATE titles
  SET type = 'self help',
      pages = NULL
  WHERE type = 'psychology';
```

Listing 10.10 For psychology books, set the type to *self help* and the number of pages to null. See Figure 10.10 for the result.

```
UPDATE titles
  SET sales = sales * 0.5
  WHERE sales >
    (SELECT AVG(sales)
       FROM titles);
```

Listing 10.11 Cut the sales of books with above-average sales in half. See Figure 10.10 for the result.

```
UPDATE titles
  SET pubdate = DATE '2003-01-01'
  WHERE title_id IN
    (SELECT title_id
       FROM title_authors
       WHERE au_id IN
         (SELECT au_id
            FROM authors
            WHERE au_fname = 'Sarah'
              AND au_lname = 'Buchman'));
```

Listing 10.12 Change the publication date of all of Sarah Buchman's books to January 1, 2003. See Figure 10.10 for the result.

Listing 10.10 updates the columns *type* and *pages* for psychology books. You use only a single SET clause to update multiple columns, with *column = expr* expressions separated by commas. (Don't put a comma after the last expression.) This statement updates three rows; see Figure 10.10 for the result.

Listing 10.11 uses a subquery and an aggregate function to cut the sales of books with above-average sales in half. This statement updates two rows; see Figure 10.10 for the result.

You can update values in a given table based on the values stored in another table. Listing 10.12 uses nested subqueries to update the publication date for all the books written (or cowritten) by Sarah Buchman. This statement updates three rows; see Figure 10.10 for the result.

Suppose that Abatis Publishers (publisher P01) swallows Tenterhooks Press (P04) in a merger, so now, all the Tenterhooks Press books are published by Abatis Publishers. Listing 10.13 works in a bottom-up fashion to change the publisher IDs in *titles* from P04 to P01. The WHERE subquery retrieves the *pub_id* for Tenterhooks Press. The DBMS uses this *pub_id* to retrieve the books in the table *titles* whose publisher is Tenterhooks Press. Finally, the DBMS uses the value returned by the SET subquery to update the appropriate rows in the table *titles*. Because the subqueries are used with an unmodified comparison operator, they must be scalar subqueries that return a single value (that is, a one-row, one-column result); see "Comparing a Subquery Value by Using a Comparison Operator" on page 261. Listing 10.13 updates five rows; see Figure 10.10 for the result.

Figure 10.10 shows the table *titles* after Listings 10.8 through 10.13 are run. Each listing updates values in a different column (or columns) from those in the other listings. The updated values in each column are highlighted.

```
UPDATE titles
  SET pub_id =
    (SELECT pub_id
       FROM publishers
       WHERE pub_name = 'Abatis Publishers')
  WHERE pub_id =
    (SELECT pub_id
       FROM publishers
       WHERE pub_name = 'Tenterhooks Press');
```

Listing 10.13 Change the publisher of all of Tenterhooks Press's books to Abatis Publishers. See Figure 10.10 for the result.

title_id	title_name	type	pub_id	pages	price	sales	pubdate	contract
T01	1977!	history	P01	107	**43.98**	566	**2003-01-01**	0
T02	200 Years of German Humor	history	P03	14	**39.90**	9566	**2003-01-01**	0
T03	Ask Your System Administrator	computer	P02	1226	39.95	25667	2000-09-01	0
T04	But I Did It Unconsciously	**self help**	**P01**	NULL	12.99	13001	1999-05-31	0
T05	Exchange of Platitudes	**self help**	**P01**	NULL	6.95	**100720**	2001-01-01	0
T06	How About Never?	biography	P01	473	19.95	11320	2000-07-31	0
T07	I Blame My Mother	biography	P03	333	23.95	**750100**	1999-10-01	0
T08	Just Wait Until After School	children	**P01**	86	10.00	4095	2001-06-01	0
T09	Kiss My Boo-Boo	children	**P01**	22	13.95	5000	2002-05-31	0
T10	Not Without My Faberge Egg	biography	P01	NULL	NULL	NULL	NULL	0
T11	Perhaps It's a Glandular Problem	**self help**	**P01**	NULL	7.99	94123	2000-11-30	0
T12	Spontaneous, Not Annoying	biography	P01	507	12.99	100001	2000-08-31	0
T13	What Are The Civilian Applications?	history	P03	802	**59.98**	10467	**2003-01-01**	0

Figure 10.10 The table *titles* after I run Listings 10.8 through 10.13. The updated values are highlighted.

Tips for UPDATE

- A DBMS will evaluate expressions in a SET or WHERE clause by using the values that the referenced columns had *before* any updates. Consider this UPDATE statement:

```
UPDATE mytable
  SET col1 = col1 * 2,
      col2 = col1 * 4,
      col3 = col2 * 8
  WHERE col1 = 1
    AND col2 = 2;
```

For the rows matching the WHERE conditions, the DBMS sets *col1* to 2, *col2* to 4 (1 × 4, not 2 × 4), and *col3* to 16 (2 × 8, not 4 × 8).

This evaluation scheme lets you swap the values of compatible columns with:

```
UPDATE mytable
  SET col1 = col2,
      col2 = col1;
```

(This trick won't work in **MySQL**.)

- If you want to be extra-careful before you update rows, then you can test your UPDATE statement on a temporary copy of the target table; see "Creating a Temporary Table with CREATE TEMPORARY TABLE" on page 352 and "Creating a New Table from an Existing One with CREATE TABLE AS" on page 355.

- You also can UPDATE rows through a view; see "Updating Data Through a View" on page 378.

- If you're using transactions, then you must use a COMMIT statement after your final UPDATE statement to make the changes to the table permanent. For information about transactions, see Chapter 14.

- The SQL:2003 standard introduced the MERGE statement as a convenient way to combine multiple UPDATE and INSERT operations in a single statement. These operations informally are called **upserts**. **Microsoft SQL Server, Oracle, Db2**, and **PostgreSQL** support MERGE. **MySQL** has the simplified MERGE variants REPLACE INTO and INSERT...ON DUPLICATE KEY UPDATE.

continues on next page

- DBMS In **Microsoft Access** date literals, omit the DATE keyword and surround the literal with # characters instead of quotes. To run Listing 10.12, change the date literal to #2003-01-01#.

  Microsoft Access doesn't support scalar subqueries in the SET clause. To run Listing 10.13, split the UPDATE statement into two statements: one that SELECTs the *pub_id* for Abatis Publishers from *publishers* and one that uses this *pub_id* to change the *pub_id* of all the Tenterhooks Press books in *titles*. Then run the statements programmatically (in a host language such as Visual Basic or C#), using the result of the first statement as the input for the second statement.

  In **Microsoft SQL Server** and **Db2** date literals, omit the DATE keyword. To run Listing 10.12, change the date literal to '2003-01-01'.

  MySQL 4.1 and later support subqueries but won't run Listing 10.11 because MySQL won't let you use the same table (*titles*, in this case) for both the subquery's FROM clause and the update target. Earlier MySQL versions don't support subqueries and won't run Listings 10.11, 10.12, and 10.13; for workarounds, see the DBMS tip in "Tips for Subqueries" on page 241 in Chapter 8.

  For **MySQL**, see also the DBMS tip in "Tips for INSERT" on page 312.

  To run Listings 10.9 and 10.11 in older **PostgreSQL** versions, convert the floating-point numbers to DECIMAL (see "Converting Data Types with CAST()" on page 145). The changes are (Listing 10.9):

  ```
  CAST(2.0 AS DECIMAL)
  ```

  and (Listing 10.11):

  ```
  CAST(0.5 AS DECIMAL)
  ```

  For **all DBMSs**, check the documentation to see how your DBMS handles updating values in columns whose data type generates a unique row identifier automatically (see "Unique Identifiers" on page 70).

Deleting Rows with DELETE

The DELETE statement removes rows from a table. You can use DELETE to remove:

- All rows in a table
- Specific rows in a table

To delete rows, you specify:

- The table whose rows to delete
- An optional search condition that specifies which rows to delete

The important characteristics of DELETE are:

- Unlike INSERT and UPDATE, DELETE takes no column names because it removes entire rows.

- DELETE removes rows from a table, but it never deletes the table's definition. Even if you remove all rows from a table, the table itself still exists. If you want to delete a table definition (and all its associated data, indexes, and so on), then see "Dropping a Table with DROP TABLE" on page 362.

- DELETE takes an optional WHERE clause that specifies which rows to delete. Without a WHERE clause, DELETE removes *all* the rows in the table.

- DELETE is dangerous because it's easy to omit the WHERE clause mistakenly (and remove all rows) or misspecify the WHERE search condition (and remove the wrong rows). It's wise to run a SELECT statement that uses the same WHERE clause before running the actual DELETE statement. Use SELECT * to display all rows that the DBMS will remove when you run DELETE, or use SELECT COUNT(*) to display only the number of rows that will disappear.

- To preserve referential integrity, you can define the action the DBMS takes automatically when you try to DELETE a key value to which foreign-key values point; see "Tips for FOREIGN KEY" on page 343.

- No expression can cause an arithmetic error (an overflow or divide-by-zero error, for example).

- Recall from "Tables, Columns, and Rows" on page 22 that the order of rows in a table is unimportant and that you have no control over the physical location of rows, so a deletion might reorder the positions of the rows remaining in a table.

To delete rows:

- Type:

  ```
  DELETE FROM table
    [WHERE search_condition];
  ```

  table is the name of a table to delete rows from.

  search_condition specifies the conditions to be met for the rows that are deleted. The *search_condition* conditions can be WHERE conditions (comparison operators, LIKE, BETWEEN, IN, or IS NULL; see Chapter 4) or subquery conditions (comparison operators, IN, ALL, ANY, or EXISTS; see Chapter 8), combined with AND, OR, or NOT. If the WHERE clause is omitted, then every row in *table* is deleted.

In the following examples, I'm going to ignore referential-integrity constraints—which I wouldn't do in a production database, of course.

Listing 10.14 deletes every row in *royalties*. The lack of a WHERE clause tells the DBMS to delete all the rows. This statement deletes 13 rows; see Figure 10.11 for the result.

The WHERE clause in Listing 10.15 tells the DBMS to remove the authors with the last name Hull from *authors*. This statement deletes two rows; see Figure 10.12 for the result.

```
DELETE FROM royalties;
```

Listing 10.14 Delete all rows from the table *royalties*. See Figure 10.11 for the result.

```
title_id advance royalty_rate
-------- ------- ------------
```

Figure 10.11 Result of Listing 10.14.

```
DELETE FROM authors
  WHERE au_lname = 'Hull';
```

Listing 10.15 Delete the rows in which the author's last name is Hull from the table *authors*. See Figure 10.12 for the result.

au_id	au_fname	au_lname	phone	address	city	state	zip
A01	Sarah	Buchman	718-496-7223	75 West 205 St	Bronx	NY	10468
A02	Wendy	Heydemark	303-986-7020	2922 Baseline Rd	Boulder	CO	80303
A05	Christian	Kells	212-771-4680	114 Horatio St	New York	NY	10014
A06		Kellsey	650-836-7128	390 Serra Mall	Palo Alto	CA	94305
A07	Paddy	O'Furniture	941-925-0752	1442 Main St	Sarasota	FL	34236

Figure 10.12 Result of Listing 10.15.

```
DELETE FROM title_authors
  WHERE title_id IN
    (SELECT title_id
       FROM titles
       WHERE pub_id IN ('P01', 'P04'));
```

Listing 10.16 Delete the rows for books published by publisher P01 or P04 from the table *title_authors*. See Figure 10.13 for the result.

```
title_id au_id au_order royalty_share
-------- ----- -------- -------------
T02      A01         1          1.00
T03      A05         1          1.00
T07      A02         1          0.50
T07      A04         2          0.50
T13      A01         1          1.00
```

Figure 10.13 Result of Listing 10.16.

You can delete rows in a given table based on the values stored in another table. Listing 10.16 uses a subquery to remove all the books published by publishers P01 or P04 from *title_authors*. This statement deletes 12 rows; see Figure 10.13 for the result.

Tips for DELETE

- If you want to be extra-careful before you remove rows, then you can test your DELETE statement on a temporary copy of the target table; see "Creating a Temporary Table with CREATE TEMPORARY TABLE" on page 352 and "Creating a New Table from an Existing One with CREATE TABLE AS" on page 355.

- You also can DELETE rows through a view; see "Updating Data Through a View" on page 378.

- If you're using transactions, then you must use a COMMIT statement after your final DELETE statement to make the changes to the table permanent. For information about transactions, see Chapter 14.

- You can use a NOT EXISTS or NOT IN subquery to delete rows from one table that refer to nonexistent rows in another table (useful for removing orphaned rows or referential-integrity violations). The following statements remove all rows from the table *titles* for which no publisher exists in the table *publishers*:

```
DELETE FROM titles
  WHERE NOT EXISTS
    (SELECT * FROM publishers
       WHERE publishers.pub_id =
             titles.pub_id);
```

or

```
DELETE FROM titles
  WHERE pub_id NOT IN
    (SELECT pub_id FROM publishers);
```

- **DBMS** In some DBMSs, the FROM keyword is optional in a DELETE statement, but you should always include it for portability.

  MySQL 4.1 and later support subqueries and will run Listing 10.16. Earlier MySQL versions don't support subqueries and won't run it; for workarounds, see the DBMS tip in "Tips for Subqueries" on page 241.

  For **MySQL**, see also the DBMS tip in "Tips for INSERT" on page 312.

Truncating Tables

If you want to delete all the rows in a table, then the TRUNCATE statement is faster than DELETE. The SQL:2008 standard introduced TRUNCATE, and **Microsoft SQL Server, Oracle, Db2, MySQL, and PostgreSQL** support it. TRUNCATE works like a DELETE statement with no WHERE clause: Both remove all rows in a table. But TRUNCATE is faster and uses fewer system resources than DELETE because TRUNCATE doesn't scan the entire table and record changes in the transaction log (see Chapter 14). The trade-off is that with TRUNCATE, you can't recover (roll back) your changes if you make a mistake. The syntax is:

TRUNCATE TABLE *table*;

table is the name of the table to be truncated. For information about TRUNCATE, search your DBMS documentation for *truncate*.

DBMS Older versions of **Db2** don't support TRUNCATE; instead, run LOAD with the REPLACE option, using a zero-byte file as input.

CHAPTER 11

Creating, Altering, and Dropping Tables

Many DBMSs have interactive, graphical tools that let you create and manage tables and table properties such as column definitions and constraints. This chapter explains how to perform those tasks programmatically by using SQL:

- The CREATE TABLE statement creates a new table.

- The ALTER TABLE statement modifies the structure of an existing table.

- The DROP TABLE statement destroys a table and all its data.

- The CREATE TEMPORARY TABLE statement creates a table that the DBMS destroys automatically when it's no longer in use.

- The CREATE TABLE AS statement creates a new table from an existing one.

These statements don't return a result, but your DBMS might print a message indicating whether the statement ran successfully. To see the actual effect the statement had on a table, examine the table's structure by using one of the commands described in "Displaying Table Definitions" on page 302.

These statements modify database objects and data, so your database administrator might need to grant you permission to run them.

Creating Tables

Database designers spend considerable time normalizing tables and defining relationships and constraints before they write a line of SQL code. If you're going to create tables for production databases, then study database design and relational-model principles beyond those presented in Chapter 2.

Recall from "Tables, Columns, and Rows" on page 22 that a database is organized around tables. To a user or an SQL programmer, a database appears to be a collection of one or more tables (and nothing but tables). To create a table, you specify the following:

- Table name

- Column names

- Data types of the columns

- Default values of columns

- Constraints

The table name and the column names must conform to the rules for SQL identifiers; see "Identifiers" on page 54. The data type of each column is a character, numeric, datetime, or other data type; see "Data Types" on page 56. A **default** is the value the column takes if you don't specify a value explicitly. **Constraints** define properties such as nullability, keys, and permissible values.

You create a new table by using the CREATE TABLE statement, whose general syntax is:

```
CREATE TABLE table
  (
  column1 data_type1 [col_constraints1],
  column2 data_type2 [col_constraints2],
  ...
  columnN data_typeN [col_constraintsN]
  [, table_constraint1]
  [, table_constraint2]
  ...
  [, table_constraintM]
  );
```

Each column definition has a column name, a data type, and an optional list of one or more column constraints. An optional list of table constraints follows the final column definition. By convention, I start each column definition and table constraint on its own line.

Table 11.1 Constraints

Constraint	Description
NOT NULL	Prevents nulls from being inserted into a column
PRIMARY KEY	Sets the table's primary-key column(s)
FOREIGN KEY	Sets the table's foreign-key column(s)
UNIQUE	Prevents duplicate values from being inserted into a column
CHECK	Limits the values that can be inserted into a column by using logical (boolean) expressions

Understanding Constraints

Constraints let you define rules for values allowed in columns (Table 11.1). Your DBMS uses these rules to enforce the integrity of information in the database automatically.

Constraints come in two flavors:

- A **column constraint** is part of a column definition and imposes a condition on that column only.

- A **table constraint** is declared independently of a column definition and can impose a condition on more than one column in a table. You must use a table constraint to include more than one column in a single constraint.

You can specify some constraints as either column or table constraints, depending on the context in which they're used. If a primary key contains one column, for example, then you can define it as either a column constraint or a table constraint. If the primary key has two or more columns, then you must use a table constraint.

Assigning names to constraints lets you manage them efficiently; you can change or delete a named constraint by using the ALTER TABLE statement, for example. Constraint names are optional, but many SQL programmers and database designers name *all* constraints. It's not uncommon to leave a NOT NULL constraint unnamed, but you always should name other types of constraints (even if I don't do so in some of the examples).

If you don't name a constraint explicitly, then your DBMS will generate a name and assign it to the constraint quietly and automatically. System-assigned names often contain strings of random characters and are cumbersome to use, so use the CONSTRAINT clause to assign your own name instead. Constraint names also appear in warnings, error messages, and logs, which is another good reason to name constraints yourself.

To name a constraint:

- Preceding a constraint definition, type:

    CONSTRAINT *constraint_name*

    constraint_name is the name of the constraint and is a valid SQL identifier. Constraints names must be unique within a table.

```
CREATE TABLE titles
  (
  title_id    CHAR(3)      ,
  title_name  VARCHAR(40)  ,
  type        VARCHAR(10)  ,
  pub_id      CHAR(3)      ,
  pages       INTEGER      ,
  price       DECIMAL(5,2) ,
  sales       INTEGER      ,
  pubdate     DATE         ,
  contract    SMALLINT
  );
```

Listing 11.1 Create the sample-database table *titles*.

```
CREATE TABLE title_authors
  (
  title_id       CHAR(3)      ,
  au_id          CHAR(3)      ,
  au_order       SMALLINT     ,
  royalty_share  DECIMAL(5,2)
  );
```

Listing 11.2 Create the sample-database table *title_authors*.

Creating a New Table with CREATE TABLE

This section describes how to create a new table by using a minimal CREATE TABLE statement. Subsequent sections show you how to add column and table constraints to CREATE TABLE.

To create a new table:

* Type:

    CREATE TABLE *table*
      (
      column1 data_type1,
      column2 data_type2,
      ...
      columnN data_typeN
      );

    table is the name of the new table to create.

    column1, column2,…, columnN are the names of the columns in *table*. You must create at least one column.

    data_type1, data_type2,…, data_typeN specify the SQL data type of each corresponding column. A data type can specify a length, scale, or precision, where applicable; see "Data Types" and subsequent sections in Chapter 3.

    The table name must be unique within the database, and each column name must be unique within the table.

    Listing 11.1 creates the sample-database table *titles*.
    Listing 11.2 creates the sample-database table *title_authors*.

Tips for CREATE TABLE

- To see the result of a CREATE TABLE statement, examine the table's structure by using one of the commands described in "Displaying Table Definitions" on page 302.

- Your DBMS will generate an error if you try to create a table with a name that already exists in the database. To prevent you from overwriting a table accidentally, SQL requires that you destroy a table explicitly with DROP TABLE before creating a new table with the same name; see "Dropping a Table with DROP TABLE" on page 362.

- A newly created table is empty (has zero rows). To populate the table with data, use the INSERT statement; see "Inserting Rows with INSERT" on page 305.

- Columns allow nulls by default. If you don't want to allow nulls, then see "Forbidding Nulls with NOT NULL" on page 329.

- To modify the structure of an existing table, see "Altering a Table with ALTER TABLE" on page 359.

- To create a table by using the structure and data of an existing table, see "Creating a New Table from an Existing One with CREATE TABLE AS" on page 355.

- DBMS **Microsoft SQL Server** doesn't support the data type DATE. To run Listing 11.1, change the data type of the column *pubdate* to DATETIME.

    MySQL might change the type of a CHAR or VARCHAR column silently when creating a table. VARCHAR columns with a length less than four are changed to CHAR, for example.

Forbidding Nulls with NOT NULL

A column's nullability determines whether its rows can contain nulls—that is, whether values are required or optional in the column. I described nulls and their effects in "Nulls" on page 72, but I'll review the basics here:

- A null is not a value but a marker that means no value has been entered.

- A null represents a missing, unknown, or inapplicable value. A null in the column *price* doesn't mean that an item has no price or that its price is zero; it means that the price is unknown or has not been set.

- A null isn't the same as zero (0), a blank, or an empty string ('').

- Nulls belong to no data type and can be inserted into any column that allows nulls.

- In SQL statements, the keyword NULL represents a null.

When you're defining a nullability constraint, some important considerations are:

- A nullability constraint always is a column constraint and not a table constraint; see "Understanding Constraints" on page 325.

- You define a nullability constraint by using the keywords NOT NULL in a CREATE TABLE column definition.

- In general, avoid allowing nulls because they complicate queries, insertions, and updates.

- Forbidding nulls in a column can help maintain data integrity by ensuring that users entering data must enter a value in the column. The DBMS won't insert or update a row if a non-nullable column contains a null.

- Some other constraints, such as a PRIMARY KEY constraint, can't be used with nullable columns.

- Nulls affect referential-integrity checks in foreign keys; see "Specifying a Foreign Key with FOREIGN KEY" on page 339.

- If you INSERT a row but include no value for a column that allows null values, then your DBMS supplies a null (unless a DEFAULT clause exists); see "Inserting Rows with INSERT" on page 305 and "Specifying a Default Value with DEFAULT" on page 332.

- A user can enter NULL explicitly in a nullable column, no matter what data type or default value the column has.

- If you don't specify a NOT NULL constraint, then the column accepts nulls by default.

To specify a column's nullability:

- Add the following column constraint to a CRE-
ATE TABLE column definition:

```
[CONSTRAINT constraint_name]
  NOT NULL
```

NOT NULL forbids nulls in a column. If the nullability constraint is omitted, then the column
accepts nulls. For the general syntax of CREATE
TABLE, see "Creating Tables" on page 324.

The CONSTRAINT clause is optional, and con-
straint_name is the name of the column's nullability constraint; see "Understanding Constraints" on page 325.

Listing 11.3 creates the sample-database table
authors, forbidding nulls in some columns. Missing
addresses and telephone numbers are common, so
I've allowed nulls in those columns.

Notice that I've forbidden nulls in both the first-
name and last-name columns. If the author's name
has only a single word (like author A06, Kellsey),
then I'll insert the name into au_lname and insert
an empty string (") into au_fname. Or I could have
allowed nulls in au_fname and inserted a null into
au_fname for one-named authors. Or I could have
allowed nulls in both au_fname and au_lname and
added a check constraint that required at least one
of the two columns to contain a non-null, non-empty
string. The database designer makes these types
of decisions before creating a table.

Most DBMSs let you specify only the NULL keyword (without the NOT) to allow nulls. Listing 11.4
creates the sample-database table titles.

```
CREATE TABLE authors
  (
  au_id     CHAR(3)     NOT NULL,
  au_fname  VARCHAR(15) NOT NULL,
  au_lname  VARCHAR(15) NOT NULL,
  phone     VARCHAR(12)          ,
  address   VARCHAR(20)          ,
  city      VARCHAR(15)          ,
  state     CHAR(2)              ,
  zip       CHAR(5)
  );
```

Listing 11.3 Create the sample-database table *authors*.
Where omitted, the nullability constraint defaults to allow
nulls.

```
CREATE TABLE titles
  (
  title_id    CHAR(3)       NOT NULL,
  title_name  VARCHAR(40)   NOT NULL,
  type        VARCHAR(10)   NULL    ,
  pub_id      CHAR(3)       NOT NULL,
  pages       INTEGER       NULL    ,
  price       DECIMAL(5,2)  NULL    ,
  sales       INTEGER       NULL    ,
  pubdate     DATE          NULL    ,
  contract    SMALLINT      NOT NULL
  );
```

Listing 11.4 Create the sample-database table *titles* and
assign nullability constraints to each column explicitly.

Tips for NOT NULL

- To see the result of a CREATE TABLE statement, examine the table's structure by using one of the commands described in "Displaying Table Definitions" on page 302.

- When you insert a row into a table, you must provide values explicitly for columns that prohibit nulls (and have no default value). For the table *authors* created by Listing 11.3, for example, the minimal INSERT statement looks like this:

```
INSERT INTO authors(
  au_id,
  au_fname,
  au_lname)
  VALUES(
  'A08',
  'Michael',
  'Polk');
```

The DBMS assigns nulls automatically to the columns in *authors* that aren't listed in the INSERT column list (*phone*, *address*, and so on); see "Inserting Rows with INSERT" on page 305.

- When INSERTing a null into a row, don't quote the keyword NULL; your DBMS will interpret it as the character string 'NULL' rather than as a null.

- See also "Testing for Nulls with IS NULL" on page 112, and "Checking for Nulls with CO-ALESCE()" on page 153 and "Comparing Expressions with NULLIF()" on page 154.

- DBMS **Microsoft SQL Server** doesn't support the data type DATE. To run Listing 11.4, change the data type of the column *pubdate* to DATETIME.

  Oracle treats an empty string ('') as a null; see DBMS tip in "Tips for Nulls" on page 72.

  Db2 doesn't accept a stand-alone NULL keyword (without a NOT) in a nullability constraint. To run Listing 11.4, omit each nullability constraint that isn't NOT NULL.

  Db2 and **MySQL** don't accept named NOT NULL constraints. Omit the clause CONSTRAINT *constraint_name* from NOT NULL column definitions.

  Nullability constraints for the DBMSs covered in this book are optional (and allow nulls by default), but other DBMSs might behave differently.

  For **all DBMSs**, check the documentation to see how your DBMS handles nullability constraints for columns whose data type generates a unique row identifier automatically; see "Other Data Types" on page 71.

Specifying a Default Value with DEFAULT

A **default** specifies a value that your DBMS assigns to a column if you omit a value for the column when inserting a row; see "Inserting Rows with INSERT" on page 305. When you're defining a default value, some important considerations are:

- A default applies to a single column.

- You define a default by using the keyword DEFAULT in a CREATE TABLE column definition.

- A default value can be any expression that evaluates to a constant.

- The default must have the same data type or must be implicitly convertible to the same type as its column; see "Converting Data Types with CAST()" on page 145.

- The column must be long enough to hold the default value.

- If you INSERT a row without specifying a value for a column, then that column's default is used. If the column definition has no DEFAULT, then the default is null.

- If a column has no DEFAULT and is declared NOT NULL, then you should specify the column's value explicitly when you INSERT a row (see "Inserting Rows with INSERT" on page 305). If you omit an explicit value in this situation, then some DBMSs will refuse to INSERT the row, whereas others will assign a default automatically based on the column's date type. **MySQL**, for example, assigns a default value of zero to numeric, non-nullable columns without explicit defaults.

To specify a column's default value:

- Add the following clause to a CREATE TABLE column definition:

  DEFAULT *expr*

  expr is an expression that evaluates to a constant, such as a literal, a built-in function, a mathematical expression, or NULL. If no default is specified, then NULL is assumed. For the general syntax of CREATE TABLE, see "Creating Tables" on page 324.

Listing 11.5 assigns defaults to some of the columns in the sample-database table *titles*. The columns *title_id* and *pub_id* are NOT NULL and have no default values, so you must provide explicit values for them in an INSERT statement. The *pages* clause DEFAULT NULL is equivalent to omitting the DEFAULT. The *pubdate* and *contract* defaults show that the defaults can be expressions more complex than plain literals.

Listing 11.6 shows the minimal INSERT statement that you can use to insert a row into the table *titles* (as created by Listing 11.5). Figure 11.1 shows the inserted row, with default values highlighted. The *title_name* default, an empty string (''), is invisible.

```
CREATE TABLE titles
  (
  title_id    CHAR(3)      NOT NULL                     ,
  title_name  VARCHAR(40)  NOT NULL DEFAULT ''          ,
  type        VARCHAR(10)           DEFAULT 'undefined' ,
  pub_id      CHAR(3)      NOT NULL                     ,
  pages       INTEGER               DEFAULT NULL         ,
  price       DECIMAL(5,2) NOT NULL DEFAULT 0.00         ,
  sales       INTEGER                                    ,
  pubdate     DATE                  DEFAULT CURRENT_DATE,
  contract    SMALLINT     NOT NULL DEFAULT (3*7)-21
  );
```

Listing 11.5 Set default values for some of the columns in the sample-database table *titles*.

```
INSERT INTO titles(title_id, pub_id)
  VALUES('T14','P01');
```

Listing 11.6 The DBMS inserts default values into columns omitted from this INSERT statement. Where no default is specified, the DBMS inserts a null. See Figure 11.1 for the result.

title_id	title_name	type	pub_id	pages	price	sales	pubdate	contract
T14		undefined	P01	NULL	0.00	NULL	2005-02-21	0

Figure 11.1 Listing 11.6 inserts this row into the table *titles*.

Tips for DEFAULT

- To see the result of a CREATE TABLE statement, examine the table's structure by using one of the commands described in "Displaying Table Definitions" on page 302.

- **DBMS** **Microsoft Access** doesn't allow arithmetic expressions in a DEFAULT clause; use a numeric literal. Use Date() instead of CURRENT_DATE to return the system date. (See the DBMS tip in "Tips for the Current Date and Time" on page 143.) To run Listing 11.5, change the default clause of the column *pubdate* to DEFAULT Date() and the default clause of the column *contract* to DEFAULT 0.

  Microsoft SQL Server doesn't support the data type DATE; use DATETIME instead. Use GETDATE() instead of CURRENT_DATE to return the system date; see the DBMS tip in "Tips for the Current Date and Time" on page 143. To run Listing 11.5, change the *pubdate* column's data type to DATETIME, and change its default clause to DEFAULT GETDATE().

In **Oracle**, the DEFAULT clause follows the data type and precedes all column constraints, including the nullability constraint. Oracle 9i and later versions support CURRENT_DATE; use SYSDATE instead of CURRENT_DATE in Oracle 8i and earlier; see the DBMS tip in "Tips for the Current Date and Time" on page 143. Oracle treats an empty string ('') as a null, so I've changed the *title_name* default to a space character (' '); see the DBMS tip in "Tips for Nulls" on page 72. See Listing 11.7 for the Oracle version of Listing 11.5.

Db2 doesn't support arithmetic expressions as default values. To run Listing 11.5, change the default clause of the column *contract* to DEFAULT 0.

In **MySQL**, a default value must be a literal and not a function or expression. This restriction means that you can't set the default of a date column to CURRENT_DATE. To run Listing 11.5, delete the DEFAULT clause of the column *pubdate* (or change the default expression to a date-time literal), and change the DEFAULT clause of the column *contract* to DEFAULT 0. (Exception: You can specify CURRENT_TIMESTAMP as the default for a TIMESTAMP column.)

For **all DBMSs**, check the documentation to see how your DBMS handles default clauses for columns whose data type generates a unique row identifier automatically; see "Other Data Types" on page 71.

```
CREATE TABLE titles
  (
  title_id    CHAR(3)                          NOT NULL,
  title_name VARCHAR(40)  DEFAULT ' '          NOT NULL,
  type        VARCHAR(10)  DEFAULT 'undefined'         ,
  pub_id      CHAR(3)                          NOT NULL,
  pages       INTEGER      DEFAULT NULL                ,
  price       DECIMAL(5,2) DEFAULT 0.00        NOT NULL,
  sales       INTEGER                                 ,
  pubdate     DATE         DEFAULT SYSDATE            ,
  contract    SMALLINT     DEFAULT (3*7)-21   NOT NULL
  );
```

Listing 11.7 In Oracle, the default clause must come before all column constraints.

Specifying a Primary Key with PRIMARY KEY

I described primary keys in "Primary Keys" on page 26, but I'll review the basics here:

- A primary key identifies each row uniquely in a table.

- No two rows can have the same primary-key value.

- Primary keys don't allow nulls.

- Each table has exactly one primary key.

- A one-column key is a simple key; a multiple-column key is a composite key.

- In a composite key, values can be duplicated within one column, but each combination of values from all the key's columns must be unique.

- A table can have more than one combination of columns that uniquely identify its rows; each combination is a candidate key. The database designer picks one of the candidate keys to be the primary key.

When you're defining a primary-key constraint, some important considerations are:

- A simple key can be a column constraint or a table constraint; a composite key always is a table constraint. See "Understanding Constraints" on page 325.

- You define a primary-key constraint by using the keywords PRIMARY KEY in a CREATE TABLE definition.

- As a table constraint, PRIMARY KEY makes you specify column name(s) explicitly. As a column constraint, PRIMARY KEY applies to the column in which it's defined.

- The SQL standard lets you create a table without a primary key (in violation of the relational model). In practice, you always should define a primary key for every table.

- No more than one primary-key constraint is allowed in a table.

- In practice, primary-key constraints almost always are named explicitly. Use a CONSTRAINT clause to do so; see "Understanding Constraints" on page 325.

- The nullability of all PRIMARY KEY columns must be NOT NULL. If you don't specify a nullability constraint, then the DBMS sets all primary-key columns to NOT NULL implicitly; see "Forbidding Nulls with NOT NULL" on page 329.

- You must specify a primary-key value explicitly when you INSERT a row unless the column's data type generates a unique row identifier automatically; see "Other Data Types" on page 71. For information about inserting rows, see "Inserting Rows with INSERT" on page 305.

- Primary-key values normally don't change after they're inserted.

- For considerations related to inserting, updating, and deleting primary keys that are referenced by foreign keys, see "Specifying a Foreign Key with FOREIGN KEY" on page 339.

- The DBMS will create a unique index for a primary key automatically (see Chapter 12).

```
CREATE TABLE publishers
  (
  pub_id    CHAR(3)      PRIMARY KEY,
  pub_name VARCHAR(20) NOT NULL   ,
  city     VARCHAR(15) NOT NULL   ,
  state     CHAR(2)                ,
  country   VARCHAR(15) NOT NULL
  );
```

Listing 11.8a Define a simple primary key for the sample-database table *publishers* by using a column constraint.

```
CREATE TABLE publishers
  (
  pub_id    CHAR(3)      NOT NULL,
  pub_name VARCHAR(20) NOT NULL,
  city     VARCHAR(15) NOT NULL,
  state     CHAR(2)              ,
  country   VARCHAR(15) NOT NULL,
  PRIMARY KEY (pub_id)
  );
```

Listing 11.8b Define a simple primary key for the sample-database table *publishers* by using an unnamed table constraint.

```
CREATE TABLE publishers
  (
  pub_id    CHAR(3)      NOT NULL,
  pub_name VARCHAR(20) NOT NULL,
  city     VARCHAR(15) NOT NULL,
  state     CHAR(2)              ,
  country   VARCHAR(15) NOT NULL,
  CONSTRAINT publishers_pk
    PRIMARY KEY (pub_id)
  );
```

Listing 11.8c Define a simple primary key for the sample-database table *publishers* by using a named table constraint.

To specify a simple primary key:

- To specify a simple primary key as a column constraint, add the following column constraint to a CREATE TABLE column definition:

  [CONSTRAINT *constraint_name*]
    PRIMARY KEY

  or

  To specify a simple primary key as a table constraint, add the following table constraint to a CREATE TABLE definition:

  [CONSTRAINT *constraint_name*]
    PRIMARY KEY (*key_column*)

  key_column is the name of the primary-key column. No more than one PRIMARY KEY constraint is allowed in a table. For the general syntax of CREATE TABLE, see "Creating Tables" on page 324.

  The CONSTRAINT clause is optional, and *constraint_name* is the name of the primary-key constraint; see "Understanding Constraints" on page 325.

Listings 11.8a, 11.8b, and 11.8c show three equivalent ways to define a simple primary key for the sample-database table *publishers*.

Listing 11.8a uses a column constraint to designate the primary-key column. This syntax shows the easiest way to create a simple primary key.

Listing 11.8b uses an unnamed table constraint to specify the primary key. I've added an explicit NOT NULL column constraint to *pub_id*, but it's unnecessary because the DBMS sets this constraint implicitly and silently (except for **Db2**; see the DBMS tip in "Tips for PRIMARY KEY" on page 338).

Listing 11.8c uses a named table constraint to specify the primary key. This syntax shows the preferred way to add a primary key; you can use the name *publishers_pk* if you decide to change or delete the key later. See "Altering a Table with ALTER TABLE" on page 359.

To specify a composite primary key:

- Add the following table constraint to a CREATE TABLE definition:

```
[CONSTRAINT constraint_name]
  PRIMARY KEY (key_columns)
```

key_columns is a list of comma-separated names of the primary-key columns. No more than one PRIMARY KEY constraint is allowed in a table. For the general syntax of CREATE TABLE, see "Creating Tables" on page 324.

The CONSTRAINT clause is optional, and *constraint_name* is the name of the primary-key constraint; see "Understanding Constraints" on page 325.

Listing 11.9 defines a composite primary key for the sample-database table *title_authors*. The primary-key columns are *title_id* and *au_id*, and the key is named *title_authors_pk*.

Tips for PRIMARY KEY

- To see the result of a CREATE TABLE statement, examine the table's structure by using one of the commands described in "Displaying Table Definitions" on page 302.

- To define a column that contains unique values but isn't a primary key, see "Forcing Unique Values with UNIQUE" on page 345.

- It's illegal to specify two or more PRIMARY KEY column constraints in the same table. You can't use the following statement, for example, to specify the composite key for *title_authors*:

```
CREATE TABLE title_authors(
  title_id CHAR(3) PRIMARY KEY,
  au_id CHAR(3) PRIMARY KEY,
  au_order SMALLINT NOT NULL,
  ...
);                        --Illegal
```

- **DBMS** **Db2** makes you set the nullability constraint to NOT NULL explicitly for PRIMARY KEY columns; see "Forbidding Nulls with NOT NULL" on page 329. To run Listing 11.8a, add NOT NULL to *pub_id*'s column constraint.

  Oracle treats an empty string ('') as a null; see the DBMS tip in "Tips for Nulls" on page 72.

```
CREATE TABLE title_authors
  (
  title_id      CHAR(3)      NOT NULL,
  au_id         CHAR(3)      NOT NULL,
  au_order      SMALLINT     NOT NULL,
  royalty_share DECIMAL(5,2) NOT NULL,
  CONSTRAINT title_authors_pk
    PRIMARY KEY (title_id, au_id)
  );
```

Listing 11.9 Define a composite primary key for the sample-database table *title_authors* by using a named table constraint.

Specifying a Foreign Key with FOREIGN KEY

I described foreign keys in "Foreign Keys" on page 28, but I'll review the basics here:

- A foreign key is a mechanism that associates two tables.

- A foreign key is a column (or set of columns) in a table whose values relate to, or reference, values in some other table.

- A foreign key ensures that rows in one table have corresponding rows in another table, called the **referenced table** or **parent table**.

- A foreign key establishes a direct relationship to a primary key or candidate key in the referenced table, so foreign-key values are restricted to parent-key values that already exist. This restriction is called **referential integrity**.

- A foreign key, unlike a primary key, can allow nulls.

- A table can have zero or more foreign keys.

- Foreign-key values generally aren't unique in their own table.

- Foreign-key columns in different tables can reference the same column in a parent table.

- A one-column key is a simple key; a multiple-column key is a composite key.

When you're defining a foreign-key constraint, some important considerations are:

- A simple key can be a column constraint or a table constraint; a composite key always is a table constraint. See "Understanding Constraints" on page 325.

- You define a foreign-key constraint by using the keywords FOREIGN KEY or REFERENCES in a CREATE TABLE definition.

- A foreign key and its parent key can have different column names.

- The foreign key's data type must have the same data type or must be convertible implicitly to the same type as its parent key; see "Converting Data Types with CAST()" on page 145.

- A FOREIGN KEY column doesn't have to reference only a PRIMARY KEY column in another table; it also can reference a UNIQUE column in another table. See "Forcing Unique Values with UNIQUE" on page 345.

- A table can have any number of foreign-key constraints (or none at all).

- In practice, foreign-key constraints almost always are named explicitly. Use a CONSTRAINT clause to name a constraint; see "Understanding Constraints" on page 325.

- Foreign-key constraints simplify updates and deletions and make it difficult to introduce inconsistencies into a database, but the topology of relations in even a medium-size database can become astonishingly complex. Poor design can lead to time-consuming routine queries, circular rules, tricky backup-and-restore operations, and psychotically ambitious cascading deletes.

To preserve referential integrity, your DBMS won't let you create orphan rows or make existing rows **orphans** (rows in a foreign-key table without an associated row in a parent table). When you INSERT, UPDATE, or DELETE a row with a FOREIGN KEY column that references a PRIMARY KEY column in a parent table, your DBMS performs the following referential-integrity checks:

Inserting a row into the foreign-key table. The DBMS checks that the new FOREIGN KEY value matches a PRIMARY KEY value in the parent table. If no match exists, then the DBMS won't INSERT the row.

Updating a row in the foreign-key table. The DBMS checks that the updated FOREIGN KEY value matches a PRIMARY KEY value in the parent table. If no match exists, then the DBMS won't UPDATE the row.

Deleting a row in the foreign-key table. A referential-integrity check is unnecessary.

Inserting a row into the parent table. A referential-integrity check is unnecessary.

Updating a row in the parent table. The DBMS checks that none of the FOREIGN KEY values matches the PRIMARY KEY value to be updated. If a match exists, then the DBMS won't UPDATE the row.

Deleting a row from the parent table. The DBMS checks that none of the FOREIGN KEY values matches the PRIMARY KEY value to be deleted. If a match exists, then the DBMS won't DELETE the row.

The DBMS skips the referential-integrity check for rows with a null in the FOREIGN KEY column.

```
CREATE TABLE titles
  (
  title_id   CHAR(3)       NOT NULL
    PRIMARY KEY                     ,
  title_name VARCHAR(40)  NOT NULL,
  type       VARCHAR(10)           ,
  pub_id     CHAR(3)       NOT NULL
    REFERENCES publishers(pub_id) ,
  pages      INTEGER               ,
  price      DECIMAL(5,2)          ,
  sales      INTEGER               ,
  pubdate    DATE                  ,
  contract   SMALLINT      NOT NULL
  );
```

Listing 11.10 Define a simple foreign key for the sample-database table *titles* by using a column constraint.

```
CREATE TABLE royalties
  (
  title_id     CHAR(3)       NOT NULL,
  advance      DECIMAL(9,2)          ,
  royalty_rate DECIMAL(5,2)          ,
  CONSTRAINT royalties_pk
    PRIMARY KEY (title_id),
  CONSTRAINT royalties_title_id_fk
    FOREIGN KEY (title_id)
    REFERENCES titles(title_id)
  );
```

Listing 11.11 Define a simple foreign key for the sample-database table *royalties* by using a named table constraint.

To specify a simple foreign key:

• To specify a simple foreign key as a column constraint, add the following column constraint to a CREATE TABLE column definition:

  [CONSTRAINT *constraint_name*]
    REFERENCES *ref_table(ref_column)*

  or

  To specify a simple foreign key as a table constraint, add the following table constraint to a CREATE TABLE definition:

  [CONSTRAINT *constraint_name*]
    FOREIGN KEY (*key_column*)
    REFERENCES *ref_table(ref_column)*

  key_column is the name of the foreign-key column. *ref_table* is the name of the parent table referenced by the FOREIGN KEY constraint. *ref_column* is the name of the column in *ref_table* that is the referenced key. Zero or more FOREIGN KEY constraints are allowed in a table. For the general syntax of CREATE TABLE, see "Creating Tables" on page 324.

  The CONSTRAINT clause is optional, and *constraint_name* is the name of the foreign-key constraint; see "Understanding Constraints" on page 325.

  Listing 11.10 uses a column constraint to designate a foreign-key column in the table *titles*. This syntax shows the easiest way to create a simple foreign key. After you run this statement, the DBMS will ensure that values inserted into the column *pub_id* in *titles* already exist in the column *pub_id* in *publishers*. Note that nulls aren't allowed in the foreign-key column, so every book must have a publisher.

  The table *royalties* has a one-to-one relationship with the table *titles*, so Listing 11.11 defines the column *title_id* to be both the primary key and a foreign key that points to *title_id* in *titles*. For information about relationships, see "Relationships" on page 30.

Listing 11.12 uses named table constraints to create two foreign keys. This syntax shows the preferred way to add foreign keys; you can use the names if you decide to change or delete the keys later. (See "Altering a Table with ALTER TABLE" on page 359.) Each foreign-key column is an individual key and *not* part of a single composite key. Note that foreign keys together, however, comprise the table's composite primary key.

To specify a composite foreign key:

* Add the following table constraint to a CREATE TABLE definition:

```
[CONSTRAINT constraint_name]
  FOREIGN KEY (key_columns)
  REFERENCES ref_table(ref_columns)
```

key_columns is a list of comma-separated names of the foreign-key columns. *ref_table* is the name of the parent table referenced by the FOREIGN KEY constraint. *ref_columns* is a list of comma-separated names of the columns in *ref_table* that are the referenced keys. *key_columns* and *ref_columns* must have the same number of columns, listed in corresponding order. Zero or more FOREIGN KEY constraints are allowed in a table. For the general syntax of CREATE TABLE, see "Creating Tables" on page 324.

The CONSTRAINT clause is optional, and *constraint_name* is the name of the foreign-key constraint; see "Understanding Constraints" on page 325.

The sample database contains no composite foreign keys, but suppose that I create a table named *out_of_print* to store information about each author's out-of-print books. The table *title_authors* has a composite primary key. This constraint shows how to reference this key from the table *out_of_print*:

```
CONSTRAINT out_of_print_fk
  FOREIGN KEY (title_id, au_id)
  REFERENCES title_authors(title_id, au_id)
```

```
CREATE TABLE title_authors
  (
  title_id      CHAR(3)       NOT NULL,
  au_id         CHAR(3)       NOT NULL,
  au_order      SMALLINT      NOT NULL,
  royalty_share DECIMAL(5,2) NOT NULL,
  CONSTRAINT title_authors_pk
    PRIMARY KEY (title_id, au_id),
  CONSTRAINT title_authors_fk1
    FOREIGN KEY (title_id)
    REFERENCES titles(title_id),
  CONSTRAINT title_authors_fk2
    FOREIGN KEY (au_id)
    REFERENCES authors(au_id)
  );
```

Listing 11.12 Define simple foreign keys for the sample-database table *title_authors* by using named table constraints.

Tips for FOREIGN KEY

- To see the result of a CREATE TABLE statement, examine the table's structure by using one of the commands described in "Displaying Table Definitions" on page 302.

- You can omit the (*ref_column*) or (*ref_columns*) expression in the REFERENCES clause if the referenced column(s) is the primary key of *ref_table*.

- A FOREIGN KEY constraint can reference another column in the same table (a self-reference). Recall from "Creating a Self-Join" on page 233 that the table *employees* is self-referencing.

  employees has three columns: *emp_id*, *emp_name*, and *boss_id*. *emp_id* is a primary key that uniquely identifies an employee, and *boss_id* is an employee ID that identifies the employee's manager. Each manager also is an employee, so to ensure that each manager ID that is added to the table matches an existing employee ID, *boss_id* is defined as a foreign key of *emp_id*:

  ```
  CREATE TABLE employees
    (
    emp_id CHAR(3) NOT NULL,
    emp_name CHAR(20) NOT NULL,
    boss_id CHAR(3) NULL,
    CONSTRAINT employees_pk
      PRIMARY KEY (emp_id),
    CONSTRAINT employees_fk
      FOREIGN KEY (boss_id)
      REFERENCES employees(emp_id)
    );
  ```

  continues on next page

- SQL lets you define the action the DBMS takes when you try to UPDATE or DELETE a key value (in a parent table) to which foreign-key values point. To trigger a referential action, specify an ON UPDATE or ON DELETE clause in the FOREIGN KEY constraint. Support for these clauses varies by DBMS; search your DBMS documentation for *foreign key* or *referential integrity*. The next two tips explain the SQL standard's definition of these clauses.

- The ON UPDATE *action* clause specifies what the DBMS does if you attempt to UPDATE a key value in a row (in a parent table) where the key value is referenced by foreign keys in rows in other tables. *action* takes one of four values:

  CASCADE updates the dependent foreign-key values to the new parent-key value.

  SET NULL sets the dependent foreign-key values to nulls.

  SET DEFAULT sets the dependent foreign-key values to their default values; see "Specifying a Default Value with DEFAULT" on page 332.

  NO ACTION generates an error on a foreign-key violation. This action is the default.

- The ON DELETE *action* clause specifies what the DBMS does if you attempt to DELETE a key value in a row (in a parent table) where the key value is referenced by foreign keys in rows in other tables. *action* takes one of four values:

  CASCADE deletes the rows that contain foreign-key values that match the deleted parent-key value.

  SET NULL sets the dependent foreign-key values to null.

  SET DEFAULT sets the dependent foreign-key values to their default values; see "Specifying a Default Value with DEFAULT" on page 332.

  NO ACTION generates an error on a foreign-key violation. This action is the default.

- DBMS **Microsoft SQL Server** doesn't support the data type DATE. To run Listing 11.10, change the data type of the column *pubdate* to DATETIME.

  Oracle treats an empty string ('') as a null; see the DBMS tip in "Tips for Nulls" on page 72.

  MySQL enforces foreign-key constraints through InnoDB tables; search MySQL documentation for *foreign key*. InnoDB FOREIGN KEY syntax is more restrictive than standard CREATE TABLE syntax.

Forcing Unique Values with UNIQUE

A unique constraint ensures that a column (or set of columns) contains no duplicate values. A unique constraint is similar to a primary-key constraint, except that a unique column can contain nulls and a table can have multiple unique columns. (For information about primary-key constraints, see "Specifying a Primary Key with PRIMARY KEY" on page 336.)

Suppose that I add the column *isbn* to the table *titles* to hold a book's ISBN. An ISBN is a unique, standardized identification number that marks a book unmistakably. *titles* already has a primary key (*title_id*), so to ensure that each ISBN value is unique, I can define a unique constraint on the column *isbn*.

When you're defining a unique constraint, some important considerations are:

- A one-column key is a simple constraint; a multiple-column key is a composite constraint.

- In a composite constraint, values can be duplicated within one column, but each combination of values from all the columns must be unique.

- A simple unique constraint can be a column constraint or a table constraint; a composite unique constraint always is a table constraint. See "Understanding Constraints" on page 325.

- You define a unique constraint by using the keyword UNIQUE in a CREATE TABLE definition.

- As a table constraint, UNIQUE makes you specify column name(s). As a column constraint, UNIQUE applies to the column in which it's defined.

- A table can have zero or more unique constraints.

- In practice, unique constraints almost always are named explicitly. Use a CONSTRAINT clause to name a constraint; see "Understanding Constraints" on page 325.

- A UNIQUE column can forbid nulls; see "Forbidding Nulls with NOT NULL" on page 329.

To specify a simple unique constraint:

- To specify a simple unique constraint as a column constraint, add the following column constraint to a CREATE TABLE column definition:

```
[CONSTRAINT constraint_name]
  UNIQUE
```

or

To specify a simple unique constraint as a table constraint, add the following table constraint to a CREATE TABLE definition:

```
[CONSTRAINT constraint_name]
  UNIQUE (unique_column)
```

unique_column is the name of the column that forbids duplicate values. Zero or more UNIQUE constraints are allowed in a table. For the general syntax of CREATE TABLE, see "Creating Tables" on page 324.

The CONSTRAINT clause is optional, and *constraint_name* is the name of the unique constraint; see "Understanding Constraints" on page 325.

Listings 11.13a and 11.13b show two equivalent ways to define a simple unique constraint for the sample-database table *titles*.

Listing 11.13a uses a column constraint to designate a unique column. This syntax shows the easiest way to create a simple unique constraint.

Listing 11.13b uses a named table constraint to specify a unique column. This syntax shows the preferred way to add a unique constraint; you can use the name if you decide to change or delete the constraint later. See "Altering a Table with ALTER TABLE" on page 359.

```
CREATE TABLE titles
  (
  title_id    CHAR(3)       PRIMARY KEY   ,
  title_name  VARCHAR(40)   NOT NULL UNIQUE,
  type        VARCHAR(10)                 ,
  pub_id      CHAR(3)       NOT NULL      ,
  pages       INTEGER                     ,
  price       DECIMAL(5,2)                ,
  sales       INTEGER                     ,
  pubdate     DATE                        ,
  contract    SMALLINT      NOT NULL
  );
```

Listing 11.13a Define a simple unique constraint on the column *title_name* for the sample-database table *titles* by using a column constraint.

```
CREATE TABLE titles
  (
  title_id    CHAR(3)       NOT NULL,
  title_name  VARCHAR(40)   NOT NULL,
  type        VARCHAR(10)           ,
  pub_id      CHAR(3)       NOT NULL,
  pages       INTEGER               ,
  price       DECIMAL(5,2)          ,
  sales       INTEGER               ,
  pubdate     DATE                  ,
  contract    SMALLINT      NOT NULL,
  CONSTRAINT titles_pk
    PRIMARY KEY (title_id),
  CONSTRAINT titles_unique1
    UNIQUE (title_name)
  );
```

Listing 11.13b Define a simple unique constraint on the column *title_name* for the sample-database table *titles* by using a named table constraint.

```
CREATE TABLE authors
  (
  au_id    CHAR(3)     NOT NULL,
  au_fname VARCHAR(15) NOT NULL,
  au_lname VARCHAR(15) NOT NULL,
  phone    VARCHAR(12)        ,
  address  VARCHAR(20)        ,
  city     VARCHAR(15)        ,
  state    CHAR(2)            ,
  zip      CHAR(5)            ,
  CONSTRAINT authors_pk
    PRIMARY KEY (au_id),
  CONSTRAINT authors_unique1
    UNIQUE (au_fname, au_lname)
  );
```

Listing 11.14 Define a composite unique constraint on the columns *au_fname* and *au_lname* for the sample-database table *authors* by using a named table constraint.

To specify a composite unique constraint:

- Add the following table constraint to a CREATE TABLE definition:

  [CONSTRAINT *constraint_name*]
    UNIQUE (*unique_columns*)

  unique_columns is a list of comma-separated names of the columns that forbid duplicate values. Zero or more unique constraints are allowed in a table. For the general syntax of CREATE TABLE, see "Creating Tables" on page 324.

  The CONSTRAINT clause is optional, and *constraint_name* is the name of the unique constraint; see "Understanding Constraints" on page 325.

  Listing 11.14 defines a multicolumn unique constraint for the sample-database table *authors*. This constraint forces the combination of each author's first and last name to be unique.

Tips for UNIQUE

- To see the result of a CREATE TABLE statement, examine the table's structure by using one of the commands described in "Displaying Table Definitions" on page 302.

- A foreign-key column can point to a UNIQUE column; see "Specifying a Foreign Key with FOREIGN KEY" on page 339.

- You should assign non-nullable unique constraints to alternate keys; see "Primary Keys" on page 26.

- You can create a unique index instead of a unique constraint; see "Creating an Index with CREATE INDEX" on page 364. To determine whether your DBMS prefers an index or a constraint, search your DBMS documentation for *unique*, *index*, or *constraint*.

- **DBMS** **Microsoft SQL Server** doesn't support the data type DATE. To run Listings 11.13a and 11.13b, change the data type of the column *pubdate* to DATETIME.

  Oracle treats an empty string ('') as a null; see the DBMS tip in "Tips for Nulls" on page 72.

  Db2 makes you set the nullability constraint to NOT NULL explicitly for PRIMARY KEY columns. To run Listing 11.13a, add NOT NULL to *title_id*'s column constraint.

  The SQL standard allows any number of nulls in a nullable, unique column. **Microsoft SQL Server** allows only one null in such a column, and **Db2** allows none.

Adding a Check Constraint with CHECK

So far, the only restrictions on an inserted value are that it have the proper data type, size, and range for its column. You can use check constraints to further limit the values that a column (or set of columns) accepts. Check constraints commonly are used to check the following:

Minimum or maximum values. Prevent sales of fewer than zero items, for example.

Specific values. Allow only 'biology', 'chemistry', or 'physics' in the column *science*, for example.

A range of values. Make sure that an author's royalty rate is between 2 percent and 20 percent, for example.

A check constraint resembles a foreign-key constraint in that both restrict the values that can be placed in a column (see "Specifying a Foreign Key with FOREIGN KEY" on page 339). They differ in how they determine which values are allowed. A foreign-key constraint gets the list of valid values from another table, whereas a check constraint determines the valid values by using a logical (boolean) expression. The following check constraint, for example, ensures that no employee's salary exceeds $50000:

```
CHECK (salary <= 50000)
```

When you're defining a check constraint, some important considerations are:

- A check constraint that applies to a single column can be a column constraint or a table constraint; a check constraint that applies to multiple columns always is a table constraint. See "Understanding Constraints" on page 325.

- You define a check constraint by using the keyword CHECK in a CREATE TABLE definition.

- A column can have zero or more check constraints associated with it.

- If you create multiple check constraints for a column, then design them carefully so that their purposes don't conflict. Don't assume that the DBMS will evaluate the constraints in any particular order or will verify that the constraints are mutually exclusive.

- In practice, check constraints almost always are named explicitly. Use a CONSTRAINT clause to name a constraint; see "Understanding Constraints" on page 325.

- The check constraint's condition is almost any valid WHERE condition, such as a comparison (=, <>, <, <=, >, >=), LIKE, BETWEEN, IN, or IS NULL condition. (Most DBMSs don't allow subqueries in check constraints.) You can join multiple conditions with AND, OR, or NOT. For information about conditions, see "Filtering Rows with WHERE" on page 89.

- A check constraint's condition can refer to any column in the table, but it can't refer to columns in other tables.

- Although it's possible to add check constraints after a table has been populated, it's a better practice to impose check constraints before populating the table to detect input errors as early as possible.

To add a check constraint:

- To add a check constraint as a column constraint or table constraint, add the following constraint to a CREATE TABLE definition:

  [CONSTRAINT *constraint_name*]
    CHECK (*condition*)

  condition is a logical (boolean) condition that the DBMS evaluates each time an INSERT, UP-DATE, or DELETE statement modifies the contents of the table. If *condition* evaluates to true or unknown (due to a null) after the modification, then the DBMS allows the change. If *condition* evaluates to false, then the DBMS undoes the change and returns an error. For the general syntax of CREATE TABLE, see "Creating Tables" on page 324.

  The CONSTRAINT clause is optional, and *constraint_name* is the name of the primary-key constraint; see "Understanding Constraints" on page 325.

  Listing 11.15 shows various column and table check constraints for the sample-database table *titles*. The constraint *title_id_chk* makes sure the each primary-key value takes the form 'T*nn*', in which *nn* represents an integer between 00 and 99, inclusive.

```
CREATE TABLE titles
  (
  title_id    CHAR(3)     NOT NULL,
  title_name VARCHAR(40)  NOT NULL,
  type        VARCHAR(10)
    CONSTRAINT type_chk
      CHECK (type IN ('biography',
        'children','computer',
        'history','psychology'))  ,
  pub_id      CHAR(3)     NOT NULL,
  pages       INTEGER
    CHECK (pages > 0)              ,
  price       DECIMAL(5,2)         ,
  sales       INTEGER              ,
  pubdate     DATE                 ,
  contract    SMALLINT    NOT NULL,
  CONSTRAINT titles_pk
    PRIMARY KEY (title_id),
  CONSTRAINT titles_pub_id_fk
    FOREIGN KEY (pub_id)
    REFERENCES publishers(pub_id),
  CONSTRAINT title_id_chk
    CHECK (
    (SUBSTRING(title_id FROM 1 FOR 1) = 'T')
    AND
    (CAST(SUBSTRING(title_id FROM 2 FOR 2)
    AS INTEGER) BETWEEN 0 AND 99)),
  CONSTRAINT price_chk
    CHECK (price >= 0.00
    AND price < 100.00),
  CONSTRAINT sales_chk
    CHECK (sales >= 0),
  CONSTRAINT pubdate_chk
    CHECK (pubdate >= DATE '1950-01-01'),
  CONSTRAINT title_name_chk
    CHECK (title_name <> ''
    AND contract >= 0),
  CONSTRAINT revenue_chk
    CHECK (price * sales >= 0.00)
  );
```

Listing 11.15 Define some check constraints for the sample-database table *titles*.

Tips for CHECK

- To see the result of a CREATE TABLE statement, examine the table's structure by using one of the commands described in "Displaying Table Definitions" on page 302.

- The SQL standard says that a check condition can't reference the datetime and user functions (CURRENT_TIMESTAMP, CURRENT_USER, and so on), but some DBMSs, such as **Microsoft Access**, **Microsoft SQL Server**, and **PostgreSQL**, allow them, for example:

  ```
  CHECK(ship_time >= CURRENT_TIMESTAMP)
  ```

  These functions are described in "Getting the Current Date and Time" on page 142 and "Getting User Information" on page 144.

- **DBMS** To run Listing 11.15 in **Microsoft Access**, convert the two column constraints (for the columns *type* and *pages*) to table constraints by moving them after the last column definition. Change the first substring expression to Mid(title_id, 1, 1); change the CAST expression to CInt(Mid(title_id, 2, 2)); and drop the keyword DATE from the date literal and surround it with # characters (#1950-01-01#) instead of quotes.

  To run Listing 11.15 in **Microsoft SQL Server**, change the data type of the column *pubdate* to DATETIME; change the two substring expressions to SUBSTRING(title_id, 1, 1) and SUBSTRING(title_id, 2, 2); and drop the keyword DATE from the date literal ('1950-01-01').

  To run Listing 11.15 in **Oracle**, change the two substring expressions to SUBSTR(title_id, 1, 1) and SUBSTR(title_id, 2, 2).

  To run Listing 11.15 in **Db2**, change the two substring expressions to SUBSTR(title_id, 1, 1) and SUBSTR(title_id, 2, 2) and drop the keyword DATE from the date literal ('1950-01-01').

  MySQL 8.0 and later support named, enforced CHECK column constraints, whereas earlier versions do not. To run Listing 11.15 in earlier MySQL versions, remove CONSTRAINT type_chk. Also, in all versions, change the CAST data type from INTEGER to SIGNED.

  To run Listing 11.15 in older **PostgreSQL** versions, change the floating-point literals 0.00 and 100.00 to CAST(0.00 AS DECIMAL) and CAST(100.00 AS DECIMAL); see "Converting Data Types with CAST()" on page 145.

  In **Microsoft SQL Server**, you can specify the check constraint *title_id_chk* alternatively as CHECK (title_id LIKE '[T][0-9][0-9]'); search SQL Server Help for *pattern* or *wildcard*.

  Oracle treats an empty string ('') as a null; see the DBMS tip in "Tips for Nulls" on page 72.

Creating a Temporary Table with CREATE TEMPORARY TABLE

Every table I've created so far has been a permanent table, called a **base table**, which stores data persistently until you destroy (DROP) the table explicitly. SQL also lets you create temporary tables to use for working storage or intermediate results. Temporary tables commonly are used to:

- Store the result of a complex, time-consuming query once and use the result repeatedly in subsequent queries, improving performance greatly.

- Create an image, or **snapshot**, of a table at a particular moment in time. (You can add a column with the DEFAULT value CURRENT_TIMESTAMP to record the time.)

- Hold the result of a subquery.

- Hold intermediate results of long or complex calculations.

A **temporary table** is a table that the DBMS empties automatically at the end of a session or transaction. (The table's data are destroyed along with the table.) A **session** is the time during which you're connected to a DBMS—between logon and logoff—and the DBMS accepts and executes your commands.

When you're creating a temporary table, some important considerations are:

- Temporary tables follow the same rules as base tables with regard to table names, column names, date types, and so on.

- You define a temporary table by using a standard CREATE TABLE statement with a bit of extra syntax. Add the keywords GLOBAL TEMPORARY or LOCAL TEMPORARY before the keyword TABLE.

- A temporary table has no rows initially. You can INSERT, UPDATE, and DELETE rows as you would in a base table (see Chapter 10).

- If you create a large temporary table, then you can free memory by destroying it yourself rather than waiting for the DBMS to do so; see "Dropping a Table with DROP TABLE" on page 362.

- CREATE TEMPORARY TABLE lets database administrators give users working storage space without giving them (potentially disastrous) CREATE TABLE, ALTER TABLE, or DROP TABLE privileges.

```
CREATE LOCAL TEMPORARY TABLE editors
  (
  ed_id    CHAR(3)    ,
  ed_fname VARCHAR(15),
  ed_lname VARCHAR(15),
  phone    VARCHAR(12),
  pub_id   CHAR(3)
  );
```

Listing 11.16 A local temporary table is available to only you. It dematerializes when your DBMS session ends.

```
CREATE GLOBAL TEMPORARY TABLE editors
  (
  ed_id    CHAR(3)    ,
  ed_fname VARCHAR(15),
  ed_lname VARCHAR(15),
  phone    VARCHAR(12),
  pub_id   CHAR(3)
  );
```

Listing 11.17 A global temporary table can be accessed by you and other users. It dematerializes when your DBMS session ends and all other tasks have stopped referencing it.

To create a temporary table:

- Type:

  CREATE {LOCAL | GLOBAL} TEMPORARY
  TABLE *table*
    (
    column1 data_type1 [*constraints1*],
    column2 data_type2 [*constraints2*],
    . . .
    columnN data_typeN [*constraintsN*]
    [, *table_constraints*]
    );

  table is the name of the temporary table to create. LOCAL specifies that *table* is a local temporary table. GLOBAL specifies that *table* is a global temporary table (Listings 11.16 and 11.17).

  column1, column2,..., columnN are the names of the columns in *table. data_type1, data_type2,..., data_typeN* specify the SQL data type of each corresponding column.

  The permissible column constraints and table constraints for temporary tables vary by DBMS; search your DBMS documentation for *temporary tables*. For general information about constraints, see "Understanding Constraints" on page 325.

Tips for CREATE TEMPORARY TABLE

- To see the result of a CREATE TEMPORARY TABLE statement, examine the table's structure by using one of the commands described in "Displaying Table Definitions" on page 302.

- To modify a temporary table, see "Altering a Table with ALTER TABLE" on page 359.

- To create a temporary copy of an existing table, see "Creating a New Table from an Existing One with CREATE TABLE AS" on page 355.

- DBMS **Microsoft Access** doesn't support temporary tables.

  The **Microsoft SQL Server** syntax to create a temporary table is, for a local table:

  ```
  CREATE TABLE #table (...);
  ```

  or, for a global table:

  ```
  CREATE TABLE ##table (...);
  ```

  You must include the # character(s) whenever you refer to a temporary table by name.

  The **Oracle** syntax to create a temporary table is:

  ```
  CREATE GLOBAL TEMPORARY
  TABLE table (...);
  ```

  The **Db2** syntax to create a temporary table is:

  ```
  DECLARE GLOBAL TEMPORARY
  TABLE table (...);
  ```

MySQL doesn't distinguish between local and global temporary tables; omit the keyword LOCAL or GLOBAL.

PostgreSQL supports (but ignores) the GLOBAL and LOCAL keywords and creates only one type of temporary table.

Your DBMS might support the optional ON COMMIT clause that is defined by the SQL standard. ON COMMIT PRESERVE ROWS preserves any data modifications to the temporary table on a COMMIT, whereas ON COMMIT DELETE ROWS empties the table after a COMMIT. For information about COMMIT, see Chapter 14.

For all **DBMSs**, check the documentation to see how the DBMS handles a temporary table that has the same name as a base table. In some cases, for example, a temporary table will hide, or **occlude**, the like-named base table until the temporary table is dropped.

As you can see, the SQL standard's definition of the behavior of temporary tables is widely ignored. DBMSs vary in how they implement temporary tables with respect to their persistence, visibility, constraints, foreign keys (referential integrity), indexes, and views; search your DBMS documentation for *temporary tables*.

Creating a New Table from an Existing One with CREATE TABLE AS

The CREATE TABLE AS statement creates a new table and populates it with the result of a SELECT. It's similar to creating an empty table with CREATE TABLE and then populating the table with INSERT SELECT (see "Inserting Rows with INSERT" on page 305). CREATE TABLE AS commonly is used to:

- Archive specific rows

- Make backup copies of tables

- Create a snapshot of a table at a particular moment in time

- Quickly duplicate a table's structure but not its data

- Create test data

- Copy a table to test INSERT, UPDATE, and DE-LETE operations before modifying production data

When you're using CREATE TABLE AS, some important considerations are:

- You can choose rows for the new table by using the standard SELECT clauses WHERE, JOIN, GROUP BY, and HAVING or any of the SELECT options described in Chapters 4 through 9.

- CREATE TABLE AS inserts rows into a single table regardless of how many source tables the SELECT references.

- The properties of the columns and expressions in the SELECT-clause list define the new table's structure.

- When you include a derived (computed) column in the SELECT-clause list, the values in the new table's corresponding column are the values that were computed at the time CREATE TABLE AS was executed. See "Creating Derived Columns" on page 116.

- The new table must have a different name from the existing table.

- You must have CREATE TABLE permission from your database administrator.

To create a new table from an existing table:

- Type:

  ```
  CREATE TABLE new_table
    AS subquery;
  ```

  new_table is the name of the table to create. *subquery* is a SELECT statement that returns rows to insert into *new_table*. The DBMS uses the result of *subquery* to determine the structure of *new_table* and the order, names, data types, and values of its columns.

  Listing 11.18 copies the structure and data of the existing table *authors* to a new table named *authors2*.

  Listing 11.19 uses a WHERE condition that's always false to copy only the structure (but not the data) of the existing table *publishers* to a new table named *publishers2*.

  Listing 11.20 creates a global temporary table named *titles2* that contains the titles and sales of books published by publisher P01; see "Creating a Temporary Table with CREATE TEMPORARY TABLE" on page 352.

  Listing 11.21 uses joins to create a new table named *author_title_names* that contains the names of the authors who aren't from New York State or California and the titles of their books.

```
CREATE TABLE authors2 AS
  SELECT *
    FROM authors;
```

Listing 11.18 Copy the structure and data of the existing table *authors* to a new table named *authors2*.

```
CREATE TABLE publishers2 AS
  SELECT *
    FROM publishers
    WHERE 1 = 2;
```

Listing 11.19 Copy the structure (but not the data) of the existing table *publishers* to a new table named *publishers2*.

```
CREATE GLOBAL TEMPORARY TABLE titles2 AS
  SELECT title_name, sales
    FROM titles
    WHERE pub_id = 'P01';
```

Listing 11.20 Create a global temporary table named *titles2* that contains the titles and sales of books published by publisher P01.

```
CREATE TABLE author_title_names AS
  SELECT a.au_fname, a.au_lname, t.title_name
    FROM authors a
    INNER JOIN title_authors ta
      ON a.au_id = ta.au_id
    INNER JOIN titles t
      ON ta.title_id = t.title_id
    WHERE a.state NOT IN ('CA', 'NY');
```

Listing 11.21 Create a new table named *author_title_names* that contains the names of the authors who aren't from New York state or California and the titles of their books.

Tips for CREATE TABLE AS

- To examine the new table's structure, use one of the commands described in "Displaying Table Definitions" on page 302.

- It's common to create a temporary table that contains data for the current date. For example:

```
CREATE GLOBAL TEMPORARY TABLE
    sales_today AS
  SELECT *
    FROM orders
    WHERE order_date = CURRENT_DATE;
```

- DBMS | The SQL:2003 standard introduced CREATE TABLE AS, but **Microsoft Access** and **Microsoft SQL Server** use SELECT INTO to create a new table from an existing one:

```
SELECT columns
  INTO new_table
  FROM existing_table
  [WHERE search_condition];
```

The SQL standard's version of SELECT INTO isn't the same thing—it selects a value into a scalar variable in a host program rather than creating a new table. The **Oracle, Db2**, and **MySQL** implementations of SELECT INTO work in the standard way. For portability, you shouldn't use CREATE TABLE AS or SELECT INTO. Instead, create a new, empty table with CREATE TABLE and then populate it with INSERT SELECT.

To run Listings 11.18 through 11.21 in **Microsoft Access**, type (Listing 11.18):

```
SELECT *
  INTO authors2
  FROM authors;
```

and (Listing 11.19):

```
SELECT *
  INTO publishers2
  FROM publishers
  WHERE 1=2;
```

and (Listing 11.20):

```
SELECT title_name, sales
  INTO titles2
  FROM titles
  WHERE pub_id='P01';
```

and (Listing 11.21):

```
SELECT a.au_fname, a.au_lname,
    t.title_name
  INTO author_title_names
  FROM titles t
  INNER JOIN (authors a
    INNER JOIN title_authors ta
      ON a.au_id = ta.au_id)
    ON t.title_id = ta.title_id
  WHERE a.state NOT IN ('NY','CA');
```

To run Listings 11.18 through 11.21 in **Microsoft SQL Server**, type (Listing 11.18):

```
SELECT *
  INTO authors2
  FROM authors;
```

and (Listing 11.19):

```
SELECT *
  INTO publishers2
  FROM publishers
  WHERE 1=2;
```

and (Listing 11.20):

```
SELECT title_name, sales
  INTO ##titles2
  FROM titles
  WHERE pub_id = 'P01';
```

and (Listing 11.21):

```
SELECT a.au_fname, a.au_lname,
    t.title_name
  INTO author_title_names
  FROM authors a
  INNER JOIN title_authors ta
    ON a.au_id = ta.au_id
  INNER JOIN titles t
    ON ta.title_id = t.title_id
  WHERE a.state NOT IN ('CA', 'NY');
```

In **Oracle** 8i, use WHERE syntax instead of JOIN syntax in Listing 11.21:

```
CREATE TABLE author_title_names AS
  SELECT a.au_fname, a.au_lname,
    t.title_name
  FROM authors a, title_authors ta,
    titles t
  WHERE a.au_id = ta.au_id
    AND ta.title_id = t.title_id
    AND a.state NOT IN ('CA', 'NY');
```

Db2's CREATE TABLE AS syntax is:

```
CREATE TABLE new_table AS
  (subquery) options;
```

The Db2 documentation describes the available *options*. To run Listing 11.19, for example, type:

```
CREATE TABLE publishers2 AS
  (SELECT * FROM publishers)
  WITH NO DATA;
```

Db2 also supports

```
CREATE TABLE new_table LIKE existing_table
```

to use one table as the pattern for creating another.

To run Listing 11.20 in **MySQL**, delete the keyword GLOBAL.

PostgreSQL also lets you use SELECT INTO to define a new table from a query result but recommends that you use CREATE TABLE AS.

CREATE TABLE AS is similar to what some vendors call **materialized tables** or **materialized views**, except that the standard's statement doesn't create a linkage between the new and old tables.

Altering a Table with ALTER TABLE

Use the ALTER TABLE statement to modify a table definition by adding, altering, or dropping columns and constraints.

DBMS Despite the SQL standard, the implementation of ALTER TABLE varies greatly by DBMS. To determine what you can alter and the conditions under which alterations are allowed, search your DBMS documentation for *ALTER TABLE*. Depending on your DBMS, some of the modifications that you can make by using ALTER TABLE are:

- Add or drop a column
- Alter a column's data type
- Add, alter, or drop a column's default value or nullability constraint
- Add, alter, or drop column or table constraints such as primary-key, foreign-key, unique, and check constraints
- Rename a column
- Rename a table

To alter a table:

- Type:

  ```
  ALTER TABLE table
    alter_table_action;
  ```

  table is the name of the table to alter. *alter_table_action* is a clause that specifies the action to take and begins with the keyword ADD, ALTER, or DROP. Some example actions are:

  ```
  ADD COLUMN column type [constraints]

  ALTER COLUMN column SET DEFAULT expr

  DROP COLUMN column [RESTRICT|CASCADE]

  ADD table_constraint

  DROP CONSTRAINT constraint_name
  ```

Listings 11.22 and 11.23 add and drop the column *email_address* from the table *authors*.

```
ALTER TABLE authors
  ADD email_address CHAR(25);
```

Listing 11.22 Add the column *email_address* to the table authors.

```
ALTER TABLE authors
  DROP COLUMN email_address;
```

Listing 11.23 Drop the column *email_address* from the table authors.

If your DBMS's ALTER TABLE statement doesn't support an action that you need (such as, say, dropping or renaming a column or constraint), then check whether your DBMS offers the action in a different SQL statement or as a separate (non-SQL) command via the command line or graphical user interface. As a last resort, you can re-create and repopulate the table in its desired state manually.

To re-create and repopulate a table:

1. Use CREATE TABLE to create a new table with the new column definitions, column constraints, and table constraints; see "Creating a New Table with CREATE TABLE" and subsequent sections earlier in this chapter.

2. Use INSERT SELECT to copy rows (from the appropriate columns) from the old table into the new table; see "Inserting Rows with INSERT" on page 305.

3. Use SELECT * FROM new_table to confirm that the new table has the proper rows; see "Retrieving Columns with SELECT and FROM" on page 76.

4. Use DROP TABLE to drop the old table; see "Dropping a Table with DROP TABLE" on page 362.

5. Rename the new table to the name of the old table; see the DBMS tip in "Tips for ALTER TABLE".

6. Re-create indexes as needed; see "Creating an Index with CREATE INDEX" on page 364.

You also need to re-create any other properties that were dropped along with the old table, such as permissions and triggers.

Tips for ALTER TABLE

- To see the result of an ALTER TABLE statement, examine the table's structure by using one of the commands described in "Displaying Table Definitions" on page 302.

- You can't drop a table's only remaining column.

- To alter or drop a constraint, use the name that you specified in the CONSTRAINT clause when you created the constraint; see "Understanding Constraints" on page 325. If you didn't name the constraint, then use the constraint name that your DBMS generated automatically.

- DBMSs typically enforce fewer modification restrictions on empty tables than they do on populated tables. When you add a new column to a table that already has one or more rows, for example, that column can't have a NOT NULL constraint, whereas a new column in an empty table can be non-nullable.

- DBMS Older versions of **Db2** won't let you drop a column with ALTER TABLE, and so won't run Listing 11.23.

  Table 11.2 lists the commands that rename tables in the current database.

Table 11.2 Renaming Tables

DBMS	Command
Access	Right-click a table in the Navigation pane and then click Rename
SQL Server	EXEC sp_rename 'old_name', 'new_name'
Oracle	RENAME old_name TO new_name;
Db2	RENAME TABLE old_name TO new_name;
MySQL	RENAME TABLE old_name TO new_name;
PostgreSQL	ALTER TABLE old_name RENAME TO new_name;

Dropping a Table with DROP TABLE

Use the DROP TABLE statement to remove a table from a database. When you're dropping a table, some important considerations are:

- You can drop a base table or a temporary table.

- Some DBMSs let you recover a dropped table by rolling back a transaction (see Chapter 14). If a dropped table wasn't part of a transaction, then you can restore the table from the most recent backup (although it might be out of date).

- Dropping a table destroys its structure, data, indexes, constraints, permissions, and so on.

- Dropping a table isn't the same as deleting all its rows. You can empty a table of rows, but not destroy it, with DELETE FROM *table*;. See "Deleting Rows with DELETE" on page 319.

- Dropping a table doesn't drop views that reference that table; see Chapter 13.

- You'll have problems with foreign keys or views that reference a dropped table unless they're altered or dropped as well.

To drop a table:

- Type:

  DROP TABLE *table*;

  table is the name of the table to drop (Listing 11.24).

```
DROP TABLE royalties;
```

Listing 11.24 Drop the table *royalties*.

Tips for DROP TABLE

- **DBMS** Some DBMSs make you drop or alter certain other properties before dropping the table itself. In **Microsoft SQL Server**, for example, you can't use DROP TABLE to drop a table referenced by a FOREIGN KEY constraint until the referencing FOREIGN KEY constraint or the referencing table is dropped first.

  Standard SQL lets you specify RESTRICT or CASCADE drop behavior. RESTRICT (which is safe) prevents you from dropping a table that's referenced by views or other constraints. CASCADE (which is dangerous) causes referencing objects to be dropped along with the table. To find out whether your DBMS supports this feature or a similar one, search your DBMS documentation for *DROP TABLE*.

CHAPTER 12

Indexes

Recall from "Tables, Columns, and Rows" on page 22 that rows stored in a table are unordered, as required by the relational model. This lack of order makes it easy for the DBMS to INSERT, UPDATE, and DELETE rows quickly, but its unfortunate side effect is that it makes searching and sorting inefficient. Suppose that you run this query:

```
SELECT *
  FROM authors
  WHERE au_lname = 'Hull';
```

To execute this query, the DBMS must search the entire table *authors* sequentially, comparing the value in each row's *au_lname* column to the string *Hull*. Searching an entire table in a small database is trivial, but production database tables can have millions of rows.

DBMSs provide a mechanism called an **index** that has the same purpose as its book or library counterpart: speeding data retrieval. At a simplified level, an index is a sorted list in which every distinct value in an indexed column (or set of columns) is stored with the drive address (physical location) of the rows containing that value. Instead of reading an entire table to locate specific rows, the DBMS scans only the index for addresses to access directly. Indexed searches typically are orders of magnitude faster than sequential searches, but some tradeoffs are involved, as explained in this chapter.

Creating an Index with CREATE INDEX

Indexes are complex; their design and effects on performance depend on the idiosyncrasies of your DBMS's optimizer. I'll provide guidelines in this section, but search your DBMS documentation for *index* to learn how your DBMS implements and uses indexes. In general, indexes are *appropriate* for columns that are frequently:

- Searched (WHERE)
- Sorted (ORDER BY)
- Grouped (GROUP BY)
- Used in joins (JOIN)
- Used to calculate order statistics (MIN(), MAX(), or the median, for example)

In general, indexes are *inappropriate* for columns that:

- Accept only a few distinct values (*gender, state,* or *marital_status*, for example)
- Are used rarely in queries
- Are part of a small table with few rows

When you're creating an index, some important considerations are:

- SQL's indexing statements modify database objects, so your database administrator might need to grant you permission to run them.
- An index never changes data; it's merely a fast access path to the data.
- A table can have zero or more indexes.

- Ideally, you create all a table's indexes when you create the table. In practice, index management is an iterative process. Typically, only vital indexes are created along with the table. Other indexes are added or deleted over time as performance problems grow or ebb and users' access patterns change. DBMSs provide testing and benchmarking tools to determine the effectiveness of indexes.

- Don't create any more indexes than you need. The DBMS must update (and possibly reorganize) an index after you INSERT, UPDATE, or DELETE rows in a table (see Chapter 10). As the number of indexes on a table grows, row-modification performance degrades as the DBMS spends more and more time maintaining indexes. In general, you shouldn't create more than about a dozen indexes for a table.

- Your DBMS will maintain and use indexes automatically after they're created. No additional actions are required by users or SQL programmers to reflect data changes in all relevant indexes.

- Indexes are transparent to the user and SQL programmer. The absence or presence of an index doesn't require a change in the wording of any SQL statement.

- An index can reference one or more columns in a table. An index that references a single column is a **simple index**; an index that references multiple columns is a **composite index**. Columns in a composite index need not be adjacent in the table. A single index can't span multiple tables.

- The order in which columns appear in a composite index is significant. A composite index applies only to the group of columns on which it's defined, not to each column individually or the same columns in different order.

- You can create multiple composite indexes that use the same columns if you specify distinctly different combinations of the columns. The following two statements, for example, specify valid combinations for the same table:

```
CREATE INDEX au_name_idx1
  ON authors (au_fname, au_lname);
```

```
CREATE INDEX au_name_idx2
  ON authors (au_lname, au_fname);
```

- In addition to allowing rapid sorts and searches, an index can ensure uniqueness. A **unique index** forces the value of the column (or columns) upon which the index is based to be distinct in the table. If you try to create a unique index for column(s) in which duplicate values already exist, then your DBMS will generate an error and refuse to create the index. DBMSs create unique indexes automatically when you define a primary-key constraint or unique constraint.

- A DBMS may or may not create indexes for foreign keys automatically. If not, then you should create these indexes yourself because most joins involve a foreign key.

- All DBMSs implement indexes even though indexes aren't part of the relational model (and don't violate any of the model's rules).

Indexes aren't part of the SQL standard, so index-related SQL statements vary by DBMS, although the syntax for the minimal CREATE INDEX statement is the same for the DBMSs covered in this book.

To create an index:

- Type:

  ```
  CREATE [UNIQUE] INDEX index
    ON table (index_columns);
  ```

  index is the name of the index to create and is a valid SQL identifier. Index names must be unique within a table. For **Oracle**, **Db2**, and **PostgreSQL**, index names must be unique within a database.

  table is the name of the table to create the index for, and *index_columns* is a list of one or more comma-separated names of the columns to index.

  Specify UNIQUE to create a unique index. UNIQUE causes the DBMS to check for duplicates in *index_columns*. If *table* already contains rows with duplicates in *index_columns*, then the DBMS won't create the index. If you attempt to INSERT or UPDATE duplicate values in unique *index_columns*, the DBMS generates an error and cancels the operation.

  Listing 12.1 creates a simple index named *pub_id_idx* on the column *pub_id* for the table *titles*. *pub_id* is a foreign key and is a good candidate for an index because:

- Changes to PRIMARY KEY constraints are checked with FOREIGN KEY constraints in related tables.

- Foreign-key columns often are used in join criteria when the data from related tables are combined in queries by matching the FOREIGN KEY column(s) of one table with the PRIMARY KEY or UNIQUE column(s) in the other table.

```
CREATE INDEX pub_id_idx
  ON titles (pub_id);
```

Listing 12.1 Create a simple index on the column *pub_id* for the table *titles*.

```
CREATE UNIQUE INDEX title_name_idx
  ON titles (title_name);
```

Listing 12.2 Create a simple unique index on the column *title_name* for the table *titles*.

```
CREATE INDEX state_city_idx
  ON authors (state, city);
```

Listing 12.3 Create a composite index on the columns *state* and *city* for the table authors.

Listing 12.2 creates a simple unique index named *title_name_idx* on the column *title_name* for the table *titles*. The DBMS will create this index only if no duplicates already exist in the column *title_name*. This index also prohibits nondistinct title names from being INSERTed or UPDATEd in *titles*.

Listing 12.3 creates a composite index named *state_city_idx* on the columns *state* and *city* for the table *authors*. The DBMS uses this index when you sort rows in *state* plus *city* order. This index is useless for sorts and searches on *state* alone, *city* alone, or *city* plus *state*; you must create separate indexes for those purposes.

Tips for CREATE INDEX

- Don't use the terms *index* and *key* interchangeably. An index is a *physical* (hardware-related) mechanism that the DBMS uses to improve performance. A key is a *logical* (based on data) concept that the DBMS uses to enforce referential integrity and update through views.

- You also can use a unique constraint to prevent duplicate column values; see "Forcing Unique Values with UNIQUE" on page 345.

- Indexes are files stored on-drive and so occupy storage space (possibly a lot of space). But when used properly, indexes are the primary means of reducing drive wear by obviating the need to read large tables sequentially. While a DBMS is creating an index, it uses as much as 1.5 times the space that the associated table occupies (make sure you have room). Most of that space is released after the index is complete.

- Searching a table sequentially (for lack of an index) is called a **table scan**.

- A **clustered index**, or clustering index, is an index in which the logical order of the key values determines the physical order of the corresponding rows in a table. In a **nonclustered index**, the index's logical order differs from the physical, stored order of the on-drive rows. A table can have at most one clustered index. Clustered indexes usually improve performance, but in some cases they make searches much faster but INSERTs, UPDATEs, and DELETEs much slower.

- Most indexes are implemented as **balanced trees**, or **B-trees**. A B-tree is an advanced data structure that minimizes drive read/write operations. Some DBMSs let you specify the data structure to use when constructing an index.

- DBMS **Microsoft SQL Server** and **Db2** consider multiple nulls to be duplicates when UNIQUE is specified and allow no more than one null in columns with a unique index. **Microsoft Access**, **Oracle**, **MySQL**, and **PostgreSQL** allow multiple nulls in such columns.

Some DBMSs let you create indexes on views (Chapter 13) as well as tables.

Dropping an Index with DROP INDEX

Use the DROP INDEX statement to destroy an index. Because an index is logically and physically independent of the data in its associated table, you can drop the index at any time without affecting the table (or other indexes). All SQL programs and other applications will continue to work if you drop an index, but access to previously indexed data will be slower.

The usual reasons for dropping an index are:

- The index is no longer needed because the associated table is much smaller (or was dropped), or users don't access the index's columns much anymore.

- The extra time it takes the DBMS to maintain the index after INSERT, UPDATE, or DELETE operations outweighs the speed improvement in retrieval operations that the index provides.

DBMS | The SQL standard omits indexes, so index-related SQL statements vary by DBMS. This section describes how to drop an index for each DBMS covered in this book. If you're using a different DBMS, then search the documentation for *index* to learn how to drop an index.

In **Oracle**, **Db2**, and **PostgreSQL**, index names must be unique within a database, so you don't specify a table name when you drop an index. In **Microsoft Access**, **Microsoft SQL Server**, and **MySQL**, index names must be unique within a table but can be reused in other tables, so you must specify a table along with the index to be dropped. The examples in this section drop the index created by Listing 12.1 in the preceding section.

Tips for DROP INDEX

- You can't drop indexes that the DBMS creates automatically for PRIMARY KEY and UNIQUE constraints (Chapter 11).

To drop an index in Microsoft Access or MySQL:

- Type:

  ```
  DROP INDEX index
    ON table;
  ```

  index is the name of the index to drop, and *table* is the name of the index's associated table (Listing 12.4a).

To drop an index in Microsoft SQL Server:

- Type:

  ```
  DROP INDEX table.index;
  ```

  index is the name of the index to drop, and *table* is the name of the index's associated table (Listing 12.4b).

To drop an index in Oracle Database, IBM Db2 Database, or PostgreSQL:

- Type:

  ```
  DROP INDEX index;
  ```

  index is the name of the index to drop (Listing 12.4c).

```
DROP INDEX pub_id_idx
  ON titles;
```

Listing 12.4a Drop the index *pub_id_idx* (Microsoft Access or MySQL).

```
DROP INDEX titles.pub_id_idx;
```

Listing 12.4b Drop the index *pub_id_idx* (Microsoft SQL Server).

```
DROP INDEX pub_id_idx;
```

Listing 12.4c Drop the index *pub_id_idx* (Oracle, Db2, or PostgreSQL).

CHAPTER 13

Views

A **view** is a stored SELECT statement that returns a table whose data are derived from one or more other tables (called **underlying tables**). Some important characteristics of a view are:

- A view's underlying tables can be base tables, temporary tables, or other views.

- A view is called a **virtual table** or **derived table** to distinguish it from a base or temporary table.

- The DBMS stores a view as *only* a SELECT statement, *not* as a set of data values, thus preventing data redundancy.

- A view materializes dynamically as a physical table when referenced by name in an SQL statement. It exists only for the duration of the statement and vanishes when the statement finishes.

- A view is a set of named columns and rows of data, so you can use it almost anywhere you'd use a real table.

- You have no restrictions on querying (SELECTing) through views. In some cases, views can be updated, causing the data changes to be passed through to the underlying base tables.

- Because of closure, a view always is a single table no matter how many underlying tables it references or how those tables are combined; see "Tips for Tables, Columns, and Rows" on page 24.

Creating a View with CREATE VIEW

Think of a view as being a tailored presentation that provides a tabular window into one or more base tables. The window can display an entire base table, part of a base table, or a combination of base tables (or parts thereof). A view also can reflect the data in base tables through other views—windows into windows. Generally, SQL programmers use views to present data to end-users in database applications. Views offer these advantages:

Simplified data access. Views hide data complexity and simplify statements, so users can perform operations on a view more easily than on the base tables directly. If you create a complex view—one that involves, say, multiple base tables, joins, and subqueries—then users can query this view without having to understand complex relational concepts or even knowing that multiple tables are involved.

Automatic updating. When a base table is updated, all views that reference the table reflect the change automatically. If you insert a row representing a new author into the table *authors*, for example, then all views defined over *authors* will reflect the new author automatically. This scheme saves storage space and prevents redundancy because, without views, the DBMS would have to store derived data to keep it synchronized.

Increased security. One of the most common uses of views is to hide data from users by filtering the underlying tables. Suppose that the table *employees* contains the columns *salary* and *commission*. If you create a view on *employees* that omits these two columns but contains other innocuous columns (such as *email_address*), then the database administrator can grant users permission to see the view but not see the underlying table, thereby hiding compensation data from the curious.

Logical data independence. Base tables provide a **real view** of a database. But when you use SQL to build a database application, you want to present end users not the real view, but a **virtual view** specific to the application. The virtual view hides the parts of the database (entire tables or specific rows or columns) that aren't relevant to the application. Thus, users interact with the virtual view, which is derived from—although independent of—the real view presented by the base tables.

A virtual view immunizes an application from logical changes in the design of the database. Suppose that many applications access the table *titles*. Books go out of print over time, so the database designer decides to reduce the system load by segregating out-of-print books. He splits *titles* into two tables: *in_print_titles* and *out_of_print_titles*. Consequently, all the applications break because they expect the now-unavailable table *titles*.

But if those applications had accessed a *view* of *titles* instead of the real table, then that view could be redefined to be the UNION of *in_print_titles* and *out_of_print_titles* (see "Combining Rows with UNION" on page 290). The applications transparently would see the two new tables as though they were the one original table and continue to work as though the split never happened. (You can't use views to immunize an application against *all* changes, however. Views can't compensate for dropped tables or columns, for example.)

When you're creating a view, some important considerations are:

- View-related SQL statements modify database objects and data, so your database administrator might need to grant you permission to run them.

- View names follow the same rules that table names do.

- View names must be unique within a database (or schema). They can't have the same name as any other table or view.

- The columns in a view inherit the default column names from the underlying tables. You can give view columns different names by using AS; see "Creating Column Aliases with AS" on page 79.

- You must specify a new name for a column in a view that would have the same name as another column in the view (usually because the view definition includes a join and the columns from two or more different underlying tables have the same name).

- A column defined in a view can be a simple column reference, a literal, or an expression that involves calculations or aggregate functions.

- In some DBMSs, you must specify explicitly the name of a column in a view if the column is derived from an arithmetic expression, a built-in function, or a literal.

- A view column inherits the data type of the column or expression from which it is derived.

- You have no practical limit on the number of views that you can create. Generally, you want to create views on subsets of data that are of interest to many users.

- Some DBMSs don't allow views on temporary tables.

- Almost any valid SELECT statement can define a view, although an ORDER BY clause usually is prohibited.

- You can nest views—that is, a view's SELECT statement can retrieve data from another view. Nested views eventually must resolve to base tables (otherwise, you'd be viewing nothing). The maximum number of nesting levels varies by DBMS.

- You can use views as a convenience to save complex queries. By saving a query that performs extensive calculations as a view, you can recalculate each time the view is queried.

- A view can express a query that you'd otherwise be unable to run. You can define a view that joins a GROUP BY view with a base table, for example, or define a view that joins a UNION view with a base table.

- A view definition can't reference itself because it doesn't exist yet.

- Views can display data formatted differently from those in the underlying tables.

- Unlike a base table, a view doesn't support constraints. Some DBMSs let you index views.

- When you define a view by using SELECT *, SQL converts the * to a list of all columns internally. This conversion occurs only once, at view creation (not at execution), so the definition of your view won't change if someone adds a column to an underlying table (by using ALTER TABLE).

- Because views store no data, the DBMS must execute them every time they're referenced. Complex views—particularly nested views—can degrade performance seriously.

To create a view:

- Type:

  ```
  CREATE VIEW view [(view_columns)]
    AS select_query;
  ```

  view is the name of the view to create. The view name must be unique within the database.

  view_columns is an optional, parenthesized list of one or more comma-separated names to be used for the columns in *view*. The number of columns in *view_columns* must match the number of columns in the SELECT clause of *select_query*. (If you name one column this way, then you must name them all this way.) Specify *view_columns* when a column in *select_query* is derived from an arithmetic expression, a function, or a literal; when two or more view columns would otherwise have the same name (usually because of a join); or to give a column in view a name different from that of the column from which it was derived. If *view_columns* is omitted, then *view* inherits column names from *select_query*. Column names also can be assigned in *select_query* via AS clauses. Each column name must be unique within the view.

  select_query is a SELECT query that identifies the columns and rows of the table(s) that the view is based on. *select_query* can be arbitrarily complex and use more than one table or other views. An ORDER BY clause usually is prohibited. For information about the SELECT statement, see Chapters 4 through 9. For DBMS-specific restrictions on SELECT in views, search your DBMS's documentation for *CREATE VIEW* (Listings 13.1 through 13.5).

```
CREATE VIEW au_names
  AS
  SELECT au_id, au_fname, au_lname
    FROM authors;
```

Listing 13.1 Create a view that hides the authors' personal information (telephone numbers and addresses).

```
CREATE VIEW cities
  (au_id, au_city, pub_id, pub_city)
  AS
  SELECT a.au_id, a.city, p.pub_id, p.city
    FROM authors a
    INNER JOIN publishers p
      ON a.city = p.city;
```

Listing 13.2 Create a view that lists the authors who live in a city in which a publisher is located. Note that I use the column names *au_city* and *pub_city* in the view. Renaming these columns resolves the ambiguity that would arise if both columns inherited the same column name *city* from the underlying tables.

```
CREATE VIEW revenues
  (Publisher, BookType, Revenue)
  AS
  SELECT pub_id, type, SUM(price * sales)
    FROM titles
    GROUP BY pub_id, type;
```

Listing 13.3 Create a view that lists total revenue (= price × sales) grouped by book type within publisher. This view will be easy to query later because I name the result of an arithmetic expression explicitly rather than let the DBMS assign a default name.

```
CREATE VIEW mailing_labels
  AS
  SELECT
    TRIM(au_fname || ' ' || au_lname)
      AS "address1",
    TRIM(address)
      AS "address2",
    TRIM(city) || ', ' || TRIM(state) || ' ' ||
        TRIM(zip)
      AS "address3"
    FROM authors;
```

Listing 13.4 Create a view that makes it easy to print mailing labels for authors. Note that I assigned column names in the SELECT clause rather than in the CREATE VIEW clause.

```
CREATE VIEW au_titles (LastName, Title)
  AS
  SELECT an.au_lname, t.title_name
    FROM title_authors ta
    INNER JOIN au_names an
      ON ta.au_id = an.au_id
    INNER JOIN titles t
      ON t.title_id = ta.title_id
    WHERE an.au_id in ('A02','A05');
```

Listing 13.5 Create a view that lists the last names of authors A02 and A05, and the books that each one wrote (or cowrote). Note that this statement uses a nested view: it references the view *au_names* created by Listing 13.1.

Tips for CREATE VIEW

- You can't create temporary views. Views and temporary tables differ in their persistence. A view exists for the duration of an SQL statement; a temporary table exists for the duration of a session. See "Creating a Temporary Table with CREATE TEMPORARY TABLE" on page 352.

- Standard SQL has no ALTER VIEW statement. If the underlying table(s) or view(s) have changed since a view was created, then drop and re-create the view. **Microsoft SQL Server**, **Oracle**, **Db2**, **MySQL**, and **PostgreSQL**, however, support a nonstandard ALTER VIEW statement.

continues on next page

-

  DBMS When you run a CREATE VIEW statement in **Microsoft Access**, the view appears as a query object in the Database window. To run Listing 13.4, change every occurrence of ‖ to +; see the DBMS tip in "Tips for Concatenating Strings" on page 123. To run Listing 13.5, type:

```
CREATE VIEW au_titles
  (LastName, Title)
  AS
  SELECT an.au_lname, t.title_name
    FROM au_names an
    INNER JOIN (titles t
      INNER JOIN title_authors ta
        ON t.title_id = ta.title_id)
      ON an.au_id = ta.au_id
      WHERE an.au_id IN ('A02','A05');
```

To run Listings 13.1 through 13.5 in **Microsoft SQL Server**, remove the terminating semicolon from each statement. Additionally, to run Listing 13.4, change every occurrence of ‖ to + and every occurrence of TRIM(x) to LTRIM(RTRIM(x)); see the DBMS tips in "Tips for Concatenating Strings" on page 123 and "Tips for Trimming Characters" on page 133.

To run Listings 13.2 and 13.5 in **Oracle** 8i and earlier, use WHERE syntax instead of JOIN syntax. Type (Listing 13.2):

```
CREATE VIEW cities
  (au_id, au_city, pub_id, pub_city)
  AS
  SELECT a.au_id, a.city, p.pub_id, p.city
    FROM authors a, publishers p
    WHERE a.city = p.city;
```

and (Listing 13.5):

```
CREATE VIEW au_titles
  (LastName, Title)
  AS
  SELECT an.au_lname, t.title_name
    FROM title_authors ta,
      au_names an, titles t
    WHERE ta.au_id = an.au_id
      AND t.title_id = ta.title_id
      AND an.au_id in ('A02','A05');
```

To run Listing 13.4 in **Db2**, change every occurrence of TRIM(x) to LTRIM(RTRIM(x)); see the DBMS tip in "Tips for Trimming Characters" on page 133.

To run Listing 13.4 in **MySQL**, use the function CONCAT() instead of the concatenation operator ‖; see the DBMS tip in "Tips for Concatenating Strings" on page 123. MySQL 5.0 and later support views. Earlier versions won't run the listings in this section. (To hide data in earlier versions, use MySQL's privilege system to restrict column access.)

In **Microsoft SQL Server**, **Oracle**, **Db2**, **MySQL**, and **PostgreSQL**, you can add the optional clause WITH [CASCADED | LOCAL] CHECK OPTION when you create a view. This clause applies to only updateable views and ensures that only data that can be read by the view can be inserted, updated, or deleted; see "Updating Data Through a View" later in this chapter. If a view shows authors from only New York state, for example, then it would be impossible to insert, update, or delete non–New York authors through that view. The CASCADED and LOCAL options apply to nested views only. CASCADED performs the check for the current view and all the views it references. LOCAL performs the check for the current view only.

Retrieving Data Through a View

Creating a view displays nothing. All that CREATE VIEW does is cause the DBMS to save the view as a named SELECT statement. To see data through a view, query the view by using SELECT, just as you would query a table. You can:

- Rearrange the order of the displayed columns with the SELECT clause

- Use operators and functions to perform calculations

- Change column headings with AS

- Filter rows with WHERE

- Group rows with GROUP BY

- Filter grouped rows with HAVING

- Join the view to other views, tables, and temporary tables with JOIN

- Sort the result with ORDER BY

To retrieve data through a view:

- Type:

```
SELECT columns
  FROM view
  [JOIN joins]
  [WHERE search_condition]
  [GROUP BY group_columns]
  [HAVING search_condition]
  [ORDER BY sort_columns];
```

view is the name of the view to query. The clauses work with views the same way that they work with tables, as described in Chapters 4 through 9.

Listings 13.6 through 13.11 and Figures 13.1 through 13.6 show how to retrieve data through the views created by Listings 13.1 through 13.5 in "Creating a View with CREATE VIEW" earlier in this chapter.

Tips for Retrieving Data Through Views

- **DBMS** To run Listing 13.9 in **Microsoft Access**, enclose the view's column names in double quotes and brackets:

```
SELECT ["address3"]
  FROM mailing_labels
  WHERE ["address1"] LIKE '%Kell%';
```

To run Listing 13.9 in **Oracle** and **Db2**, enclose the view's column names in double quotes:

```
SELECT "address3"
  FROM mailing_labels
  WHERE "address1" LIKE '%Kell%';
```

MySQL 5.0 and later support views. Earlier versions won't run the listings in this section.

```
SELECT *
  FROM au_titles;
```

Listing 13.6 List all the rows and columns of the view *au_titles*. See Figure 13.1 for the result.

```
LastName   Title
---------  -----------------------------
Kells      Ask Your System Administrator
Heydemark  How About Never?
Heydemark  I Blame My Mother
Heydemark  Not Without My Faberge Egg
Heydemark  Spontaneous, Not Annoying
```

Figure 13.1 Result of Listing 13.6.

```
SELECT DISTINCT au_city
  FROM cities;
```

Listing 13.7 List the distinct cities in the view *cities*. See Figure 13.2 for the result.

```
au_city
-------------
New York
San Francisco
```

Figure 13.2 Result of Listing 13.7.

```
SELECT BookType,
    AVG(Revenue) AS "AVG(Revenue)"
  FROM revenues
  GROUP BY BookType
  HAVING AVG(Revenue) > 1000000;
```

Listing 13.8 List the types of books whose average revenue exceeds $1 million. See Figure 13.3 for the result.

```
BookType   AVG(Revenue)
--------- ------------
biography 18727318.50
computer   1025396.65
psychology 2320933.76
```

Figure 13.3 Result of Listing 13.8.

```
SELECT address3
  FROM mailing_labels
  WHERE address1 LIKE '%Kell%';
```

Listing 13.9 List the third line of the mailing address of each author whose name contains the string *Kell*. See Figure 13.4 for the result.

```
address3
-------------------
New York, NY 10014
Palo Alto, CA 94305
```

Figure 13.4 Result of Listing 13.9.

```
SELECT DISTINCT an.au_fname, an.au_lname
  FROM au_names an
  INNER JOIN title_authors ta
    ON an.au_id = ta.au_id
  WHERE ta.au_order > 1;
```

Listing 13.10 List the name of each author who wasn't the lead author of at least one book. See Figure 13.5 for the result.

```
au_fname au_lname
-------- --------
Hallie   Hull
Klee     Hull
```

Figure 13.5 Result of Listing 13.10.

```
SELECT au_fname, au_lname
  FROM au_names
  WHERE state = 'CA';
```

Listing 13.11 List the names of the authors from California. See Figure 13.6 for the result.

```
ERROR: Invalid column name 'state'.
```

Figure 13.6 Result of Listing 13.11. The view *au_names* references *authors* but hides the column *state*, so referring to *state* through the view causes an error.

Updating Data Through a View

An **updateable view** is a view to which you can apply INSERT, UPDATE, and DELETE operations to modify data in the underlying table(s). Any changes made in an updateable view always pass through to the base table(s) unambiguously. The syntax for the INSERT, UPDATE, and DELETE statements is the same for views as it is for tables; see Chapter 10.

A **nonupdateable view** (or **read-only view**) view is one that doesn't support INSERT, UPDATE, and DELETE operations because changes would be ambiguous. To change the data that appear in a read-only view, you must change the underlying table(s) directly (or through another, nonambiguous view).

Each row in an updateable view is associated with exactly one row in an underlying base table. A view isn't updateable if its SELECT statement uses GROUP BY, HAVING, DISTINCT, or aggregate functions, for example.

The SQL-92 standard said that an updateable view must be defined over only one table, which is stringent but very safe. The SQL:1999 standard relaxed that restriction because many more types of updateable views exist. By the time that standard was released, the DBMS vendors already offered an expanded set of updateable views. Single-table views always are updateable. DBMSs also examine the underlying tables' joins and referential-integrity constraints of a multitable view to determine whether the view is updateable. Here are some of the types of queries that can define updateable views:

- One-to-one inner joins
- One-to-one outer joins
- One-to-many inner joins
- One-to-many outer joins
- Many-to-many joins
- UNION and EXCEPT queries

The examples in this section use updateable views that reference only one underlying table. See your DBMS documentation to find out which multitable views you can update and how those updates affect each base table.

```
CREATE VIEW ny_authors
  AS
  SELECT au_id, au_fname, au_lname, state
    FROM authors
    WHERE state = 'NY';

SELECT *
  FROM ny_authors;
```

Listing 13.12 Create and display the view *ny_authors*, which lists the IDs, names, and states of only those authors from New York state. See Figure 13.7 for the result.

```
au_id au_fname  au_lname state
----- --------- -------- -----
A01   Sarah     Buchman  NY
A05   Christian Kells    NY
```

Figure 13.7 Result of Listing 13.12: the view *ny_authors*.

```
INSERT INTO ny_authors
  VALUES('A08','Don','Dawson','NY');
```

Listing 13.13 Insert a new row through the view *ny_authors*.

```
INSERT INTO ny_authors
  VALUES('A09','Jill','LeFlore','CA');
```

Listing 13.14 Insert a new row through the view *ny_authors*. The DBMS would cancel this insertion if WITH CHECK OPTION had been used when *ny_authors* was created.

Inserting a Row Through a View

Consider the view *ny_authors*, which consists of the IDs, names, and states of only those authors from New York State (Listing 13.12 and Figure 13.7). *ny_authors* references only the base table *authors*.

Listing 13.13 inserts a new row through a view. The DBMS inserts a new row into the table *authors*. The row contains A08 in the column *au_id*, Don in *au_fname*, Dawson in *au_lname*, and NY in *state*. The other columns in the row—*phone*, *address*, *city*, and *zip*—are set to null (or their default values, if DEFAULT constraints exist).

Listing 13.14, like Listing 13.13, inserts a new row through a view. But this time, the new author is from California, not New York, which violates the WHERE condition in the view's definition. Does the DBMS insert the row or cancel the operation? The answer depends on how the view was created. In this particular example, the insertion is allowed because the CREATE VIEW statement (see Listing 13.12) lacks a WITH CHECK OPTION clause, so the DBMS isn't forced to maintain consistency with the view's original definition. For information about WITH CHECK OPTION, see the DBMS tip in "Tips for CREATE VIEW" earlier in this chapter. The DBMS would have canceled the insertion if *ny_authors* were defined as:

```
CREATE VIEW ny_authors AS
  SELECT au_id, au_fname, au_lname, state
    FROM authors
    WHERE state = 'NY'
  WITH CHECK OPTION;
```

Updating a Row Through a View

Listing 13.15 updates an existing row through a view. The DBMS updates the row for author A01 in the table authors by changing the author's name from Sarah Buchman to Yasmin Howcomely. The values in the other columns in the row—*au_id*, *phone*, *address*, *city*, *state*, and *zip*—don't change.

But suppose that Listing 13.15 looked like this:

```
UPDATE ny_authors
  SET au_fname = 'Yasmin',
      au_lname = 'Howcomely',
      state = 'CA'
  WHERE au_id = 'A01';
```

This statement presents the same problem as Listing 13.14: the desired change would cause Yasmin's row to no longer meet the conditions for membership in the view. Again, the DBMS will accept or reject the UPDATE depending on whether the WITH CHECK OPTION clause was specified when the view was created. If WITH CHECK OPTION is used, then rows can't be modified in a way that causes them to disappear from the view.

```
UPDATE ny_authors
  SET au_fname = 'Yasmin',
      au_lname = 'Howcomely'
  WHERE au_id = 'A01';
```

Listing 13.15 Update an existing row through the view *ny_authors*.

```
DELETE FROM ny_authors
  WHERE au_id = 'A05';
```

Listing 13.16 Delete a row through the view *ny_authors*.

Deleting a Row Through a View

Listing 13.16 deletes a row through a view. The DBMS deletes the row for author A05 in the table *authors*. (Every column in the row is deleted, not just those in the view.) In turn, the row disappears from the view *ny_authors*.

View updates can have integrity repercussions, of course. The DBMS will disallow a deletion if removing a row violates a referential-integrity constraint; see "Specifying a Foreign Key with FOREIGN KEY" on page 339. If you delete a row, then all the underlying FOREIGN KEY constraints in related tables must still be satisfied for the deletion to succeed. Some updating can be handled by the CASCADE option (if specified) of a FOREIGN KEY constraint, not by the view definition.

In Listing 13.16, for example, the DBMS will cancel the DELETE if I don't first change or delete the foreign-key values in the table *title_authors* that point to author A05 in *authors*.

Tips for Updating Data Through a View

- An updateable view must contain a key of the base table to ensure that each view row maps back to only one row in the base table.

- Any column excluded from an updateable view must be nullable or have a DEFAULT constraint in the base table, so that the DBMS can construct the entire row for insertion.

- Updated values must adhere to the base table's column restrictions, such as data type, nullability, and other constraints.

- Some arithmetically derived columns are (theoretically) updateable. In a view with the derived column *bonus = 0.1 * salary*, for example, you'd expect to be able to update bonus and have SQL apply the inverse function (*bonus/0.1*) to update *salary* in the base table. Sadly, SQL won't back-propagate updates in derived columns.

- For complex updateable views, one type of operation can involve other types. A view UPDATE, for example, might involve INSERTing new base rows.

- **DBMS** To run Listing 13.12 in **Microsoft SQL Server**, omit the terminating semicolon from the CREATE VIEW statement and run the two statements separately.

  MySQL 5.0 and later support views. Earlier versions won't run the listings in this section.

  In **PostgreSQL**, simple views are automatically updatable. For complex views, you can create the effect of an updateable view by creating TRIGGERs or RULEs for INSERTs, UPDATEs, and DELETEs. Search PostgreSQL documentation for *CREATE VIEW*.

  For **all DBMSs**, check the documentation to see how your DBMS handles updateable views for columns whose data type generates a unique row identifier automatically; see "Unique Identifiers" on page 70.

Dropping a View with DROP VIEW

Use the DROP VIEW statement to destroy a view. Because a view is physically independent of its underlying table(s), you can drop the view at any time without affecting those table(s). All SQL programs, applications, and other views that reference the dropped view will break, however.

To drop a view:

- Type:

  DROP VIEW *view*;

  view is the name of the view to drop (Listing 13.17).

Tips for DROP VIEW

- Dropping a table doesn't drop the views that reference that table, so you must drop the views with DROP VIEW explicitly; see "Dropping a Table with DROP TABLE" on page 362.

- DBMS MySQL 5.0 and later support views. Earlier versions won't run the listing in this section.

```
DROP VIEW ny_authors;
```

Listing 13.17 Drop the view *ny_authors*.

CHAPTER 14

Transactions

```
UPDATE savings_accounts
  SET balance = balance - 500.00
  WHERE account_number = 208998628;

UPDATE checking_accounts
  SET balance = balance + 500.00
  WHERE account_number = 786783165;
```

Figure 14.1 Two SQL statements are needed when a banking customer transfers money from savings to checking.

A **transaction** is a sequence of one or more SQL statements executed as a single logical unit of work. The DBMS considers a transaction to be an indivisible, all-or-nothing proposition: it executes all the transaction's statements as a group, or it executes none of them.

For example, suppose that a bank customer transfers $500 from her savings account to her checking account. This operation consists of two separate actions, executed sequentially:

1. Decrement savings balance by $500.

2. Increment checking balance by $500.

Figure 14.1 shows the two SQL statements for this transaction. Now imagine that the DBMS fails—power outage, system crash, hardware problem—after it executes the first statement but before the second. The accounts would be out of balance without your knowledge. Accusations of malfeasance and prison time would soon follow.

To avoid legal problems, use a transaction to guarantee that both SQL statements are performed to maintain the accounts in proper balance. When something prevents one of the statements in a transaction from executing, the DBMS undoes (rolls back) the other statements of the transaction. If no error occurs, then the changes are made permanent (committed).

Executing a Transaction

To learn how transactions work, you need to learn a few terms:

Commit. Committing a transaction makes all data modifications performed since the start of the transaction a permanent part of the database. After a transaction is committed, all changes made by the transaction become visible to other users and are guaranteed to be permanent if a crash or other failure occurs.

Roll back. Rolling back a transaction retracts any of the changes resulting from the SQL statements in the transaction. After a transaction is rolled back, the affected data are left unchanged, as though the SQL statements in the transaction were never executed.

Transaction log. The **transaction log file**, or just **log**, is a serial record of all modifications that have occurred in a database via transactions. The transaction log records the start of each transaction, the changes to the data, and enough information to undo or redo the changes made by the transaction (if necessary later). The log grows continually as transactions occur in the database.

Although it's the DBMS's responsibility to ensure the *physical* integrity of each transaction, it's your responsibility to start and end transactions at points that enforce the *logical* consistency of the data, according to the rules of your organization or business. A transaction should contain only the SQL statements necessary to make a consistent change—no more and no fewer. Data in all referenced tables must be in a consistent state before the transaction begins and after it ends.

When you're designing and executing transactions, some important considerations are:

- Transaction-related SQL statements modify data, so your database administrator might need to grant you permission to run them.

- Transaction processing applies to statements that change data or database objects (INSERT, UPDATE, DELETE, CREATE, ALTER, DROP—the list varies by DBMS). For production databases, every such statement should be executed as part of a transaction.

- A committed transaction is said to be **durable**, meaning that its changes remain in place permanently, persisting even if the system fails.

- A DBMS's data-recovery mechanism depends on transactions. When the DBMS is brought back online following a failure, the DBMS checks its transaction log to see whether all transactions were committed to the database. If it finds uncommitted (partially executed) transactions, then it rolls them back based on the log. You must resubmit the rolled-back transactions (although some DBMSs can complete unfinished transactions automatically).

- A DBMS's backup/restore facility depends on transactions. The backup facility takes regular snapshots of the database and stores them with (subsequent) transaction logs on a backup drive.

Suppose that a crash damages a production drive in a way that renders the data and transaction log unreadable. You can invoke the restore facility, which will use the most recent database backup and then execute, or **roll forward**, all *committed* transactions in the log from the time the snapshot was taken to the last transaction preceding the failure. This restore operation brings the database to its correct state before the crash. (Again, you'll have to resubmit uncommitted transactions.)

- For obvious reasons, you should store a database and its transaction log on separate physical drives.

Concurrency Control

To humans, computers appear to carry out two or more processes at the same time. In reality, computer operations occur not concurrently, but in sequence. The illusion of simultaneity appears because a microprocessor works with much smaller time slices than people can perceive. In a DBMS, **concurrency control** is a group of strategies that prevents loss of data integrity caused by interference between two or more users trying to access or change the same data simultaneously.

DBMSs use locking strategies to ensure transactional integrity and database consistency. **Locking** restricts data access during read and write operations; thus, it prevents users from reading data that are being changed by other users and prevents multiple users from changing the same data at the same time. Without locking, data can become logically incorrect, and statements executed against those data can return unexpected results. Occasionally you'll end up in a **deadlock**, where you and another user, each having locked a piece of data needed for the other's transaction, attempt to get a lock on each other's piece. Most DBMSs can detect and resolve deadlocks by rolling back one user's transaction so that the other can proceed (otherwise, you'd both wait forever for the other to release the lock). Locking mechanisms are very sophisticated; search your DBMS documentation for *locking*.

Concurrency transparency is the appearance from a transaction's perspective that it's the only transaction operating on the database. A DBMS isolates a transaction's changes from changes made by any other concurrent transactions. Consequently, a transaction never sees data in an intermediate state; either it sees data in the state they were in before another concurrent transaction changed them, or it sees the data after the other transaction has completed. Isolated transactions let you reload starting data and replay (roll forward) a series of transactions to end up with the data in the same state they were in after the original transactions were executed.

For a transaction to be executed in all-or-nothing fashion, the transaction's boundaries (starting and ending points) must be clear. These boundaries let the DBMS execute the statements as one atomic unit of work. A transaction can start **implicitly** with the first executable SQL statement or **explicitly** with the START TRANSACTION statement. A transaction ends explicitly with a COMMIT or ROLLBACK statement (it never ends implicitly). You can't roll back a transaction after you commit it.

DBMS Oracle and **Db2** transactions always start implicitly, so those DBMSs have no statement that marks the start of a transaction. In **Microsoft Access**, **Microsoft SQL Server**, **MySQL**, and **PostgreSQL**, you can (or must) start a transaction explicitly by using the BEGIN statement. The SQL:1999 standard introduced the START TRANSACTION statement—long after these DBMSs already were using BEGIN to start transactions, so the extended BEGIN syntax varies by DBMS. **MySQL** and **PostgreSQL** support START TRANSACTION (as a synonym for BEGIN).

To start a transaction explicitly:

- In **Microsoft Access** or **Microsoft SQL Server**, type:

  ```
  BEGIN TRANSACTION;
  ```

  or

  In **MySQL** or **PostgreSQL**, type:

  ```
  START TRANSACTION;
  ```

To commit a transaction:

- Type:

  ```
  COMMIT;
  ```

To roll back a transaction:

- Type:

  ```
  ROLLBACK;
  ```

The SELECT statements in Listing 14.1 show that the UPDATE operations are performed by the DBMS and then undone by a ROLLBACK statement. See Figure 14.2 for the result.

```
SELECT SUM(pages), AVG(price) FROM titles;

BEGIN TRANSACTION;
  UPDATE titles SET pages = 0;
  UPDATE titles SET price = price * 2;
  SELECT SUM(pages), AVG(price) FROM titles;
ROLLBACK;

SELECT SUM(pages), AVG(price) FROM titles;
```

Listing 14.1 Within a transaction block, UPDATE operations (like INSERT and DELETE operations) are never final. See Figure 14.2 for the result.

```
SUM(pages) AVG(price)
---------- ----------
      5107    18.3875

SUM(pages) AVG(price)
---------- ----------
         0    36.7750

SUM(pages) AVG(price)
---------- ----------
      5107    18.3875
```

Figure 14.2 Result of Listing 14.1. The results of the SELECT statements show that the DBMS cancelled the transaction.

```
BEGIN TRANSACTION;

  DELETE FROM title_authors
    WHERE title_id IN
      (SELECT title_id
         FROM titles
         WHERE pub_id = 'P04');

  DELETE FROM royalties
    WHERE title_id IN
      (SELECT title_id
         FROM titles
         WHERE pub_id = 'P04');

  DELETE FROM titles
    WHERE pub_id = 'P04';

  DELETE FROM publishers
    WHERE pub_id = 'P04';

COMMIT;
```

Listing 14.2 Use a transaction to delete publisher P04 from the table *publishers* and delete P04's related rows in other tables.

Listing 14.2 shows a more practical example of a transaction. I want to delete the publisher P04 from the table *publishers* without generating a referential-integrity error. Because some of the foreign-key values in *titles* point to publisher P04 in *publishers*, I first need to delete the related rows from the tables *titles*, *titles_authors*, and *royalties*. I use a transaction to be certain that *all* the DELETE statements are executed. If only some of the statements were successful, then the data would be left inconsistent. (For information about referential-integrity checks, see "Specifying a Foreign Key with FOREIGN KEY" on page 339.)

ACID

ACID is an acronym that summarizes the properties of a transaction:

Atomicity. Either all of a transaction's data modifications are performed, or none of them are.

Consistency. A completed transaction leaves all data in a consistent state that maintains all data integrity. A consistent state satisfies all defined database constraints. (Note that consistency isn't necessarily preserved at any intermediate point *within* a transaction.)

Isolation. A transaction's effects are isolated (or concealed) from those of all other transactions. See "Concurrency Control" on page 385.

Durability. After a transaction completes, its effects are permanent and persist even if the system fails.

Transaction theory is a big topic, separate from the relational model. A good (if sometimes dated) reference is *Transaction Processing: Concepts and Techniques* by Jim Gray and Andreas Reuter.

Tips for Transactions

- Don't forget to end transactions explicitly with either COMMIT or ROLLBACK. A missing endpoint could lead to huge transactions with unpredictable results on the data or, on abnormal program termination, rollback of the last uncommitted transaction. Keep your transactions as small as possible because they can lock rows, entire tables, indexes, and other resources for their duration. COMMIT or ROLLBACK releases the resources for other transactions.

- You can nest transactions. The maximum number of nesting levels depends on the DBMS.

- It's faster to UPDATE multiple columns with a single SET clause than to use multiple UPDATEs. For example, the query

```
UPDATE mytable
  SET col1 = 1
      col2 = 2
      col3 = 3
  WHERE col1 <> 1
     OR col2 <> 2
     OR col3 <> 3;
```

is better than three UPDATE statements because it decreases logging (although it increases locking).

- By default, DBMSs run in **autocommit mode** unless overridden by either explicit or implicit transactions (or turned off with a system setting). In this mode, each statement is executed as its own transaction. If a statement completes successfully, then the DBMS commits it; if the DBMS encounters any error, then it rolls back the statement.

- For long transactions, you can set arbitrary intermediate markers, called **savepoints**, to divide a transaction into smaller parts. Savepoints let you roll back changes made from the current point in the transaction to a location earlier in the transaction (provided that the transaction hasn't been committed). Imagine a session in which you've made a complex series of uncommitted INSERTs, UPDATEs, and DELETEs and then realize that the last few changes are incorrect or unnecessary. You can use savepoints to avoid resubmitting every statement. **Microsoft Access** doesn't support savepoints. For **Oracle, Db2, MySQL,** and **PostgreSQL**, use the statement

SAVEPOINT *savepoint_name;*

For **Microsoft SQL Server**, use the statement

SAVE TRANSACTION *savepoint_name;*

See your DBMS documentation for information about savepoint locking subtleties and how to COMMIT or ROLLBACK to a particular savepoint.

- **DBMS** In **Microsoft Access**, you can't execute transactions in a SQL View window or via DAO; you must use the Microsoft Jet OLE DB Provider and ADO.

  Oracle and **Db2** transactions begin implicitly. To run Listing 14.1 and Listing 14.2 in Oracle and Db2, omit the statement BEGIN TRANSACTION;.

  To run Listing 14.1 and Listing 14.2 in **MySQL**, change the statement BEGIN TRANSACTION; to START TRANSACTION; (or to BEGIN;).

  MySQL supports transactions through InnoDB and NDB tables; search the MySQL documentation for *transactions.*

  Microsoft SQL Server, Oracle, MySQL, and **PostgreSQL** support the statement SET TRANSACTION to set the characteristics of the upcoming transaction. **Db2** transaction characteristics are controlled via server-level and connection initialization settings.

CHAPTER 15

Advanced SQL

This chapter describes how to solve common problems with SQL programs that

- Contain subtle or clever combinations of standard SQL elements, or

- Use nonstandard (DBMS-specific) SQL elements that obviate the need for convoluted solutions in standard SQL

Calculating Running Statistics

A **running statistic**, or **cumulative statistic**, is a row-by-row calculation that uses progressively more data values, starting with a single value (the first value), continuing with more values in the order in which they're supplied, and ending with all the values. The **running sum** (total) and **running average** (arithmetic mean) are the most common running statistics.

Listing 15.1 calculates the running sum and running average of book sales, along with a cumulative count of data items. The query cross-joins two instances of the table *titles*, grouping the result by the first-table (*t1*) title IDs and limiting the second-table (*t2*) rows to ID values smaller than or equal to the *t1* row to which they're joined. The intermediate cross-joined table, to which SUM(), AVG(), and COUNT() are applied, looks like this:

```
t1.id t1.sales t2.id t2.sales
----- -------- ----- --------

T01        566 T01        566
T02       9566 T01        566
T02       9566 T02       9566
T03      25667 T01        566
T03      25667 T02       9566
T03      25667 T03      25667
T04      13001 T01        566
T04      13001 T02       9566
T04      13001 T03      25667
T04      13001 T04      13001
T05     201440 T01        566
...
```

Note that the running statistics don't change for title T10 because its *sales* value is null. The ORDER BY clause is necessary because GROUP BY doesn't sort the result implicitly. See Figure 15.1 for the result.

```
SELECT
    t1.title_id,
    SUM(t2.sales) AS RunSum,
    AVG(t2.sales) AS RunAvg,
    COUNT(t2.sales) AS RunCount
  FROM titles t1, titles t2
  WHERE t1.title_id >= t2.title_id
  GROUP BY t1.title_id
  ORDER BY t1.title_id;
```

Listing 15.1 Calculate the running sum, average, and count of book sales. See Figure 15.1 for the result.

title_id	RunSum	RunAvg	RunCount
T01	566	566	1
T02	10132	5066	2
T03	35799	11933	3
T04	48800	12200	4
T05	250240	50048	5
T06	261560	43593	6
T07	1761760	251680	7
T08	1765855	220731	8
T09	1770855	196761	9
T10	1770855	196761	9
T11	1864978	186497	10
T12	1964979	178634	11
T13	1975446	164620	12

Figure 15.1 Result of Listing 15.1.

```
SELECT t1.seq, AVG(t2.price) AS MovingAvg
  FROM time_series t1, time_series t2
  WHERE t1.seq >= 5
    AND t1.seq BETWEEN t2.seq AND t2.seq + 4
  GROUP BY t1.seq
  ORDER BY t1.seq;
```

Listing 15.2 Calculate a moving average with a five-point window. See Figure 15.2 for the result.

```
seq MovingAvg
--- ---------
  5      10.6
  6      10.9
  7      11.2
  8      11.6
  9      12.4
 10      13.0
 11      13.3
 12      13.4
 13      13.2
 14      12.7
 15      12.2
```

Figure 15.2 Result of Listing 15.2.

A **moving average** is a way of smoothing a time series (such as a list of prices changing over time) by replacing each value by an average of that value and its nearest neighbors. Calculating a moving average is easy if you have a column that contains a sequence of integers or dates, such as in this table, named *time_series*:

```
seq price
--- -----
  1  10.0
  2  10.5
  3  11.0
  4  11.0
  5  10.5
  6  11.5
  7  12.0
  8  13.0
  9  15.0
 10  13.5
 11  13.0
 12  12.5
 13  12.0
 14  12.5
 15  11.0
```

Listing 15.2 calculates the moving average of *price*. See Figure 15.2 for the result. Each value in the result's moving-average column is the average of five values: the price in the current row and the prices in the four preceding rows (as ordered by *seq*). The first four rows are omitted because they don't have the required number of preceding values. You can adjust the values in the WHERE clause to cover any size averaging window. To make Listing 15.2 calculate a five-point moving average that averages each price with the two prices before it and the two prices after it, for example, change the WHERE clause to:

```
WHERE t1.seq >= 3
  AND t1.seq <= 13
  AND t1.seq BETWEEN t2.seq - 2
                AND t2.seq + 2
```

If you have a table that already has running totals, then you can calculate the differences between pairs of successive rows. Listing 15.3 backs out the intercity distances from the following table, named *roadtrip*, which contains the cumulative distances for each leg of a trip from Seattle, Washington, to San Diego, California. See Figure 15.3 for the result.

```
seq city               miles
--- ----------------   -----
  1 Seattle, WA            0
  2 Portland, OR         174
  3 San Francisco, CA    808
  4 Monterey, CA         926
  5 Los Angeles, CA     1251
  6 San Diego, CA       1372
```

```
SELECT
    t1.seq AS seq1,
    t2.seq AS seq2,
    t1.city AS city1,
    t2.city AS city2,
    t1.miles AS miles1,
    t2.miles AS miles2,
    t2.miles - t1.miles AS dist
  FROM roadtrip t1, roadtrip t2
  WHERE t1.seq + 1 = t2.seq
  ORDER BY t1.seq;
```

Listing 15.3 Calculate intercity distances from cumulative distances. See Figure 15.3 for the result.

Tips for Running Statistics

- Listing 15.1 and Listing 15.2 give inaccurate results if the grouping column contains duplicate values.

- See Listing 8.21 on page 259 for another way to calculate a running statistic.

- **DBMS** In **Microsoft SQL Server**, **Oracle**, **Db2**, **MySQL**, and **PostgreSQL** you can use window functions to calculate running statistics; for example:

```
SELECT title_id, sales,
  SUM(sales) OVER (ORDER BY title_id)
    AS RunSum
  FROM titles
  ORDER BY title_id;
```

```
seq1 seq2 city1               city2               miles1 miles2 dist
---- ---- ----------------    ----------------    ------ ------ ----
   1    2 Seattle, WA         Portland, OR             0    174  174
   2    3 Portland, OR        San Francisco, CA      174    808  634
   3    4 San Francisco, CA   Monterey, CA           808    926  118
   4    5 Monterey, CA        Los Angeles, CA        926   1251  325
   5    6 Los Angeles, CA     San Diego, CA         1251   1372  121
```

Figure 15.3 Result of Listing 15.3.

Generating Sequences

Recall from "Unique Identifiers" on page 70 that you can use sequences of autogenerated integers to create identity columns (typically for primary keys). The SQL standard provides **sequence generators** to create them.

To define a sequence generator:

• Type:

```
CREATE SEQUENCE seq_name
  [INCREMENT [BY] increment]
  [MINVALUE min | NO MINVALUE]
  [MAXVALUE max | NO MAXVALUE]
  [START [WITH] start]
  [[NO] CYCLE];
```

seq_name is the name (a unique identifier) of the sequence to create.

increment specifies which value is added to the current sequence value to create a new value. A positive value will make an **ascending sequence**; a negative one, a **descending sequence**. The value of *increment* can't be zero. If the clause INCREMENT BY is omitted, then the default increment is 1.

min specifies the minimum value that a sequence can generate. If the clause MINVALUE is omitted or NO MINVALUE is specified, then a default minimum is used. The defaults vary by DBMS, but they're typically 1 for an ascending sequence or a very large number for a descending one.

max (>*min*) specifies the maximum value that a sequence can generate. If the clause MAXVALUE is omitted or NO MAXVALUE is specified, then a default maximum is used. The defaults vary by DBMS, but they're typically a very large number for an ascending sequence or −1 for a descending one.

start specifies the first value of the sequence. If the clause START WITH is omitted, then the default starting value is *min* for an ascending sequence or *max* for a descending one.

CYCLE indicates that the sequence continues to generate values after reaching either its *min* or *max*. After an ascending sequence reaches its maximum value, it then generates its minimum value. After a descending sequence reaches its minimum value, it then generates its maximum value. NO CYCLE (the default) indicates that the sequence can't generate more values after reaching its maximum or minimum value.

Listing 15.4 defines the sequence shown in Figure 15.4.

You can use a sequence generator in a few ways. Standard SQL provides the built-in function NEXT VALUE FOR to increment a sequence value, as in:

```
INSERT INTO shipment(
    part_num, desc, quantity)
  VALUES(
    NEXT VALUE FOR part_seq,
    'motherboard',
    5);
```

If you're creating a column of unique values, then you can use the keyword IDENTITY to define a sequence right in the CREATE TABLE statement:

```
CREATE TABLE parts (
  part_num INTEGER AS
    IDENTITY(
      INCREMENT BY 1
      MINVALUE 1
      MAXVALUE 10000
      START WITH 1
      NO CYCLE),
  desc AS VARCHAR(100),
  quantity INTEGER;
```

This table definition lets you omit NEXT VALUE FOR when you insert a row:

```
INSERT INTO shipment(desc, quantity)
  VALUES('motherboard', 5);
```

SQL also provides ALTER SEQUENCE and DROP SEQUENCE to change and remove sequence generators.

DBMS | **Microsoft SQL Server, Oracle, Db2**, and **PostgreSQL** support CREATE SEQUENCE, ALTER SEQUENCE, and DROP SEQUENCE. In **Oracle**, use NOCYCLE instead of NO CYCLE. See your DBMS documentation to see how sequences are used in your system.

Most DBMSs don't support IDENTITY columns because they have other (pre-standard) ways that define columns with unique values; see "Unique Identifiers" on page 70. **PostgreSQL**'s generate_series() function offers a quick way to generate numbered rows.

```
CREATE SEQUENCE part_seq
  INCREMENT BY 1
  MINVALUE 1
  MAXVALUE 10000
  START WITH 1
  NO CYCLE;
```

Listing 15.4 Create a sequence generator for the consecutive integers 1 to 10000. See Figure 15.4 for the result.

```
1
2
3
...
9998
9999
10000
```

Figure 15.4 The sequence that Listing 15.4 generates.

```
CREATE TABLE temp09 (
  i CHAR(1) NOT NULL PRIMARY KEY
  );

INSERT INTO temp09 VALUES('0');
INSERT INTO temp09 VALUES('1');
INSERT INTO temp09 VALUES('2');
INSERT INTO temp09 VALUES('3');
INSERT INTO temp09 VALUES('4');
INSERT INTO temp09 VALUES('5');
INSERT INTO temp09 VALUES('6');
INSERT INTO temp09 VALUES('7');
INSERT INTO temp09 VALUES('8');
INSERT INTO temp09 VALUES('9');

CREATE TABLE seq (
  i INTEGER NOT NULL PRIMARY KEY
  );

INSERT INTO seq
  SELECT CAST(t1.i || t2.i ||
      t3.i || t4.i AS INTEGER)
    FROM temp09 t1, temp09 t2,
      temp09 t3, temp09 t4;

DROP TABLE temp09;
```

Listing 15.5 Create a one-column table that contains consecutive integers. See Figure 15.5 for the result.

```
i
-----
0
1
2
3
4
...
9996
9997
9998
9999
```

Figure 15.5 Result of Listing 15.5.

A one-column table containing a sequence of consecutive integers makes it easy to solve problems that would otherwise be difficult with SQL's limited computational power. **Sequence tables** aren't actually part of the data model—they're auxiliary tables that are adjuncts to queries and other "real" tables.

You can create a sequence table by using one of the methods just described. Alternatively, you can create one by using Listing 15.5, which creates the sequence table *seq* by cross-joining the intermediate table *temp09* with itself. The CAST expression concatenates digit characters into sequential numbers and then casts them as integers. You can drop the table *temp09* after *seq* is created. Figure 15.5 shows the result. The table *seq* contains the integer sequence 0, 1, 2,…, 9999. You can shrink or grow this sequence by changing the SELECT and FROM expressions in the INSERT INTO seq statement.

A sequence table is especially useful for enumerative and datetime functions. Listing 15.6 lists the 95 printable characters in the ASCII character set (if that's the character set in use). See Figure 15.6 for the result.

```
SELECT
    i AS CharCode,
    CHR(i) AS Ch
  FROM seq
  WHERE i BETWEEN 32 AND 126;
```

Listing 15.6 List the characters associated with a set of character codes. See Figure 15.6 for the result.

```
CharCode Ch
-------- --
      32
      33  !
      34  "
      35  #
      36  $
      37  %
      38  &
      39  '
      40  (
      41  )
      42  *
      43  +
      44  ,
      45  -
      46  .
      47  /
      48  0
      49  1
      50  2
      51  3
      52  4
...
```

Figure 15.6 Result of Listing 15.6.

```
SELECT
    i AS MonthsAhead,
    DATEADD("m", i, CURRENT_TIMESTAMP)
      AS FutureDate
  FROM seq
  WHERE i BETWEEN 1 AND 6;
```

Listing 15.7 Increment today's date to six months hence, in one-month intervals. See Figure 15.7 for the result.

```
MonthsAhead FutureDate
----------- ----------
          1 2005-04-07
          2 2005-05-07
          3 2005-06-07
          4 2005-07-07
          5 2005-08-07
          6 2005-09-07
```

Figure 15.7 Result of Listing 15.7.

Listing 15.7 adds monthly intervals to today's date (7-March-2005) for the next six months. See Figure 15.7 for the result. This example works on **Microsoft SQL Server**; other DBMSs have similar functions that increment dates (see "Working with Dates" on page 427).

Sequence tables are handy for normalizing data that you've imported from a nonrelational source such as a spreadsheet or accounting package. Suppose that you have the following non-normalized table, named *au_orders*, showing the order of the authors' names on each book's cover:

```
title_id author1 author2 author3
-------- ------- ------- -------
T01      A01     NULL    NULL
T02      A01     NULL    NULL
T03      A05     NULL    NULL
T04      A03     A04     NULL
T05      A04     NULL    NULL
T06      A02     NULL    NULL
T07      A02     A04     NULL
T08      A06     NULL    NULL
T09      A06     NULL    NULL
T10      A02     NULL    NULL
T11      A06     A03     A04
T12      A02     NULL    NULL
T13      A01     NULL    NULL
```

Listing 15.8 cross-joins *au_orders* with *seq* to produce Figure 15.8. You can DELETE the result rows with nulls in the column *au_id*, leaving the result set looking like the table *title_authors* in the sample database. Note that Listing 15.8 does the reverse of Listing 8.18 on page 257.

```
SELECT title_id,
    (CASE WHEN i=1 THEN '1'
          WHEN i=2 THEN '2'
          WHEN i=3 THEN '3'
     END) AS au_order,
    (CASE WHEN i=1 THEN author1
          WHEN i=2 THEN author2
          WHEN i=3 THEN author3
     END) AS au_id
  FROM au_orders, seq
  WHERE i BETWEEN 1 AND 3
  ORDER BY title_id, i;
```

Listing 15.8 Normalize the table *au_orders*. See Figure 15.8 for the result.

```
title_id au_order au_id
-------- -------- -----
T01      1        A01
T01      2        NULL
T01      3        NULL
T02      1        A01
T02      2        NULL
T02      3        NULL
T03      1        A05
T03      2        NULL
T03      3        NULL
T04      1        A03
T04      2        A04
T04      3        NULL
T05      1        A04
T05      2        NULL
T05      3        NULL
T06      1        A02
T06      2        NULL
T06      3        NULL
T07      1        A02
T07      2        A04
T07      3        NULL
T08      1        A06
T08      2        NULL
T08      3        NULL
T09      1        A06
T09      2        NULL
T09      3        NULL
T10      1        A02
T10      2        NULL
T10      3        NULL
T11      1        A06
T11      2        A03
T11      3        A04
T12      1        A02
T12      2        NULL
T12      3        NULL
T13      1        A01
T13      2        NULL
T13      3        NULL
```

Figure 15.8 Result of Listing 15.8.

Calendar Tables

Another useful auxiliary table is a **calendar table**. One type of calendar table has a primary-key column that contains a row for each calendar date (past and future) and other columns that indicate the date's attributes: business day, holiday, international holiday, fiscal-month end, fiscal-year end, Julian date, business-day offsets, and so on. Another type of calendar table stores the starting and ending dates of events (in the columns *event_id*, *start_date*, and *end_date*, for example). Spreadsheets have more date-arithmetic functions than DBMSs, so it might be easier to build a calendar table in a spreadsheet and then import it as a database table.

Even if your DBMS has plenty of date-arithmetic functions, it might be faster to look up data in a calendar table than to call these functions in a query.

Tips for Generating Sequences

- If you have a column of sequential integers that's missing some numbers, then you can fill in the gaps by EXCEPTing the column with a sequence column. See "Finding Different Rows with EXCEPT" on page 298.

- **DBMS** To run Listing 15.5 in **Microsoft Access** and **Microsoft SQL Server**, change the CAST expression to:

```
t1.i + t2.i + t3.i + t4.i
```

To run Listing 15.5 in **MySQL**, change the CAST expression to:

```
CONCAT(t1.i, t2.i, t3.i, t4.i)
```

To run Listing 15.6 in **Microsoft SQL Server** and **MySQL**, change CHR(i) to CHAR(i).

To run Listing 15.8 in **Microsoft Access**, change the CASE expressions to Switch() function calls:

```
(Switch(i=1, '1', i=2, '2', i=3, '3'))
AS au_order,

(Switch(i=1, author1, i=2, author2, i=3,
author3)) AS au_id
```

Finding Sequences, Runs, and Regions

A **sequence** is a series of consecutive values without gaps. A **run** is like a sequence, but the values don't have to be consecutive, just increasing (that is, gaps are allowed). A **region** is an unbroken series of values that all are equal.

Finding sequences, runs, and regions requires a table that has at least two columns: a primary-key column that holds a sequence of consecutive integers and a column that holds the values of interest. The table *temps* (Listing 15.9 and Figure 15.9) shows a series of high temperatures over 15 days.

As a set-oriented language, SQL isn't a good choice for finding series of values. The following queries won't run very fast, so if you have a lot of data to analyze, then consider exporting it to a statistical package or using a procedural host language.

Listing 15.10 finds all the sequences in *temps* and lists each sequence's start position, end position, and length. See Figure 15.10 for the result.

Listing 15.10 is a lot to take in at first glance, but it's easier to understand it if you look at it piecemeal. Then you'll be able to understand the rest of the queries in this section.

The subquery's WHERE clause subtracts *id* from *hi_temp*, yielding (internally):

```
id hi_temp diff
-- ------- ----
 1      49   48
 2      46   44
 3      48   45
 4      50   46
 5      50   45
 6      50   44
 7      51   44
 8      52   44
 9      53   44
10      50   40
11      50   39
12      47   35
13      50   37
14      51   37
15      52   37
```

```
SELECT *
  FROM temps;
```

Listing 15.9 List all the columns in the table *temps*. See Figure 15.9 for the result.

```
id hi_temp
-- -------
 1      49
 2      46
 3      48
 4      50
 5      50
 6      50
 7      51
 8      52
 9      53
10      50
11      50
12      47
13      50
14      51
15      52
```

Figure 15.9 Result of Listing 15.9.

```
SELECT
    t1.id AS StartSeq,
    t2.id AS EndSeq,
    t2.id - t1.id + 1 AS SeqLen
  FROM temps t1, temps t2
  WHERE (t1.id < t2.id)
    AND NOT EXISTS(
      SELECT *
        FROM temps t3
        WHERE (t3.hi_temp - t3.id <>
                t1.hi_temp - t1.id
                AND t3.id BETWEEN
                    t1.id AND t2.id)
          OR (t3.id = t1.id - 1
              AND t3.hi_temp - t3.id =
                  t1.hi_temp - t1.id)
          OR (t3.id = t2.id + 1
              AND t3.hi_temp - t3.id =
                  t1.hi_temp - t1.id)
    );
```

Listing 15.10 List the starting point, ending point, and length of each sequence in the table *temps*. See Figure 15.10 for the result.

```
StartSeq EndSeq SeqSize
-------- ------ -------
       6      9       4
      13     15       3
```

Figure 15.10 Result of Listing 15.10.

In the column *diff*, note that successive differences are constant for sequences (50 − 6 = 44, 51 − 7 = 44, and so on). To find neighboring rows, the outer query cross-joins two instances of the same table (*t1* and *t2*), as described in "Calculating Running Statistics" on page 390. The condition

```
WHERE (t1.id < t2.id)
```

guarantees that any *t1* row represents an element with an index (*id*) lower than the corresponding *t2* row.

The subquery detects sequence breaks with the condition

```
t3.hi_temp - t3.id <> t1.hi_temp - t1.id
```

The third instance of *temps* (*t3*) in the subquery is used to determine whether any row in a candidate sequence (*t3*) has the same difference as the sequence's first row (*t1*). If so, then it's a sequence member. If not, then the candidate pair (*t1* and *t2*) is rejected.

The last two OR conditions determine whether the candidate sequence's borders can expand. A row that satisfies these conditions means the current candidate sequence can be extended and is rejected in favor of a longer one.

To find only sequences larger than *n* rows, add the WHERE condition

```
AND (t2.id - t1.id) >= n - 1
```

To change Listing 15.10 to find all sequences of four or more rows, for example, replace

```
WHERE (t1.id < t2.id)
```

with

```
WHERE (t1.id < t2.id)
    AND (t2.id - t1.id) >= 3
```

The result is:

```
StartSeq EndSeq SeqSize
-------- ------ -------
       6      9       4
```

Listing 15.11 finds all the runs in *temps* and lists each run's start position, end position, and length. See Figure 15.11 for the result.

The logic of this query is similar to that of the preceding one but accounts for run values needing only to increase, not (necessarily) be consecutive. The difference between *id* and *hi_temp* values doesn't have to be constant, so a fourth instance of *temps* (*t4*) is needed. The subquery cross-joins *t3* and *t4* to check rows in the middle of a candidate run, whose borders are *t1* and *t2*. For every element between *t1* and *t2* (limited by BETWEEN), *t3* and its predecessor *t4* are compared to see whether their values are increasing.

```
SELECT
    t1.id AS StartRun,
    t2.id AS EndRun,
    t2.id - t1.id + 1 AS RunLen
  FROM temps t1, temps t2
  WHERE (t1.id < t2.id)
    AND NOT EXISTS(
      SELECT *
        FROM temps t3, temps t4
        WHERE (t3.hi_temp <= t4.hi_temp
                AND t4.id = t3.id - 1
                AND t3.id BETWEEN
                    t1.id + 1 AND t2.id)
            OR (t3.id = t1.id - 1
                AND t3.hi_temp < t1.hi_temp)
            OR (t3.id = t2.id + 1
                AND t3.hi_temp > t2.hi_temp)
    );
```

Listing 15.11 List the starting point, ending point, and length of each run in the table *temps*. See Figure 15.11 for the result.

```
StartRun EndRun RunLen
-------- ------ ------
       2      4      3
       6      9      4
      12     15      4
```

Figure 15.11 Result of Listing 15.11.

```
SELECT
    t1.id AS StartReg,
    t2.id AS EndReg,
    t2.id - t1.id + 1 AS RegLen
  FROM temps t1, temps t2
  WHERE (t1.id < t2.id)
    AND NOT EXISTS(
      SELECT *
        FROM temps t3
        WHERE (t3.hi_temp <> 50
               AND t3.id BETWEEN
                   t1.id AND t2.id)
          OR (t3.id = t1.id - 1
              AND t3.hi_temp = 50)
          OR (t3.id = t2.id + 1
              AND t3.hi_temp = 50)
    );
```

Listing 15.12 List the starting point, ending point, and length of each region (with value 50) in the table *temps*. See Figure 15.12 for the result.

```
StartReg EndReg RegLen
-------- ------ ------
       4      6      3
      10     11      2
```

Figure 15.12 Result of Listing 15.12.

Listing 15.12 finds all regions in *temps* with a high temperature of 50 and lists each region's start position, end position, and length. See Figure 15.12 for the result.

Listing 15.13 is a variation of Listing 15.12 that finds all regions of length 2. See Figure 15.13 for the result. Note that overlapping subregions are listed. To return regions of length n, change the WHERE clause's second condition to:

```
AND t2.id - t1.id = n - 1
```

Tips for Sequences, Runs, and Regions

- To rank regions by length, add an ORDER BY clause to the outer query:

  ```
  ORDER BY t2.id - t1.id DESC
  ```

- To list the individual *id*s that fall in a region (with value 50), type:

  ```
  SELECT DISTINCT t1.id
    FROM temps t1, temps t2
   WHERE t1.hi_temp = 50
     AND t2.hi_temp = 50
     AND ABS(t1.id - t2.id) = 1;
  ```

The standard function ABS(), which all DBMSs support, returns the absolute value of its argument. The result is:

```
id
--
 4
 5
 6
10
11
```

```
SELECT
    t1.id AS StartReg,
    t2.id AS EndReg,
    t2.id - t1.id + 1 AS RegLen
  FROM temps t1, temps t2
 WHERE (t1.id < t2.id)
   AND t2.id - t1.id = 1
   AND NOT EXISTS(
     SELECT *
       FROM temps t3
       WHERE (t3.hi_temp <> 50
         AND t3.id BETWEEN t1.id AND t2.id)
   );
```

Listing 15.13 List all regions of length 2. See Figure 15.13 for the result.

```
StartReg EndReg RegLen
-------- ------ ------
       4      5      2
       5      6      2
      10     11      2
```

Figure 15.13 Result of Listing 15.13.

```
SELECT emp_id, sales
  FROM empsales
  ORDER BY sales DESC;
```

Listing 15.14 List employees by descending sales. See Figure 15.14 for the result.

```
emp_id sales
------ -----
E09      900
E02      800
E10      700
E05      700
E01      600
E04      500
E03      500
E06      500
E08      400
E07      300
```

Figure 15.14 Result of Listing 15.14.

Limiting the Number of Rows Returned

In practice it's common to use queries that return a certain number (*n*) of rows that fall at the top or the bottom of a range specified by an ORDER BY clause. SQL doesn't require an ORDER BY clause, but if you omit it, then the query will return an unsorted set of rows (because SQL doesn't promise to deliver query results in any particular order without an ORDER BY clause).

The examples in this section use the table *empsales* (Listing 15.14 and Figure 15.14), which lists sales figures by employee. Note that some employees have the same sales amounts. A correct query for the top three salespeople in *empsales* actually will return four rows: employees E09, E02, E10, and E05. Ties shouldn't force the query to choose arbitrarily between equal values (E10 and E05 in this case). No standard terminology exists, but queries that return at most *n* rows (regardless of ties) sometimes are called **limit queries**. Queries that include ties and return possibly more than *n* rows are **top-n queries** or **quota queries**.

You can also use limit and quota queries to limit the number of rows affected by an UPDATE or DELETE statement. Some limit and quota queries might be invalid in some contexts (such as in subqueries or views); see your DBMS documentation.

DBMS | The SQL:2003 standard introduced the functions ROW_NUMBER() and RANK() to use in limit and top-n queries. **Microsoft SQL Server, Oracle**, and **Db2** support both functions. Queries that use pre-2003 SQL are complex, unintuitive, and run slowly (see the tips at the end of this section for an SQL-92 example). The SQL standard has lagged DBMSs, which for years have offered nonstandard extensions to create these types of queries. Some DBMSs also let you return a percentage of rows (rather than a fixed *n*) or return offsets by skipping a specified number of initial rows (returning rows 3–8 instead of 1–5, for example). This section covers the DBMS extensions individually.

Microsoft Access

Listing 15.15 lists the top three salespeople, including ties. See Figure 15.15 for the result. This query orders highest to lowest; to reverse the order, change DESC to ASC in the ORDER BY clause.

The TOP clause always includes ties. Its syntax is:

```
TOP n [PERCENT]
```

Listing 15.16 lists the bottom 40 percent of salespeople, including ties. See Figure 15.16 for the result. This query orders lowest to highest; to reverse the order, change ASC to DESC in the ORDER BY clause.

Tips for Microsoft Access

- The following offset query returns *n* rows but excludes the topmost *skip* rows from the result. This query orders highest to lowest; to reverse the order, change ASC to DESC and DESC to ASC in each ORDER BY clause.

```
SELECT *
  FROM (
    SELECT TOP n *
      FROM (
        SELECT TOP n + skip *
          FROM table
          ORDER BY sort_col DESC)
      ORDER BY sort_col ASC)
  ORDER BY sort_col DESC;
```

```
SELECT TOP 3 emp_id, sales
  FROM empsales
  ORDER BY sales DESC;
```

Listing 15.15 List the top three salespeople, with ties. See Figure 15.15 for the result.

```
emp_id sales
------ -----
E09      900
E02      800
E10      700
E05      700
```

Figure 15.15 Result of Listing 15.15.

```
SELECT TOP 40 PERCENT emp_id, sales
  FROM empsales
  ORDER BY sales ASC;
```

Listing 15.16 List the bottom 40 percent of salespeople, with ties. See Figure 15.16 for the result.

```
emp_id sales
------ -----
E07      300
E08      400
E06      500
E04      500
E03      500
```

Figure 15.16 Result of Listing 15.16.

```
SELECT TOP 3 emp_id, sales
  FROM empsales
  ORDER BY sales DESC;
```

Listing 15.17 List the top three salespeople, without ties.
See Figure 15.17 for the result.

```
emp_id sales
------ -----
E09      900
E02      800
E05      700
```

Figure 15.17 Result of Listing 15.17.

```
SELECT TOP 3 WITH TIES emp_id, sales
  FROM empsales
  ORDER BY sales DESC;
```

Listing 15.18 List the top three salespeople, with ties. See
Figure 15.18 for the result.

```
emp_id sales
------ -----
E09      900
E02      800
E05      700
E10      700
```

Figure 15.18 Result of Listing 15.18.

Microsoft SQL Server

Listing 15.17 lists the top three salespeople, not in-cluding ties. See Figure 15.17 for the result. Note that this query is inconsistent when ties exist; rerunning it can return either E10 or E05, depending on how ORDER BY sorts the table. This query orders highest to lowest; to reverse the order, change DESC to ASC in the ORDER BY clause.

The TOP clause's syntax is:

```
TOP n [PERCENT] [WITH TIES]
```

Listing 15.18 lists the top three salespeople, in-cluding ties. See Figure 15.18 for the result. This query orders highest to lowest; to reverse the order, change DESC to ASC in the ORDER BY clause.

Listing 15.19 lists the bottom 40 percent of sales-people, including ties. See Figure 15.19 for the result. This query orders lowest to highest; to reverse the order, change ASC to DESC in the ORDER BY clause.

Tips for Microsoft SQL Server

- The statement SET ROWCOUNT *n* provides an alternative method returning *n* rows.

- The following offset query returns *n* rows but excludes the topmost *skip* rows from the result. This query orders highest to lowest; to reverse the order, change ASC to DESC and DESC to ASC in each ORDER BY clause.

```
SELECT *
  FROM (
    SELECT TOP n *
      FROM (
        SELECT TOP n + skip *
          FROM table
          ORDER BY sort_col DESC)
            AS any_name1
      ORDER BY sort_col ASC)
        AS any_name2
  ORDER BY sort_col DESC;
```

```
SELECT TOP 40 PERCENT WITH TIES
    emp_id, sales
  FROM empsales
  ORDER BY sales ASC;
```

Listing 15.19 List the bottom 40 percent of salespeople, with ties. See Figure 15.19 for the result.

```
emp_id sales
------ -----
E07     300
E08     400
E06     500
E03     500
E04     500
```

Figure 15.19 Result of Listing 15.19.

```
SELECT emp_id, sales
  FROM (
    SELECT *
      FROM empsales
      ORDER BY sales DESC)
  WHERE ROWNUM <= 3;
```

Listing 15.20 List the top three salespeople, without ties.
See Figure 15.20 for the result.

```
emp_id sales
------ -----

E09     900
E02     800
E05     700
```

Figure 15.20 Result of Listing 15.20.

```
SELECT emp_id, sales
  FROM (
    SELECT
      RANK() OVER
        (ORDER BY sales DESC)
          AS sales_rank,
      emp_id,
      sales
    FROM empsales)
  WHERE sales_rank <= 3;
```

Listing 15.21 List the top three salespeople, with ties. See
Figure 15.21 for the result.

```
emp_id sales
------ -----

E09     900
E02     800
E05     700
E10     700
```

Figure 15.21 Result of Listing 15.21.

Oracle Database

Use the built-in ROWNUM pseudocolumn to limit the number of rows returned. The first row selected has a ROWNUM of 1, the second has 2, and so on. Use the window function RANK() to include ties.

Listing 15.20 lists the top three salespeople, not including ties. See Figure 15.20 for the result. Note that this query is inconsistent when ties exist; rerunning it can return either E10 or E05, depending on how ORDER BY sorts the table. This query orders highest to lowest; to reverse the order, change DESC to ASC in the ORDER BY clause.

Listing 15.21 lists the top three salespeople, including ties. See Figure 15.21 for the result. This query orders highest to lowest; to reverse the order, change DESC to ASC in the ORDER BY clause.

Tips for Oracle Database

- The function ROW_NUMBER() provides an alternative method of assigning unique numbers to rows.

- The following offset query returns *n* rows but excludes the topmost *skip* rows from the result. This query orders highest to lowest; to reverse the order, change DESC to ASC in the ORDER BY clause.

```
SELECT *
  FROM (
    SELECT
      ROW_NUMBER() OVER
        (ORDER BY sort_col DESC)
          AS rnum,
      columns
    FROM table)
  WHERE rnum > skip
    AND rnum <= (n + skip);
```

IBM Db2 Database

Listing 15.22 lists the top three salespeople, not including ties. See Figure 15.22 for the result. Note that this query is inconsistent when ties exist; rerunning it can return either E10 or E05, depending on how ORDER BY sorts the table. This query orders highest to lowest; to reverse the order, change DESC to ASC in the ORDER BY clause.

The FETCH clause's syntax is:

```
FETCH FIRST n ROW[S] ONLY
```

Listing 15.23 lists the top three salespeople, including ties. See Figure 15.23 for the result. This query orders highest to lowest; to reverse the order, change DESC to ASC in the ORDER BY clause.

Tips for IBM Db2 Database

- The following offset query returns n rows but excludes the topmost *skip* rows from the result. This query orders highest to lowest; to reverse the order, change DESC to ASC in the ORDER BY clause.

```
SELECT *
  FROM (
    SELECT
        ROW_NUMBER() OVER
          (ORDER BY sort_col DESC)
            AS rnum,
        columns
      FROM table)
        AS any_name
  WHERE rnum > skip
    AND rnum <= n + skip;
```

```
SELECT emp_id, sales
  FROM empsales
  ORDER BY sales DESC
  FETCH FIRST 3 ROWS ONLY;
```

Listing 15.22 List the top three salespeople, without ties. See Figure 15.22 for the result.

```
emp_id sales
------ -----
E09      900
E02      800
E05      700
```

Figure 15.22 Result of Listing 15.22.

```
SELECT emp_id, sales
  FROM (
    SELECT
      RANK() OVER
        (ORDER BY sales DESC)
          AS sales_rank,
      emp_id,
      sales
    FROM empsales)
      AS any_name
  WHERE sales_rank <= 3;
```

Listing 15.23 List the top three salespeople, with ties. See Figure 15.23 for the result.

```
emp_id sales
------ -----
E09      900
E02      800
E05      700
E10      700
```

Figure 15.23 Result of Listing 15.23.

```
SELECT emp_id, sales
  FROM empsales
  ORDER BY sales DESC
  LIMIT 3;
```

Listing 15.24 List the top three salespeople, without ties.
See Figure 15.24 for the result.

```
emp_id sales
------ -----
 E09     900
 E02     800
 E10     700
```

Figure 15.24 Result of Listing 15.24.

```
SELECT emp_id, sales
  FROM empsales
  WHERE sales >= COALESCE(
    (SELECT sales
       FROM empsales
       ORDER BY sales DESC
       LIMIT 1 OFFSET 2),
    (SELECT MIN(sales)
       FROM empsales))
  ORDER BY sales DESC;
```

Listing 15.25 List the top three salespeople, with ties. See
Figure 15.25 for the result.

```
emp_id sales
------ -----
 E09     900
 E02     800
 E05     700
 E10     700
```

Figure 15.25 Result of Listing 15.25.

MySQL

Listing 15.24 lists the top three salespeople, not including ties. See Figure 15.24 for the result. Note that this query is inconsistent when ties exist; re-running it can return either E10 or E05, depending on how ORDER BY sorts the table. This query orders highest to lowest; to reverse the order, change DESC to ASC in the ORDER BY clause.

The LIMIT clause's syntax is:

LIMIT *n* [OFFSET *skip*]

or

LIMIT [*skip*,] *n*

The offset of the initial row is 0 (not 1).

Listing 15.25 lists the top three salespeople, including ties. The OFFSET value is $n − 1 = 2$. COALESCE()'s second argument lets the query work in case the table has fewer than *n* rows; see "Checking for Nulls with COALESCE()" on page 153. See Figure 15.25 for the result. This query orders highest to lowest; to reverse the order, change >= to <= in the comparison, change MIN() to MAX() in the second subquery, and change DESC to ASC in each ORDER BY clause.

Listing 15.26 lists the top three salespeople, skipping the initial four rows. See Figure 15.26 for the result. Note that this query is inconsistent when ties exist. This query orders highest to lowest; to reverse the order, change DESC to ASC in the ORDER BY clause.

```
SELECT emp_id, sales
  FROM empsales
  ORDER BY sales DESC
  LIMIT 3 OFFSET 4;
```

Listing 15.26 List the top three salespeople, skipping the initial four rows. See Figure 15.26 for the result.

```
emp_id sales
------ -----
E01      600
E04      500
E03      500
```

Figure 15.26 Result of Listing 15.26.

```
SELECT emp_id, sales
  FROM empsales
  ORDER BY sales DESC
  LIMIT 3;
```

Listing 15.27 List the top three salespeople, without ties.
See Figure 15.27 for the result.

```
emp_id sales

------ -----

E09       900
E02       800
E05       700
```

Figure 15.27 Result of Listing 15.27.

```
SELECT emp_id, sales
  FROM empsales
  WHERE (
    sales >= (
      SELECT sales
        FROM empsales
        ORDER BY sales DESC
        LIMIT 1 OFFSET 2)
  ) IS NOT FALSE
  ORDER BY sales DESC;
```

Listing 15.28 List the top three salespeople, with ties. See
Figure 15.28 for the result.

```
emp_id sales

------ -----

E09       900
E02       800
E10       700
E05       700
```

Figure 15.28 Result of Listing 15.28.

PostgreSQL

Listing 15.27 lists the top three salespeople, not
including ties. See Figure 15.27 for the result. Note
that this query is inconsistent when ties exist; rerunning it can return either E10 or E05, depending
on how ORDER BY sorts the table. This query orders highest to lowest; to reverse the order, change
DESC to ASC in the ORDER BY clause.

The LIMIT clause's syntax is:

LIMIT *n* [OFFSET *skip*]

The offset of the initial row is 0 (not 1).

Listing 15.28 lists the top three salespeople,
including ties. The OFFSET value is $n - 1 = 2$. See
Figure 15.28 for the result. This query orders highest
to lowest; to reverse the order, change >= to <= in
the comparison and change DESC to ASC in each
ORDER BY clause.

Listing 15.29 lists the top three salespeople, skipping the initial four rows. See Figure 15.29 for the result. Note that this query is inconsistent when ties exist. This query orders highest to lowest; to reverse the order, change DESC to ASC in the ORDER BY clause.

Tips for Limiting the Number of Rows Returned

- When using a inconsistent query to present results to end-users, it's a good practice to include a tie-breaking ORDER BY column so that users see ties ranked consistently across queries. Adding *emp_id* after *sales* in the (outermost) ORDER BY clause in the queries in this section, for example, guarantees that employees with the same *sales* value always will sort the same way.

- Fabian Pascal's *Practical Issues in Database Management* discusses quota queries. His SQL-92 solution (which is too slow for practical use) to list the top three salespeople, including ties, is:

```
SELECT emp_id, sales
  FROM empsales e1
  WHERE (
    SELECT COUNT(*)
      FROM empsales e2
      WHERE e2.sales > e1.sales
  ) < 3;
```

This query orders highest to lowest; to reverse the order, change > to < in the innermost WHERE clause.

- DBMS You can also use a cursor to retrieve a specific subset of ordered rows in **Microsoft SQL Server, Oracle, Db2, MySQL**, and **PostgreSQL**. A cursor allows a result set to be processed one row at a time; search your DBMS documentation for *cursor*.

```
SELECT emp_id, sales
  FROM empsales
  ORDER BY sales DESC
  LIMIT 3 OFFSET 4;
```

Listing 15.29 List the top three salespeople, skipping the initial four rows. See Figure 15.29 for the result.

```
emp_id sales
------ -----
E01      600
E06      500
E03      500
```

Figure 15.29 Result of Listing 15.29.

```
SELECT e1.emp_id, e1.sales,
    (SELECT COUNT(sales)
        FROM empsales e2
        WHERE e2.sales >= e1.sales)
            AS ranking
    FROM empsales e1;
```

Listing **15.30a** Rank employees by sales (method *a*). See Figure 15.30 for the result.

```
SELECT e1.emp_id, e1.sales,
    (SELECT COUNT(sales)
        FROM empsales e2
        WHERE e2.sales > e1.sales) + 1
            AS ranking
    FROM empsales e1;
```

Listing **15.30b** Rank employees by sales (method *b*). See Figure 15.30 for the result.

```
SELECT e1.emp_id, e1.sales,
    (SELECT COUNT(sales)
        FROM empsales e2
        WHERE e2.sales > e1.sales)
            AS ranking
    FROM empsales e1;
```

Listing **15.30c** Rank employees by sales (method *c*). See Figure 15.30 for the result.

```
SELECT e1.emp_id, e1.sales,
    (SELECT COUNT(DISTINCT sales)
        FROM empsales e2
        WHERE e2.sales >= e1.sales)
            AS ranking
    FROM empsales e1;
```

Listing **15.30d** Rank employees by sales (method *d*). See Figure 15.30 for the result.

```
SELECT e1.emp_id, e1.sales,
    (SELECT COUNT(DISTINCT sales)
        FROM empsales e2
        WHERE e2.sales > e1.sales)
            AS ranking
    FROM empsales e1;
```

Listing **15.30e** Rank employees by sales (method *e*). See Figure 15.30 for the result.

Assigning Ranks

Ranking, which allocates the numbers 1, 2, 3, … to sorted values, is related to top-n queries and shares the problem of interpreting ties (see "Limiting the Number of Rows Returned" on page 405). The following queries calculate ranks for sales values in the table *empsales* (page 405).

Listings 15.30a to 15.30e rank employees by sales. The first two queries show the most commonly accepted ways to rank values. The other queries show variations on them. Figure 15.30 shows the result of each ranking method, *a* to *e*, combined for brevity and ease of comparison. These queries rank highest to lowest; to reverse the order, change > (or >=) to < (or <=) in the WHERE comparisons. You can add the clause ORDER BY ranking ASC to a query's outer SELECT to sort the results by rank.

```
emp_id sales a  b  c  d  e
------ ----- -- -- -- -- --
E09      900  1  1  0  1  0
E02      800  2  2  1  2  1
E10      700  4  3  2  3  2
E05      700  4  3  2  3  2
E01      600  5  5  4  4  3
E04      500  8  6  5  5  4
E03      500  8  6  5  5  4
E06      500  8  6  5  5  4
E08      400  9  9  8  6  5
E07      300 10 10  9  7  6
```

Figure 15.30 Compilation of results of Listings 15.30a to 15.30e.

DBMS These ranking queries use correlated subqueries and so run slowly. If you're ranking a large number of items, then you should use a built-in rank function, if available. The SQL:2003 standard introduced the functions RANK() and DENSE_RANK(), which **Microsoft SQL Server**, **Oracle, Db2, MySQL**, and **PostgreSQL** support. Alternatively, you can use your DBMS's SQL extensions to calculate ranks efficiently. The following **MySQL** script, for example, is equivalent to Listing 15.30b:

```
SET @rownum = 0;
SET @rank = 0;
SET @prev_val = NULL;
SELECT
    @rownum := @rownum + 1 AS row,
    @rank := IF(@prev_val <> sales,
      @rownum, @rank) AS rank,
    @prev_val := sales AS sales
  FROM empsales
  ORDER BY sales DESC;
```

Microsoft Access doesn't support COUNT(DISTINCT) and won't run Listing 15.30d and Listing 15.30e. For a workaround, see "Aggregating Distinct Values with DISTINCT" on page 166.

```
SELECT AVG(sales) AS TrimmedMean
  FROM titles t1
  WHERE
    (SELECT COUNT(*)
       FROM titles t2
       WHERE t2.sales <= t1.sales) > 3
    AND
    (SELECT COUNT(*)
       FROM titles t3
       WHERE t3.sales >= t1.sales) > 3;
```

Listing 15.31 Calculate the trimmed mean for *k* = 3. See Figure 15.31 for the result.

```
TrimmedMean
-----------
 27357.3333
```

Figure 15.31 Result of Listing 15.31.

```
SELECT AVG(sales) AS TrimmedMean
  FROM titles t1
  WHERE
    (SELECT COUNT(*)
       FROM titles t2
       WHERE t2.sales <= t1.sales) >=
         (SELECT 0.25 * COUNT(*)
            FROM titles)
    AND
    (SELECT COUNT(*)
       FROM titles t3
       WHERE t3.sales >= t1.sales) >=
         (SELECT 0.25 * COUNT(*)
            FROM titles);
```

Listing 15.32 Calculate the trimmed mean by discarding the lower and upper 25% of values. See Figure 15.32 for the result.

```
TrimmedMean
-----------
 27357.3333
```

Figure 15.32 Result of Listing 15.32.

Calculating a Trimmed Mean

The **trimmed mean** is a robust order statistic that is the arithmetic mean (average) of the data if the *k* smallest values and *k* largest values are discarded. The goal is to avoid the influence of extreme observations.

Listing 15.31 calculates the trimmed mean of book sales in the sample database by omitting the top three and bottom three sales figures. See Figure 15.31 for the result. For reference, the 12 sorted sales values are 566, 4095, 5000, 9566, 10467, 11320, 13001, 25667, 94123, 100001, 201440, and 1500200. This query discards 566, 4095, 5000, 100001, 201440, and 1500200 and then calculates the mean in the usual way by using the remaining six middle values. Nulls are ignored. Duplicate values are either all removed or all retained. (If all sales are the same, for example, then none of them will be trimmed no matter what *k* is.)

Listing 15.32 is similar to Listing 15.31 but trims a fixed percentage of the extreme values rather than a fixed number. Trimming by 0.25 (25%), for example, discards the sales in the top and bottom quartiles and averages what's left. See Figure 15.32 for the result.

> **DBMS** **Microsoft SQL Server** and **Db2** return an integer for the trimmed mean because the column *sales* is defined as an INTEGER. To get a floating-point value, change AVG(sales) to AVG(CAST(sales AS FLOAT)). For more information, see "Converting Data Types with CAST()" on page 145.

Picking Random Rows

Some databases are so large, and queries on them so complex, that often it's impractical (and unnecessary) to retrieve all the data relevant to a query. If you're interested in finding an overall trend or pattern, for example, then an approximate answer within some margin of error will usually suffice. One way to speed such queries is to select a random sample of rows. An efficient sample can improve performance by orders of magnitude yet still yield accurate results.

Standard SQL's TABLESAMPLE clause returns a random subset of rows. **Microsoft SQL Server, Db2**, and **PostgreSQL** support TABLESAMPLE, and **Oracle** has something similar. For the other DBMSs, use a (nonstandard) function that returns a uniform random number between 0 and 1 (Table 15.1).

Listing 15.33a randomly picks about 25% (0.25) of the rows from the sample-database table *titles*. If necessary, change RAND() to the function that appears in Table 15.1 for your DBMS. For **Oracle**, use Listing 15.33b. For **Microsoft SQL Server, Db2**, and **PostgreSQL**, use Listing 15.33c.

Figure 15.33 shows one possible result of a random selection. The rows and the number of rows returned will change every time that you run the query. If you need an exact number of random rows, then increase the sampling percentage and use one of the techniques described in "Limiting the Number of Rows Returned" on page 405.

Table 15.1 Randomization Features

DBMS	Clause or Function
Access	RND() function
SQL Server	TABLESAMPLE clause
Oracle	SAMPLE clause or DBMS_RANDOM package
Db2	TABLESAMPLE clause
MySQL	RAND() function
PostgreSQL	TABLESAMPLE clause

```
SELECT title_id, type, sales
  FROM titles
  WHERE RAND() < 0.25;
```

Listing 15.33a Select about 25% percent of the rows in the table *titles* at random. See Figure 15.33 for a possible result.

```
SELECT title_id, type, sales
  FROM titles
  SAMPLE (25);
```

Listing 15.33b Select about 25% percent of the rows in the table *titles* at random (Oracle only). See Figure 15.33 for a possible result.

```
SELECT title_id, type, sales
  FROM titles
  TABLESAMPLE SYSTEM (25);
```

Listing 15.33c Select about 25% percent of the rows in the table *titles* at random (Microsoft SQL Server, Db2, and PostgreSQL only). See Figure 15.33 for a possible result.

```
title_id type          sales
-------- ----------    -----
T03      computer      25667
T04      psychology    13001
T11      psychology    94123
```

Figure 15.33 One possible result of Listing 15.33a/b/c.

Tips for Picking Random Rows

- Randomizers take an optional **seed** argument or setting that sets the starting value for a random-number sequence. Identical seeds yield identical sequences (handy for testing). By default, the DBMS sets the seed based on the system time to generate different sequences every time.

- **DBMS** Listing 15.33a won't run correctly in **Microsoft Access** because the random-number function returns the same "random" number for every selected row. In Access, use Visual Basic or C# to pick random rows.

To use the NEWID() function to pick *n* random rows in **Microsoft SQL Server**, type:

```
SELECT TOP n title_id, type, sales
  FROM titles
  ORDER BY NEWID();
```

To use the VALUE() function in the DBMS_RANDOM package to pick *n* random rows in **Oracle**, type:

```
SELECT * FROM
  (SELECT title_id, type, sales
     FROM titles
     ORDER BY DBMS_RANDOM.VALUE())
  WHERE ROWNUM <= n;
```

Selecting Every *n*th Row

Instead of picking random rows, you can pick every *n*th row by using a modulo expression:

- *m* MOD *n* (**Microsoft Access**)
- *m* % *n* (**Microsoft SQL Server**)
- MOD(*m*, *n*) (**other DBMSs**)

This expression returns the remainder of *m* divided by *n*. For example, MOD(20, 6) is 2 because 20 equals (3 × 6) + 2. MOD(*a*, 2) is 0 if *a* is an even number.

The condition MOD(*rownumber*, *n*) = 0 picks every *n*th row, where *rownumber* is a column of consecutive integers or row identifiers. This **Oracle** query, for example, picks every third row in a table:

```
SELECT *
  FROM table
  WHERE (ROWID,0) IN
    (SELECT ROWID, MOD(ROWNUM,3)
       FROM table);
```

Note that *rownumber* imposes a row order that doesn't exist implicitly in a relational-database table.

Handling Duplicates

Normally you use SQL's PRIMARY KEY (page 336) or UNIQUE (page 345) constraints to prevent duplicate rows from appearing in production tables. But you need to know how to handle duplicates that appear when you accidentally import the same data twice or import data from a nonrelational source such as a spreadsheet or accounting package, where redundant information is rampant. This section describes how to detect, count, and remove duplicates.

Suppose that you import rows into a staging table to detect and eliminate any duplicates before inserting the data into a production table (Listing 15.34 and Figure 15.34). The column *id* is a unique row identifier that lets you identify and select rows that otherwise would be duplicates. If your imported rows don't already have an identity column, then you can add one yourself; see "Unique Identifiers" on page 70 and "Generating Sequences" on page 393. It's a good practice to add an identity column to even short-lived working tables, but in this case it also makes deleting duplicates easy. The imported data might include other columns too, but you've decided that the combination of only book title, book type, and price determines whether a row is a duplicate, regardless of the values in any other columns. Before you identify or delete duplicates, you must define exactly what it means for two rows to be considered "duplicates" of each other.

Listing 15.35 lists only the duplicates by counting the number of occurrences of each unique combination of *title_name*, *type*, and *price*. See Figure 15.35 for the result. If this query returns an empty result, then the table contains no duplicates. To list only the nonduplicates, change COUNT(*) > 1 to COUNT(*) = 1.

```
SELECT id, title_name, type, price
  FROM dups;
```

Listing 15.34 List the imported rows. See Figure 15.34 for the result.

```
id title_name    type        price
-- ------------  ---------   -----
 1 Book Title 5 children    15.00
 2 Book Title 3 biography    7.00
 3 Book Title 1 history     10.00
 4 Book Title 2 children    20.00
 5 Book Title 4 history     15.00
 6 Book Title 1 history     10.00
 7 Book Title 3 biography    7.00
 8 Book Title 1 history     10.00
```

Figure 15.34 Result of Listing 15.34.

```
SELECT title_name, type, price
  FROM dups
  GROUP BY title_name, type, price
  HAVING COUNT(*) > 1;
```

Listing 15.35 List only duplicates. See Figure 15.35 for the result.

```
title_name    type        price
------------  ---------   -----
Book Title 1 history     10.00
Book Title 3 biography    7.00
```

Figure 15.35 Result of Listing 15.35.

```
SELECT title_name, type, price,
    COUNT(*) AS NumDups
  FROM dups
  GROUP BY title_name, type, price
  HAVING COUNT(*) >= 1
  ORDER BY COUNT(*) DESC;
```

Listing 15.36 List each row and its number of repetitions.
See Figure 15.36 for the result.

```
title_name    type       price NumDups
------------  ---------  ----- -------
Book Title 1  history    10.00       3
Book Title 3  biography   7.00       2
Book Title 4  history    15.00       1
Book Title 2  children   20.00       1
Book Title 5  children   15.00       1
```

Figure 15.36 Result of Listing 15.36.

```
DELETE FROM dups
  WHERE id < (
    SELECT MAX(d.id)
      FROM dups d
      WHERE dups.title_name = d.title_name
        AND dups.type = d.type
        AND dups.price = d.price);
```

Listing 15.37 Remove the redundant duplicates in place.
See Figure 15.37 for the result.

```
id  title_name    type       price
--  ------------  ---------  -----
 1  Book Title 5  children   15.00
 4  Book Title 2  children   20.00
 5  Book Title 4  history    15.00
 7  Book Title 3  biography   7.00
 8  Book Title 1  history    10.00
```

Figure 15.37 Result of Listing 15.37.

Listing 15.36 uses a similar technique to list each row and its duplicate count. See Figure 15.36 for the result. To list only the duplicates, change COUNT(*) >= 1 to COUNT(*) > 1.

Listing 15.37 deletes duplicate rows from *dups* in place. This statement uses the column *id* to leave exactly one occurrence (the one with the highest ID) of each duplicate. Figure 15.37 shows the table *dups* after running this statement. See also "Deleting Rows with DELETE" on page 319.

Tips for Handling Duplicates

- If you define a duplicate to span *every* column in a row (not just a subset of columns), then you can drop the column *id* and use `SELECT DISTINCT * FROM table` to delete duplicates. See "Eliminating Duplicate Rows with DISTINCT" on page 81.

- **DBMS** If your DBMS offers a built-in unique row identifier, then you can drop the column *id* and still delete duplicates in place. In **Oracle**, for example, you can replace *id* with the ROWID pseudocolumn in Listing 15.37; change the outer WHERE clause to:

```
WHERE ROWID < (SELECT
  MAX(d.ROWID)...
```

To run Listing 15.36 in **MySQL**, change `ORDER BY COUNT(*) DESC` to `ORDER BY NumDups DESC`. You can't use Listing 15.37 to do an in-place deletion because MySQL won't let you use same table for both the subquery's FROM clause and the DELETE target.

Messy Data

Deleting duplicates gets harder as data get messier. It's not unusual to buy a mailing list containing entries that look like this:

```
name          address1
----------    ------------------
John Smith    123 Main St
John Smith    123 Main St, Apt 1
Jack Smiht    121 Main Rd
John Symthe   123 Main St.
Jon Smith     123 Mian Street
```

DBMSs offer nonstandard tools such as **Soundex** (phonetic) functions to suppress spelling variations, but creating an automated deletion program that works over thousands or millions of rows is a major project.

```
SELECT
    a.au_id AS "ID",
    a.au_fname AS "FirstName",
    a.au_lname AS "LastName",
    COALESCE(twork.tel_no, thome.tel_no)
      AS "TelNo",
    COALESCE(twork.tel_type, thome.tel_type)
      AS "TelType"
  FROM authors a
  LEFT OUTER JOIN telephones twork
    ON a.au_id = twork.au_id
    AND twork.tel_type = 'W'
  LEFT OUTER JOIN telephones thome
    ON a.au_id = thome.au_id
    AND thome.tel_type = 'H'
  WHERE COALESCE(twork.tel_no, thome.tel_no)
    IS NOT NULL
  ORDER BY a.au_fname ASC, a.au_lname ASC;
```

Listing 15.38 Lists the authors' names and telephone numbers, favoring work numbers over home numbers. See Figure 15.38 for the result.

```
ID   FirstName  LastName   TelNo          TelType
---  ---------  ---------  ------------   -------
A05  Christian  Kells      666-666-6666   H
A04  Klee       Hull       555-555-5555   W
A01  Sarah      Buchman    222-222-2222   W
A02  Wendy      Heydemark  333-333-3333   W
```

Figure 15.38 Result of Listing 15.38.

Creating a Telephone List

You can use the function COALESCE() (page 153) with a left outer join (page 221) to create a convenient telephone listing from a normalized table of telephone numbers.

Suppose that the sample database has an extra table named *telephones* that stores the authors' work and home telephone numbers:

au_id	tel_type	tel_no
A01	H	111-111-1111
A01	W	222-222-2222
A02	W	333-333-3333
A04	H	444-444-4444
A04	W	555-555-5555
A05	H	666-666-6666

The table's composite primary key is (*au_id*, *tel_type*), where *tel_type* indicates whether *tel_no* is a work (W) or home (H) number. Listing 15.38 lists the authors' names and numbers. If an author has only one number, then that number is listed. If an author has both home and work numbers, then only the work number is listed. Authors with no numbers aren't listed. See Figure 15.38 for the result.

The first left join picks out the work numbers, and the second picks out the home numbers. The WHERE clause filters out authors with no numbers. (You can extend this query to add mobile and other numbers.)

DBMS **Microsoft Access** won't run Listing 15.38 because of the restrictions Access puts on join expressions.

Retrieving Metadata

Metadata are data about data. In DBMSs, metadata include information about schemas, databases, users (page 144), tables (page 302), columns, and so on. When meeting a new database, inspect its metadata: What's in the database? How big is it? How are the tables organized?

Metadata, like other data, are stored in tables and so can be accessed via SELECT queries. Metadata also can be accessed, often more conveniently, by using command-line and graphical tools. The following listings show DBMS-specific examples for viewing metadata. The DBMS itself maintains metadata—look, but don't touch.

> **DBMS** The SQL standard calls a set of metadata a **catalog** and specifies that it be accessed through the schema INFORMATION_SCHEMA. Not all DBMSs implement this schema or use the same terms. In **Microsoft SQL Server**, for example, the equivalent term for a *catalog* is a *database* and for a *schema*, an *owner*. In **Oracle**, the repository of metadata is the *data dictionary*.

Microsoft Access

Microsoft Access metadata are available graphically through the Design View of each database object and programmatically through the Visual Basic for Applications (VBA) or C# language. Access also creates and maintains hidden system tables in each database.

To show system tables in Microsoft Access:

- Choose File tab > Options > Current Database (in the left pane). Scroll to Navigation, click Navigation Options, and then select Show System Objects.

The system tables begin with *MSys* and are commingled with the database's other tables. You can open and query them as you would ordinary tables. The most interesting system table is MSysObjects, which catalogs all the objects in the database. Listing 15.39 lists all the tables in the current database. Note that system tables don't have to be visible to be used in queries.

```
SELECT Name
  FROM MSysObjects
  WHERE Type = 1;
```

Listing 15.39 List the tables in the current Microsoft Access database. To list queries instead, change Type = 1 to Type = 5.

```
-- List the databases.
exec sp_helpdb;

-- List the schemas.
SELECT schema_name
  FROM information_schema.schemata;

-- List the tables (Method 1).
SELECT *
  FROM information_schema.tables
  WHERE table_type = 'BASE TABLE'
    AND table_schema = 'schema_name';

-- List the tables (Method 2).
exec sp_tables;

-- Describe a table (Method 1).
SELECT *
  FROM information_schema.columns
  WHERE table_catalog = 'db_name'
    AND table_schema = 'schema_name'
    AND table_name = 'table_name';

-- Describe a table (Method 2).
exec sp_help table_name;
```

Listing 15.40 Metadata statements and commands for Microsoft SQL Server

```
-- List the schemas (users).
SELECT *
  FROM all_users;

-- List the tables.
SELECT table_name
  FROM all_tables
  WHERE owner = 'user_name';

-- Describe a table (Method 1).
SELECT *
  FROM all_tab_columns
  WHERE owner = 'user_name'
    AND table_name = 'table_name';

-- Describe a table (Method 2, in sqlplus).
DESCRIBE table_name;
```

Listing 15.41 Metadata statements and commands for Oracle Database.

```
-- List the databases (in db2).
LIST DATABASE DIRECTORY;

-- List the schemas.
SELECT schemaname
  FROM syscat.schemata;

-- List the tables (Method 1).
SELECT tabname
  FROM syscat.tables
  WHERE tabschema = 'schema_name';

-- List the tables (Method 2, in db2).
LIST TABLES;

-- List the tables (Method 3, in db2).
LIST TABLES FOR SCHEMA schema_name;

-- Describe a table (Method 1).
SELECT *
  FROM syscat.columns
  WHERE tabname = 'table_name'
    AND tabschema = 'schema_name';

-- Describe a table (Method 2, in db2).
DESCRIBE TABLE table_name SHOW DETAIL;
```

Listing 15.42 Metadata statements and commands for IBM Db2 Database

Microsoft SQL Server

Microsoft SQL Server metadata are available through the schema INFORMATION_SCHEMA and via system stored procedures (Listing 15.40).

Oracle Database

Oracle metadata are available through data dictionary views and via the sqlplus command-line tool (Listing 15.41). To list data dictionary views, run this query in sqlplus:

```
SELECT table_name, comments
  FROM dictionary
  ORDER BY table_name;
```

For a list of Oracle databases (instances) in Unix or Linux, look in the file *oratab* located in the directory */etc* or */var/opt/oracle*. In Windows, run this command at a command prompt:

```
net start | find /i "OracleService"
```

Or choose Start > Run (Windows logo key + R), type `services.msc`, press Enter, and then inspect the Services list for entries that begin with *OracleService*.

IBM Db2 Database

Db2 metadata are available through the system catalog SYSCAT and via the db2 command-line tool (Listing 15.42).

MySQL

MySQL metadata are available through the schema INFORMATION_SCHEMA and via the mysql command-line tool (Listing 15.43).

```
-- List the databases (Method 1).
SELECT schema_name
  FROM information_schema.schemata;

-- List the databases (Method 2, in mysql).
SHOW DATABASES;

-- List the tables (Method 1).
SELECT table_name
  FROM information_schema.tables
  WHERE table_schema = 'db_name';

-- List the tables (Method 2, in mysql).
SHOW TABLES;

-- Describe a table (Method 1).
SELECT *
  FROM information_schema.columns
  WHERE table_schema = 'db_name'
    AND table_name = 'table_name';

-- Describe a table (Method 2, in mysql).
DESCRIBE table_name;
```

Listing 15.43 Metadata statements and commands for MySQL.

PostgreSQL

PostgreSQL metadata are available through the schema INFORMATION_SCHEMA and via the psql command-line tool (Listing 15.44).

```
-- List the databases (Method 1).
psql --list

-- List the databases (Method 2, in psql).
\l

-- List the schemas.
SELECT schema_name
  FROM information_schema.schemata;

-- List the tables (Method 1).
SELECT table_name
  FROM information_schema.tables
  WHERE table_schema = 'schema_name';

-- List the tables (Method 2, in psql).
\dt

-- Describe a table (Method 1).
SELECT *
  FROM information_schema.columns
  WHERE table_schema = 'schema_name'
    AND table_name = 'table_name';

-- Describe a table (Method 2, in psql).
\d table_name;
```

Listing 15.44 Metadata statements and commands for PostgreSQL

```
-- Extract parts of the current datetime.
SELECT
  datepart("s",    now()) AS sec_pt,
  datepart("n",    now()) AS min_pt,
  datepart("h",    now()) AS hr_pt,
  datepart("d",    now()) AS day_pt,
  datepart("m",    now()) AS mon_pt,
  datepart("yyyy",now()) AS yr_pt;


-- Add or subtract days, months, and years.
SELECT
    dateadd("d",     2,pubdate) AS p2d,
    dateadd("d",    -2,pubdate) AS m2d,
    dateadd("m",     2,pubdate) AS p2m,
    dateadd("m",    -2,pubdate) AS m2m,
    dateadd("yyyy", 2,pubdate) AS p2y,
    dateadd("yyyy",-2,pubdate) AS m2y
  FROM titles
  WHERE title_id = 'T05';


-- Count the days between two dates.
SELECT datediff("d",date1,date2) AS days
  FROM
    (SELECT pubdate as date1
       FROM titles
       WHERE title_id = 'T05') t1,
    (SELECT pubdate as date2
       FROM titles
       WHERE title_id = 'T06') t2;


-- Count the months between two dates.
SELECT datediff("m",date1,date2) AS months
  FROM
    (SELECT
         MIN(pubdate) AS date1,
         MAX(pubdate) AS date2
       FROM titles) t1;
```

Listing 15.45 Working with dates in Microsoft Access.

Working with Dates

As pointed out in "Performing Datetime and Interval Arithmetic" on page 140 and "Getting the Current Date and Time" on page 142, DBMSs provide their own extended (nonstandard) functions for manipulating dates and times. This section explains how to use built-in functions to do simple date arithmetic. The queries in each listing:

- Extract parts (hour, day, month, and so on) of the current (system) datetime and return them as numbers.

- Add and subtract intervals of days, months, and years from a date.

- Count the days between two dates in different rows of the same column. The result is positive, zero, or negative depending on whether the first date falls before, on, or after the second date.

- Count the months between the earliest and latest dates in the same column.

Microsoft Access

The function datepart() extracts the specified part of a datetime. now() returns the current (system) date and time. dateadd() adds a specified time interval to a date. datediff() returns the number of specified time intervals between two dates (Listing 15.45). Alternatives to datepart() are the extraction functions second(), day(), month(), and so on.

Microsoft SQL Server

The function datepart() extracts the specified part of a datetime. getdate() returns the current (system) date and time. dateadd() adds a specified time interval to a date. datediff() returns the number of specified time intervals between two dates (Listing 15.46). Alternatives to datepart() are the extraction functions day(), month(), and year().

```
-- Extract parts of the current datetime.
SELECT
  datepart("s",   getdate()) AS sec_pt,
  datepart("n",   getdate()) AS min_pt,
  datepart("hh",  getdate()) AS hr_pt,
  datepart("d",   getdate()) AS day_pt,
  datepart("m",   getdate()) AS mon_pt,
  datepart("yyyy",getdate()) AS yr_pt;

-- Add or subtract days, months, and years.
SELECT
    dateadd("d",     2,pubdate) AS p2d,
    dateadd("d",    -2,pubdate) AS m2d,
    dateadd("m",     2,pubdate) AS p2m,
    dateadd("m",    -2,pubdate) AS m2m,
    dateadd("yyyy",  2,pubdate) AS p2y,
    dateadd("yyyy",-2,pubdate) AS m2y
  FROM titles
  WHERE title_id = 'T05';

-- Count the days between two dates.
SELECT datediff("d",date1,date2) AS days
  FROM
    (SELECT pubdate as date1
       FROM titles
       WHERE title_id = 'T05') t1,
    (SELECT pubdate as date2
       FROM titles
       WHERE title_id = 'T06') t2;

-- Count the months between two dates.
SELECT datediff("m",date1,date2) AS months
  FROM
    (SELECT
         MIN(pubdate) AS date1,
         MAX(pubdate) AS date2
       FROM titles) t1;
```

Listing 15.46 Working with dates in Microsoft SQL Server.

```
-- Extract parts of the current datetime.
SELECT
    to_number(to_char(sysdate,'ss'))
      AS sec_pt,
    to_number(to_char(sysdate,'mi'))
      AS min_pt,
    to_number(to_char(sysdate,'hh24'))
      AS hr_pt,
    to_number(to_char(sysdate,'dd'))
      AS day_pt,
    to_number(to_char(sysdate,'mm'))
      AS mon_pt,
    to_number(to_char(sysdate,'yyyy'))
      AS yr_pt
  FROM dual;

-- Add or subtract days, months, and years.
SELECT
    pubdate+2             AS p2d,
    pubdate-2             AS m2d,
    add_months(pubdate, +2) AS p2m,
    add_months(pubdate, -2) AS m2m,
    add_months(pubdate,+24) AS p2y,
    add_months(pubdate,-24) AS m2y
  FROM titles
  WHERE title_id = 'T05';

-- Count the days between two dates.
SELECT date2 - date1 AS days
  FROM
    (SELECT pubdate as date1
       FROM titles
       WHERE title_id = 'T05') t1,
    (SELECT pubdate as date2
       FROM titles
       WHERE title_id = 'T06') t2;

-- Count the months between two dates.
SELECT months_between(date2,date1) AS months
  FROM
    (SELECT
         MIN(pubdate) AS date1,
         MAX(pubdate) AS date2
       FROM titles) t1;
```

Listing 15.47 Working with dates in Oracle Database.

Oracle Database

The function to_char() converts a datetime to a character value in the given format. to_number() converts its argument to a number. sysdate returns the current (system) date and time. The standard addition and subtraction operators add and subtract days from a date. add_months() adds a specified number of months to a date. Subtracting one date from another yields the number of days between them. months_between() returns the number of months between two dates (Listing 15.47).

IBM Db2 Database

The functions second(), day(), month(), and so on, extract part of a datetime. `current_timestamp` returns the current (system) date and time. The standard addition and subtraction operators add and subtract time intervals from a date. days() converts a date to an integer serial number (Listing 15.48).

```
-- Extract parts of the current datetime.
SELECT
    second(current_timestamp) AS sec_pt,
    minute(current_timestamp) AS min_pt,
    hour(current_timestamp)   AS hr_pt,
    day(current_timestamp)    AS day_pt,
    month(current_timestamp)  AS mon_pt,
    year(current_timestamp)   AS yr_pt
  FROM SYSIBM.SYSDUMMY1;

-- Add or subtract days, months, and years.
SELECT
    pubdate + 2 DAY   AS p2d,
    pubdate - 2 DAY   AS m2d,
    pubdate + 2 MONTH AS p2m,
    pubdate - 2 MONTH AS m2m,
    pubdate + 2 YEAR  AS p2y,
    pubdate - 2 YEAR  AS m2y
  FROM titles
  WHERE title_id = 'T05';

-- Count the days between two dates.
SELECT days(date2) - days(date1) AS days
  FROM
    (SELECT pubdate as date1
       FROM titles
       WHERE title_id = 'T05') t1,
    (SELECT pubdate as date2
       FROM titles
       WHERE title_id = 'T06') t2;

-- Count the months between two dates.
SELECT
    (year(date2) * 12 + month(date2)) -
    (year(date1) * 12 + month(date1))
      AS months
  FROM
    (SELECT
        MIN(pubdate) AS date1,
        MAX(pubdate) AS date2
      FROM titles) t1;
```

Listing 15.48 Working with dates in IBM Db2 Database.

```
-- Extract parts of the current datetime.
SELECT
  date_format(current_timestamp,'%s')
    AS sec_pt,
  date_format(current_timestamp,'%i')
    AS min_pt,
  date_format(current_timestamp,'%k')
    AS hr_pt,
  date_format(current_timestamp,'%d')
    AS day_pt,
  date_format(current_timestamp,'%m')
    AS mon_pt,
  date_format(current_timestamp,'%Y')
    AS yr_pt;

-- Add or subtract days, months, and years.
SELECT
    pubdate + INTERVAL 2 DAY   AS p2d,
    pubdate - INTERVAL 2 DAY   AS m2d,
    pubdate + INTERVAL 2 MONTH AS p2m,
    pubdate - INTERVAL 2 MONTH AS m2m,
    pubdate + INTERVAL 2 YEAR  AS p2y,
    pubdate - INTERVAL 2 YEAR  AS m2y
  FROM titles
  WHERE title_id = 'T05';

-- Count the days between two dates.
SELECT datediff(date2,date1) AS days
  FROM
    (SELECT pubdate as date1
      FROM titles
      WHERE title_id = 'T05') t1,
    (SELECT pubdate as date2
      FROM titles
      WHERE title_id = 'T06') t2;

-- Count the months between two dates.
SELECT
    (year(date2) * 12 + month(date2)) -
    (year(date1) * 12 + month(date1))
      AS months
  FROM
    (SELECT
        MIN(pubdate) AS date1,
        MAX(pubdate) AS date2
      FROM titles) t1;
```

Listing 15.49 Working with dates in MySQL.

MySQL

The function date_format() formats a datetime according to the specified format. `current_timestamp` returns the current (system) date and time. The standard addition and subtraction operators add and subtract time intervals from a date. datediff() returns the number of days between two dates (Listing 15.49). Alternatives to date_format() are the extraction functions extract(), second(), day(), month(), and so on.

PostgreSQL

The function date_part() extracts the specified part of a datetime. `current_timestamp` returns the current (system) date and time. The standard addition and subtraction operators add and subtract time intervals from a date. Subtracting one date from another yields the number of days between them (Listing 15.50). An alternative to date_part() is extract().

```
-- Extract parts of the current datetime.
SELECT
  date_part('second',current_timestamp)
    AS sec_pt,
  date_part('minute',current_timestamp)
    AS min_pt,
  date_part('hour',current_timestamp)
    AS hr_pt,
  date_part('day',current_timestamp)
    AS day_pt,
  date_part('month',current_timestamp)
    AS mon_pt,
  date_part('year',current_timestamp)
    AS yr_pt;

-- Add or subtract days, months, and years.
SELECT
    pubdate + INTERVAL '2 DAY'   AS p2d,
    pubdate - INTERVAL '2 DAY'   AS m2d,
    pubdate + INTERVAL '2 MONTH' AS p2m,
    pubdate - INTERVAL '2 MONTH' AS m2m,
    pubdate + INTERVAL '2 YEAR'  AS p2y,
    pubdate - INTERVAL '2 YEAR'  AS m2y
  FROM titles
  WHERE title_id = 'T05';

-- Count the days between two dates.
SELECT date2 - date1 AS days
  FROM
    (SELECT pubdate as date1
       FROM titles
       WHERE title_id = 'T05') t1,
    (SELECT pubdate as date2
       FROM titles
       WHERE title_id = 'T06') t2;

-- Count the months between two dates.
SELECT
    (date_part('year', date2) * 12 +
    date_part('month',date2)) -
    (date_part('year', date1) * 12 +
    date_part('month',date1))
      AS months
  FROM
    (SELECT
        MIN(pubdate) AS date1,
        MAX(pubdate) AS date2
      FROM titles) t1;
```

Listing 15.50 Working with dates in PostgreSQL.

```
emp_id  sales
------  -----
E07       300
E08       400
E03       500
E04       500
E06       500
E01       600
E05       700
E10       700
E02       800
E09       900
```

Figure 15.39 The table *empsales*, sorted by ascending sales.

```
SELECT AVG(sales) AS median
    FROM
        (SELECT e1.sales
            FROM empsales e1, empsales e2
            GROUP BY e1.sales
            HAVING
                SUM(CASE WHEN e1.sales = e2.sales
                    THEN 1 ELSE 0 END) >=
                ABS(SUM(SIGN(e1.sales -
                                e2.sales)))) t1;
```

Listing 15.51 Calculate the median of *sales* in standard SQL.

Calculating a Median

The **median** describes the center of the data as the middle point of *n* (sorted) values. If *n* is odd, then the median is the observation number $(n + 1)/2$. If *n* is even, then the median is the midpoint (average) of observations $n/2$ and $(n/2) + 1$.

The examples in this section calculate the median of the column *sales* in the table *empsales* (Figure 15.39). The median is 550—the average of the middle two numbers, 500 and 600, in the sorted list.

Search the web and you'll find many standard and DBMS-specific ways to calculate the median. Listing 15.51 shows one way—it uses a self-join and GROUP BY to create a Cartesian product (*e1* and *e2*) without duplicates and then uses HAVING and SUM to find the row (containing the median) where the number of times *e1.sales* = *e2.sales* equals (or exceeds) the number of times *e1.sales* > *e2.sales*. Like all methods that use standard (or near-standard) SQL, it's cumbersome, it's hard to understand, and it runs slowly because it's difficult to pick the middle value of an ordered set when SQL is about *un*ordered sets.

DBMS To run Listing 15.51 in **Microsoft Access**, change the CASE expression to iif(e1. sales = e2.sales, 1, 0) and change SIGN to SGN.

Median vs. Mean

The median is a popular statistic because it's robust, meaning it's not affected seriously by extreme high or low values, either legitimate or caused by errors. The arithmetic mean (average), on the other hand, is so sensitive that it can swing wildly with the addition or removal of even a single extreme value. That's why you see the median applied to skewed (lopsided) distributions such as wealth, house prices, military budgets, and gene expression. The median is also known as the **50th percentile** or the **second quartile**. See also "Finding Extreme Values" on page 435.

```
-- Method 1.
-- Works in Microsoft SQL Server.
SELECT
  (
    (SELECT MAX(sales) FROM
      (SELECT TOP 50 PERCENT sales
        FROM empsales
        ORDER BY sales ASC) AS t1)
    +
    (SELECT MIN(sales) FROM
      (SELECT TOP 50 PERCENT sales
        FROM empsales
        ORDER BY sales DESC) AS t2)
  )/2 AS median;


-- Method 2.
-- Works in Microsoft SQL Server and Db2.
SELECT AVG(sales) AS median
  FROM
    (SELECT
      sales,
      ROW_NUMBER() OVER (ORDER BY sales)
        AS rownum,
      COUNT(*) OVER () AS cnt
    FROM empsales) t1
  WHERE rownum IN ((cnt+1)/2, (cnt+2)/2);
```

Listing 15.52 Here are two ways to calculate the median in Microsoft SQL Server. The second method, which also works in Db2, is faster than the first.

```
-- Method 1.
-- Works in Oracle.
SELECT
    percentile_cont(0.5)
      WITHIN GROUP (ORDER BY sales)
      AS median
  FROM empsales;

-- Method 2.
-- Works in Oracle and Db2.
SELECT median(sales) AS median
  FROM empsales;
```

Listing 15.53 Here are two to calculate the median in Oracle. The second method, which also works in Db2, is faster than the first.

DBMS It's faster and more efficient to calculate the median by using DBMS-specific functions. In **Microsoft Access**, use Visual Basic or C# to call Excel's MEDIAN() function from within Access. Listing 15.52 calculates the median in **Microsoft SQL Server** in two ways. Listing 15.53 calculates it in **Oracle** in two ways. The second query in Listing 15.52 and Listing 15.53 also works in **Db2**,

If you use an alternate method to compute the median, then make sure that it doesn't eliminate duplicate values during calculations and averages the two middle observations for an even n (rather than just lazily choosing one of them as the median).

See also "Statistics in SQL" on page 164.

```
SELECT title_id, advance
  FROM royalties
  WHERE advance IN (
    (SELECT MIN(advance) FROM royalties),
    (SELECT MAX(advance) FROM royalties));
```

Listing 15.54 List the books with the highest and lowest advances. See Figure 15.40 for the result.

```
title_id advance
-------- ----------
T07       1000000.00
T08             0.00
T09             0.00
```

Figure 15.40 Result of Listing 15.54.

```
SELECT title_id, advance
  FROM
    (SELECT title_id, advance,
          MIN(advance) OVER () min_adv,
          MAX(advance) OVER () max_adv
      FROM royalties) t1
  WHERE advance IN (min_adv, max_adv);
```

Listing 15.55 List the books with the highest and lowest advances, using window functions.

Finding Extreme Values

You can use aggregate functions in a subquery to find the highest and lowest values in a column.

Listing 15.54 finds the rows with the highest and lowest values (ties included) of the column *advance* in the table *royalties*. Figure 15.40 shows the result.

You also can use the queries in "Limiting the Number of Rows Returned" on page 405 to find extremes, although not both highs and lows in the same query.

DBMS In **Microsoft SQL Server, Oracle, Db2, MySQL**, and **PostgreSQL** you can replicate Listing 15.54 by using the window functions MIN OVER and MAX OVER (Listing 15.55).

Changing Running Statistics Midstream

You can modify values of an in-progress running statistic depending on values in another column. First, review Listing 15.1 in "Calculating Running Statistics" on page 390.

Listing 15.56 calculates the running sum of book sales, ignoring biographies. The scalar subquery computes the running sum, and the inner CASE expression identifies biographies and changes their *sales* value to NULL, which is ignored by the aggregate function SUM(). The outer CASE expression merely creates a label column in the result; it's not part of the running-sum logic. Figure 15.41 shows the result.

In the inner CASE expression, you can set the value being summed to any number, not only NULL. If you were summing bank transactions, for example, then you could make the deposits positive and withdrawals negative.

```
SELECT
    t1.title_id,
    CASE WHEN t1.type = 'biography'
      THEN '*IGNORED*'
      ELSE t1.type END
        AS title_type,
    t1.sales,
    (SELECT
        SUM(CASE WHEN t2.type = 'biography'
            THEN NULL
            ELSE t2.sales END)
      FROM titles t2
      WHERE t1.title_id >= t2.title_id)
        AS RunSum
  FROM titles t1;
```

Listing 15.56 Calculate the running sum of book sales, ignoring biographies. See Figure 15.41 for the result.

```
title_id title_type sales    RunSum
-------- ---------- -------  ------

T01      history        566     566
T02      history       9566   10132
T03      computer     25667   35799
T04      psychology   13001   48800
T05      psychology  201440  250240
T06      *IGNORED*    11320  250240
T07      *IGNORED*  1500200  250240
T08      children      4095  254335
T09      children      5000  259335
T10      *IGNORED*     NULL  259335
T11      psychology   94123  353458
T12      *IGNORED*   100001  353458
T13      history      10467  363925
```

Figure 15.41 Result of Listing 15.56.

```
SELECT
    title_id,
    CASE WHEN type = 'biography'
      THEN '*IGNORED*'
      ELSE type END
        AS title_type,
    sales,
    SUM(CASE WHEN type = 'biography'
            THEN NULL
            ELSE sales END)
            OVER (ORDER BY title_id, sales)
        AS RunSum
  FROM titles;
```

Listing 15.57 Calculate the running sum of book sales, ignoring biographies and using window functions.

DBMS To run Listing 15.56 in **Microsoft Access**, change the two CASE expressions to

```
iif(t1.type = 'biography', '*IGNORED*',
  t1.type)
```

and

```
iif(t2.type = 'biography', NULL, t2.sales)
```

In **Microsoft SQL Server, Oracle, Db2 , MySQL**, and **PostgreSQL** you can replicate Listing 15.56 by using the window function SUM OVER (Listing 15.57).

Pivoting Results

Pivoting a table swaps its columns and rows, typically to display data in a compact format on a report.

Listing 15.58 uses SUM functions and CASE expressions to list the number of books each author wrote (or cowrote). But instead of displaying the result in the usual way (see Listing 6.9 on page 169, for example), like this:

```
au_id  num_books
-----  ---------
A01    3
A02    4
A03    2
A04    4
A05    1
A06    3
A07    0
```

Listing 15.58 produces a pivoted result:

```
A01 A02 A03 A04 A05 A06 A07
--- --- --- --- --- --- ---
  3   4   2   4   1   3   0
```

```sql
SELECT
    SUM(CASE WHEN au_id='A01'
        THEN 1 ELSE 0 END) AS A01,
    SUM(CASE WHEN au_id='A02'
        THEN 1 ELSE 0 END) AS A02,
    SUM(CASE WHEN au_id='A03'
        THEN 1 ELSE 0 END) AS A03,
    SUM(CASE WHEN au_id='A04'
        THEN 1 ELSE 0 END) AS A04,
    SUM(CASE WHEN au_id='A05'
        THEN 1 ELSE 0 END) AS A05,
    SUM(CASE WHEN au_id='A06'
        THEN 1 ELSE 0 END) AS A06,
    SUM(CASE WHEN au_id='A07'
        THEN 1 ELSE 0 END) AS A07
  FROM title_authors;
```

Listing 15.58 List the number of books each author wrote (or cowrote), pivoting the result.

```
SELECT
    au_ids.au_id,
    CASE au_ids.au_id
      WHEN 'A01' THEN num_books.A01
      WHEN 'A02' THEN num_books.A02
      WHEN 'A03' THEN num_books.A03
      WHEN 'A04' THEN num_books.A04
      WHEN 'A05' THEN num_books.A05
      WHEN 'A06' THEN num_books.A06
      WHEN 'A07' THEN num_books.A07
    END
      AS num_books
  FROM
    (SELECT au_id FROM authors) au_ids,
    (SELECT
      SUM(CASE WHEN au_id='A01'
        THEN 1 ELSE 0 END) AS A01,
      SUM(CASE WHEN au_id='A02'
        THEN 1 ELSE 0 END) AS A02,
      SUM(CASE WHEN au_id='A03'
        THEN 1 ELSE 0 END) AS A03,
      SUM(CASE WHEN au_id='A04'
        THEN 1 ELSE 0 END) AS A04,
      SUM(CASE WHEN au_id='A05'
        THEN 1 ELSE 0 END) AS A05,
      SUM(CASE WHEN au_id='A06'
        THEN 1 ELSE 0 END) AS A06,
      SUM(CASE WHEN au_id='A07'
        THEN 1 ELSE 0 END) AS A07
    FROM title_authors) num_books;
```

Listing 15.59 List the number of books each author wrote (or cowrote), reverse-pivoting the result.

Listing 15.59 reverses the pivot. The first subquery in the FROM clause returns the unique authors' IDs. The second subquery reproduces the result of Listing 15.58.

DBMS To run Listing 15.58 and Listing 15.59 in **Microsoft Access**, change the simple CASE expressions to iif functions. For example, change the first CASE expression in Listing 15.58 to

```
iif(au_id = 'A01', 1, 0)
```

Also, change the searched CASE expression to a switch() function (see the DBMS tip in "Evaluating Conditional Values with CASE" on page 149).

Working with Hierarchies

You can use SQL to traverse elements that are organized in a hierarchy. A **hierarchy** ranks and organizes people or things within a system. Each element (except the top one) is a subordinate to a single other element. Figure 15.42 is a tree diagram of a corporate pecking order, with the chief executive officer (CEO) at top, above vice presidents (VP), directors (DIR), and wage slaves (WS).

Hierarchical trees come with their own vocabulary. Each element in the tree is a **node**. Nodes are connected by **branches**. Two connected nodes form a **parent–child relationship** (three connected nodes form a grandparent–parent–child relationship, and so on). At the top of the pyramid is the **root node** (CEO, in this example). Nodes without children are **end nodes** or **leaf nodes** (DIR2 and all the WSs). **Branch nodes** connect to leaf nodes or other branch nodes (VP1, VP2, DIR1, and DIR3— middle management).

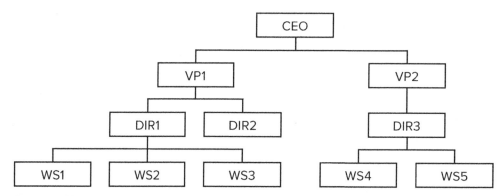

Figure 15.42 An organization chart showing a simple company hierarchy.

```
emp_id  emp_title  boss_id
------  ---------  -------
E01     CEO        NULL
E02     VP1        E01
E03     VP2        E01
E04     DIR1       E02
E05     DIR2       E02
E06     DIR3       E03
E07     WS1        E04
E08     WS2        E04
E09     WS3        E04
E10     WS4        E06
E11     WS5        E06
```

Figure 15.43 The result of the query SELECT * FROM hier;. The table *hier* represents the organization chart in Figure 15.42.

```
SELECT
    h1.emp_title ||
    ' obeys '    ||
    h2.emp_title
      AS power_structure
  FROM hier h1, hier h2
  WHERE h1.boss_id = h2.emp_id;
```

Listing 15.60 List the parent–child relationships. See Figure 15.44 for the result.

```
power_structure
---------------
VP1 obeys CEO
VP2 obeys CEO
DIR1 obeys VP1
DIR2 obeys VP1
DIR3 obeys VP2
WS1 obeys DIR1
WS2 obeys DIR1
WS3 obeys DIR1
WS4 obeys DIR3
WS5 obeys DIR3
```

Figure 15.44 Result of Listing 15.60.

The table *hier* (Figure 15.43) represents the tree in Figure 15.42. The table *hier* has the same structure as the table *employees* in "Creating a Self-Join" on page 233. Review that section for the basics of using self-joins with hierarchies.

Listing 15.60 uses a self-join to list who works for whom. See Figure 15.44 for the result.

DBMS To run Listing 15.60 in **Microsoft Access** and **Microsoft SQL Server**, change each || to +. In **MySQL**, use CONCAT() to concatenate strings. See "Concatenating Strings with ||" on page 122.

Listing 15.61 traverses the hierarchy by using multiple self-joins to trace the chain of command from employee WS3 to the top of the tree. See Figure 15.45 for the result. Unfortunately, you must know the depth of the hierarchy before you write this query; use one of the alternatives given next, if possible.

```
SELECT
    h1.emp_title || ' < ' ||
    h2.emp_title || ' < ' ||
    h3.emp_title || ' < ' ||
    h4.emp_title
      AS chain_of_command
  FROM hier h1, hier h2, hier h3, hier h4
  WHERE h1.emp_title = 'WS3'
    AND h1.boss_id = h2.emp_id
    AND h2.boss_id = h3.emp_id
    AND h3.boss_id = h4.emp_id;
```

Listing 15.61 Show the full hierarchical relationship of employee WS3. See Figure 15.45 for the result.

```
chain_of_command
----------------------
WS3 < DIR1 < VP1 < CEO
```

Figure 15.45 Result of Listing 15.61.

To run Listing 15.61 in **Microsoft Access** and **Microsoft SQL Server**, change each ‖ to +. In **MySQL**, use CONCAT() to concatenate strings. See "Concatenating Strings with ‖" on page 122.

In **Microsoft SQL Server** and **Db2**, use the (standard) recursive WITH clause to traverse a hierarchy. The following query is equivalent to Listing 15.61 (in Microsoft SQL Server, change each ‖ to +):

```
WITH recurse (chain, emp_level, boss_id) AS
  (SELECT
      CAST(emp_title AS VARCHAR(50)),
      0,
      boss_id
   FROM hier
   WHERE emp_title = 'WS3'
  UNION ALL
  SELECT
      CAST(recurse.chain || ' < ' ||
        hier.emp_title AS VARCHAR(50)),
      recurse.emp_level + 1,
      hier.boss_id
   FROM hier, recurse
   WHERE recurse.boss_id = hier.emp_id
  )
SELECT chain AS chain_of_command
  FROM recurse
  WHERE emp_level = 3;
```

In **Microsoft SQL Server** and **Db2**, to list everyone who reports to a particular employee (VP1, in this example), either directly or indirectly (through a boss's boss), use this query:

```
WITH recurse (emp_title, emp_id) AS
  (SELECT emp_title,emp_id
     FROM hier
     WHERE emp_title = 'VP1'
  UNION ALL
  SELECT hier.emp_title, hier.emp_id
     FROM hier, recurse
     WHERE recurse.emp_id = hier.boss_id
  )
SELECT emp_title AS "Works for VP1"
  FROM recurse
  WHERE emp_title <> 'VP1';
```

In **Oracle**, use the (nonstandard) CONNECT BY syntax to traverse a hierarchy. The following query is equivalent to Listing 15.61:

```
SELECT LTRIM(SYS_CONNECT_BY_PATH(
  emp_title, ' < '), ' < ')
    AS chain_of_command
FROM hier
WHERE LEVEL = 4
START WITH emp_title = 'WS3'
CONNECT BY PRIOR boss_id = emp_id;
```

In **Oracle**, to list everyone who reports to a particular employee (VP1, in this example), either directly or indirectly (through a boss's boss), use this query:

```
SELECT emp_title AS "Works for VP1"
  FROM hier
  WHERE emp_title <> 'VP1'
  START WITH emp_title = 'VP1'
  CONNECT BY PRIOR emp_id = boss_id;
```

Listing 15.62 traverses the hierarchy by using multiple UNIONs and self-joins to trace the chain of command for every employee. See Figure 15.46 for the result. Unfortunately, you must know the maximum depth of the hierarchy before you write this query; use one of the alternatives given next, if possible.

```
SELECT chain AS chains_of_command
  FROM
    (SELECT emp_title as chain
      FROM hier
      WHERE boss_id IS NULL
    UNION
    SELECT
        h1.emp_title || ' > ' ||
        h2.emp_title
      FROM hier h1
      INNER JOIN hier h2
        ON (h1.emp_id = h2.boss_id)
      WHERE h1.boss_id IS NULL
    UNION
    SELECT
        h1.emp_title || ' > ' ||
        h2.emp_title || ' > ' ||
        h3.emp_title
      FROM hier h1
      INNER JOIN hier h2
        ON (h1.emp_id = h2.boss_id)
      LEFT OUTER JOIN hier h3
        ON (h2.emp_id = h3.boss_id)
      WHERE h1.emp_title = 'CEO'
    UNION
    SELECT
        h1.emp_title || ' > ' ||
        h2.emp_title || ' > ' ||
        h3.emp_title || ' > ' ||
        h4.emp_title
      FROM hier h1
      INNER JOIN hier h2
        ON (h1.emp_id = h2.boss_id)
      INNER JOIN hier h3
        ON (h2.emp_id = h3.boss_id)
      LEFT OUTER JOIN hier h4
        ON (h3.emp_id = h4.boss_id)
      WHERE h1.emp_title = 'CEO'
    ) chains
  WHERE chain IS NOT NULL
  ORDER BY chain;
```

Listing 15.62 Show the full hierarchal relationship of every employee. See Figure 15.46 for the result.

```
chains_of_command
----------------------
CEO
CEO > VP1
CEO > VP1 > DIR1
CEO > VP1 > DIR1 > WS1
CEO > VP1 > DIR1 > WS2
CEO > VP1 > DIR1 > WS3
CEO > VP1 > DIR2
CEO > VP2
CEO > VP2 > DIR3
CEO > VP2 > DIR3 > WS4
CEO > VP2 > DIR3 > WS5
```

Figure 15.46 Result of Listing 15.62.

DBMS **Microsoft Access** won't run Listing 15.62 because of the restrictions Access puts on join expressions.

To run Listing 15.62 in **Microsoft SQL Server**, change each || to +.

To run Listing 15.62 in **MySQL**, use CONCAT() instead of || to concatenate strings.

In **Microsoft SQL Server** and **Db2**, use the (standard) recursive WITH clause to traverse a hierarchy. The following query is equivalent to Listing 15.62 (in Microsoft SQL Server, change each || to +):

```
WITH recurse (emp_title, emp_id) AS
  (SELECT
      CAST(emp_title AS VARCHAR(50)),
      emp_id
    FROM hier
    WHERE boss_id IS NULL
  UNION ALL
  SELECT
      CAST(recurse.emp_title || ' > ' ||
        h1.emp_title AS VARCHAR(50)),
      h1.emp_id
    FROM hier h1, recurse
    WHERE h1.boss_id = recurse.emp_id
  )
SELECT emp_title emp_tree
  FROM recurse;
```

In **Oracle**, use the (nonstandard) CONNECT BY syntax to traverse a hierarchy. The following query is equivalent to Listing 15.62:

```
SELECT ltrim(SYS_CONNECT_BY_PATH(
    emp_title, ' > '),' > ')
      AS chains_of_command
  FROM hier
  START WITH boss_id IS NULL
  CONNECT BY PRIOR emp_id = boss_id;
```

Listing 15.63 uses scalar subqueries to determine whether each node in the hierarchy is a root, branch, or leaf node. See Figure 15.47 for the result. A zero in the result denotes True; nonzero, False.

DBMS To run Listing 15.63 in **Microsoft Access**, change each SIGN to SGN.

In **Oracle**, use the (nonstandard) CONNECT BY syntax to traverse a hierarchy. The following query is equivalent to Listing 15.63:

```
SELECT
    emp_title,
    (CASE CONNECT_BY_ROOT(emp_title)
    WHEN emp_title THEN 1
    ELSE 0 END)
      AS root_node,
    (SELECT COUNT(*)
      FROM hier h1
      WHERE h1.boss_id = hier.emp_id
        AND hier.boss_id IS NOT NULL
        AND rownum = 1)
          AS branch_node,
    CONNECT_BY_ISLEAF AS leaf_node
FROM hier
START WITH boss_id IS NULL
CONNECT BY PRIOR emp_id = boss_id
ORDER BY root_node DESC,
        branch_node DESC;
```

```
SELECT h1.emp_title,
  (SELECT SIGN(COUNT(*))
    FROM hier h2
    WHERE h1.emp_id = h2.emp_id
      AND h2.boss_id IS NULL)
        AS root_node,
  (SELECT SIGN(COUNT(*))
    FROM hier h2
    WHERE h1.emp_id = h2.boss_id
      AND h1.boss_id IS NOT NULL)
        AS branch_node,
  (SELECT SIGN(COUNT(*))
    FROM hier h2
    WHERE 0 =
      (SELECT COUNT(*)
        FROM hier h3
        WHERE h1.emp_id = h3.boss_id))
          AS leaf_node
  FROM hier h1;
```

Listing 15.63 Determine whether each node is a root, branch, or leaf node. See Figure 15.47 for the result.

emp_title	root_node	branch_node	leaf_node
CEO	1	0	0
VP1	0	1	0
VP2	0	1	0
DIR1	0	1	0
DIR2	0	0	1
DIR3	0	1	0
WS1	0	0	1
WS2	0	0	1
WS3	0	0	1
WS4	0	0	1
WS5	0	0	1

Figure 15.47 Result of Listing 15.63.

Index

Made in the USA
Las Vegas, NV
12 September 2022

55172678R00256